ALSO BY DAVID TRAXEL

1898: The Birth of the American Century

An American Saga: The Life and Times of Rockwell Kent

CRUSADER NATION

CRUSADER NATION

The United States in Peace and the Great War, 1898–1920

———◦———

DAVID TRAXEL

ALFRED A. KNOPF NEW YORK 2006

THIS IS A BORZOI BOOK
PUBLISHED BY ALFRED A. KNOPF

Copyright © 2006 by David Traxel
Published in the United States by Alfred A. Knopf,
a division of Random House, Inc., New York, and in
Canada by Random House of Canada Limited, Toronto.
www.aaknopf.com

Knopf, Borzoi Books, and the colophon are
registered trademarks of Random House, Inc.

Library of Congress Cataloging-in-Publication Data

Traxel, David.
Crusader nation : the United States in peace and the Great War, 1898–1920 /
David Traxel.—1st ed.
        p.   cm.
Includes bibliographical references.
ISBN 0-375-41078-3
1. United States—Politics and government—1897–1901.   2. United States—Politics and
government—1901–1953.   3. Progressivism (United States politics).   4. United States—
Social conditions—1865–1918.   5. Social movements—United States—History.
6. World War, 1914–1918—United States.   7. World War, 1914–1918—Political aspects.
8. World War, 1914–1918—Social aspects.   I. Title.

E743.T73 2005
973.8'9—dc22   2004063246

Manufactured in the United States of America
First Edition

For Rosemary:
And you wait, are awaiting the one thing
that will infinitely enhance your life;
the powerful, the uncommon,
the awakening of stones,
depths turning toward you.

—Rilke

Contents

Preface

There are few periods in American history filled with such troublesome, adventurous, and challenging events as the first decades of the American Century. The United States had undergone enormous economic and social upheaval in the 1880s and 1890s as a ruthless industrial manufacturing system evolved while millions of impoverished immigrants poured in to work and suffer in factories and mines. The sins of uncontrolled industrial development inspired passionate crusades for reform that had many goals: stop child labor and other exploitive employer practices, extend democracy through votes for women, rein in irresponsible plutocrats, expel corrupt big-city machines, and prohibit the social evil of alcohol. Crusaders ranged from foot soldiers of the Democratic and Republican parties to ardent Socialists, to members of even more radical organizations such as the Industrial Workers of the World and antiorganizations such as Emma Goldman's anarchists. All had faith in their particular visions for the good society and fought to establish these with a passionate intensity that often blinded them to other points of view.

This Age of Progress was also marked by the wide range of articulate and dedicated people who were both participants and witnesses to the momentous transformations taking place. There were colorful politicians such as Theodore Roosevelt and Woodrow Wilson trying not only to control the giant corporations dominating the new economy but also to contain and direct the forces of reform that had been unleashed. These men, though once admirers of each other, became bitter enemies over questions of political philosophy, and their relationship was made even worse by personal jealousy. The radical journalist John Reed is another of the individuals whose lives illuminate the times. A graduate of Harvard, he was one of the early bohemians of Greenwich Village, enjoying numerous love affairs and great success in his writing about revolutionaries here and abroad. Young America was rebelling against the strictures of the Victorians, a rebellion that was reflected in all aspects of life, from the new sexual mores, dance crazes, and jazz music to politics. It was a time of old certainties under attack from those who were just as certain about what *they* believed.

The outbreak of the European war in August 1914 began to shift the attention of Americans to international concerns. Most were sure that their country could avoid becoming involved, and felt morally superior to the belligerents, though they were grateful for the flood of war orders that turned a stagnant economy into roaring prosperity. Great Britain, controlling the sea-lanes, benefited most from American productivity, but that was countered by Germany's submarine fleet. Woodrow Wilson, recognizing the dangers of involvement, pleaded in vain with his fellow citizens to stay neutral, but for a nation of immigrants with ties of blood and culture to the warring nations, that proved impossible. Social activists such as Jane Addams organized a peace movement, finding an ally in Henry Ford, who revolutionized American life during these years through his Model T. The automaker launched his own crusade to stop the war, financing the Peace Ship of December 1915 and accompanying it to Europe, naively assuring the public that he would end the war in a few weeks.

But soon the country was drawn into the war itself by acts that included the sinking of the *Lusitania* and a German sabotage campaign against American industry directed by Franz von Papen, military attaché at the German embassy, who a couple of decades later would play a role in the rise of Adolf Hitler. Germany was also involved in fomenting deadly raids along the Mexican border, so that when the kaiser proposed that Mexico and Japan join with him to make war on the United States, the threat was taken very seriously. The country entered on a crusade in 1917 that, typically, was not just to defend the country's interests, but to "make the world safe for democracy," a struggle that would make war impossible in the future. The results of that great campaign are in some ways both the culmination and the defeat of progressivism. America relied on many of the same tactics that had been used to such effect in the reform campaigns, such as morally charged publicity to generate support for the cause. Progressive goals, including prohibition and votes for women, were achieved partly because of the war, as is the extraordinary, and brief, use of government power to contain capitalists accustomed to the freedoms of laissez-faire. Unfortunately, crusades also lead to a moral self-righteousness that makes dissent intolerable, and civil liberties were sup-pressed for the duration. Such passionate commitment could not last. The reality of a victory for idealism that later seemed much like a defeat is one of the factors that brought Warren G. Harding and conservative Republi-cans back to power through the election of 1920. As H. L. Mencken wrote that year, people "were weary of hearing highfalutin and meaningless words; they sicken of an idealism that is oblique, confusing, dishonest and ferocious." The American crusades that had been dedicated to changing first the nation and then the world had been, temporarily, defeated.

CRUSADER NATION

———◇———

CHAPTER ONE

American Renascence

*Looking back . . . I have thought of the period in America, includ-
ing the last few years of the nineteenth century and the early years
of the twentieth, as the American Renascence, even the Great
American Renascence.*

Ray Stannard Baker[1]

*You see, getting down to the bottom of things, this is a pretty raw,
crude civilization of ours—pretty wasteful, pretty cruel, which
often comes to the same thing, doesn't it? And in a lot of respects we
Americans are the rawest and crudest of all. Our production, our
factory laws, our charities, our relations between capital and labor,
our distribution—all wrong, out of gear. We've stumbled along for
a while, trying to run a new civilization in old ways, but we've got
to start to make this world over.*

Thomas Edison, 1912[2]

IN 1898 the United States stepped into the realm of international power
politics for the first time. The country had already become a global economic presence, and was feared as a competitor because of its tremendous
natural resources and industrial efficiency. Militarily, however, it was
viewed with condescension by the Great Powers until it quickly and deci-
sively thrashed Spain in 1898, seizing as the fruits of victory the colonies
remaining in that faded empire: Cuba, which was soon given a limited
independence, Puerto Rico, Guam, and the Philippines. Mixed into this
rather amateurish adventure were motives of economic gain, national prestige, fear of German or other European expansion into the Caribbean,
desire for strategic naval bases, and anger over the blowing up of the battleship *Maine*. But there was also a strong sense of moral outrage about the
way the Spanish had been mistreating Cuban civilians while suppressing a

3

revolt on the island. Hundreds of thousands of men, women, and children had died in concentration camps just ninety miles off the American shore, and the public demanded that an end be put to such horrors.

America was encouraged to take the path to a world role by Great Britain, looking for allies against the rising and aggressive strength of Germany. Rudyard Kipling, celebratory poet of the world-circling British Empire, wrote a widely distributed poem urging Americans to "Take up the White Man's burden" of civilizing "sullen peoples, half devil and half child."

The challenge was taken up, and yet, in this American assumption of global responsibilities there was a shyness and uncertainty even among those such as Theodore Roosevelt who urged a "large" policy on the United States. The country needed to take a more active role in international affairs, these men believed, if only to protect itself in a Darwinian world where the strong devoured the weak. China, one of the countries being picked apart by stronger nations, provided a negative example for such Americans. The United States could not, argued Roosevelt's close friend and political ally Senator Henry Cabot Lodge, "allow itself to become a hermit nation hiding a defenseless, feeble body within a huge shell . . . shut up and kept from its share of the world's commerce until it was smothered by a power hostile to it in every conception of justice and liberty."[3] At the same time, the policy of extending the country's reach across the seas invited attack on these "hostages to fortune," as Roosevelt recognized by calling the new Philippine colony "our Achilles' heel." A newspaper doggerel writer spoke for many who were unhappy with imperialism:

> We've taken up the white man's burden
> of ebony and brown;
> Now will you tell us, Rudyard
> how we may put it down?[4]

Roosevelt had been the Man of the Year in 1898, and also for the decade that followed, the ideal spokesman for his generation and a worthy representative of their ambitions. These were roles for which he was both born, in 1856, and self-made. His father was a member of a wealthy old New York "Dutch" family, his mother came from plantation-owning stock in Georgia, and young "Teedie" had grown up during the Civil War in a household reflecting the regional differences. He had enjoyed a childhood replete with all the good things money could buy, but marred by ill health and poor eyesight, his own weak body making him defenseless against bullies until he overcame these physical disabilities through exercise and will. Some of that exercise had come from long expeditions running through Long Island fields and woods with butterfly net and rifle to collect natural-history specimens, and some through steady work with dumbbells and other such instruments of torture taken up at the urging of his father, who told him, "You have the mind but not the body, and without the help of the body the mind cannot go as far as it should. You must *make* your body. It is hard drudgery to make one's body, but I know you will do it."[5] He did, and kept doing so all his life. He also worked at making his mind; in adulthood he could speak three languages besides English with some facility, and could read seven, while he continued his intense, if rather bloodstained, study of birds, animals, and nature, and became a prolific historian and writer as well.

After graduating from Harvard and after an early marriage, Roosevelt entered politics, much to the dismay of friends and family, who regarded that line of work as appropriate only for saloon keepers, corrupt hacks, and Irishmen. "I answered that if this were so it merely meant that the people I knew did not belong to the governing class, and that the other people did—and that I intended to be one of the governing class; that if they proved too hard-bit for me I supposed I would have to quit, but that I certainly would not quit until I had made the effort and found out whether I really was too weak to hold my own in the rough and tumble."[6] He more than held his own, serving three terms in the New York assembly, where he became an important part of the reform element in the Republican Party. But then both his beloved wife, Alice, and his mother died within hours of each other on February 14, 1884, and he fled to the frontier West to raise cattle, shoot big game, and mourn. A few years later, Roosevelt remarried and returned to politics, running unsuccessfully for mayor of New York, then serving as U.S. civil service commissioner before winning public attention as the aggressive president of New York's police commission. His intelligence, honesty, and energy had gained him many admiring allies, but his combative temperament and impatient self-righteousness had also bred enemies. President Benjamin Harrison observed about his civil service commissioner that he "wanted to put an end to all the evil in the world between sunrise and sunset."[7]

It looked for a while as if the firebrand's career would go no further. He had campaigned strenuously for William McKinley in the hard-fought and divisive election of 1896, but, even so, after the victory McKinley was hesitant to appoint him assistant secretary of the navy. "I want peace," the new president told one of Roosevelt's supporters, "and I am told that your friend

Theodore—whom I know only slightly—is always getting into rows with everybody. I am afraid he is too pugnacious."[8] These doubts were overcome, allowing Roosevelt to perform superbly in preparing the navy for the war with Spain. As soon as he felt he had done all he could for that service, he resigned to organize the First Volunteer Cavalry, popularly known as Roosevelt's Rough Riders, which he dashingly led to victory in Cuba.

The young politician had a genius for publicity. He knew how to charm and manipulate the press, while journalists appreciated his glamour, outspokenness, and charismatic flair for action. Coming back from the war as one of the most famous men in the country, he was able to mount a winning campaign for governor of New York in that fall of 1898. Two years later, having alienated state Republican bosses with his modest attempts at regulating business and protecting New York's natural resources, he was kicked upstairs to join William McKinley's ticket as vice-presidential candidate. They won the election easily against William Jennings Bryan and Adlai Stevenson, but on September 6, 1901, McKinley was shot twice in the stomach by an anarchist named Leon Czolgosz, and died eight days later from the resulting infection. Theodore Roosevelt became president; at just forty-two years old he was the youngest before or since to hold that office.

Men and women of the new president's generation had been waiting impatiently for their turn at the levers of power. They had grown up both inspired and burdened by their fathers' glory, a glory won first on the battlefields of the Civil War and then enhanced by their own part in the prodigious growth of the American economy and American industrial might in the decades after that struggle. But social disruptions and suffering on the same enormous scale had accompanied that growth: abject poverty, especially in the burgeoning cities; women and children working long hours at dangerous tasks; fathers who could not earn enough even when laboring thirteen- or fourteen-hour days in mines and factories to support their families. In the middle of the nineteenth century there had been only a few millionaires; now there were thousands. Such were the disparities in wealth that while children went unfed, the rich would spend tens of thousands of dollars on dinner parties where guests dined off solid-gold plates or, as at one given by Caroline Astor, would use sterling-silver trowels to dig through heaps of sand arranged on the table to find buried treasure troves of diamonds and rubies.

Sometimes these galas were presented as benefits for the poor. In the winter of 1896, during the depths of the worst economic depression up to that time in American history, Mr. and Mrs. Bradley Bradley-Martin, perturbed by what they were reading in newspapers about the misery of the unemployed, decided to give a costume ball to help them find work. Mrs. Bradley-Martin reportedly exclaimed, "It would give such impetus to trade!"

The couple was wealthy enough to enjoy an elaborate mansion in New York, a town house in London, and a shooting estate in Scotland; a notable social coup had been achieved in marrying their sixteen-year-old daughter to an English aristocrat, Lord Craven. Louis XIV's glittering eighteenth-century court provided the theme for their costume ball, and the luxurious Waldorf-Astoria hotel was the chosen venue, its Grand Ballroom transformed into the Great Hall of Mirrors at Versailles. Employment was undoubtedly provided for hairdressers, jewelers, musicians, couturieres, and even some historians of fashion as the seven hundred guests arrived on February 10, 1897, dressed as Renaissance, Elizabethan, French, and a few American historical figures. European royalty were particular favorites, though Anne Morgan, youngest daughter of the powerful financier J.P., came as Pocahontas in a beautifully beaded costume reportedly made by "real Indians." August Belmont, financier and star of New York society, wore a full suit of steel armor inlaid with gold that cost him $10,000. Mrs. Theodore Roosevelt attended, while her husband, police commissioner at the time, oversaw 250 of New York's finest as they ensured that anarchists and other unruly elements did not intrude. The overall expenses were paid for by the Bradley-Martins, and amounted to a stunning $369,000.[9] This at a time when the average workman, if he could find work, earned $500 a year. It is no wonder that just two years later, in 1899, the sociologist Thorstein Veblen would write about "conspicuous consumption" in his book *The Theory of the Leisure Class,* noting, "To gain and to hold the esteem of men, it is not sufficient merely to possess wealth or power. The wealth or power must be put in evidence."

Such a vulgar display, covered in great detail in contemporary newspapers, called down upon the Bradley-Martins a storm of criticism from both press and pulpit alike. While there were few public defenders of the hosts, who ended up fleeing to a more understanding Europe for refuge, there were certainly those who supported the inequality brought about by the raw capitalism of the time. Two such were the English philosopher Herbert Spencer and the American sociologist William Graham Sumner, who argued that society was just like the wilderness of nature where Darwinian evolution took place, and that only those who were strong and adaptable, those who were "fittest," should survive, flourish, and grow rich—or at least comfortable. This philosophy of social Darwinism was used as a scientific basis for arguing against laws to ameliorate the conditions of poverty or restrain competition. Any attempt to interfere would be against "natural law."

John D. Rockefeller, one of the richest of all Americans, wrote that all "failures which a man makes in his life are due almost always to some defect in his personality, some weakness of body, or mind, or character, will, or temperament."[10] And there were spiritual authorities who argued that this was the way God wanted the world. Russell H. Conwell, Baptist minister and founder of Temple University, had an acclaimed speech, or sermon, entitled "Acres of Diamonds," that he recited more than five thousand times in the years at the end of the nineteenth century. In the course of two hours, he would exhort his listeners to "get rich, and it is your duty to get rich . . . to make money honestly is to preach the gospel. . . . If you can honestly attain unto riches . . . it is your Christian and godly duty to do so." Those who suffered poverty deserved their lot. "To sympathize with a man whom God has punished for his sins, thus to help him when God would still continue a just punishment, is to do wrong, no doubt about it." All should remember that "there is not a poor person in the United States who has not been made poor by his own shortcomings, or by the shortcomings of some one else."[11]

But many of Roosevelt's generation, born around the time of the Civil War, worried by and feeling guilty over the great contrast between wealth and poverty that had become so obvious in American cities, were determined to tame social and economic chaos and restore a sense of justice to the system. The name usually given to the general movement to reform and realign American society is *progressivism*. Though there were different hopes and expectations, as well as contradictions, in the various groups called progressive, they all shared the optimistic belief that society not only could be improved through peaceful, reasoned action, but might actually be made perfect—though definition of that perfection varied greatly. This desire to better the world was also reflected in the arts: in literature, where writers such as Theodore Dreiser, Frank Norris, and Upton Sinclair revealed the sordid side of urban and industrial life; in painting, where Robert Henri's "Ashcan" school also depicted factories, grimy allies, and slums; even in the new art of motion pictures, which joined the fight with films that exposed the misuse of prison labor or the evils of the white slave traffic. The reform city government of Cleveland, Ohio, financed a semi-documentary to raise money for its battle against the diseases of the slums.

For many, one of the principal motivations of this crusade for improvement was religious, but not the old-time fundamentalist religion of their ancestors, though that was still strong and growing stronger in rural parts of the country. The Social Gospel aspect of the progressive movement hoped to return to American life an emphasis on Protestant morals that had been lost in an economic system that worshipped mammon more than Christ. Charles M. Sheldon's 1896 novel *In His Steps* told the edifying story of a group of people who pledge to make all important decisions in their lives by asking what Jesus would have done in the same situation; the editor of the town's daily newspaper wonders if Jesus would print a story about a prizefight, while a novelist realizes that his success is empty because it is based only on an ability to amuse rather than spread the Word of Christ. The most daring of the characters, a young girl, takes a drunken prostitute home to convert her to the path of virtue. Millions of copies of the uplifting tale were sold, making it the most popular book published in the United States between 1880 and 1935.[12] This and other imaginative tracts such as William T. Stead's *If Christ Came to Chicago* inspired young people to take up a life of service in the hope that perhaps God's Kingdom could be established here on earth. Progressivism for such people became a mission, a holy war, a crusade for virtue and the betterment of mankind.

Women were particularly well represented among these activists, since they not only were strongly moved by the moral and ethical dilemmas of their time, but also found an outlet for their talents working among the poor that the broader society denied them. In contrast to social Darwinism's belief that inherited qualities determined success or failure, the Social Gospel argued that environment was the important factor; consequently, effort was put into improving the living conditions of immigrants in slums and ghettos.

Jane Addams was one of the earliest pioneers here, as she was in many things, starting Hull House in Chicago with her friend and Rockford College classmate Ellen Gates Starr in the fall of 1889, a settlement house that grew into a complex of thirteen buildings with a staff of more than fifty and a yearly budget of $100,000 by the first decade of the twentieth century. Hull House, Addams wrote in 1910, was "an experimental effort to aid in the solution of the social and industrial problems which are engendered by the modern conditions of life in a great city."[13] She went on to explain why she and Starr had taken up their burden: "First, the desire to interpret democracy in social terms; secondly, the impulse . . . urging us to aid in the race progress; and, thirdly, the Christian movement toward humanitarianism."

Hull House provided a model for others concerned with improving the lives of immigrants and poor people, and in making them an important part of the democratic system. Unmarried working women were provided with housing, as well as child care, a kindergarten, and a safe playground. There were classes for adults in how to become American citizens and about other practical aspects of their new life, but they could also study book-binding, painting, and music, and put on plays and ethnic festivals. By the beginning of the Great War, there were more than four hundred settlement houses in cities and towns around the country, trying to bring reform to local government and improve the lives of slum dwellers. Their greatest successes came as social centers for women and children; men preferred their traditional saloons.

Restoring and extending a working democracy was an important goal for activists such as Addams. They saw evidence all around them that the growth of giant corporations and large, impersonal cities had limited the people's access to power, and that both local and national political reforms, such as the direct election of U.S. senators, were necessary so that laws could be passed eradicating child labor and requiring children to attend school, and reduce the number of hours their mothers worked. Women's suffrage was part of the campaign because reformers were confident that women, the great moral force in American life, would provide the votes necessary to pass progressive legislation to protect vulnerable citizens, including the prohibition of alcohol, a substance that was viewed as the cause of much of the misery of the poor.

Another great driving force behind the progressive movement was the desire to organize society along rational and efficient "scientific" lines, a belief that experts could bring order to the complex chaos of industrial society. Thorstein Veblen best articulated this vision. Contemptuously amused by the excesses of the newly rich and the way the rising middle class was aping their conspicuously profligate ways, he satirized them in *A Theory of the Leisure Class*. Veblen believed that the role of technology in shaping human values was little appreciated. In later books he argued that instead of leaving the direction of the new technological society to scientif-ically ignorant and status-hungry businessmen, it would be better if trained engineers, the practical designers and makers of things, served as guides to modern life, for they understood machines and thus could rationally organize their use.

Frederick Winslow Taylor provides a good example of the practical kind of expertise that knew machines and their uses. He was both an engi-neer and an inventor who held a hundred patents. One of the processes he developed, high speed steel, enabled cutting tools in lathes to keep their edge longer and operate three times faster, tripling the output of machine shops. But his greatest contribution to the new industrial economy came through his studies of the workplace.

The fast new machines being built would never be used to full potential unless their operators also worked efficiently, and he argued that if properly trained and managed, fewer men could produce more than ever before. He began his studies in 1898 at the Bethlehem Steel Company by using stopwatches to time crews of ten to fifteen men as they performed their labors. By eliminating, he argued, "all false movements, slow movements, and useless movements" and training the men to make "the quickest and best movements" while equipped with the best tools for the job, the same amount of work could be done by 140 men that had previously taken 600. True, many workers had lost their jobs, but those remaining had received a 60 percent increase in pay.

"In the past," Taylor wrote in *The Principles of Scientific Management,* "the man has been first; in the future the system must be first." This system would bring, he was sure, a golden age as efficient production washed away all social tensions and hatreds between races, creeds, classes, and sections of the country, the material abundance allowing every American to find happiness, for he felt that his principles "applied with equal force to all our social activities; to the management of our homes; the management of our farms; the management of the business of our tradesmen, . . . of our churches, our philanthropic institutions, our universities, and our governmental departments."[14]

Many of his contemporaries agreed with him, seeing, as Thomas Edison indicated in the quote at the beginning of this chapter, that much social cruelty came out of inefficiency. Only unions, whose members rightly feared being held to machinelike standards, some political radicals, and the new "bohemians" would rebel against such standardization and mechanization of society. The scientific management, or "time and motion," approach spread across the country in the young century as businessmen hired scientists and engineers to develop new tools and design innovative products in company laboratories. Henry Ford would be the great pioneer in applying these developments, along with the revolutionary power of electricity, to achieve true mass production, though he would also provide a good example of how a narrow engineering point of view could lead to social dangers as well as economic efficiencies. The whole industrial establishment was picking up speed. Between 1899 and 1914, American productivity increased by 75 percent while the workforce grew by only 36 percent. The cornucopia was beginning its flow; the question to be determined was who would most benefit.

There were obvious parallels between the ideas of Veblen and Taylor about how to bring the industrial forces that had so disrupted modern life under control, and "Taylorism" also affected how intellectuals formed their critiques of modern society. When the political writer Herbert Croly, author of *The Promise of American Life* and *Progressive Democracy,* helped found *The New Republic* magazine in 1914, one of his goals was to make politics more rational by applying Taylor's ideas about expertise and organization to the American system of government.

Progressives believed that government at every level—local, state, and federal—had to be enrolled in the fight through the direct participation of the people. "In the people," they were sure, in spite of evidence to the contrary, resided all political virtue. Legislation was necessary to protect woman and child workers, to clean up slums, improve housing, and control the great corporations, but first government itself had to be reformed. And to do that it was necessary to rescue the democratic process from interest groups whose only concern was in increasing their power and profits.

It was municipal government that had the greatest immediate power over people's lives, and yet was the most obviously corrupt. Cities, therefore, became the earliest target of reformers, and they were aided by a new breed of crusading journalists who began exposing the sins of the political machines controlling American local governments. Technological revolutions had reduced the costs of printing during the 1890s, and geniuses of mass circulation such as Joseph Pulitzer and William Randolph Hearst built great newspaper empires on sensationalist exploitation of the tragedies of urban life; after the turn of the century, they, especially Hearst, turned their energies to informing their working-class readers about the scandalous activities of city bosses.

At the same time, American magazines entered their golden age, gaining unprecedented power. S. S. McClure was the pioneering innovator in low-priced, intellectually respectable mass-circulation magazines. With his formula of light fiction and well-written articles on travel, contemporary history, and the latest scientific discoveries, he had won an educated middle-class readership that was national in scope; by 1907, *McClure's* had a circulation of nearly half a million. Publishers of other magazines including *Cosmopolitan, Everybody's,* and *Collier's* quickly copied the pattern he had designed, and they also followed him in the series of exposés he allowed his talented reporters to investigate and write: Lincoln Steffens first on "The Shame of the Cities," which delved into the combination of dishonest interests that led to tainted government, then a second series about state corruption; Ida Tarbell on the sordid history of John D. Rockefeller's Standard Oil Company, which made the plutocrat one of the most hated men in the nation; Ray Stannard Baker on the misery of life in Pennsylvania's coal regions. Baker thought of himself as a "maker of understanding," believing that if the people knew of the evil deeds being perpetrated in business and politics they would rise up and smite the sinners.[15] This was a view widely shared by the other investigative journalists, soon to be labeled *muckrakers* by someone they had regarded as an ally, and also by the active political reformers themselves. Robert "Battling Bob" La Follette, the insurgent Republican governor of Wisconsin who became a national hero thanks to Steffens's series on state governments, edited and published his own magazine, whose motto was the biblical "Ye shall know the truth and the truth shall make you free." And, to some extent, their faith was rewarded. The middle class, which throughout the latter part of the nineteenth century had scorned politics as vulgar and debased, re-entered the arena.

William Allen White, editor of the *Emporia Gazette* of Kansas, was an acute observer of as well as an activist in the progressive movement; decades later he wrote,

> We and all the world in those days were deeply stirred. Our sympathies were responding excitedly to a sense of injustice that had become a part of the new glittering, gaudy machine age. Machines of steel and copper and wood and stone, and bookkeeping and managerial talent, were creating a new order. It looked glamorous. It seemed permanent; yet, because someway the masses of the world, not the proletariat but the middle class, had qualms and squeamish doubts about the way things were going, discontent rose in the hearts of the people and appeared in world politics.[16]

The world to be changed eventually, but first the local bosses had to be tamed. Progressives found that the bosses' "machine" rule in the cities often proved difficult if not impossible to dislodge, for though they were corrupt they were also intelligent, dynamic, and flexible and actually provided important services to their immigrant and poor constituents, while the "goo-goos," or good-government reformers, were too often naive or lacked any real concern for the day-to-day needs of lower-class urban dwellers. Theodore Roosevelt had learned these political lessons in the tough school of practical experience and noted that many reform leaders "excited almost as much derision among the plain people as the machine itself excited anger or dislike" because of the unqualified candidates they often ran: "some rather inefficient, well-meaning person, who bathed every day, and didn't steal, but whose only good point was 'respectability.' " These leaders also lacked the "slightest understanding of the needs, interests, ways of thought, and convictions of the average small man," and they "did not offer him anything materially better from his point of view than the machine."[17] In other words, he recognized that "bread and butter" issues were at least as important as moral ones for most voters.

However, many of the clean-government campaigns were for a while victorious when they did broaden their concerns. Samuel "Golden Rule" Jones and Brand Whitlock had been successful in cleaning up Toledo; Tom Johnson and Newton D. Baker had earned Cleveland the reputation as the best-governed city in the nation.[18]

But state governments offered even greater prizes. Here was the seat of power capable of passing laws against child labor and the exploitation of women in the workplace. State legislatures were often incompetent or subject to bribery or pressure from corporations, especially railroads, so ways around them were devised to put power directly into the hands of the people through direct democracy. The primary and the initiative were two innovations that were designed to raise the quality of elected officials. The primary system was an attempt to avoid the power of the machines in selecting candidates; the recall allowed voters to remove corrupt or incompetent officials at a special election. But if the houses of representative government could not be fully cleansed, there were two other measures to restore democracy. The initiative allowed voters to pass legislation on their own, while the referendum let them repeal bad laws. Oregon in 1902 became the first state to enact these latter reforms, and nineteen others had followed suit by 1918. Two issues that were quickly put to state voters were suffrage for women and the sometimes related campaign to ban alcoholic beverages. These proposals enjoyed occasional success, women winning the vote in California, Kansas, Oregon, and other states, while losing in Michigan and Wisconsin due to the strong opposition of brewers, who feared with good reason that women would support prohibition. That cause also made headway in individual states, especially in those that allowed counties to declare themselves dry, but increasingly leaders in both crusades felt that what were needed were national laws, that the federal government should be the true field of battle.

Theodore Roosevelt had made no secret of his reform instincts, and his rise to the presidency after the assassination of McKinley in 1901 was welcomed by men and women of liberal thought, just as it had been opposed by the pro-business wing of the Republican Party. Senator Mark Hanna, millionaire industrialist and leader of the conservatives, had fought ferociously against Roosevelt's nomination as vice president, shouting, "Don't any of you realize that there's only one life between this madman and the White House?"[19] After that life was taken, Hanna remembered his earlier warnings and was said to have lamented, "I told William McKinley that it was a mistake to nominate that wild man. . . . Now look, that damned cowboy is President of the United States."

But the mad cowboy was not really as wild as feared, and he had the wit to recognize that his position was not strong. No previous vice president assuming the presidency upon the death of the incumbent had ever then won the office; he dearly wanted to break that tradition, so it was necessary to build a power base of his own. Both the Senate and the House of Representatives were controlled by the conservative wing of his party, who saw themselves as guardians of corporate interests, and they might put their support behind Hanna or some other more amenable politician as the Republican candidate in 1904. Roosevelt, in spite of the fear he inspired, was himself a man of conservative instincts, but he understood that times were changing and that the people were demanding that government take a more active role in controlling big business and ameliorating the burdens of modern life. Keeping the party united while attracting the allegiance of progressives was a delicate balancing act that called on all his formidable political skills.

Caution was the watchword during his first term, but Roosevelt did fight some notable battles, two of which took place in 1902. "Trusts" and holding companies were tight combinations of businesses in a particular industry controlled by a central board of trustees that determined production quotas and prices for all. This arrangement produced efficiencies by cutting overhead and duplication, and great profits through the elimination of competition. Rockefeller's Standard Oil Company was one of the earliest and most effective of these arrangements. By the turn of the century, such combinations were being formed at an alarming rate, and they were of a size to dominate the whole economy; in 1899 alone more than 1,200 companies were absorbed in mergers. In 1901, J. P. Morgan organized the United States Steel Corporation, capitalized at an astounding $1.4 billion and controlling 80 percent of the nation's steel production.

Governmental tools for controlling the formation of such behemoths were limited. The Sherman Antitrust Act became law in 1890, but had been poorly written, never clearly defining a trust. When the American Sugar Refining Company managed to control 98 percent of sugar production in 1895, and was prosecuted under the Sherman Act, the Supreme Court, strong defender of laissez-faire business practices, in *U.S. v. E. C. Knight* declared that the law applied strictly to commerce, not manufacture or production. The act fell into disuse.

But in early 1902, J. P. Morgan combined two railroad lines into the Northern Securities Company, a giant that would have given the financier and his partners monopoly control over transportation between Chicago and the Pacific coast. Nothing mattered more to the economy than the railroads, the only effective means of taking goods to market and therefore touching everyone's lives: farmers and grain dealers, miners and manufacturers, consumers and merchants, lumber barons as well as lumberjacks, and the chambers of commerce of every village, town, and city in the land. Roosevelt ordered his attorney general to use the Sherman Act to stop the combination.

Morgan was shocked by the unfriendly action, and came quickly to the White House, accompanied by two powerful senators, to plead his case the old-fashioned way. "If we have done anything wrong," he told Roosevelt, "send your man to my man and they can fix it up."[20] The president, unmoved, responded, "That can't be done." He had the Justice Department continue to prosecute the case, and in 1904 the Supreme Court decided in the government's favor.

Coal mining also affected every part of the economy, since that potent material powered the steam engines that did the work of the nation, fired the furnaces that made steel for rails and skyscrapers, and heated homes and cooking stoves. It was even more troubled by labor problems than other industries, which is saying a lot. In 1902, the United Mine Workers, under the leadership of thirty-two-year-old John Mitchell, struck the anthracite, or hard coal, mines for better wages, an eight-hour day, and recognition of the union. The mine operators, even more arrogant than other industrial chieftains, which is also saying a lot, refused to negotiate; their position, and that of their peers in other businesses, is best expressed by a quote from George F. Baer, railroad multimillionaire, mine owner, and their spokesman: "The rights and interests of the laboring man will be protected and cared for—not by the labor agitators, but by the Christian men to whom God in His infinite wisdom has given the control of the property interests of this country."[21]

The coming of fall and the threat of a winter without coal brought Roosevelt into the struggle. He asked for a meeting in Washington with both

*Breaker boys at mine head in South Pittson, Pennsylvania. Photographed
by Lewis Hine for the National Child Labor Committee sometime
between 1907 and 1913.*

sides, though the White House was torn up during remodeling, and he was confined to a wheelchair due to an accident involving his carriage and a trolley that had killed the Secret Service agent sitting next to him. Mitchell willingly came, but Baer and his fellows showed up only after pressure was exerted by J. P. Morgan. The mine owners still refused to negotiate, one complaining that there were many young children working in his mines, and that their youthful innocence would be corrupted if they were exposed to the radical ranting of Mitchell and the United Mine Workers. Baer, on the defensive, seemed to argue that the miners were merely brutes: they "don't suffer, why, they can't even speak English."[22]

The first modern president, Roosevelt saw himself as an active mediator representing the public, and an equal to the lords of both labor and industry. He was impressed with Mitchell, whom he thought a true gentleman, and furious with what he saw as the self-defeating stupidity of the men who owned the mines. By threatening to seize and operate the coal works with army troops, and with further aid from Morgan, who had financed many of these enterprises, Roosevelt was able to bring the owners to arbitration. The strikers won increased wages and a nine-hour day, but not what they had wanted most: union recognition.[23] Still, it was seen as a breakthrough victory for labor. Never before had a president refused to actively support the capitalist side in such a dispute; in fact, they had usually backed that side with federal troops, as the Democrat Grover Cleveland had in the Pullman strike of 1894.

Roosevelt was a progressive, but a moderate one, and a major motivation in his challenging of the corporations was to prevent more radical programs from gaining strength; the growing socialist movement, under the leadership of the dynamic Eugene Debs, took 3 percent of the vote in 1904. TR also respected the economic efficiency of the giants. "I am in no sense hostile to corporations," he said in his State of the Union message to Congress in 1905. "This is an age of combination, and any effort to prevent all combination will be not only useless, but in the end vicious." Democratic Party candidates, for example, publisher William Randolph Hearst and William Jennings Bryan, were seen as irresponsible demagogues, and even Republican "insurgents" such as Robert La Follette could be dangerous. "An insurgent," Roosevelt remarked somewhat anxiously, "is a Progressive who is exceeding the speed limit."[24] By 1906 he had also grown annoyed with the increasing press criticism of political and business life and attacked reporters for concentrating only on the negative. "Muckrakers" he called them in 1906, referring to the character in John Bunyan's *Pilgrim's Progress* who never lifted his eyes from the vile and debasing to admire the good.

As far as Roosevelt was concerned, there was nothing inherently wrong with bigness or concentration of power in a business enterprise, as long as it did nothing illegal and was subject to reasonable government supervision. The sage Irish American saloon keeper Mr. Dooley, the brilliant creation of Finley Peter Dunne and voice of the people, caught the contradictions in the president's position. " 'The trusts,' says he, 'are . . . monsthers built up be the inlightened intherprise iv th' men that have done so much to advance progress in our beloved country,' he says. 'On wan hand I wud stamp thim undher fut; on th' ohter hand not so fast.' "[25]

Roosevelt, in a campaign promising the American people a "Square Deal," won overwhelming election on his own in 1904, receiving more than 57 percent of the popular vote while beating the dull, conservative Democrat Alton B. Parker. Part of his appeal was personal, due to his vigor, outspokenness, and personal toughness, and part came from his program for reining in the trusts; he pushed for strong regulatory legislation and prosecuted more than forty antitrust cases in his second term, but his greater militancy in two additional areas, conservation and international affairs, also added to his popularity among the general public.

His lifelong love of natural history and hunting, and his experiences in the West, gave him insight into the rapacious looting of the timber, mineral, and soil resources of the nation. Soon after becoming president, he had camped in the Sierra Nevada Mountains of California with John Muir, founder of the Sierra Club and eloquent and mystical defender of wilderness. Roosevelt loved the challenge of wilderness, but he also was convinced that the riches of nature needed to be exploited, though rationally and efficiently rather than with the traditional greedy chaos. Here was another area of American life that would be improved through scientific expertise. With the help of men such as James R. Garfield, secretary of the interior, and Gifford Pinchot, wealthy progressive and the first trained forester in America, Roosevelt was able to protect vast stretches of the West through executive action, bypassing the congressional old guard. By 1907, though, the Republican conservatives were fully aroused, and passed legislation to take such power away from him; Roosevelt held off signing the measure, and he, Garfield, and Pinchot, working around the clock, managed to protect even more of the forests and rivers just hours before the law took effect. They hoped that through government regulation the common people, not just the rich, would have access to natural resources and that the power that came with the concentration of wealth would not grow so strong that it excluded all other values. "No man," wrote Pinchot, "can make his life what it ought to be by living it merely on a business basis. There are things higher than business."[26] By the time he left the presidency in 1909, Roosevelt had added almost fifty million acres to the national forest system, extended tighter federal control over mineral resources, founded fifty-one wildlife refuges, created sixteen national monuments, and added five new national parks to the system.

Roosevelt believed it was America's destiny to rise to be one of the Great Powers of the world, and that it was his task to lead it there. Weaknesses like sectionalism and the evils of class warfare had to be overcome, but appropriate instruments of strength also had to be built. Elihu Root, his secretary of war, made attempts at reforming the army, but a far more important instrument was a strong navy, which Roosevelt had argued for even while a Harvard undergraduate; by 1906, the American navy was second only to Great Britain's, and in December 1907, Roosevelt dispatched it on a voyage around the world, a "big stick" to impress foreign nations.

As part of this strategy to increase American power, he pushed ahead on construction of the canal through Panama, which would not only facili-

tate commerce but also allow naval squadrons to concentrate quickly in
either the Pacific or Atlantic, a need that had also become evident in 1898
during the Spanish-American War. He was convinced that the only way for
the country to survive and flourish was to be so strong that no other nation
would dare attack her. Part of this strategy demanded that European
nations not be allowed to extend their influence to Latin America, especially the Caribbean. After Germany threatened naval action to collect
debts from Venezuela, the president issued the "Roosevelt Corollary" to the
Monroe Doctrine, warning that the United States was ready to become an
"international police power" to keep the countries of the Western Hemisphere well behaved and "civilized" so that the Europeans could not use
debt or other misbehavior as grounds for intervention or seizing territory in
the hemisphere.

The long, though increasingly fragile, peace of Europe had been maintained by complex arrangements balancing the powers against one another,
a system that Roosevelt supported. In 1905–6, he helped defuse a crisis
involving Great Britain, France, and Germany over imperialist aims in
northern Africa: "The Kaiser's pipe dream this week takes the form of
Morocco," he wrote William Howard Taft. "I do not care to take sides
between France and Germany in the matter. At the same time if I can find
out what Germany wants I shall be glad to oblige her if possible, and I am
sincerely anxious to bring about a better state of feeling between England
and Germany."[27] He also tried to establish some sort of balance in the
Pacific since that region was growing ever more unstable as the powers jostled for position and colonies. Japan and Russia went to war in 1904 over
who would control Manchuria and Korea, Japan striking first with a surprise attack on Russian ships at Port Arthur, Manchuria, then sinking the
Russian fleet that had been sent from Europe to exact revenge. The land
campaign fell into a stalemate, and Roosevelt was able to bring both sides
to negotiations at Portsmouth, New Hampshire, that ended the conflict.
For these efforts, he was awarded the Nobel Peace Prize in 1906.

He loved being president; wielding power in the fight for The Good
was what he had been born to do, he was convinced, and the power of
words was a respected part of his arsenal. From the "bully pulpit" he would
hector, harangue, and inspire his people, not allowing them to relax into
complacency. But he also had a respect for words as literature, and a love
of the other lively arts and sciences. Days were spent working with politicians and bureaucrats, who were often more narrowly focused, so in the
evenings, and other free moments, scholars, scientists, writers, artists, and
musicians were his guests. "Distinguished civilized men and charming civ-

ilized women came as a habit to the White House while Roosevelt was there," noted Owen Wister, his friend and the author of *The Virginian*. "For that once in our history, we had an American *salon*."[28] His manner was to become intensely absorbed in conversation with an expert in any of the wide range of fields of interest to him, pulling the man or woman off to a corner and temporarily ignoring his other guests. "So much of his time was spent among the bookless that many people never suspected either the range of his literary culture or his learned interest in the natural sciences," wrote another admiring friend, the novelist Edith Wharton, remembering that "he was so alive at all points, and so gifted with the rare faculty of living intensely and entirely in every moment as it passed, that each of those encounters glows in me like a tiny morsel of radium."[29]

In spite of the power and of the access to the great minds of his age that the presidency afforded him, in the flush of good feeling and responsibility following his victory in 1904, he had announced that he would not seek reelection in 1908. The American tradition, established by George Washington, had always limited presidents to two terms, and TR considered this a "wise custom." As the end of his time in office drew near, Roosevelt, only fifty years old, probably realized he was being overfastidious; he had, after all, not really served his *own* full two terms, but he felt bound to live up to his word. Besides, during the second term he had grown increasingly radical in the eyes of conservative Republicans—arguing for, among other progressive proposals, an eight-hour workday, regulation of the stock market, downward revision of the tariff, and graduated inheritance and income taxes—and they would have fought hard against his renomination. Ironically, his support for these propositions sprang from his conservatism. "I am a radical," he wrote later, "who most earnestly desires the radical programme to be carried out by conservatives. I wish to see industrial and social reforms of a far-reaching nature accomplished in this country, . . . but I want to see that movement take place under sober and responsible men, not under demagogues."[30] He saw himself as advocate of a middle way between the "Robespierre type" and the "Bourbon type."

Some satisfaction came from using his political skills and control of the party apparatus to engineer the nomination of William Howard Taft, the man he selected as worthy of being his successor. Conservatives such as Senator Nelson Aldrich did not stand in the way, for they read this candidate better than TR did. Taft had considerable experience, having served as solicitor general, a federal circuit court judge, first civilian governor of the Philippines, and secretary of war. Though he also had considerable physical presence, standing over six feet tall and weighing more than three hundred pounds, he was not a riveting speaker or charismatic campaigner like his patron. Nor was he comfortable playing the "game" of politics; all his previous governmental positions had been appointive, and he was more a judge than a wheeling, dealing politician. Still, there was public affection for him, as indicated by a popular joke of the time that pointed out that Taft was a model gentleman, having given up his seat in a streetcar to three women.

William Jennings Bryan, running for the third and last time as the Democratic hopeful, was Taft's major opponent. Bryan, who crisscrossed the country on a chartered train, just as he had in 1896 and 1900, set the pattern in these elections for later twentieth-century candidates by his tireless, wide-ranging campaigning. A brilliant orator who held even the baggage handlers on his "special" in thrall (they would rush through the loading and unloading so they could then listen to his speech, perhaps for the twelfth or thirteenth time that day), Bryan was not able to improve much on previous Democratic showings: the lethargic but well-financed Taft won almost 52 percent of the total vote. This, however, was 5 percent less than Roosevelt had achieved in 1904, a fact noted by enemies and friends alike, as well as by the new president himself. Just after taking office, Taft wrote to TR:

> When I am addressed as, "Mr. President," I turn to see whether you are not at my elbow. . . . I have not the facility for educating the public as you had, . . . and so I fear that a large part of the public will feel as if I had fallen away from your ideals; but you know me better and will understand that I am still working away on the same old plan.[31]

Roosevelt responded, "Everything will surely turn out all right, old man," then departed for an extended safari in Africa, taking along his twenty-year-old son, Kermit, numerous rifles and books, and nine pairs of glasses. He was followed by his enemies' jokes about "may every lion do his duty."[32] Those who knew the man, however, worried more for the lions' sake.

CHAPTER TWO

The Battle

The New Nationalism regards the executive power as the steward of the public welfare.

Theodore Roosevelt[1]

We do not want big-brother government. . . . I do not want a government that will take care of me. I want a government that will make other men take their hands off so I can take care of myself.

Woodrow Wilson[2]

UNFORTUNATELY, despite Roosevelt's assurances, things did not turn out all right. William Howard Taft's judicial temperament, his dislike of campaigning and "politicking," limited his effectiveness as chief executive. He did prosecute twice as many antitrust cases as Roosevelt, but was not very agile in defending his legislative proposals before Congress. The first test came early in 1909 when Taft summoned Congress into a special session to revise and lower the tariff, called the "mother of trusts" because high rates protected the monopoly power of businesses. This was particularly timely because the cost of living was rising. Taft found himself outmaneuvered by Speaker of the House "Uncle Joe" Cannon and Senator Aldrich, then, to the anger of the insurgent Republicans who had looked to him for help, he acquiesced all too readily with the resulting Payne-Aldrich bill, which contained a tariff schedule that actually raised some rates. The disillusionment of the reformers became complete when Taft, in an address in Winona, Minnesota, that fall, called it "on the whole . . . the best [tariff] bill that the Republican Party ever passed."[3] It seemed obvious to them that his allegiance had been captured by the eastern conservatives. But western conservatives also had their influence on the president, and the trouble he fell into trying to please their demands for immediate economic development with little regard for conservation was going to be the greatest cause of his unhappy split with Theodore Roosevelt.

As a lawyer, Taft had been discomforted by what he regarded as TR's cavalier disregard for legal niceties in pursuing his aggressive policies in conservation. He surprised Roosevelt, and set about changing some of those policies, by replacing James R. Garfield as secretary of the interior with the Seattle corporate lawyer Richard Ballinger. Further alarm among conservationists was raised when Ballinger quickly reversed some of Roosevelt's decisions about public lands, reopening almost a million acres to private development, saying he preferred doing so rather than follow the "socialist" policies that had been established under Garfield. Gifford Pinchot, still serving as head of the National Forest Service, protested vigorously, but Taft remained unmoved. The chief forester then helped found the National Conservation Association to encourage public support for the policies he and Roosevelt had pursued. This did not charm Taft, who regarded Pinchot as "too much the radical and the crank," and who still had strong doubts about the legality of those policies.[4] "Pinchot is not a lawyer," the president complained, "and I am afraid he is quite willing to camp outside the law to accomplish his beneficent purposes."[5] The chief forester had his own complaints, writing later: "After TR came Taft. It was as though a sharp sword had been succeeded by a roll of paper, legal size."[6]

However, Pinchot himself thought he had sighted something lurking outside the law when Louis R. Glavis, an employee of the Department of the Interior, came to him with charges that Ballinger, when earlier serving as commissioner of the General Land Office, had colluded with a syndicate put together by J. P. Morgan and Daniel Guggenheim to illegally claim rich coal lands in Alaska. Pinchot presented the evidence to Taft, who, deciding that it had been distorted, fired Glavis. Pinchot, who was almost as adept as TR at using the press, then leaked the information to Collier's, one of the most active of the muckraking magazines, which published a long article by Glavis casting doubt on Ballinger's integrity. The case became a national affair, and Taft ended up firing Pinchot for insubordination. A congressional investigation followed; Ballinger was more or less cleared, but Republican insurgents and Democrats decried the process as a whitewash, while newspaper editors across the country called for Pinchot's nomination for president in 1912.[7]

Roosevelt, in his hunting camp in Africa, had trouble at first understanding Taft's motivations, and was made "most uneasy" by the developments in Washington. When he returned to Europe in April 1910, Pinchot met him at Porto Maurizio in Italy and explained his side of the controversy, buttressed with letters from other progressives in the Republican Party. It became clear to TR that the "Taft-Aldrich-Cannon regime" had "twisted around the policies I advocated and acted upon." TR had attended law school briefly, but dropped out because he felt that he was being trained only to defend unfair privilege and corporate interests. Now he thought that part of the problem was that Taft's was "an Administration which is primarily a lawyers' Administration" and as such was "totally unfit" to lead the nation. What the country needed were not the fine points of law but an aggressive fight for justice. If the right kind of leadership was not given, then the country would turn to demagogues and extremists. "I might be able to *guide* this movement, but I should be wholly unable to *stop* it, even if I were to try."[8]

Europe gave the ex-president an uproarious welcome, and his return to civilization resembled the tour of a conquering hero; Oxford awarded him an honorary degree, the Sorbonne invited him to lecture, and Kaiser Wilhelm II had him attend German military maneuvers, where the monarch signed a photograph of the two, "President Roosevelt shows the Emperor of Germany how to command an attack."[9] TR was not very impressed with the royalty he met: "A king is a kind of cross between a vice-president and a leader of the Four Hundred."[10] New York seemed determined to match the European honors; fireboats in full fountain greeted his ocean liner, and he was smothered in ticker tape in a parade through the city streets.

Taft's unpopularity had now reached national proportions, and the split between Republican factions grew worse. Delegations of insurgents and other progressive-minded folk came calling on Roosevelt, hoping that he could be convinced to enter the lists for the Republican presidential nomination in 1912. He resisted at first, in spite of resenting the continued bull-headed fighting by the party's old guard against needed reforms. "Our own party leaders," he wrote his friend Henry Cabot Lodge, "did not realize that I was able to hold the Republican party in power only because I insisted on a steady advance, and dragged them along with me. Now the advance has been stopped."[11] On a speaking tour of the West late in the summer of 1910, he was greeted by crowds of enthusiastic farmers and workers at every city, small town, and station stop, and he responded with some of his most fiery rhetoric, deliberately attacking the Supreme Court as reactionary for its decisions overturning federal and state efforts to regulate working conditions and control giant corporations.

This attack on judicial review and against property rights in favor of human rights drove the old guard to distraction, but he followed it with an even stronger plea at a ceremony honoring the antislavery radical John

Brown at Osawatomie, Kansas, on August 31. "The essence of any struggle for liberty has always been, and must always be, to take from some one man or class of men the right to enjoy power, or wealth, or position, or immunity, which has not been earned by service to his or their fellows." As support for his position, he quoted a previous president: "Labor is prior to, and independent of, capital. Capital is only the fruit of labor. . . . Labor is the superior of capital, and deserves much the higher consideration." And TR explained, "If that remark was original with me, I should be even more strongly denounced as a Communist agitator than I shall be anyhow. It is Lincoln's. I am only quoting it."[12] He was, of course, not a communist agitator, but a moderate progressive, arguing that the country needed to "destroy privilege, and give to the life and citizenship of every individual the highest possible value both to himself and to the commonwealth." This must be done, however, without going to the extremes that the socialists and La Follette–type reformers proposed, which would destroy the economic engines that had brought such prosperity to the country. It was time for a "New Nationalism," he argued, that would put the common interest before sectional, class, or individual ambitions. "The New Nationalism regards the executive power as the steward of the public welfare."

Many in the western United States were convinced after this tour that Theodore Roosevelt would be the Republican candidate for president in 1912; the man himself still was not. He continued to try to mend the breach between insurgents and regulars in the party, but with decreasing ardor. When the congressional elections of 1910 returned a humiliating defeat for Taft and the old guard, who had deliberately set out to battle the progressive wing in primaries and the general election, TR seemed resigned to Taft losing the 1912 contest. The Democrats, offering their own progressive candidates, won control of the House of Representatives for the first time since 1892 with a majority of sixty-six seats, and also took important Senate and state elections, including the governorship of New Jersey, which was won by the president of Princeton University, a historian named Woodrow Wilson who had never before run for office. After such a miserable failure, Roosevelt probably expected the conservatives to see the political sense in his positions, to recognize that they had to change, and then to support his presidential nomination as the only candidate who could bring both wings of the party back together in 1916. He would still be only fifty-eight years old that year.

But this was not to be. The mutual alienation between Roosevelt and Taft grew more bitter during the next year and a half as the new president continued to reverse policies Roosevelt had established. In January 1911, the insurgents formed the National Progressive Republican League to fight for their program of reform. They approached Roosevelt about the 1912 nomination; he demurred, but did not make an outright refusal. Robert La Follette, now a senator from Wisconsin and a founder of the league, stepped forward and actually began to campaign for the nomination in the spring of 1911. La Follette, however, was seen as too much a provincial as well as a radical, tied to his region of the upper Midwest and its problems, and so fierce in attacking the sins of corporations and the wealthy that it was unlikely that he could wrest the nomination away from Taft. Then, in early February 1912, La Follette himself put it far beyond his own reach.

La Follette had been invited to address the Periodical Publishers Association in Philadelphia along with Woodrow Wilson, a candidate for the Democratic nomination. Both men were known as gifted speakers; Wilson lived up to his reputation, speaking briefly and urbanely of his ideas on progressivism and what it offered the nation. "Never was he in better form," wrote the liberal editor Oswald Garrison Villard. "He made one of his great speeches, and swept everything before him. The audience, largely composed of Republican reactionaries, was thrilled by him."[13]

Unfortunately, La Follette, whom Wilson respected as a champion of progressive ideas, at this moment cracked under the strain of overwork and the frustrations of his campaign. There were rumors later that he was suffering from ptomaine poisoning, or that he, ordinarily a teetotaler, had taken a few nips. Whatever the cause, he rose, and, unusual for him, pulled out a typescript of his speech, then proceeded to read the same pages over and over again for more than two hours, crudely denouncing the daily press for mendacity, irresponsibility, and lack of concern for society's needy. Shouts from the audience of "Sit down" finally penetrated, and he sank weakly into his chair, but not before most guests had left the hall. Even friendly reporters were shocked by the performance: "Senator La Follette is a sick man—this is the explanation of his failure at Philadelphia last night," wrote Angus McSween of the Philadelphia *North American*.[14] As a form of vengeance, the rest of the press played the story of La Follette's nervous breakdown for days, and his campaign, for all practical purposes, was over. The National Progressive Republican League again turned to Roosevelt, and on February 22, 1912, he announced, "My hat is in the ring! The fight is on and I'm stripped to the buff." Newspapers across the nation ran cartoons of his Rough Rider hat in a boxing ring.

Roosevelt appears to have had no illusions about his chances. He knew the power of the presidency to control the party organization, having used it so skillfully himself, and he recognized that the conservatives would not be overly bound by scruples in denying him the nomination. Close friends, and his eldest son, Theodore Jr., tried to convince him of the wisdom of waiting until 1916, but political wisdom was not now the issue, principles were. He judged that his philosophy of, and record as, a strong president who would serve as the aggressive defender of the common good had been betrayed by Taft and his conservative supporters, while Roosevelt felt personally dishonored by their attacks on his decisions.

TR campaigned with his usual vigor, giving speeches across the country, arguing that he was fighting for the progressive cause, and in the interests "of the crippled brakeman on a railroad, of the overworked girl in a factory, of the stunted child toiling at inhuman labor, of all who work excessively or in unhealthy surroundings, of the family dwelling in the squalor of a noisome tenement, of the worn-out farmer in regions where the farms are worn out also."[15] Those interests were being betrayed by a political and judicial system that lacked the wisdom and the courage to change, and he came out for the right of voters to "recall" the decisions of state courts in cases that had overturned progressive legislation, though he opposed the position taken by more extreme elements to recall the judges themselves. The explanation of his position was muddled, however, and brought forth widespread condemnation not just from reactionaries but also from moderates and allies. Even his close friend Henry Cabot Lodge refused to support him because of his stance, and this speech may, like La Follette's performance before the Periodical Publishers, have been the blunder that cost him the nomination.[16]

Less energetically effective was President Taft, who pushed himself to take to the road to win renomination, though tradition dictated that an incumbent president should not campaign very actively, but should instead remain above the fray. At one time he had evidently thought of withdrawing, but that hesitation ended after TR openly challenged him. He had been wounded by the break with his former patron, and by the slashing attacks that had followed. "Mr. Taft means well but he means well feebly," went one of Roosevelt's gentler comments. "It is this quality of feebleness in a normally amiable man which preeminently fits such a man for use in high office by the powers of evil."[17] One night the *New York World* reporter John Siebold came across the president in the campaign train "slumped over, with his head between his hands." Taft looked up as Siebold entered. "Roosevelt was my closest friend," he said, then started weeping.[18] He made speeches that he hoped would show the differences between himself and his major opponent; they, however, often showed his lack of campaign skills: "I am a man of peace, and I don't want to fight. But when I do fight I want to hit hard," which is the sort of toughness American male voters like, but then he added: "Even a rat in a corner will fight."[19] Roosevelt's people made sure that the analogy received wide distribution.

TR began piling up the primary victories; even in the president's own state of Ohio, Roosevelt took thirty-seven of the forty-eight delegates, then followed with an overwhelming win in New Jersey. By the end, he had won 1,157,397 votes in the primaries, while Taft had managed a mere 761,716. But most states still used the convention system to select candidates, and these bodies were usually in the hands of party professionals. He won Kansas, Maine, and Oklahoma, but lost the other contests manipulated by the president's men. This was especially true in the "rotten boroughs" of the South, where federal largess provided the only patronage for Republican loyalists, mostly African Americans.

By the time the convention convened in Chicago in June, Roosevelt was contesting 252 delegates. The National Committee, however, began deciding case after case in favor of Taft, while Roosevelt's people futilely protested the "steamroller" tactics so vociferously that the newspapers ran cartoons of such machines squashing insurgents, and poems such as one entitled "The Steam Roller" published in the *Baltimore Sun,* which began:

> Oh, they threw the throttle open
> And they jammed 'er full of coke
> And they watched 'er as she gathered up her steam.
> A lot o' men were hopin'
> That she wouldn't stir a stroke
> When they jerked the rope and let the whistles scream.[20]

The parallel between these powerful monsters and the political machine rolling over TR so caught the public imagination that an enterprising, if overly optimistic, Hearst newspaperman hired a steamroller, parked it in front of the convention, and unsuccessfully tried to talk party leaders into clambering behind the controls to be photographed.

Roosevelt fought the irresistible force as best he could, even breaking long-standing tradition by showing up himself at the convention site, the Coliseum. There were a thousand Chicago police on duty because of the charged atmosphere, and the platform was surrounded by barbed wire hidden under the red, white, and blue bunting.[21] Bands marched to and fro playing the jolly hit tune by Irving Berlin "Everybody's Doin' It, Doin' It, Doin' It," which TR's supporters changed to "Everybody's Sayin' It, Roosevelt, Roosevelt." Journalists interpreted the fistfights that kept breaking out as visible signs of the hate that was seething on both sides. Florence Harriman, social worker and Democrat, was there as a reporter. "The sultry air was charged with dynamite. Delegates talked of drawing pistols and knives over disputed seats. Everybody jostled, pushed, whispered. Day and night the excitement grew, monotonous, continuous."[22] William Jennings Bryan, the Democrat of Democrats, was also in Chicago, as a reporter, and he assured the official in charge of issuing press passes, "I will agree not to say anything worse about Taft and Roosevelt than they say about each other—a promise I feel sure I can live up to."[23]

But, of course, some of the anger was going beyond words. Roosevelt personally was called upon to restrain some of his followers. One half-drunk former Rough Rider burst into TR's room threatening to wreak havoc on the opposition, and wouldn't listen when his colonel tried to calm him. "Say, Teddy," he broke in, "don't you fool yourself. . . . They're goin' to run that Steam Roller right over your body." After some more ranting, he pulled two enormous pistols out from under his long-tailed coat and threatened to fill enemy leaders "full of lead." Unable to charm or order him to stay away, Roosevelt's people finally assisted him into such a drunken state that he was unable to attend the convention the next day, when the Steam Roller completed its run.[24]

Other supporters were just as angry as the Rough Rider, even if less violently inclined. They stormed out of the hall, vowing vengeance. Filled with self-righteous wrath, Roosevelt tried to decide the proper response to what he called a "successful fraud."[25] They had not been "steamrolled," he told the public, but "robbed." But could he really abandon the party he had led so skillfully for so many years? Abandon the art of compromise that he had perfected? But where was the room to compromise, and wouldn't it be immoral to do so? As he and his advisers met, two of the wealthiest, publisher Frank Munsey and industrialist and former J. P. Morgan partner George Perkins, assured him of financial support if he started a new party, saying, "Colonel, we will see you through." Amos Pinchot, who, along with his brother Gifford, was also wealthy enough to contribute financially, remembered, "At that precise moment the Progressive Party was born."[26] A convention was called for early August.

Roosevelt and his new party had a chance to win, but only if the Democrats, who suffered from their own contending factions, were foolish enough to nominate a party hack or a conservative, as they had in 1904 with Alton B. Parker. Progressive elements of both parties would then see Roosevelt as the bright and shining hope for their cause; for a while it looked as if the Democrats would cooperate. As was evident from the results of the elections of 1910, they had been enjoying a resurgence as Republicans fell into open warfare. When the Democrats met in Baltimore in late June, the front-runner was Speaker of the House Champ Clark from Missouri, a wily, if bibulous, professional who enjoyed close ties to the party machines in Kansas City and St. Louis and was backed by William Randolph Hearst. Clark did not have a very distinguished political record and was not widely known, though he had gained some notoriety by endorsing a patent medicine called Electric Bitters that had the allure of a high alcoholic content. But he had swept eleven primaries and could boast hundreds of enthusiastic delegates, a host of whom spent their time marching up and down the aisles chanting, yelling, sometimes screaming a refrain from the Missourian's campaign song:

> *I don't care if he is a houn',*
> *You gotta quit kickin' my dawg aroun'.*

A worker for Woodrow Wilson grew so maddened by this constant refrain that he told his campaign manager, William Gibbs McAdoo, "I'm going to get a hound dog, take him out on the street, and kick him around—just to see what happens."

"Do you want to be lynched?" was the reply.[27]

The strongest alternative candidate was the Virginia-born governor of New Jersey, Woodrow Wilson, who had a reputation for stern, upright morality, and who had enjoyed surprising success in his brief political career; the governorship was his first elected office, yet this former professor had boldly applied his book learning to practical politics, outmaneuvering the New Jersey political machine, then guiding a divided legislature into passing a range of progressive reforms, including direct primaries, regulation of public utilities, workmen's compensation, and school improvements, without incurring debts to party hacks. His eloquent speech before the Periodical Publishers had helped his cause, and he had then spent much of the spring campaigning across the nation.

Candidates traditionally tried to preserve their dignity and stay above the fray, so Wilson didn't go to Baltimore, but remained at the official governor's summer residence in Sea Girt, New Jersey, while his managers, McAdoo and William McCombs, helped by Pennsylvania congressman A. Mitchell Palmer, led a valiant floor fight in the raucous, circuslike atmosphere of the convention. After a dozen ballots, no candidate had the necessary two-thirds majority, though Clark was leading. That worthy's daughter, Genevieve, was parading around the armory wrapped in the

American flag, which prompted Wilson, when he learned of the display, to tell his own daughters, "Now you will understand why I wouldn't allow any of you to go to the convention."[28]

The Great Commoner, William Jennings Bryan, still a major force in the party despite his three defeats, had not run for the nomination this year, though rumors circulated that he would accept if drafted. However, he admitted to Florence Harriman, who was a Wilson supporter, that he could never again be a candidate, for three reasons: "first my stand on prohibition, second my attitude toward the Roman Catholic Church, and third because I am considered a hoo-

Woodrow Wilson:
the scholar as politician

doo to the party."[29] William Allen White, covering the story for his *Emporia Gazette* and other papers, noted that Bryan "was a strange figure in that convention, a ridiculous man with tremendous power."[30]

Bryan was also no longer the "Boy Orator of the Platte," slender, dashing, and graceful. Sixteen years of good living and little exercise had thickened his body, doubled his chin, and softened his muscles, but he retained a core of steel and great influence among the delegates. Amid all the dramatic, "spontaneous" demonstrations, the loud bands playing competing campaign songs, mysterious women releasing white doves to soar among the rafters, and the operatic flights of oratory, Bryan kept struggling against what he perceived as a conspiracy to place another Wall Street conservative like Parker at the head of the ticket. Wearing his traditional outfit of baggy trousers and wrinkled alpaca jacket, bald pate topped with a Panama hat, arm waving a palm-leaf fan like a metronome against the humid southern heat, he attacked over and over again the New York delegation, which had as members two of the nation's wealthiest financiers, August Belmont and Thomas Fortune Ryan, and which was controlled by the corrupt Tammany Hall machine. Here was the voice of the embittered West and South against the money power of the East; here, too, was the voice of rural

America protesting the strength of the city and its immigrant citizenry. After Bryan tried to have Belmont and Ryan expelled from the convention, a near riot ensued, with cries of "Lynch him!" from conservative opponents, while one man climbed onto a chair to shout that he would pay $25,000 to anyone who would shoot the Commoner. In response, some supporters gave rebel yells that "ripped through the applause like a scythe down the swath," as White wrote.[31] Bryan, however, sitting calmly with his pale fan beating time and sipping from an ever present glass of water, had made his point, headed off any conspiracy; southern and western supporters, such as "Alfalfa Bill" Murray of Oklahoma, waving red bandannas, took up the cry: "We won't put our stamp of approval on Wall Street!"[32]

Wilson, whose aides in Sea Girt had special telegraph and telephone equipment installed, was in touch with the Baltimore managers. When Bryan asked for support in some of these maneuvers, one of Wilson's people advised caution, but his greatest and most consistent adviser, his wife, Ellen, told him that "there must be no hedging" when principle was involved. Wilson had originally been a conservative Democrat, and in fact had earlier regarded Bryan as an embarrassment and encumbrance to the party. "Would that we could do something," he had written to a friend in 1907 in a letter that would later be made public at an inopportune moment, "at once dignified and effective, to knock Mr. Bryan . . . into a cocked hat."[33] But over the years the differences had been made up, and his present hewing to progressive ideals helped convince Bryan that here was the candidate worthy of his support. Other delegates then began maneuvering, as one explained to Bernard Baruch, a Wilson partisan: "I saw that my man Clark was dead. I wasn't going to lay down on that ice and get political pneumonia. No, Sir! I got up and cut some fancy didoes and came out for Wilson."[34] On the forty-sixth ballot, Woodrow Wilson became the Democratic candidate for president. Well-wishers and reporters came pouring across his lawn when word reached the Jersey Shore, and a brass band that his secretary, Joe Tumulty, had hidden in some nearby bushes came marching forth playing "Hail, the Conquering Hero Comes!," which caused Wilson to ask what tune would have been played if the effort had failed. When things quieted down enough, he sent an assistant to buy a celebratory box of cigars for his friends to smoke, though he never indulged himself.

Theodore Roosevelt arrived at his National Progressive Party's convention in Chicago on August 4, announcing that he felt "as strong as a bull moose," which the delighted reporters quickly used as a sobriquet for the new organization. There were no staged demonstrations, parades, or dove-liberating women of mystery at this convention, which more resembled a revivalist camp meeting, nor any uncertainty about who the nominee would be. When TR appeared on the platform, the fifteen thousand attendees, whom one reporter described as "crusaders," gave him a spontaneous fifty-two-minute standing ovation, waving red bandannas and cheering themselves hoarse when not singing:

> *Thou wilt not cower in the dust,*
> *Roosevelt, O Roosevelt!*
> *Thy gleaming sword shall never rust,*
> *Roosevelt, O Roosevelt.*

The Progressive, or Bull Moose, candidate, the first of any party to accept such a nomination in person, gave his people a rousing evangelical speech—interrupted 145 times by applause—that he admitted was a "Confession of Faith." "I hope we shall win. . . . But win, or lose, we shall not falter. . . . Our cause is based on the eternal principle of righteousness; and even though we who now lead may for the time fail, in the end the cause itself shall triumph. . . . We stand at Armageddon, and we battle for the Lord."[35] Joining him on the battlefield were such prominent progressives as Jane Addams, who in her speech seconding TR's nomination gave particular praise to the plank in the party platform supporting women's suffrage.

That struck a responsive chord in an audience that, William Allen White wrote, had many successful women sitting among the successful men, "women doctors, women lawyers, women teachers, college professors, middle-aged leaders of civic movements, or rich young girls who had gone in for settlement work." White, studying the well-dressed crowd, estimated "that there was not a man or woman on the floor who was making less than two thousand a year, and not one . . . who was topping ten thousand."[36] A solidly middle-class crowd, yet one moved by passion as the convention theme song of "Onward Christian Soldiers" was played, and when the party platform was approved, they broke into "Praise God from Whom All Blessings Flow." That platform included, among its many proposed reforms, calls for the tight regulation of corporations, a tariff commission, minimum-wage and workers' compensation laws, the direct election of senators, and the banning of child labor.[37] The campaign slogan that most moved them and that seemed to sum up the platform was "using government as an agency of human welfare."

But even amid all this fervor, Roosevelt, as a professional politician, recognized that the selection of Wilson instead of Clark or some Democratic reactionary combined with the fact that few Republican Party professionals had bolted with him doomed the campaign to failure before it even began. The intense religious spirit of the convention seemed to puzzle him at times. As a *New York Times* reporter explained, not completely accurately, "They were crusaders; he was not."[38]

When the full campaign began, Wilson charged that it would be denying necessary change to vote for either "Tweedledum" or "Tweedledee," who, he said, merely represented different wings of the Republican Party. However, the election of 1912 was far more complicated than that; not simply a choice between conservatives and reformers, but also between two different types of progressivism, or "liberalism." Taft stayed in the race more as a spoiler than a true candidate; everyone recognized that the real contest was between Roosevelt, offering his New Nationalism, and Wilson, with what was being called the New Freedom.

Policy toward the enormous concentration of economic power in the trusts was one of the points of contention in their differing visions of America's future. Roosevelt believed that this increase in size and power of corporations was inevitable under modern economic conditions; they were here to stay, and the way to control them was through an equally strong central government armed with clear regulatory powers. Wilson, advised by the brilliant Boston lawyer Louis Brandeis, argued that these huge entities should be dismantled, not regulated. Only then would small entrepreneurs and businessmen have a chance to make their own fortunes. "I am for the man on the make," Wilson pronounced, "not the already made man." Roosevelt's scheme, he argued, would diminish American freedom by promoting big government that would serve to protect big business. "This is a second struggle for emancipation. If America is not to have free enterprise, then she can have freedom of no sort whatever."[39] And if a certain measure of industrial inefficiency resulted, then so be it.

There was also a difference in their view of the place of the individual in American society. Roosevelt had been worrying for years over the selfishness of sectional and individual drive, envy, and ambition. The New Nationalism called for a greater unity in American life, a deferring of individual and sectional interests to the greater good of the nation. Wilson emphasized a greater freedom for individuals under the traditional decentralized government of states' rights that would allow people to devote their energies to their own advancement, believing such liberty would benefit the whole.

Both candidates were articulate and energetic speakers, though Roosevelt's nervous energy and heroic glamour contrasted strongly with Wilson's reserved self-possession and professorial dignity. Wilson had made a lifelong study of oratory, and had, in his quiet way, become a master who was unafraid to speak his mind to any audience. Ray Stannard Baker, a journalist who would become a scholar of Wilson's life and first editor of his papers, met him when Wilson addressed a group of powerful bankers: "the veritable kingpins of the American earth." Wilson was not shy in lecturing them about their failings: "Banking is founded on a moral basis and not on a financial basis. The trouble today is that you bankers are too narrow-minded. You don't know the country or what is going on in it and the country doesn't trust you. You are not interested in the development of the country, but in what has been developed. You take no interest in the small borrower and the small enterprise which affect the future of the country, but you give every attention to the big borrower and the rich enterprise which has already arrived." When Wilson sat down, an irritated J. P. Morgan let him know that the remarks had been taken personally.[40]

George Creel, another journalist who would later serve Wilson, was also drawn by his skills as an orator. "What thrilled me was not merely the clarity of his thought, the beauty of his phrasing, but the shining faith of the man in the *practicality* of ideals. More than any other, it seemed to me that he voiced the true America—not the songs that people sing when they remember the words, but the dream of liberty, justice, and fraternity."[41]

But there was also a fourth contender in the battle, and a fierce one. Eugene Victor Debs was the son of immigrant shopkeepers from the Alsace. Going to work on the railroad at the age of fourteen, he had become a union organizer, and during the Pullman strike of 1894 he was jailed for contempt of court. This, he later said, gave him the opportunity for six months of reading and thinking that convinced him that the solution to the problems of the workingman and the broader society lay with the Socialist Party. Debs, like TR and Wilson, was a skilled public speaker, though rather more flowery than his competitors. This was his third run for the presidency, and in spite of recognizing that there was little chance for victory, he campaigned with all the fervor of a true believer, sure that the future would bring a socialist utopia where the workers would control natural resources and the means of production for the betterment of all society. Debs urged workers to overturn the traditional capitalist system, to "tear up privilege by the roots, and consecrate the earth and all its fullness to the joy and service of all humanity."[42] Here, indeed, was an election with choices.

Wilson was surprised, given the importance of the issues, that the candidates' views on national politics fought a sometimes losing competition with newspaper space reserved for baseball's World Series (in which the

Boston Red Sox would beat the New York Giants in seven games). He was also taken aback when his long face with its bony features received more attention than he thought appropriate, and a frequently overheard phrase used by people at his speeches became a running joke between the candidate and reporters accompanying him: "Well, he may be all right, but he ain't good-looking."[43] Perhaps he wasn't very pretty, but malicious rumors were deliberately circulated that he had indulged in an affair with a woman friend, Mary Allen Peck, who was going through a messy divorce. Theodore Roosevelt scoffed at the idea: "You can't cast a man as Romeo who looks and acts so much like an apothecary's clerk."[44] Romeo Wilson was not, but the danger presented by the rumors came from the painful truth behind them. However, the stories did not catch fire with the public, perhaps because most people shared TR's reaction to the candidate's seemingly dry personality and craggy homeliness.

Wilson found that he enjoyed the grueling pace of the campaign, gaining more than seven pounds, though he also had to endure the dangers of the road: a freight car smashed into his Pullman, shattering the windows and narrowly missing him; then while being driven in an "autocar" along one of the nation's notoriously bad roads, the driver hit a rut, throwing the candidate into the roof so hard that stitches were needed to close his bleeding scalp.

By far the greater injury, however, came to Roosevelt on October 14 as he was climbing into an automobile in Milwaukee on his way to give a campaign speech. John Schrank, unemployed and mentally ill, had been stalking TR for days. Now, seeing his opportunity, he rushed close and shot his prey in the chest. Roosevelt staggered back, coughed, then recovered his balance and rose to his feet as the crowd began to yell at Schrank, "Lynch him! Kill him!"

"Stand back," TR shouted. "Don't hurt him!" Once Schrank was taken off by the police, the candidate overruled his doctors and insisted on going to the hall to deliver his speech.[45]

He opened with a disjointed prologue about the shooting: "I shall ask you to be as quiet as possible. I don't know whether you fully understand that I have just been shot; but it takes more than that to kill a Bull Moose." He held up the torn manuscript of his speech, which folded into a breast pocket had kept the bullet from penetrating deeply. "The bullet is in me now. . . . And now, friends . . . I want you to understand that I am ahead of the game, anyway. No man has had a happier life than I have led. . . . I cannot understand a man fit to be a colonel who can pay any heed to his personal safety. . . . At one time I promoted five men for gallantry . . . two of them were Protestants, two Catholics, and one a Jew. . . . If all five of them had been Jews I would have promoted them. . . . I make the same appeal in our citizenship." After working off the nervous shock of the wound, he continued to speak for close to an hour, defending the idea of unions and attacking Wilson for promoting "the old flintlock, muzzle-loading doctrine of States' rights. . . . We are for the people's rights. If they can be obtained best through the National Government, then we are for national rights. . . . Mr. Wilson has distinctly declared that you shall not have a national law to prohibit the labor of children. . . . I ask you to look at our declaration and hear and read our platform about social and industrial justice."[46] After finishing, he was rushed to a hospital, where he remained for more than a week.

Woodrow Wilson did the gentlemanly thing, refusing to book any new speaking engagements while Roosevelt recuperated, publicly stating that "my thought is constantly of that gallant gentleman lying in the hospital," though he knew, as he laughingly told friends, "Teddy will have apoplexy when he hears of this."[47] At least one death threat against Wilson arrived soon after TR was shot, and at the recommendation of Wilson's political adviser Edward House, Captain Bill McDonald of the Texas Rangers became his bodyguard.

On Election Day, the expected happened: Wilson won 6,286,000 votes, Roosevelt 4,216,000, Taft 3,486,000. The only real surprise was the showing of the Socialist Eugene Debs, who polled almost 900,000, about 6 percent of the total, from Americans who felt that neither of the two front-runners went far enough in challenging the power of the great corporations. The electoral college made it a landslide: Wilson's 435 (the most ever for a candidate) to 88 for TR and a meager 8 for Taft, who managed to carry just Utah and the Republican perennial, Vermont. In addition, the Democrats won control of both houses of Congress for the first time since 1890, and won the governorship in twenty-one of the thirty-five states that held gubernatorial elections.

The president-elect fled to Bermuda with his wife and two youngest daughters in order to have the peace and quiet to absorb his victory, and think about what to do. During the election, he had written about the American people's lack of familiarity with him compared to Roosevelt. "He appeals to their imagination; I do not. He is a real, vivid person, whom they have seen and shouted themselves hoarse over and voted for, millions strong; I am a vague, conjectural personality, more made up of opinions and academic prepossessions than of human traits and red corpuscles. We shall see what will happen!"[48]

CHAPTER THREE

——◄◦►——

The New Spirit

We live in a revolutionary period and nothing is so important as to be aware of it. The dynamics of a splendid human civilization are about us.

Walter Lippmann

Oh, the ragtime of the present
Is in many ways unpleasant. . . .
It is not in music solely
That its influence unholy
Is exerted the proprieties to balk,
But it permeates existence
With insidious persistence,
And it gets into our thinking and our talk.

Life magazine, June 26, 1913

Everybody's doin' it, doin' it. Everybody's doin' it now.

Irving Berlin, 1911

THE UNITED STATES in 1913 was awash in newness that went far beyond Theodore Roosevelt's New Nationalism or Woodrow Wilson's New Freedom. There were, among many other things nouvelle, a New Music, New Theater, New Art, New Psychology, New Morals, New Immigration. A New Man strutted along the boulevards, accompanied, or on occasion brushed aside, by a New Woman. For those so inclined there was a New Marriage (along with a startling rise in something that until recently had been so rare that a "new" version need not be marked: divorce). A New Consciousness was also said to be working its way among the more advanced thinkers.

39

Music, however, affected everyone, and especially everyone in the growing cities, which pulsed with a different rhythm than the small-town agricultural communities so closely tied to nature—though these too were beginning to move to a man-made beat thanks to Thomas Edison's marvelous invention, the phonograph. Ragtime, with its jittery cadence, had first begun to be heard at the turn of the century, and now its popularity spread throughout the United States. Irving Berlin was one of the early masters of syncopated songs, and he came to symbolize how the new wave of immigrants could both absorb and form the spirit of their new country. Born Israel Baline in 1888, he came to America in 1893 when his family joined the millions of Jews fleeing pogroms and poverty in Russia. Growing up on Cherry Street in the Lower East Side of New York, he had very little formal schooling, but his father, a cantor turned poultry inspector, did give him music lessons. When his father died in 1900, leaving his wife and eight children in desperate straits, the boy, not wanting to be a burden, left home, becoming a busker on the city streets, a raspy-throated singing waiter in a Chinese restaurant, and a song "plugger" at Tony Pastor's Music Hall. All the while, he was listening to the diverse voices of the immigrant city; it was estimated that 290,000 people were crammed into every square mile of the slums on the Lower East Side. In 1907, his first song, "Marie from Sunny Italy," in comic Italian dialect, was published, and though it earned him only thirty-seven cents in royalties, it was followed by increasingly popular ethnic tunes such as "Sadie Salome, Go Home," which told the tale of a nice Jewish girl who runs off to become an actress, but who is found by her boyfriend, Moses, as a stripper. "Oy, oy, oy, oy," he laments, "where is your clothes?/You better go and get your dresses,/Everyone's got the op'ra glasses." Between 1907 and 1914, the young writer and composer would publish 190 songs, with titles such as "Oh, How That German Could Love," "Colored Romeo," "Latins Know How," "Everybody's Doin' It Now," and "Snooky Ookums." Berlin became known as the King of Ragtime, and his inability to sing or play an instrument well or even know much about the formal rules of music is an early sign of the freedom that popular music, and the popular arts in general, would enjoy in the twentieth century. No need for long, disciplined training to satisfy the growing mass audience.

Berlin's first big hit came in 1911 with the jubilant invitation of "Alexander's Ragtime Band" to "Come on and hear, come on and hear," which instantly became an anthem for the age; a million copies of the sheet music were sold in seven months, yielding its twenty-one-year-old author more than a hundred thousand dollars at a time when a few thousand a year could provide a comfortable middle-class way of life. "What was needed," wrote contemporary critic Gilbert Seldes, "was a crystallization, was one song which should take the whole dash and energy of rag-time and carry it to its apotheosis. With a characteristic turn of mind Berlin accomplished this in a song which had no other topic than rag-time itself. 'Alexander's Ragtime Band' was . . . utterly unsentimental and the whole country responded to its masterful cry, 'Come on and hear!' "[1]

Others tied that lack of sentimentality, and ragtime itself, to its birth in the African American community, where old, genteel standards such as "Home Sweet Home" were played with, jeered at, mocked. As the journalist and historian Mark Sullivan explained, African American musicians "took advantage of the pauses in this slow music to repeat the regular melody—but with the accents quickened and shifted, making an effect of comical pertness. The humor of it lay in the surprise; hearers recognized the authentic music of an old familiar favorite, but done in a quickened tempo, as far as possible from the original mood."[2] And that is why in "Alexander's Ragtime Band" you are invited to listen, while also warned that you will hear the traditional minstrel tune "Swanee River," only in ragtime. "All the old rhythm is gone," Berlin explained later, "and in its place is heard the hum of an engine, the whir of wheels, the explosion of an exhaust."[3] The term *rag*, because of this quickened tempo, became slang indicating the need for hurried action. It was the perfect music for the developing urban pace of life, and the sense of freedom that came with it.

Along with the new popular songs came dances that matched them in their jittery excitement; here was hurried action by couples on public display, and while both socialites and the "masses" loved the syncopation, traditionalists were shocked to outrage by what were being called "animal dances." There was the fox-trot, the horse-trot, the kangaroo dip, the camel walk, the chicken scratch, and the lame duck, among many others. The most famous, or infamous, were the turkey trot and the grizzly bear, which called for hugging one's partner, "backing," i.e., pushing against, the lady, and sometimes using a "strangle-hold" while moving about the floor. One well-known music critic complained that "in this year of pretended refinement, which is the year of our Lord 1913, the [ragtime dances] are threatening to force grace, decorum, and decency out of the ball rooms of America."[4] This was just fine with the young bohemians flocking into Greenwich Village that same year. Intent on liberating American society from its old Victorian ways, William Langner, one of these crusaders, wrote of the turkey trot that "as you clutched your feminine partner and led her through the crowded dance floor . . . you felt you were doing something for the progress of humanity, as well as for yourself and, in some cases, for her."[5]

These feelings must have been widely shared; in spite of much unofficial and official condemnation by both religious and secular institutions, including fines levied for frolicking to such risqué tunes, the dances won popular acceptance fairly quickly. The elegant and refined dance instructors Irene and Vernon Castle helped tone down some of the sexuality, though countering that diminution was another dancer just arrived in New York. Rodolfo Guglielmi arrived on a boat from Italy in 1913, making his way in the city first by teaching, then becoming an exhibition dancer, eventually performing before President Wilson, among other notables. After changing his name to Rudolph Valentino, he would go on to even steamier success in the movies.

America's dance craze was not limited to the forty-eight states. As Berlin wrote in that same year of 1913:

> *What did you do, America? They're after you, America!*
> *You got excited and you started something, Nations jumping all around;*
> *You've got a lot to answer for, they lay the blame right at your door,*
> *The world is ragtime crazy from shore to shore.*
> *London dropped its dignity, so has France and Germany.*
> *All hands are dancing to a raggedy melody full of originality.*

This international originality flowed both ways. In February 1913, an art exhibit opened at the Sixty-ninth Infantry Regiment Armory in New York City that gave Americans their first full look at the work produced by the European modernist movement, and the reaction here, too, was often shocked outrage.

At the turn of the century, Robert Henri and John Sloan had led the social realists of the Ashcan school in rebellion against the genteel tradition of John Singer Sargent, William Merritt Chase, John La Farge, and the National Academy of Design. It was important, Henri felt, to paint all of life, not just the pretty aspects, so the group's canvases often depicted the ordinary appearance of the city, from laundry drying on a line, to soot falling on snow, to tumbled ash cans in an alley, to everyday people doing everyday tasks and enjoying themselves on the streets.

They were seen as rebels, and many were socialists and critics of the capitalism of the age, but their technique was that of a rather traditional, though gritty, American realism. Beginning in 1906, a different line of rebellion was being led by Alfred Stieglitz at his Photo-Secession Gallery, which became known as the "291," located at 291 Fifth Avenue. Challenging traditional standards, he exhibited both photographs, which were usually disdained as works of technology rather than art, and the "modern" styles of painting and sculpture being experimented with in Europe, giving many avant-garde artists their first American showings: Rodin and Matisse drawings in 1907, and, over the next several years, works by Toulouse-Lautrec, Cézanne, and Picasso.

In November 1912, a group of New York artists decided to mount an exhibition of the new art. Intentions at first were for it to be mainly a show of American artists, but then three painters, Walter Pach, Walt Kuhn, and Arthur B. Davies, made a trip to Europe to select modern pieces there. They returned with more than five hundred of the most radically "progressive" that they could find; to these were added about eight hundred works by Americans. The organizers took as their slogan "The New Spirit."

From its grand opening in New York on the evening of February 17, 1913, the exhibition caused a sensation. Early newspaper reports were enthusiastic, calling the show "a bomb shell," and "an event not to be missed," but the uproar became strident once established art critics had time to get their views in print. The consensus was that the European part of the show consisted of "crazy" works that had little or no relationship to art. Such condemnation, not for the last time, added fuel to the fire of controversy, and attendance soared; everyone wanted to see this exciting carnival: artists, collectors, writers, amateur sketchers, and idle gawkers. One thing all could agree on was that most foreign works on display bore little relationship to what had gone before. Somewhere between seventy thousand and a hundred thousand people saw the show in New York, perhaps some ten thousand on the last day alone.

Here was the first opportunity for the broad American public to encounter work by artists such as Vincent van Gogh, Wassily Kandinsky, Paul Cézanne, Henri Matisse, Paul Gauguin, Constantin Brancusi, and Pablo Picasso; the people came, and were amused but confounded by the nonrepresentational styles. The painting that caused the greatest bewilderment, and generated the most jokes, was Marcel Duchamp's fractured image entitled *Nude Descending a Staircase,* which one wag insisted should more accurately be called an "explosion in a shingle factory" and others claimed was really a "staircase descending a nude." Newspapers were full of jokes, cartoons, and doggerel mocking it; one offered a prize to anyone who could find the nude, and there were arguments about, once found, whether it would be male or female.

Professional critics continued their attacks as the exhibit, now reduced

Duchamp's Nude Descending a
Staircase, No. 2 (1912)

to around five hundred pieces, moved to Chicago, where the faculty at that city's Art Institute convinced their students to burn effigies of Matisse, Brancusi, and Walter Pach, one of the organizers. The students also held a "Futuristic Party" where women adorned their heads with long curling wood shavings and painted their faces in Cubist colors. The *Chicago Tribune* reported that "a man with a bale of shingles fastened to his clothes danced with a girl whose face represented a spider web, or a map of a railroad yard on a foggy night."[6] Here, too, scandal worked its alluring magic as close to two hundred thousand people made their way to the show. Critics in Boston, the next and last stop on the tour, added their bits to the collective heap of scorn that traveled along with it. A. J. Philpott of the *Boston Globe* wrote: "There is scarcely a picture or a bit of sculpture in the exhibition that does not appear to be either an intentional joke, the work of an unbalanced mind, or the work of an extremely bad artist."[7]

One amateur critic had a surprisingly positive take on aspects of the show. Theodore Roosevelt, writing in *Outlook* magazine, did decry the Cubists and Futurists as part of a "lunatic fringe," and he made a point of ridiculing Duchamp's painting, "which for some reason is called 'A Naked Man Going Down Stairs,' but could just as fittingly have been called 'A Well-Dressed Man Going Up a Ladder.'" But he also, no doubt because of his own political struggles, recognized the openness to creativity and originality that the show celebrated. "It is vitally necessary to move forward and to shake off the dead hand . . . of the reactionaries." And he understood that for creative artists there "is a liability to extravagance." At the Armory Show there was nothing "of the commonplace. There was not a touch of simpering self-satisfied conventionality anywhere in the exhibition. Any sculptor or painter who had in him something to express and the power of expressing it found the field open to him. . . . There was no stunting or dwarfing, no requirement that a man whose gift lay in new directions should measure up or down to stereotyped and fossilized standards."[8]

The power of this great invasion of European creativity, whether lamented or celebrated, was widely recognized. For all the general mockery by the press and public, the exhibit sold $45,000 worth of paintings, sculpture, and prints—an impressive amount in 1913. "The press and public laughed," wrote the art historian Milton W. Brown, "the critics, with their standards crumbling around their ears, fulminated, but it was all to no avail. The Armory Show had done its job."[9] American art would never be the same, but it would take years for the changes to fully take effect.

While the more affluent were debating what style of art to buy, workers were still struggling for the means to survive. The war between capitalists and workers continued apace, and the several years just before the war were particularly violent, as well as creative. An especially bitter battle was being waged in West Virginia as the United Mine Workers tried to organize the workers there. Mine operators resisted this threat to their power, bringing in armed guards and expelling miners from company housing, forcing them to set up tent colonies. Gun battles ensued; on July 26, 1912, twelve men, eight of them guards, lost their lives, and on February 7, 1913, a train mounting machine guns and chartered by the coal companies approached workers' tents at Holly Grove in the middle of the night. Gunners on board opened up, but, fortunately making a mistake common in night firing, shot too high, killing only one miner and wounding the wife of another. This presaged a similar atrocity that would take place the next year at Rockefeller-owned mines in Colorado.

The textile industry, then located mainly in the northeastern states, was also roiled by strikes during these years. Most workers in Lawrence, Massachusetts, made only about six dollars per week for fifty-six hours' labor in the mills. In January 1912, they went on strike against the largest textile companies in the country, and within days two workers, a man and a woman, had been killed. A number of radical labor leaders came to Lawrence to take part in the fight: the anarchist Emma Goldman, Margaret Sanger, Mary "Mother" Jones, Elizabeth Gurley Flynn and William Dudley Haywood of the Industrial Workers of the World, the IWW.

"Big Bill" Haywood was a burly, one-eyed westerner born in poverty in 1869, who from his mid-teens had worked as a miner, a logger, and a cowboy, as well as a union organizer. He had taken part in some of the most violent labor struggles in the West; in 1905, he had presided over the

Anarchist Emma Goldman

formation of the IWW, nicknamed the Wobblies, which was opposed to the conservative American Federation of Labor's program of organizing within skilled crafts, and compromising with the bosses. Instead, the IWW resembled the European syndicalist movement, dedicated to bring-ing all workers—immigrants and nativeborn, skilled and unskilled—into "one big union" that would eventually launch a general strike so powerful that it would bring capitalism to its knees, placing control of production in the hands of the workers. Meanwhile, propaganda, direct action, sabotage, and strikes, rather than reformist politics, were the courses to follow.

Along with two other Wobblies, Haywood had been indicted for murder in 1906, when former Idaho governor Frank Steunenberg was killed by a bomb. They were ably defended by Clarence Darrow in a sensational trial and were acquitted. Haywood then became a leader of the American Socialist Party, but proved too radical for a group opposed to violence and was expelled from the party's Executive Committee. Margaret Sanger, a supporter of labor-organizing and promoter of modern birth-control methods, found Haywood rumpled and uncouth, a "one-eyed giant with an enormous head which he tended to hold to one side. Big Bill . . . looked like a bull about to plunge into an arena. He seemed always glancing warily this way and that with his one eye, head slightly turned as though to get the view of you. His great voice boomed; his speech was crude and so were his manners; his philosophy was that of the mining camps. . . . But I soon found out that for gentleness and sympathy he had not his equal. He was blunt because he was simple and direct. Though he was not tailor-made, he was custom-made."[10]

Lawrence was the first major effort by the Wobblies to organize workers in the East. They wanted to moderate their reputation for violent action and be seen as flexible and willing to compromise while still using the special skills that Haywood and the IWW had developed in the rough-and-ready logging and mining camps of the West. Employers relied on the language and cultural differences among workers to hinder their ability to form a union or conduct a strike, and the conservative American Federation of Labor had essentially agreed that it would be impossible to organize such diverse groups. But Haywood's charismatic personality, manly presence, and inspiring speeches helped pull the workers together, as did the impassioned leadership of Elizabeth Gurley Flynn, who was "dramatically beautiful," Sanger remembered, "with her black hair and deep blue eyes, her cream-white complexion set off by the flaming scarf she always wore about her throat."[11]

Some thirty nationalities were represented among the workers, but on this occasion, they were bound into a cohesive force. Seventy-five-year-old Mother Jones, nationally famous as a labor radical, organized the women, who took an active part in picketing and standing up to the company guards' attempts at intimidation. Even the children were enlisted in the struggle, forming an important part of a brilliant cultivation of public opinion. In this "Children's Crusade," based on a tactic used by Mother Jones in an earlier strike, the youngsters, dressed in rags, visited New York and other cities to plead for support, and one group of children testified before a congressional committee. Public sympathy was great, and grew even stronger when Lawrence police were photographed beating women and children who were trying to board a train to join the crusade.

Strong efforts were made to break the strike: an AFL trade union, the United Textile Workers of America, cooperated with the owners and tried unsuccessfully to lure support away from the IWW; dynamite was planted in one of the mills in an attempt to frame strike leaders; when a young woman was killed in a clash with local police, two IWW organizers were charged with her murder because it had happened during a union demonstration they had called. They were later acquitted, but only after an expensive court battle.

The workers held firm, and after six weeks of struggle, the strike was won. Haywood thought that "it was a wonderful strike, the most significant strike, the greatest strike that has ever been carried on in this country or any other country." That greatness came from the democratic way the fight had been made, with committees of workers from all ethnic groups making the important decisions and conducting the everyday business. A perfect symbol to Haywood was how the victory was celebrated with the anthem of the radical movement. "We sang the *Internationale* in as many tongues as were represented on the strike committee."

A NEW GENERATION, born in the 1880s and 1890s, was now laying the foundations of what would become the permanent youth culture of the United States. Most, of course, did not stray too far from the paths of their fathers and mothers, but some sought refuges from which to work their rebellion, and these were usually found in the biggest cities, especially San Francisco, St. Louis, Chicago, and New York. Greenwich Village became the national center of this young generation, an old neighborhood of New York that was shabby enough to offer charming housing at low rent and the stimulation of being close to vibrant immigrant communities. John Reed, one of the rising stars of this cohort, living with a group of friends on Washington Square, wrote enthusiastically, "Within a block of my house was all the adventure in the world; within a mile was every foreign country."

By 1913 the Village was filled with self-styled bohemians, long-haired men and short-haired women who were enjoying a ferment of new ideas, and part of their enjoyment came from attacking what they regarded as obsolete styles, mores, and thought. Reed described their optimistic attitude in a poem called "The Day in Bohemia":

> We are free who live in Washington Square
> We dare to think as Uptown wouldn't dare
> Blazing our nights with arguments uproarious
> What care we for a dull old world censorious
> When each is sure he'll fashion something glorious?[12]

Over the next few years a number of places emerged as special favorites of the rebel set: Luke O'Connor's bar at the corner of Greenwich Avenue and Christopher Street, inappropriately nicknamed "The Working Girls' Home," offered rye whiskey with beer chasers in a huge double-decked room full of tobacco smoke and decorated with stuffed elk heads; the Golden Swan on Fourth Street and Sixth Avenue, which sported a nickname that *was* appropriate, the "Hell Hole," was the hangout of a gang called the Hudson Dusters—young bohemian women found "authenticity" and local color by drinking there with the toughs; Mama Bertelotti's, an Italian restaurant on Third Street, provided inexpensive meals, as did Polly's Village Restaurant, which was in the basement of the Liberal Club at 137 MacDougal; Alfred Stieglitz's "291" gallery made the new art and

good conversation freely available; the office of Emma Goldman's anarchist magazine *Mother Earth* provided both utopian theory and hard-won
earthly insights; then, sui generis, there was Mabel Dodge's sparkling
white apartment at 23 Fifth Avenue.

She had been born to wealth and privilege in Buffalo, New York, in 1879.
Marrying early to escape her parents' stifling household, she had been wid-
owed young; then, while recuperating in Europe from the resulting nervous
breakdown, or neurasthenia, she met and married Edwin Dodge, another
man of independent means. They lived in a villa near Florence, Italy, where
they entertained visiting artists and writers such as Gertrude Stein, then
returned to the United States in 1912. On the advice of her psychiatrist,
Mrs. Dodge sent Mr. Dodge away so she would be able to conduct an unhin-
dered search for fulfillment and meaning in her life, and be free to *"live
mentally."* Among other experiences, she wanted "to know everybody. . . .
I wanted, in particular, to know the Heads of things. Heads of Movements,
Heads of Newspapers, Heads of all kinds of groups of people. I became a
Species of Head Hunter, in fact. It was not dogs or glass I collected now, it
was people. Important People."[13] She certainly had all the attributes necessary for collecting heads: attractiveness, wealth, quirky charm, an openness
to new ideas, new sensations, and new people; she added to these attributes
what Gertrude Stein described as "an old-fashioned coquetry." Max Eastman, a young philosopher who had recently taken over the radical journal
The Masses, was fascinated by her. There was, he noted, "something going
on, or going round, in Mabel's head or bosom, something that creates a mag-
netic field in which people become polarized and pulled in and made to
behave very queerly."[14]

Mabel Dodge was thirty-three when she arrived in the city, and she
carried an ambition, expressed in a metaphor very much of the time: "I was
going to dynamite New York and nothing would stop me."[15] She also
brought with her a self-consciously "modern" sensibility: one of her first
acts was to paint over the old-fashioned Victorian brown of her apartment,
covering everything—woodwork, walls, fireplace—in eggshell white, then
hanging white porcelain chandeliers and white linen drapes, with a polar-
bear rug for emphasis. Feeling that American art also needed to be dyna-
mited, she had helped finance the Armory Show. Then, on the advice of
the famous muckraking journalist Lincoln Steffens, she began hosting her
"Evenings." "All sorts of guests came to Mabel Dodge's salons," Steffens
wrote later, "poor and rich, labor skates, scabs, strikers and unemployed,
painters, musicians, reporters, editors, swells; it was the only successful
salon I have ever seen in America. By which I mean that there was conver-

sation and that the conversation developed usually out of some one theme and stayed on the floor."[16]

Some of the themes discussed in this "fresh and sparkling" setting were the new jazz music, free love, birth-control techniques, and the psychoanalytic method developed by the recently discovered Sigmund Freud, who had garnered a great deal of publicity in 1912 when he accepted an honorary degree from Clark University. (The writer Susan Glaspell complained that around this time "you could not go out to buy a bun without hearing of someone's complex.")[17] One pioneer evening involved an experiment with hallucinogenic peyote mushrooms that a visitor from the Southwest provided. In the spirit of free inquiry, buttons were avidly swallowed with little regard to what might be proper dosage. The result was what could be expected: some colorful, vibrant hallucinations, but also vomiting (which seemed to one participant like bright flames springing from his mouth), and the hurried summoning of a doctor to aid those suffering through a bad trip.[18] As the hostess put it later, "it seems as though everywhere in that year of 1913, barriers went down and people reached each other who had never been in touch before; there were all sorts of new ways to communicate as well as new communications."[19]

The most exciting adventure for these bohemian intellectuals, however, was hooking up with Big Bill Haywood and the rough-and-ready members of the Industrial Workers of the World, authentic revolutionaries who came and sat on the white rug covering the floor of Dodge's spacious drawing room. "Cross-legged, . . ." remembered Margaret Sanger, "in the best Bohemian tradition, were Wobblies with uncut hair, unshaven faces, leaning against valuable draperies. Their clothes may have been unkempt, but their eyes were ablaze with interest and intelligence. Each knew his own side of the subject as well as any scholar."[20] Intense arguments during these evenings on Fifth Avenue would often come close to breaking into fistfights as the intellectuals tried to shout one another down, each certain that he or she alone had the answer to whatever problem was being discussed. This passionate contentiousness the workmen could understand, but they must have been a bit taken aback when the big doors to the dining room were thrown open and the butler announced, "Madam, supper is served." Nevertheless, "one and all jumped up with alacrity from the floor and discussion was . . . postponed. The wide, generous table . . . was burdened with beef, cold turkey, hot ham—hearty meat for hungry souls. On a side table were pitchers of lemonade, siphons, bottles of rye and Scotch."

Haywood came in April 1913 to talk of the walkout by 25,000 workers that had taken place several months earlier in the Paterson, New Jersey, silk mills to protest changed work rules that increased their labor, and to demand an eight-hour day for a wage of twelve dollars. Big Bill spoke with charismatic energy for hours about the suffering of the workers, how their families were going hungry, how they were beaten by the police and unfairly jailed by the courts, how any criticism of the city government was bringing trials for sedition, and how none of this was appearing in the press because of a news blackout. It was necessary, Haywood told his spellbound listeners, for the strike to receive publicity in order to draw the same support the Lawrence workers had won. One of the most captivated of those listeners was John Reed, who rushed to Paterson to report the scene for a radical magazine with national distribution, *The Masses.*

Reed was an Oregonian who had graduated from Harvard in 1910, a class that had also included T. S. Eliot, Alan Seeger, Waldo Peirce, and Walter Lippmann, among others who would later become notables. After spending some time in Europe with Peirce adventuring, pulling college-style pranks, and trying to write poetry and travel pieces, Reed had landed in Greenwich Village. His father, a U.S. marshal who had suffered financial and social reverses for being a Roosevelt-allied crusader against western land fraud, asked his friend the muckraker Lincoln Steffens to look after his son: "Save him for poetry. . . . Don't let him get a conviction, like me, and become serious. . . . Keep my boy laughing, laughing and singing."[21] The young man had been a cheerleader at Harvard, but had felt rejected by the rich snobs of the school; this combined with his father's own tribulations had already made him sensitive to social injustice.

Steffens, who had made a nationwide reputation as a leading journalistic muckraker, exposing the sins and hypocrisies of contemporary America, was an inspiration, patron, and father figure to a number of the Village's young men. He questioned Reed about what he wanted to do with his life. "I said I didn't know," Reed later remembered, "except that I wanted to write."[22]

The older man smiled, and said the words that the old should always say to the talented young: "You can do anything you want to," then arranged a job for him at the *The American Magazine.* Other favors followed, as in helping Reed break an impulsive engagement he had made with a French girl while abroad. Steffens certainly agreed with Reed's father about the dangers of seriousness for a youth filled with such high animal spirits. "I had never seen anything so near to pure joy," he wrote after Reed's early death. "If only we could keep him so, we might have a poet at last who could see and sing nothing but joy. Convictions were what I was afraid of. I tried to steer him away from convictions."[23]

But Haywood steered Reed to the strike in Paterson, and the convictions came rushing in. "I couldn't help but observe the ugliness of poverty and all its train of evil," Reed wrote in explanation after much more experience, "the cruel inequality between rich people who had too many motorcars and poor people who didn't have enough to eat. It didn't come to me from books that the workers produced all the wealth of the world, which went to those who did not earn it. . . . All I know is that my happiness is built on the misery of other people, that I eat because others go hungry, that I am clothed when other people go almost naked through the frozen cities in winter; and that fact poisons me, disturbs my serenity, makes me write propaganda when I would rather play."[24]

It was just after dawn on a gray, rainy morning when Reed first visited Paterson, joining a workers' demonstration and taunting a policeman into arresting him. "Officer McCormack, who is doubtless a good, stupid Irishman in time of peace, is almost helpless in a situation that requires thinking. . . . He didn't want to arrest me, and said so with a great deal of profanity."[25]

Once in the holding tank, Reed enjoyed the singing and antiauthoritarian hell-raising, all the while feeling superior to his immigrant comrades, just as he had to an Irish cop. " 'Musica! Musica!' cried the Italians, like children." After he was sentenced to twenty days and transferred to the county jail, he came across a familiar figure. "Surrounded by a dense crowd of short, dark-faced men, Big Bill Haywood towered in the center of the room. His big hand made simple gestures as he explained something to them. His massive, rugged face, seamed and scarred like a mountain, and as calm, radiated strength. These slight, foreign-faced strikers, one of many desperate little armies in the vanguard of the battle line of labor, quickened and strengthened by Bill Haywood's face and voice, looked up at him lovingly, eloquently."

The jail also held its horrors. "Suffice it to say that 40-odd men lounged about a long corridor; . . . that the only ventilation and light came from one small skylight up a funnel shaped airshaft; that one man had syphilitic sores on his legs and was treated by the prison doctor with sugar pills for 'nervousness'; that a 17 year old boy *who had never been sentenced* had remained in that corridor without ever seeing the sun for over nine months; that a cocaine fiend was getting his 'dope' regularly from the inside, and that the background of this and much more was the monotonous and terrible shouting of a man who had lost his mind in that hell hole and who walked among us."

Perhaps less horrifying but certainly unpleasant was the greasy, often rancid, food, so Reed had a friend send edible meals to him. Also, in spite of the occasional singing and camaraderie, time began to hang heavy on the journalist's hands. There were only so many cockroach races he could bear to watch while he chain-smoked cigarettes. It must have been with some relief that he greeted the fresh air when an IWW attorney arranged his release after four days inside.

Reed immediately began writing about what he had seen and experienced. "There's a war in Paterson, New Jersey. But it's a curious kind of war. All the violence is the work of one side, the mill owners. Their servants, the police, club unresisting men and women and ride down law-abiding crowds. Their paid mercenaries, the armed detectives, shoot and kill innocent people. Their newspapers, the *Paterson Press* and the *Paterson Call,* publish incendiary and crime-inciting appeals to mob violence against the strike leaders. . . . They absolutely control the police, the press, the courts. . . . When it came time for me to go out I said goodbye to all those gentle, alert, brave men, ennobled by something greater than themselves."

This appeared in the June 1913 issue of *The Masses,* which, in its attempt to blend art, politics, and a new way of life, spoke for the young people in the Village. It had been started in 1911 with funding by Rufus Weeks, an eccentric insurance executive who believed in a gentle Christian socialism.[26] Its ideal had been to uplift the laboring classes through inspirational art and fiction, publishing stories by Leo Tolstoy and Émile Zola, but these genteel efforts at cultural improvement had not drawn much of an audience, and the effort failed after fourteen months. When a proposed merger with the feminist magazine *Progressive Woman* foundered, the publication was brought back to life by Max Eastman, who had been working toward his doctorate in philosophy from Columbia, where he had studied with the philosopher John Dewey. Eastman helped turn *The Masses* toward a kind of lyric bohemian radicalism, into a magazine that would be revolutionary not only in its politics and view of how to live free, but also in an innovative layout, designed by the artist John Sloan, that eliminated the visual clutter of establishment magazines.

Eastman, a handsome man of seductive charm, sat as an equal with a talented staff. The art editor was Sloan, whose contributors included Robert Henri, Art Young, Stuart Davis, George Bellows, and Robert Minor; the literary editor was the novelist Floyd Dell, who drew on, among others, Louis Untermeyer, Mary Heaton Vorse, and Reed. Much space was given to poetry and essays and reportage on the lives and struggles of laboring people, while the art and cartoons also supported the cause, but this support was given from an independent base, free of ideological constraints.

"We shall have no further part in the fractional disputes within the Socialist Party," one early editorial promised; "we are opposed to the dogmatic spirit which creates and sustains these disputes. Our appeal will be to the masses, both Socialist and non-Socialist, with entertainment, education, and the livelier kinds of propaganda."[27] The ambition was to be a popular political magazine that would score its points with humor, art, and good writing. *The Masses* was to be "frank, arrogant, impertinent, searching for the true causes; a magazine directed against rigidity and dogma wherever it is found; printing what is too naked or true for a money-making press; a magazine whose final policy is to do as it pleases and conciliate nobody, not even its readers."[28]

All editorial decisions were made collectively, amid much beer drinking and good talk. "The talk was radical," Eastman later wrote, "it was free-thought talk and not just socialism. There was a sense of universal revolt and regeneration, of the just-before-dawn of a new day in American art and literature and living-of-life as well as in politics. . . . I never more warmly enjoyed liking people and being liked by them."[29]

Sometimes this search for the naked truth brought pain to both readers and the editorial staff; as a number of critics pointed out, a publication for the working classes that attacked religion and argued for free love would find little support no matter how much it also attacked the bosses and upheld labor's rights to organize and strike. As one puzzled radical put it:

> *They draw nude women for the* Masses
> *Thick, fat, ungainly lasses*
> *How does that help the working classes?*[30]

Helping the working classes was the great desire, though, especially those workers who were taking the most militant stand against big capitalists: the revolutionary and, to the bohemians of the Village, romantic Wobblies, whose "dynamite" would counter the "steamroller" of the established powers.

Others followed Reed to the barricades of Paterson as the cause of "Industrial Democracy" was taken up by the Village: Walter Lippmann (also a protégé of Lincoln Steffens), Margaret Sanger, Upton Sinclair, Max Eastman, and Hutchins Hapgood joined Reed, Elizabeth Gurley Flynn, and Bill Haywood in addressing the workers. Sundays, particularly, became a time for speeches, songs, and wine drinking. Reed drew on his cheerleading days at Harvard and led them in singing the *Marseillaise* and the *Internationale*. He and the others were struck by how this collective singing brought all the different ethnic groups together, just as it had during the Lawrence, Massachusetts, walkout.

At some point during this time, it was decided that a great "mass-play of the whole strike" would be a way to make the newspapers cover the story and also raise money for the suffering workers and their families. Reed enthusiastically volunteered to write the script and direct the production, which would be mounted in Madison Square Garden. "We'll make a pageant of the Strike! The first in the World."[31]

The idea caught fire, and dozens of Villagers helped organize the show. John Sloan with a crew of volunteers painted the backdrops, and in only two weeks the affair was ready. On June 7, fifteen thousand people lined up before Madison Square Garden, which sported red electric lights ten feet tall spelling out IWW. Inside, the visitors watched a cast of more than a thousand real workers portray scenes of themselves first in the mill and then going on strike, followed by the burial of a martyred striker at which Carlo Tresca, Elizabeth Gurley Flynn, and Haywood recited the same speeches they had given at the real funeral. The strikers' children were then seen leaving home for refuge in other towns while singing "The Red Flag." The climax was a mass rally that effectively included everyone in the Garden, with a speech by Haywood that received a standing ovation from the enthusiastic audience. "This kind of thing," wrote Hutchins Hapgood in praising the birth of a revolutionary art form, "makes us hope for a real democracy, where self-expression in industry and art among the masses may become a rich reality, spreading a human glow over the whole of humanity."[32]

Cover of Paterson strike pageant program

In spite of the warm glow, widespread publicity, and the spectacular success of the pageant as theater, as a moneymaker it was a failure, losing $1,996. There were also other problems caused by the effort. Flynn appreciated it as "a unique form of proletarian art," but she thought that it had weakened the strike because it was "disastrous to solidarity."[33] Jealousy over who would participate had caused friction, and the workers' focus had been diverted from the scene of the battle, Paterson. Scabs had managed to get into the mills during pageant rehearsals, when picket lines were not maintained. There were also debilitating charges that sticky fingers among the Village sponsors caused the financial loss. Signs of weakness were suddenly obvious everywhere. Language and cultural differences between the workers resurfaced and led to increased tension, and Haywood and the IWW were criticized by some of the more radical workers as being too ready to compromise with the owners. When Haywood, hoping to convince the public that the IWW was peaceable, advised the members, "Keep your hands in your pockets, men, and nobody can say you are shooting," they charged that he was getting soft.[34] The strike was broken by the end of July, and the IWW gave up its campaign to organize workers in the Northeast and began a long period of retrenchment and reorganization.

Labor rights, political revolution, and artistic innovation were not the only upheavals of the established order that Village bohemians championed. The prevailing sexual mores were enthusiastically cast aside. "Free love," it was felt, would liberate men and women alike to fulfill their true natures. For some, such liberation meant promiscuity, but others saw it as freedom to engage in sex with those they loved without needing the sanction of marriage, an institution, they argued, that imprisoned women and men, and often stifled love. This campaign, like so many others of the time, took on the "nature of a crusade," wrote Lawrence Langner, one of the crusaders.[35]

There was a long history of such campaigners in America, springing especially from the utopian communities of the early nineteenth century, and from the anarchist and spiritualist movements. During the Victorian era, middle-class men had been expected to adhere to a high standard of virtue, but many failed and had indulged in some form of sexual license if only with prostitutes. Now, radical feminists argued not just for the right to vote and hold well-paying jobs, but also for power over biology. Birth control would make them free to live their lives as they wished. Margaret Sanger was one of the bravest of pioneers here, publishing a pamphlet, *What Every Girl Should Know,* in 1913 that would result first in her arrest, then in her having to flee the country to escape prosecution. Allies at *The Masses* supported such freedom for both men and women, calling for "a reconstruction of our customs and attitudes which will permit the sexual instinct and expression at once freer and more socially beneficent."[36] The campaign for sexual freedom held the added attraction of enraging bourgeois sensibilities.

Jack Reed certainly believed in this reforming of customs and attitudes, and delighted in skewering what he saw as middle-class hypocrisy. The charming and handsome writer had indulged in various affairs with young bohemian girls, slim-figured girls, he described in a never produced play, with a "thorough comprehension of Matisse; more than a touch of languor; a dash of economic independence; dark hair, dark eyes, dark past."[37] Then, during the hectic rush of writing and producing the pageant, a more serious romance bloomed. Mabel Dodge was one of the organizers of the spectacular, and others working with the pair noticed their mutual attraction. "When I saw the look on her face," remembered Hutchins Hapgood, "I knew it was all over for Mabel, for the time being, and also probably all over for Reed."[38]

In late June 1913, exhausted from the pageant, Mabel and Jack boarded the German liner *Amerika* for an extended trip to Europe, accompanied by her ten-year-old son and Miss Galvin, his nanny. Jack felt guilty about abandoning the strikers and enjoying the first-class accommodations of the ship, but he also discovered the mixed pleasures of living a life where money was "absolutely no object"—mixed because, of course, it was not his money. The first time he signed his patroness's name to a check on board, the steward assured him, "Oh, you're good for any amount, sir."[39]

At thirty-four, Mabel was eight years older than the writer, married twice, and in the full flush of attractiveness, but she suddenly became, he discovered to his frustration, all too conventional. She refused to consummate their affair. Part of this reluctance came from fear of scandal if he was discovered in her cabin, and he angrily tried the old line, "You shouldn't care about that. If you cared for me nothing would matter."[40]

There was also enjoyment, she thought, in the "high clear excitement of continence." She tried to explain this to him: "Oh, Reed, darling, we are just at the Threshold and nothing is ever so wonderful as the Threshold of things, don't you *know* that?"

The impatient young man did not; it wasn't until they were alone in their Parisian hotel, with the child and governess packed off to Italy, that she allowed him to come to her, and afterward the poet murmured, "I thought your fire was crimson, but you burn blue in the dark."

Mabel felt that real love had finally been found. "And in one night . . . nothing counted for me but Reed . . . to lie close to him and to empty myself over and over, flesh against flesh. And I was proud that I had saved so much to spill lavishly, without reckoning, passion unending."

They toured the French and Italian Rivieras on their way to her magnificent villa in Florence, then returned to the United States in September, their departure delayed by his being forced to the sickbed with diphtheria. Back in New York, Reed moved into the apartment on Fifth Avenue, and enthusiastically reentered the excitement of the Village. He had always cut a noticeable figure in the community, but the pageant and his writings in *The Masses*, *The American*, and other publications had fixed a golden glow about his sturdy figure. Most of his friends thought of him as a poet with a special gift for life, but he could also be an opinionated swaggerer when feeling confident, and there were some who found him arrogant and his boundless energy an irritant.

The relationship between Jack and Mabel had begun showing signs of strain. She was fickle, easily bored, and jealous, not just of other women but also of his ambition for success in the world; she was the type of wealthy neurotic who required constant and careful handling.

Reed at first was oblivious to this, feeling his own dissatisfactions in the relationship coming through her lack of real interest in the human dramas that were going on all around them, and in the embarrassments of this new deluxe life, the most galling of which was probably when she agreed to go with him on an exploration of the immigrant slums of the Lower East Side, but insisted on making the tour in the comfort of her chauffeur-driven limousine. An even greater source of frustration with his current life was the lack of meaningful writing or, now that the Paterson strike was broken, an intense engagement in any cause larger than his own happiness. He was a writer, more journalist than poet or novelist, who, lacking deep wellsprings of creativity, needed a clearly defined project, and a deadline.

Quarrels between the lovers increased. Jack was feeling suffocated, and Mabel grew more and more demanding—first threatening, then dramatically attempting, suicide. Jack left, but soon came back, only to leave again two weeks later. Lincoln Steffens had recommended him to the editor of *Metropolitan* magazine as just the fellow to cover the revolution now burning through Mexico. In true American reportorial fashion, Reed accepted the assignment, not much intimidated by his lack of Spanish, lack of knowledge about local customs, or even the shallowest understanding of Mexican history.

CHAPTER FOUR

◄◦►

A Southern Gentleman

A great many people in the United States have regarded me as a very remote and academic person. They don't know how much human nature there has been in me to give me trouble all my life.

Woodrow Wilson[1]

I am so tired of a merely talking profession. I want to do something!

Woodrow Wilson[2]

TENS OF THOUSANDS of men, women, and children lined Pennsylvania Avenue on March 4, 1913, while other multitudes gathered behind the barricades across from the Capitol to wait for the new president to be sworn in. In spite of an intermittently overcast sky, the air was balmy; trees were already in blossom, and the crowd was quite happy to be celebrating the first national Democratic government to be sworn in since Grover Cleveland in 1893. The broad-brimmed hats of southerners and westerners were far more prevalent than the bowlers or flat caps of East Coast city men.

Just after noon, Thomas Woodrow Wilson and William Howard Taft, both wearing shiny silk top hats, began making their dignified way along the traditional route in a four-horse landau escorted by the Essex Troop of cavalry from New Jersey, the clip-clopping of horses preceded by the sound of bugles. There was still some litter blowing about as well as some leftover nervous tension in the air from a chaotic suffragette demonstration held the day before.

The crowd roared a welcome all along the streets and boulevards of the District, a roar that grew even louder on Capitol Hill as the two men, after attending the swearing in of Vice President Thomas R. Marshall in the Senate chamber, mounted the reviewing stand. The outgoing president was smiling and ruddy-faced, as if happy to be relieved of the burdens of

59

office; Wilson was more subdued, with the nervous strain he was feeling obvious in his solemn expression. Gazing from the stand, the president-elect saw that a large area immediately in front of the rostrum had been kept clear, the crowd held back by uniformed cadets from the military academies, and he ordered, in words that supporters would celebrate as expressing the open philosophy of his Democratic administration: "Let the people come forward."

They came in a rush to listen as Wilson, silk hat removed, took the oath of office on his wife's personal Bible before Chief Justice Edward D. White. His inaugural address, at fifteen hundred words one of the briefest ever delivered, had as its theme the enormous reshaping that American society had undergone in the decades since the Civil War, and the inventive solutions that he proposed to solve the problems those changes had brought. "It began two years ago," he pointed out in his well-trained tenor voice, "when the House of Representatives became Democratic by a decisive majority. It has now been completed. The Senate about to assemble will also be Democratic. The offices of president and vice president have been put into the hands of Democrats. What does the change mean?"

The nation was richer than ever before, with a stable political system and a people imbued with a strong moral sense. But,

> with riches has come inexcusable waste. We have squandered a great part of what we might have used, and have not stopped to conserve the exceeding bounty of nature, without which our genius for enterprise would have been worthless and impotent, scorning to be careful, shamefully prodigal as well as admirably efficient. We have been proud of our industrial achievements, but we have not hitherto stopped thoughtfully enough to count the human cost, the cost of lives snuffed out, of energies overtaxed and broken, the fearful physical and spiritual cost to the men and women and children upon whom the dead weight and burden of it all has fallen pitilessly the years through.

The nation had now taken the time for second thoughts, and had decided to return traditional moral values to American life. "Our work is a work of restoration." He listed specific reforms that would help the rebuilding, pointing out that what was at stake went beyond the interests of Democrats, or even Americans. One area that seemed to bode well for the future of the human race was the developing international understanding. There was, he declared, "a growing cordiality and sense of community of interest among the nations, foreshadowing an age of settled peace and goodwill." The new president ended with a challenge: "Who shall live up to the great trust? Who dares fail to try? I summon all honest men, all patriotic, all forward-looking men, to my side. God helping me, I will not fail them, if they will but counsel and sustain me!"[3]

Woodrow Wilson was, as he had pointed out to his family and advisers after the election, largely unknown to the American people. This was due to the meteoric suddenness of his rise from the relative obscurity of academia to the highest public office in the land; in March 1910 he had been president of Princeton University, and had never run for political office; three years later, he was taking the oath to become president of the United States.

In spite of his lack of previous practical experience, he had been fascinated by politics from his youth. Born in Staunton, Virginia, in 1856, he had spent a rather rootless childhood in several southern towns as his father, Dr. Joseph Wilson, a Presbyterian minister, moved from church to church. Though his parents had grown up in Ohio, and married there, the boy was reared as a southern gentleman. He was named after his maternal grandfather, Thomas Woodrow, who was also a Presbyterian divine. They were of Scotch-Irish stock, and some ancestors had been Covenanters, seventeenth-century Presbyterians who had single-mindedly dedicated themselves to promoting and protecting their faith. Admiring this stubborn adherence to religion, he also took pride in the Woodrows' family crest, which sported a bull's head, and a motto stressing boldness: *Audaci favit fortuna* (Fortune favors the bold). And he would later brag, "A Yankee always thinks that he is right, a Scotch-Irishman *knows* that he is right."[4]

Tommy, as he was called when young, had fifty first cousins, but they were far scattered and rarely seen as he grew up during the Civil War. Instead, most free time was spent with his two older sisters, and the brother who was born a year after him. As he later wrote, "There were in the community almost no companionable people for us."[5] This meant he was raised without the rough-and-tumble of most boyhoods; when neighborhood play became too rambunctious he would retreat to the protection of his middle-aged mother's arms, and she did not allow him to attend regular school until he was twelve years old. A gangling, awkward boy—blue-eyed, black-haired, skinny-shanked—he was plagued by poor vision and wore glasses from the age of eight. Reading came slowly to Tommy, who seems to have suffered from a learning disability, and some members of the family thought the boy rather dull-witted as a result; the difficulty made his parents, especially his mother, even more protective of their sensitive son.

Both sides of the family valued words, and, coached by his father, the boy found early that his easy verbal facility gave him a certain status among his peers, even though his athletic gifts were limited. Like many dreamy and imaginative children, he was an indifferent student at first, much given to spending time alone reading adventure novels by Frederick Marryat and James Fenimore Cooper about pirates, Indians, and wandering men of action willing to fight the good fight; the knight-errant rode through the imaginations of the middle class of his generation. But then he found God, the severe Calvinist God of his Scottish ancestors. Though he continued his fantasy reading, he also applied himself more diligently to his studies, following the Protestant belief that the more he knew of the world, the closer he would come to understanding God's Will, and thus the better he would be able to follow it. At this time, he acquired the lifelong habit of kneeling by his bed to pray every night, and also shouldered the heavy burden of constantly seeking to perfect himself, to always be right in his judgments, to somehow reach a state where his character was able to weather any storm, resist any temptation. Wilson suffered one of the unfortunate side effects of such an impossible dream and became something of a prig, judging others by his own quixotic standards of behavior.

The Civil War had not brought as much suffering to his family as it did to many in the South, though the Wilsons did have to free their slaves. Joseph Wilson, in spite of being the Ohio-born son of an abolitionist, periodically served Confederate army units as a chaplain, but most of his war was fought from a pulpit in Augusta, Georgia. In 1870, five years after peace came, Joseph and his family moved to Columbia, South Carolina, where he became a professor in the theological seminary and pastor of the First Presbyterian Church. Much of that capital city, once famed for its beauty, had been burned in Sherman's campaign, and Tommy became intimately aware of the destructive results of war: poverty, maimed bodies, the moral suffering of defeat, and corruption.

The family expected him to follow in the family line, and in 1873 he was sent to Davidson College in North Carolina to prepare for the ministry. Though very close to his father, he found the separation from his mother particularly difficult. "I remember how I clung to her," he wrote his fiancée later, "a laughed-at 'mamma's boy' till I was a great big fellow."[6] The comfort of women's company would always be preferred to the rougher companionship of men.

His dislike of male intimacy was made clear by his disdain of the crude humor of teasing, which can be used to humiliate the weak, weaken the envied, or perplex the perplexing, but men also use it to break through pomposity, relieve the tension of formality, and grow closer. "I've always regarded teasing as of doubtful gentility when ventured by any but one's nearest relatives and dearest intimate," he later explained to his fiancée, "and I am quite sure that some people who have teased me have thought me curt and disagreeable."[7]

He lasted less than a year at Davidson, retreating to his family suffering from exhaustion and severe indigestion, early signs of the physical ailments that would afflict him all his life. Controversy was roiling the haven of home, as his father, a brilliant preacher but too intellectually arrogant and cold-blooded to bring much comfort in his role as pastor to his flock, had fallen into dispute both with his congregation and students at the seminary. In 1874, Joseph resigned those positions and became minister to a church in the port city of Wilmington, North Carolina, and it was there that Tommy recuperated. Part of the youth's time was spent in reading widely and in studying Greek, and part in romantic fantasies of running away to sea, though these received rather a hard-edged setback when he tumbled into the hold of one of the dockside ships. In the fall of 1875, he embarked again for the adventure of higher education, this time bound for his father's old school, the College of New Jersey at Princeton, which offered free tuition for the sons of Presbyterian ministers.

Tommy Wilson had never felt strongly drawn to his father's calling, and at an early age, inspired by the examples of Daniel Webster and the British statesman William Gladstone, he decided he wanted to follow a political career; at Princeton, which he found "a quiet country college," he set about studying what he thought necessary to support such ambition: rhetoric, political science, and history.[8] He discovered that he possessed a talent for analyzing problems, and did well in humanities classes, though his lack of interest in science and math dragged down his overall average, as did his difficulty with timed examinations. He did manage to graduate in the top third of his class, a noteworthy achievement since his grades were maintained in spite of a severe learning disability that was probably a form of what today is called dyslexia.

Dyslexia had not yet been recognized as a distinct problem, and Wilson had to devise his own strategies for overcoming the burden: reading narrowly but intensely, developing a strong memory, rereading books and articles rather than going on to new works. It also must have aggravated the frustrations of trying to be the perfect Christian scholar and gentleman.

Respectable grades were not the only sign of his success at Princeton; he excelled at public speaking and writing, founding the Liberal Debating Club and editing the student newspaper, *The Princetonian*. Joseph Wilson had coached his son well in oratory, a necessary skill for a lad ambitious for a political career. "Study manner, dearest Tommy," he wrote in one of his letters, "as much as matter." He told him that sentences in a speech "ought to resemble bullets—that is, be compact and rapid, and prepared to make clean holes."[9] Tommy Wilson and Charles Talcott, a classmate who was later elected to Congress, pledged to each other that they would make oratory the basis of their studies as a route to political power. That such power was his goal can be seen in a card he wrote out and evidently used as a page marker since it was later found in one of his books: "Thomas Woodrow Wilson, Senator from Virginia."[10]

The undergraduate also worked on developing a persuasive writing style. He produced papers for his professors, of course, editorials for *The Princetonian,* and had two critical essays on political leaders printed in the *Nassau Literary Magazine,* one on Otto von Bismarck of Prussia and the other on British statesman William Pitt. But his literary ambitions were even greater. While still a junior, he began the rough form of an article arguing that universal manhood suffrage, then under attack (by his father among others), was not responsible for the low moral and intellectual level of American politics. Instead he called for a weakening of the separation of powers so that Cabinet members could have seats in Congress, a reform that would increase the powers of the presidency and make the American system more like the British, which he admired for the quality of its leaders. "Debate," he argued, "is the essential function of a representative body," but he found little of any real interest taking place in Congress. Expanded and revised over the next months, "Cabinet Government in the United States" was published during his senior year in the *International Review,* which had as an editor another scholarly young man with political ambitions, Henry Cabot Lodge.[11]

Tommy's family seems to have quietly supported his decision not to enter the Presbyterian ministry. His father then encouraged him to consider the study of law, which would be an acceptable career for a proper southern gentleman. After graduating from Princeton in 1879, at the age of twenty-two, he unenthusiastically enrolled in the law school of the University of Virginia. "The profession I chose was politics," he wrote in 1884 to his fiancée, Ellen Axson, "the profession I entered was law. I entered the one because I thought it would lead to the other."[12] It was at about this time that his mother asked that he drop Tommy and become Woodrow in order to show both sides of his family heritage.

Though he respected his teachers, the young man was frustrated by the narrow legal particulars he was expected to learn, finding them "as monotonous as . . . Hash," but he forced himself to swallow "the vast mass of its technicalities with as good a grace and as straight a face as an offended palate will allow."[13] In spite of this distaste, he managed to do well in his classes, pleasant relief from them being found by singing in the choir and the Glee Club, and by wide reading in history, biography, and poetry. Also a happy stimulant were the debates that he entered, winning a prize and gaining a strong local reputation as an orator worth attending.

But none of these activities were enough of a diversion to save him from another collapse like the one he had suffered at Davidson College. In the middle of his second year, he again retreated to the family manse in Wilmington to recover. Sheer physical exhaustion played a role; he was never very strong. But there was also the psychological tension of his impossible quest for perfection, and the frustrations of trying to fit his ambitions into an unsatisfactory framework. Indigestion gave him the most trouble, but he also suffered from constant colds and catarrh.

Woodrow spent eighteen months with his family, much of the time reading for pleasure, but also continuing to study the law; in the fall of 1882, he passed the Georgia bar in good order. Atlanta, which was quickly becoming the commercial center of the "New South," offered a good starting place for a freshly minted attorney, but only for those with an aggressive love of the profession. There was already one lawyer for every 270 Atlantans, so enterprise would be required to build a practice. Unfortunately, Wilson, like Theodore Roosevelt, felt a strong distaste for the immorality as well as the mundane requirements of a law practice. "A man must become a mere lawyer to succeed at the Bar," he wrote a friend, "and must, moreover acquire a most ignoble shrewdness at overcoming the unprofessional tricks and underhand competition of sneaking pettifoggers."[14]

With plenty of spare time on his hands as he waited for clients to appear, and continuing to be subsidized by his father, Wilson wrote articles and a book, took part in local antitariff politicking, and let his mustache and sideburns grow. One article, on convict labor, was printed in the *New York Evening Post*, but the book was rejected by several publishers, including G. P. Putnam's Sons, the firm that had recently put out Theodore Roosevelt's *The Naval War of 1812*. Putnam was willing to publish the book if Wilson could provide a subsidy, which was effectively what Roosevelt had done.[15] Whatever else they might share, this young southerner lacked that rich New Yorker's deep pockets. "If I had the money," he wrote a friend, "I should not hesitate to close with Putnam's offer . . . but, as things now stand, I have no choice."[16]

As it became obvious that the law would provide no satisfaction, either financial or political, Woodrow Wilson searched for an alternative career and, after rejecting journalism, found teaching. At the university level this would provide encouragement and time for his writing, an intellectual status that might encourage educated people to respect his views, and an adequate if less than bountiful income. It would also be a field where his overrefined sense of dignity and lack of easy geniality would not be a hindrance. "What better can I be, therefore, than a professor, a lecturer upon subjects whose study delights me?"[17] Lecturing would allow further refinement of his skills in oratory, but it was really writing that he regarded as his way to influence the nation. "After all," he confided in Ellen Axson, "it's my *writing*, not my teaching, that must win me reputation."[18] He felt all the more need for reputation and income since he had fallen in love with this petite, blond, artistic daughter of Rome, Georgia, during his year of undertaking to be a lawyer.

She, too, was the child and grandchild of Presbyterian ministers; she, too, was a shy and reserved southerner, requiring a gentle, indirect courting that was very much of their time, place, and class, a courting that would be aggressively rejected by the following generation. Their parents were friends, but her mother had died giving birth to the last of her two younger brothers, and she, now twenty-three, had taken on the responsibility of the boys' upbringing. Woodrow began with a formal note inviting her to a concert, but she replied that she had a previous commitment. This was followed by the offer of a country ride in a hired carriage that was accepted, then by visits to her home, accompanying her to concerts, prayer meetings, and picnics, where they discussed their love of English literature. A thrilling development for the suitor came when this genteel young woman indicated a sense of intimacy by addressing him as "Mr. Woodrow," and further progress was evident when she agreed to correspond with him on his return to Atlanta. From there the relationship developed unusually quickly, but there was no way that he could immediately take on the financial responsibilities of marriage. Still, they reached an understanding that when he found his first teaching job, they would be wed; for the sexually passionate but repressed young man, it could not come soon enough, as he described himself to her, writing of "the riotous element in my blood."[19]

The Johns Hopkins University in Baltimore had been established in 1876, on the German model, as this country's first institution to stress research and graduate education in history and the social sciences. Wilson enrolled there in the fall of 1883 on the recommendation of his mother's scholarly brother, James Woodrow. Again his parents proved supporting, dipping into family savings to pay for this new path in learning. The young man found the same distasteful emphasis on narrow specialization that he had suffered through in law school, but he delighted in the "splendid library facilities," as he wrote Ellen, and he learned "a great deal from my fellow-students."[20] Wilson felt that he could not bear to follow the required course work and research project, and historian Herbert Baxter Adams, founding director, proved flexible enough to give Wilson the freedom to conduct his own studies of the practical workings of the American political system. This resulted in *Congressional Government,* a book that was quickly brought out by a first-rate publisher, Houghton Mifflin, without subsidy; it immediately established this second-year graduate student's reputation as a gifted thinker with a realistic approach to the problems of American government—the major one of which, he argued, was the unrestrained, "the supreme," power of Congress, the representative of local interests. What was needed was a growth in the strength of the presidency, the spokesman for national interests, to guide the legislative branch.[21] This was a revolution building on Theodore Roosevelt's accomplishments, that Wilson later firmly established.

Wilson felt that *Congressional Government* proved his academic qualifications, and he balked at fulfilling the other requirements for his Ph.D., arguing to Herbert Baxter Adams that he could not do well in examinations "from sheer perversity of natural disposition" and because he was not the sort who could "pull in ordinary harness." He was almost thirty, and feeling it was well past time to launch his career and to marry Ellen. Adams again proved his praiseworthy and unusual flexibility, permitting this rebel to take his degree with his book serving as thesis, and without a formal oral examination.[22]

Bryn Mawr, a new college for women near Philadelphia, offered him a position, and though it paid only $1,500 a year, barely enough to support a gentleman's way of life, he was able to marry his beloved in June 1885. He also willingly accepted into his household Ellen's eleven-year-old brother and a female cousin who needed financial support while attending the college; a lifelong pattern of such generosity to family and friends would make close domestic economy necessary until the Wilsons moved into the White House. Within ten months a daughter was added to the family, quickly followed by two more. A salary of $2,500, and the chance to teach young men, soon drew him to Wesleyan College; in 1890 he joined the faculty at his alma mater, Princeton, at $3,000 a year. These career decisions, as with all such decisions of his married life, were arrived at only after thorough discussion and agreement with Ellen.

Wilson's study of the art of public speaking had turned him into a lively lecturer, while his genuine concern for students made him popular with undergraduates. As he once explained to his wife, "Oratory is not declamation, not swelling tones and excited delivery, but the art of persuasion, the art of putting things so as to appeal irresistibly to an audience."[23] Though a demanding grader, the enrollment in his classes swelled, he was frequently voted the most popular professor at the university, and his reputation drew students to Princeton.

He also proved a popular lecturer outside the confines of academia. Most of these talks were on the subject of education, particularly higher education, which, like the rest of society, was undergoing enormous changes in the 1890s as established universities grew and fresh institutions were founded every year.[24] A new type of student was attending college, even more impatient with traditional curricular demands than previous generations had been, wanting quick and narrow professional training so they could hasten to make their prosperous way in the world. Wilson argued the need for these young men to be educated more liberally in the humanities and sciences, both for their own good and for the good of society. These addresses, often given before nonacademic groups, served to spread his reputation, and also added to the family income; in 1898 he earned $1,760 from his popular lectures. Princeton paid well, comparatively, but the family needs were growing. In 1896, when the University of Virginia tried to lure him to be its president, a group of Princeton alumni voluntarily added $2,400 to his annual salary to keep him at their alma mater.

Another appreciated addition to his income was, increasingly, his writing, and this complemented his admirable ambition to reach as wide an audience as possible in order to educate the public, especially young people, about their country. "I want to write books which will be read by the great host who don't wear spectacles, whose eyes are young and unlearned!" he had written to Ellen during their courtship. "I don't care how much contempt may look upon my pages through professors' glasses."[25] These exercises in popular history were also quite lucrative; Harper's publishing house offered him $12,000 (roughly the equivalent of $260,000 in 2005 dollars) for *A History of the American People,* run first as installments for their monthly magazine, then brought out in five volumes. "I am corrupted," he admitted to a friend, but he added, "it is a piece of work I meant to do anyway, and I alter the quality not a bit, nor dilute the stuff, neither, to suit the medium."[26] And, "I must cultivate a new style for the new venture: a quick and perfectly pellucid narrative as clear as the air and coloured with nothing but the sun, stopped in its current here and there . . . for the setting in of small pictures of men and manners, coloured variously, as life is. It must be a work of art or nothing, and I must study the art."[27] But as others have discovered, the struggle to weave such a vast and varied amount of material into an accurate, flowing historical narrative puts a great strain on one's constitution. "I pray it may grow easier or it will kill me."[28] However terrible the strain, in 1900 alone Wilson supplemented his Princeton salary with more than $7,000 from writing and lecturing.

And yet, for all this success during the 1890s, Wilson also felt discontent. Perhaps some of this had a physical cause, for there is evidence that he suffered a small stroke in May 1896, but he was also unhappy with the administration of his university. It seemed unable to change to meet the demands of the new age or manage its evolution from the small denominational College of New Jersey into Princeton University, as the institution was renamed at its 150th anniversary in 1896. This criticism was widely, and even more strongly, held by other members of the faculty. In June 1902, the trustees ousted the president, and, voting unanimously, asked Woodrow Wilson, who had turned down several such offers from other institutions, to assume the post.

Theories of leadership were all well and good, but he had long been eager for a chance to engage in the actual exercise of power. "Definite, tangible tasks" were just what he needed in order to remove "the flutter and restlessness" from the abstract thinking of his professorial life.[29] "I am so tired of a merely talking profession," he told his family. "I want to *do* something!"[30] Politics, real power on a large scale, still remained a lure, but this was an opportunity to reform an institution he loved, to put his imprimatur on education and gain a national reputation. Others seemed to recognize that this might be the first step to something grander. Wilson's father, who was dying, had come to spend his last days with him. Now, unable to rise from bed, he summoned his three granddaughters and told them: "Never forget what I tell you. Your father is the greatest man I have ever known. . . . This is just the beginning of a very great career."[31]

It certainly was the beginning of a great test. Wilson's ambition was to raise his university to the highest level, to make it able to compete with Harvard and Yale in educational leadership. Though there were joking protests that he was going to ruin a good country club, he found wide support as he informed the trustees that the university had to find money enough to fund innovations that would enable Princeton to achieve his desires. Unfortunately, Wilson, who as a gentleman disliked asking people for money, proved a poor fund-raiser, a great disadvantage for a university president's relationship with trustees.

Wilson instituted various curriculum reforms, introducing new subjects for study, but insisting that students follow an integrated, well-organized program rather than the more freewheeling elective system found at Harvard. Young faculty, or preceptors, were hired so that undergraduates would have more intimate contact with scholars, and he attracted a host of academics inspired by his vision for higher education.

Wilson, partly due to sureness in his own judgment, was not consistent in seeking counsel from his alumni, deans, or faculty. He had decided that the university's system of eating clubs, dominated by the wealthier students, was undemocratic, socially divisive, and anti-intellectual, so he presented the trustees with a plan to weaken or eliminate them. Quadrangles, or "quads," forming "colleges," would be built where all undergraduates would have their base, living and eating together without regard to cliques or class. In June 1907, once conditional approval was given by the trustees, Wilson presented this revolutionary plan to his community as an accomplished fact, without any warning or even the slightest preparation of the people affected. Alumni, who had returned to the campus for boisterous reunions, learned the news when Wilson had it read aloud at their clubs' annual banquets, turning these happy occasions into funereal feasts. The storm was immediate, and only grew in intensity over the summer.

Wilson would not retreat, nor would he compromise, and he lacked that need for easy social intercourse and feeling of brotherhood that motivate most men. At first he regarded the disturbance as a "dust cloud," and took strength from a relative's letter reminding him of the Woodrow family crest's bull's head and the motto about fortune favoring the bold. The growing strength of the resistance to his plan proved to him that he was right about the eating clubs having too much power, and that victory was morally imperative; the struggle became one over issues greater than educational reform. Evil lurked in those dens of privilege, and the university was in need of "salvation."

He took the fight on the road, speaking to audiences across the nation of his plan, trying to put pressure on the trustees. Most of the alumni opposed him but he rallied what support he could. Most of the faculty opposed him, as well. He fell out with a particularly close friend, John Grier Hibben, when that professor, feeling that he had to "save Woodrow from himself," warned him that the struggle was lost and that to continue it would split the university. Hibben and others begged him to consider a compromise that would retain the core of reform, but he refused.[32] One did not compromise with the forces of darkness; one fought.

And the fight was lost. The trustees, led by former president Grover Cleveland, rejected Wilson's plan, handing him a humiliating defeat that could probably have been avoided had he prepared his ground more carefully, been willing to meet his critics partway, and, perhaps, been more of a manipulator, willing to scheme and intrigue behind the scenes. Instead, he had donned crusader armor, and he fought as if to yield an inch of ground was to temporize with the devil. One of the costs of the defeat was his friendship with Hibben, whom he had loved as a brother; he could not forgive what he saw as a betrayal.

Part of this self-righteous rigidity came from his upbringing, but, again, a likely contributor was ill health. He constantly suffered from what he described as a "derangement of the bowels"; on New Year's Day 1904 he complained of a severe "neuralgia" attack; in May 1906 he lost the vision in his left eye and suffered from crippling neuritis in his joints and right hand and arm, evidently the result of another stroke. He taught himself to write with his left hand. Though a relaxing vacation in the Lake District, one of a number of visits to England during these years, helped him recover some vision in the eye, doctors told him that he was the victim of high blood pressure and hardening of the arteries. Yet, it was also a mark of the man that even during these torments he was able to joke of the lost fight: "I didn't get the quads, but I got the wrangles."[33]

Unfortunately, another university battle that started in 1909, this time regarding details of the new graduate school, ended in a second major defeat for the president of Princeton. Again he was faced with foes better skilled at intrigue and deal making who were backed by wealthy, socially prominent alumni. And again, with confidence in his powers of public speaking, he took to the road in an attempt to convince graduates, many of them his former students, of the correctness of his position, but again the tour ended in failure. For the good of his supporters among the faculty, students, and alumni, he did not resign immediately, but waited until October 20, 1910, when he was campaigning for the governorship of New Jersey.

At some point during this turmoil, most likely from November 1909 through January 1910, Woodrow Wilson fell into a passionate affair with Mary Peck, an attractive woman he had met on family vacations in Bermuda. She was now living close by, in New York, in the process of divorcing her second husband; Wilson, under the strain of his university troubles and drawn by her wit and liveliness, lost his self-control and gave in to the "riotous element" in his blood. It was "a passage of folly and gross impertinence," he admitted later, caused by his ignoring of "standards of honourable behavior."[34] His biographer August Heckscher sees the affair as part of the profound change that Wilson was experiencing as he began to boldly cut the ties that bound him to academia and his former life, reaching out to the broader world. "The immense energies released at the time of his campaign for the governorship and the presidency," he writes, "were generated in the fires that almost consumed his inner and outer lives during this period."[35]

Beginning after the election of 1904 and the defeat of Alton B. Parker, Wilson had become a spokesman for conservative elements in the Democratic party opposed to the resurgent western radicalism of William Jennings Bryan. Arguing that the United States, "as it moves forward in its great material progress, needs and will tolerate no party of discontent or radical experiment; but it does need a party of conservative reform acting in the spirit of law and of ancient institutions," he pleaded for a rejuvenation of the party.[36]

This role as spokesman for the states'-rights, limited-government wing of the party won him wide attention in the press, especially when combined with the reputation he was gaining at Princeton. Increasingly, he was seen as an education reformer who had gone beyond mere curriculum revision and tried to "democratize" that institution in spite of the resistance put up by wealthy snobs belonging to exclusive clubs. This publicity as a man of the people drew new progressive supporters to him, men of particular note such as the brilliant Wall Street speculator Bernard Baruch, a fellow southerner and Democrat.

Wilson did not stay within the anti-Bryan group for very long; he soon began to see the need for a more active government role in controlling big business and helping society adapt to the great changes sweeping the nation. In 1906 there was a short-lived movement for him to run for the Senate from New Jersey as a progressive candidate; in 1908 he warned, "The present conflict in this country is not between capital and labor. It is a contest between those few men in whose hands the wealth of the land is concentrated and the rest of us. . . . I believe in governmental regulation."[37] Through his personal charm and upright character, along with some shrewd but limited maneuvering on contentious issues, he managed this shift without alienating his more conservative supporters.[38]

As it happened, in 1910 the bosses of the New Jersey Democratic machine found themselves in need of a candidate whose integrity was beyond question. George Harvey, head of Harper's publishing, and several other influential members of the party convinced these bosses that Wilson was just the man, and they, sure that this naive professor could be easily handled, agreed. Ironically, the only resistance came from party reformers, but they were quickly defeated by the party hacks. They were then charmed by the candidate's eloquent acceptance speech, where he asserted his independence and promised that he would fight for a public-utilities commission like the one that the great progressive hero Robert La Follette had instituted in Wisconsin.

The Republicans had dominated New Jersey politics since the mid-1890s, but a strong progressive faction was in rebellion. Wilson united his own party, then reached out to independents and insurgent Republicans. He promised a long list of reforms regarding control of trusts, the openness of elections, and honest government, and he vowed that he would be an activist governor, giving notice that he would go out on the stump and discuss important issues with the people. These pledges won him the election, and he had lived up to them, listening to the reformers, fighting the bosses, pushing his progressive agenda through the state legislature, and gaining a national reputation that led, after just one term, to his being elected president of the United States.

At his inauguration in March 1913, Woodrow Wilson vowed to be the same kind of activist as president that he had been as governor of New Jersey. "This is not a day of triumph; it is a day of dedication. . . . Men's hearts wait upon us; men's lives hang in the balance; men's hopes call upon us to say what we will do." He then proceeded to lay out his agenda: tariff revision, banking and currency reform, the strengthening of the Sherman Antitrust Act.

Most citizens in the nation recognized that new conditions called for new responses, so that even though Wilson had won but a minority of the popular vote, the progressive vote combined had been overwhelming. But within that large group were different expectations, ranging from extreme conservatism to the radical, and these differences ran across the whole spectrum of modern American life. Many, especially older citizens or those living in regions still given to traditional values, found the national emphasis on newer, bigger, richer, faster extremely distasteful, and the intense questioning of received wisdom that went along with these developments deeply disturbing. One of the great challenges facing the president would be to bring about change in a manner that did not overly offend the traditional feelings of the members of his party, particularly those in the South and West.

Wilson had written in *Congressional Government* in 1885, as well as in other works, that the division of power between a strong but irresponsible Congress and the president was the great flaw in the American political system. But in 1900, he had written a new introduction for the book in which he recognized the effect of the Spanish-American War on that system and the enormous change it had worked on the country's relationship to the world.

The greatly increased power and opportunity for constructive leadership given the President, by the plunge into international politics and into the administration of distant dependencies, . . . has been the war's most striking and momentous consequence. . . . When foreign affairs play a prominent part in the politics and policy of a nation, its Executive must of necessity be its guide, must utter every initial judgment, take every first step of action, supply the information upon which it is to act, suggest and in large measure control its conduct. . . . Upon his choice, his character, his experience hang some of the most weighty issues of the future. . . . The President is at liberty, both in law and conscience, to be as big a man as he can. . . . He cannot escape being the leader of his party. . . . He is also the political leader of his nation . . . or has it in his choice to be. . . . His is the only national voice in affairs. Let him win the admiration and confidence of the country, and no other single force can withstand him, no combination of forces will easily overpower him. . . . His office is anything he has the sagacity and force to make.[39]

Theodore Roosevelt had provided a good example of what a forceful chief executive could do, not just in using the position as a bully pulpit, but also in increasing its powers. Wilson recognized that achievement, and soon imitated it.[40]

He would establish an amazing record of victory during his first eighteen months in office, benefiting a great deal from the strong Cabinet he had selected. The most difficult among the many choices he had faced when first elected was what to do about the Great Commoner. William Jennings Bryan had been the major power in the Democratic Party for almost twenty years, so it was necessary to keep him happy and on the administration's side. Wilson hesitated a bit, fearing both the appearance of being overly influenced by Bryan in his appointments and the actual pressure he would exert to place his loyalists in positions of power. The party had been out of national office for sixteen years, and was hungry.

Edward M. House—known to most as "the Colonel" because of a ridiculous honorary title awarded by the governor of his home state of Texas and as "the Little Wizard" to others because of his diminutive size and his success in getting things, especially political things, done—had been serving as an unofficial counselor and confidant to Wilson since they had met and become friends during the presidential campaign. Wilson trusted House, who was amiable and independently wealthy and wanted no political office, and increasingly relied on his disinterested advice in important matters such as forming his government. When Wilson offered

House a Cabinet post, the Colonel demurred, confiding to his diary, "I very much prefer being a free lance, and to advise with him regarding matters in general, and to have a roving commission to serve wherever and whenever possible."[41]

House emphasized the advantages of having Bryan in the Cabinet. When approached, Bryan, who hated war, agreed to be secretary of state as long as he was allowed to advance his great dream for promoting international peace through binational treaties that would require a non-aggression period between nations locked in disputes. He also made clear that he would not compromise his prohibitionist principles by serving wine or any other alcoholic beverage at diplomatic affairs, no matter how much press mockery this called down on the administration.

William Gibbs McAdoo, who had led the fight for the nomination at the Baltimore convention and then helped direct the presidential campaign, was appointed secretary of the treasury; he would also soon become, much to the surprise of Wilson, a presidential son-in-law, though being only seven years younger. Albert S. Burleson, a tough and experienced politician from Texas, eagerly accepted the postmaster general position, and thus was in charge of the handling of the long-denied thirst for patronage of the party faithful. Wilson, in his high-minded idealism, resisted this traditional rewards system, but Burleson was able to convince him that without intelligent use of patronage, the consulting with senators and representatives about who became, say, local postmaster, then his administration would be a failure.

William B. Wilson, born in Scotland and an organizer of the United Mine Workers, became secretary of labor, the first one ever, as Wilson established the independent office at the request of the unions. Josephus Daniels, a newspaper editor from North Carolina, like his hero William Jennings Bryan a teetotaler and, also like Bryan, close to being a Christian pacifist, assumed the post of secretary of the navy. He would offend naval officers and become, like Bryan, the butt of journalists' jokes for immediately banning wine and beer from officers' messes. The assistant secretary of the navy, Franklin Delano Roosevelt, was far more popular with officers and journalists alike. David F. Houston, president of the University of Texas, agreed to give up academia to serve as secretary of agriculture. Daniels and Houston were two of the sharpest observers in the Cabinet, and left valuable records of what they saw.

The Department of Interior went to a westerner, Franklin K. Lane; Commerce, which had just been split from Labor as one of the last acts of William Howard Taft, was awarded to William C. Redfield, a congressman from New York who had also been a business executive. Wilson had wanted to appoint Louis D. Brandeis, who had provided him with excellent counsel during the election campaign, to the Commerce position, but though this liberal Bostonian had great support from the progressives, there was so much opposition from the business wing of the party that he backed down. "Such a tremendous hullabaloo had been raised in business circles," remembered William McAdoo, "that the appointment . . . might have had, in fact, a harmful psychological effect."[42] Most of that hostility came from Brandeis's political and economic ideas, but there was also a touch of anti-Semitism in it. When someone objected that Brandeis was a Jew, Wilson snapped, "And a fine one!"[43]

Half the Cabinet were southerners, and though it could be argued that such a bedrock of support for the party deserved that much recognition, many in the West felt that their contributions to the victory were being taken for granted. Few of the members came with great political or intellectual prestige, but that was part of the price paid by a party out of power for so long. There had been little chance for leaders to gain national experience or reputation. "The country as a whole looked upon the new Cabinet as a collection of mediocrities," McAdoo later acknowledged. "This widespread opinion was created and nourished by the Republican press, which included . . . most of the wealthy and powerful newspapers in the United States."[44]

An example of the difficulty in putting together a good Cabinet is the manner in which the secretary of war was chosen, though this also gives an indication of how unimportant this post seemed to the Democrats. The first choice was A. Mitchell Palmer, a Pennsylvania Quaker and congressman who recognized, even if his president could not, that membership in the pacifistic Society of Friends might interfere with the proper carrying out of such a militaristic duty.

Joseph Tumulty had served as Wilson's private secretary and chief of staff during the governorship, and he now followed him to Washington in the same capacity, though there were protests at his Catholicism. It seemed obvious to the politically astute Tumulty that there should be someone from New Jersey in the Cabinet. After the war position had been rejected by a couple of candidates, he was leafing through the state's lawyers' directory and was reminded of New Jersey Supreme Court justice Lindley M. Garrison, who was known for his integrity. Tumulty recommended him to head the War Department; Wilson met with the surprised jurist, liked him, and convinced him to take the job.

In the hours immediately after the inauguration, the new president moved to establish himself as the political leader of his nation through the active management of large-scale domestic affairs. That same day, he called Congress into special session to tackle the first issue on his agenda, revision of the tariff. Wilson was committed to lowering the high rates that lobbyists had manipulated into the Payne-Aldrich Act. This was partly for reasons of industrial efficiency, but was also because many Democrats believed, as Secretary of the Treasury William McAdoo put it, that "the high tariff system is one of the chief causes . . . of the strikingly unequal distribution of wealth in the United States."[45] On April 8, 1913, Wilson broke with tradition by going in person to address the joint houses, the first president since John Adams to do so. His advisers had warned that this might offend old-line legislators, sensitive to their independence, and a number of Democratic senators did flare into warm enough rhetoric to move Vice President Marshall, who presided over the Senate, to declare that there was no need to vote on extending an invitation; the president had the right to come.

Wilson himself was nervous about his intrusion, and he spent the first few minutes winning over his audience by saying that he wanted them to realize that the president was "a human being trying to cooperate with other human beings in a common service" and not "a mere department of the Government hailing Congress from some isolated island of jealous power, sending messages, not speaking naturally with his own voice." He then explained the duty they now had to perform:

> Only new principles of action will save us from a final hard crystallization of monopoly and a complete loss of the influences that quicken enterprise and keep independent energy alive. It is plain what those principles must be. We must abolish everything that bears even the semblance of privilege . . . and put our businessmen . . . under the stimulation of a constant necessity to be efficient, economical, and enterprising masters of competitive supremacy, better workers and merchants than any in the world. . . . The object of the tariff duties henceforth laid must be effective competition, the whetting of American wits by contest with the wits of the rest of the world.[46]

Wilson and his supporters, especially Oscar W. Underwood of the Ways and Means Committee, took an active part in guiding the tariff revision through the House, where it passed by a two-to-one majority in just a month. The Senate, which held a number of Democrats representing states benefiting from import protection, came under siege by lobbyists aggressively trying to defeat the revision. Rumors appeared in newspapers that Wilson was going to try for a compromise, but he told reporters, "When you get a chance just say that I am not the kind that considers compromises when I once take my position."[47] It was important that this first fight be won in order to build the momentum for the rest of his reform legislation.

One of the purposes of the president's bold address to Congress had been to focus the attention of ordinary citizens on the tariff issue; now, on May 26, he made a direct attack on those who were interfering with his bill. "I think that the public ought to know the extraordinary exertions being made . . . in Washington, . . . [which] has seldom seen so numerous, so industrious, or insidious a lobby. The newspapers are being filled with paid advertisements calculated to mislead the judgment not only of public men, but also the public opinion of the country itself. There is every evidence that money without limit is being spent. . . . Great bodies of astute men seek . . . to overcome the interests of the public for private profit."[48]

This assertive defense worked, shaming wavering senators into holding their ground and ensuring passage in September of the Underwood Tariff Act, which reduced duties on hundreds of imported goods, and made many, such as sugar, wool, iron, and steel, completely free of the added cost. Walter Hines Page, American ambassador in London, saw the victory as the unleashing of his nation's economy, assuring a British editor "that the passing of commercial supremacy to the United States will be dated in the economic histories from the tariff act of 1913."[49]

Also passed was an even more revolutionary piece of legislation that provided for a direct and graduated tax on income to make up for revenue lost because of this downward tariff revision. The first such tax had been an emergency measure during the Civil War that was dropped in the 1870s. Efforts had been made since to reimpose it, but the Supreme Court had declared the income tax unconstitutional in 1894 in *Pollock v. Farmers' Loan and Trust Company*, with the argument that it was a "communistic threat" to property. William Howard Taft had helped pass the Sixteenth Amendment, which changed the Constitution to allow such a tax, and to the outraged surprise of conservatives, the necessary approval of three-fourths of the states was achieved in February 1913. Cordell Hull, a forty-two-year-old congressman from Tennessee, was given the task of guiding passage, while Wilson insisted to the legislators that no one making less than $3,000 a year should even have to file a form. Annual incomes above $20,000 would be taxed 1 percent, graduating by stages to 7 percent for incomes over $500,000.

Banking and currency reform was the next campaign, and it proved a far more difficult victory. Again, Wilson went to the Capitol to personally lay out his proposals before a joint session of Congress. A national banking system was necessary, he said, where regulation "must be public, not private, must be vested in the Government itself, so that the banks may be the instruments, not the masters, of business and of individual enterprise and initiative."[50] Working closely with Carter Glass of Virginia, and with the help of Bryan and the advice of Brandeis, Wilson was able to have the legislation passed fairly quickly by the House. The Senate, however, was where the real fight took place because both conservatives, who wanted a private system, and reformers such as La Follette, who wanted to eliminate private bankers completely, were difficult to bring into line. Still, with patience and the skillful use of patronage and political favors, Wilson guided the Federal Reserve Act to passage by December 1913. This was perhaps his greatest contribution to the domestic economy as president. The Federal Reserve System, with its twelve regional banks directed by the Federal Reserve Board, was a success as soon as it began operations in 1914, something that even the critics who had been most hostile during the fight to establish it were quick to recognize.

Another part of Wilson's legislative package was an antitrust bill. He wanted the government to have more clearly defined power to control the giant corporations, and an administrative structure, a new agency, to enforce the new law. The Clayton Antitrust Act passed fairly smoothly, though it took some battling to win a partial exemption for labor unions from antitrust laws and thus freedom from the injunctions against restraint of trade that businesses had been able to procure from friendly courts. This success won Wilson and the Democrats the gratitude of the American Federation of Labor and its leader, Samuel Gompers.

It took a greater struggle to establish the Federal Trade Commission (FTC). Resistance here came from both those opposed to government oversight of corporations and those, such as Robert La Follette and Theodore Roosevelt, who felt that the enabling legislation did not go far enough. The final stages of this battle were fought in August 1914, when Wilson was broken-hearted by the death of his wife and distracted by the opening cannons of the Great War. Still, he managed to have the FTC established, though in weaker form than he would have liked.

Bryan was of particular help in getting Wilson's progressive agenda passed. Even though there were many specifics with which he disagreed, he used his influence when necessary to support the bills. One crisis involved Democrats from the agrarian South and West who implied that

Bryan was with them in resisting the Federal Reserve bill. The secretary of state immediately issued a denial, which sped the legislation through the House.

This same spirit of support was true of the other members of the Cabinet, though they lacked Bryan's power within the party. Burleson used his patronage power effectively, and an additional aid to discipline was the long time the Democrats had spent out of national office: even the politicians most resistant to Wilson's positions and arguments recognized that it was necessary for the party to prove itself trustworthy and responsible. The greatest reason, however, for a record of such achievement was the skill, patience, and leadership of the president himself. Though forced to husband his strength because of his physical fragility, his powers of analysis, concentration, and flexibility stiffened by determination were evident to everyone with whom he dealt. He kept Congress in session for an unprecedented nineteen months, and worked his will on both his party and the nation to pass the legislation.

In spite of this record of legislative success, there was criticism of Wilson from various dissatisfied sections of the citizenry. Some progressives saw all that he had accomplished as just the bare beginnings, and complained that much more needed to be done on many fronts. The women's suffrage movement had demonstrated in Washington the day before his inauguration and continued to press him during his first years in office to support their cause. Wilson's daughters, too, tried to enlist him, but he resisted, saying that he believed the right for women to vote was a matter for the individual states to decide. He also felt that he could not be ahead of his party on such a sensitive issue—women's suffrage was strongly opposed by southern members. But there were also personal reasons for his reluctance. Raised as an old-fashioned southern gentleman, he did not find militant feminists, even those of a refined background, attractive models for American womanhood, and he also felt that women were too "rational" and direct in their politics, unwilling to wheel and deal and compromise. "We cannot enfranchise the women all at once. It would be very dangerous. Woman's mind is too logical. . . . In politics, in governmental affairs, and in life you cannot go in a straight and logical line."[51]

Nativists, too, were unhappy. A bill to restrict immigration through the use of a literacy test had passed Congress in 1912 and been vetoed by President Taft. A more restrictive bill, passed by even greater majorities in both houses, would be presented to Woodrow Wilson in early 1915. The House just barely missed subsequently overturning his veto, and nativist politicians, such as Republican senator Henry Cabot Lodge of Massachusetts, promised that the legislation would be back on his desk soon.

African Americans were another group dissatisfied with the new president, and here there was an even stronger, well justified sense of betrayal. During the campaign in 1912, Wilson had promised for blacks "absolute fair dealing" from his administration, though there were obvious signs that his white southern supporters would be less tolerant. Josephus Daniels, the secretary of the navy, as a North Carolina newspaper editor, wrote an editorial a month before the election explaining that the South voted Democratic because of "the realization that the subjection of the negro, politically, and the separation of the negro socially, are paramount to all other considerations in the South short of the preservation of the Republic itself. And we shall recognize no emancipation, nor shall we proclaim any deliverer, that falls short of these essentials to the peace and welfare of our part of the country."[52]

In spite of such signs, African American leaders such as W.E.B. DuBois and William Monroe Trotter had supported Wilson in the election of 1912, a major break with the tradition of supporting the Republicans as the party of Abraham Lincoln. Theodore Roosevelt and the Progressive Party, hoping to draw southern white support, explicitly ruled out a role for the federal government in a state's race relations, so Wilson ended up receiving more black votes than any previous presidential candidate in history. But when he tried to appoint African Americans to positions in the government, he came under attack from the southern wing of the party, many members of which had hoped for the complete elimination of African Americans from all federal jobs. Senators "Pitchfork Ben" Tillman of South Carolina and James K. Vardaman of Mississippi, among the worst of the racists, fought ferociously against one appointment, Vardaman charging that if it went through it would "create in every negro in the country a hope that he may some day stand on social and political equality with the white man."[53] Wilson, needing southern votes to pass his slate of reform measures, withdrew that nomination, but did later defy the extreme racists through the appointment of other African Americans to important posts.

As a southerner himself, the president shared the region's belief in segregation, though to a more moderate and paternalistic degree than Tillman and Vardaman. When McAdoo, a Georgian and the secretary of the treasury, along with Burleson, a Texan and the postmaster general, instituted stricter than traditional "separate but equal" policies in their departments, the president did nothing until a storm of denunciation came from both blacks and their white supporters.

Wilson met twice with delegations of African American leaders to defend the segregation, which he argued was "for the benefit of both" races, since blacks had to prove themselves independently, free from both white help and white criticism. Monroe Trotter, editor of the *Boston Guardian,* a Harvard graduate, and the first black member of the Phi Beta Kappa honor society, was an outspoken critic at both meetings. The second, on November 12, 1914, grew very heated. "Only two years ago you were heralded as perhaps the second Lincoln," Trotter charged, "and now the Afro-American leaders who supported you are hounded as false leaders and traitors to their race. What a change segregation has wrought!" Trotter then accused the president of having a "new freedom" for white Americans and only a "new slavery" for those of African descent. Furious, Wilson refused to continue the discussion, all but throwing the delegation out of his office, creating a widely publicized dramatic illustration of his lack of sympathy.[54]

Such pressures on the president were made worse by cracks that were developing in his coalition as the various Democratic factions became used to being in power, and by a growing Mexican crisis. All took a toll on his health. From his first week in office he had suffered physically from the stress of the job, feeling exhausted, and tortured by his delicate stomach. This was evident to some observers; Silas Weir Mitchell, the famous Philadelphia expert on nervous diseases, predicted that Wilson would not survive his first term. But Dr. Cary Grayson, a young naval medical officer who came highly recommended by Taft, began attending to the president and his family. Surprised by the amount of medicine his new patient took and by the fact that he had his stomach pumped out regularly, as well as by the number of ailments that he suffered from, Grayson eliminated the medications and put him on a diet of fruit juice and raw eggs. To treat the pain of neuritis, he applied heat followed by massage, and he urged his patient to find relief from the pressures he was feeling; like so many of his contemporaries, executives, and other middle-class males suffering from the increasing tensions of the modern world, he took up golf.

————◁◦▷————

CHAPTER FIVE

Testing

It would be an irony of fate if my administration had to deal chiefly with foreign affairs.

Woodrow Wilson, March 1913[1]

[I had] a terrible curiosity. . . . I felt I had to know how I would act under fire.

John Reed[2]

SECRETARY OF STATE William Jennings Bryan, silver-voiced son of the farming West, had dedicated himself to every one of the multitudinous efforts of Protestant America to raise the morality of peoples here and abroad. Premarital chastity, the suppression of alcohol, missions to convert the heathen in the Far East, and blue laws to prevent commerce from tainting the Sabbath were just a few of the crusades he had preached on the campaign trail, on the Chautauqua circuit, and in the pages of his magazine, *The Commoner.* One of his, and his constituency's, bedrock beliefs was that the age of wars had passed, and that every man and woman's duty now was to spread the vision of the Prince of Peace. In this he was very much in the American grain, representative of a nation that increasingly saw war as a European vice with little connection to its own well-being. The recent unpleasantness with Spain, in which Bryan had served, stateside, as a colonel of Nebraska volunteers, was irrelevant because that had been a Christian duty imposed by Spain's barbaric treatment of the Cubans. The crushing of Philippine guerrillas who had resisted American control of their islands had never penetrated very deeply into the country's consciousness, but Bryan had opposed that campaign, though in a rather low and confused voice. The very bloody Civil War lost much of its bloodiness as it retreated further and further into the past, blurring the suffering into an epic tale of romantic gallantry instead of the slaughter of 620,000 American men.

This drive for a world free from the barbaric anachronism of war can be seen in the establishment of the Carnegie Endowment for International Peace in 1910, founded with the enormous sum of $10 million donated by Andrew Carnegie, the retired industrialist. He made further contributions to the cause by establishing the Palace of Peace at The Hague, which opened for business on August 28, 1913. Less affluent Americans were also involved in this quest; between 1898 and 1914 they founded close to forty-five different societies seeking to establish some kind of permanent world peace.

One of Secretary Bryan's greatest ambitions was to negotiate arbitration treaties with individual nations, treaties that would impose a cooling-off period of a year on countries on the verge of hostilities, thus allowing time for impartial investigation and the resolution of grievances. Here we see another example of the contemporary American confidence in both expertise and democracy, for if one or both of the governments involved were unhappy with the results of the investigation and they threatened war, it was expected that the citizens of the countries, having witnessed the honest investigation conducted by impartial experts, would not support such threats and would force compliance.

A similar system had also been a goal of President William Howard Taft, whose secretary of state, Philander Knox, had actually negotiated and signed such treaties with France and Great Britain, only to see them torn apart in the Senate because of that body's unwillingness to give up any of its powers over war and peace.[3] Henry Cabot Lodge, with the encouragement of his good friend Theodore Roosevelt, had led the successful repulse.

Bryan launched his own arbitration campaign soon after being sworn in to office, and by early August 1913 the first treaty had been signed. True, that first signatory was the small and unthreatening nation of El Salvador, but thirty others soon followed, including China, Spain, France, and Great Britain, which inspired the secretary to predict that the treaties would "make armed conflict between the contracting nations almost, if not entirely, impossible."[4] Only Germany, of the nations approached, refused, with Kaiser Wilhelm II reported by Colonel House as boasting, "Our strength lies in being always prepared for war at a second's notice."[5]

In spite of these well-intentioned, good-hearted attempts at building a system that would ensure world peace, there were some ugly encounters in the administration's very first months that indicated that the road to that worthy goal would be a rocky one. Japan posed one problem, as it continued trying to grab parts of China, an effort that had begun decades before. American diplomatic efforts to contain Japanese aggression were complicated by the racial prejudice of Californians, who were severely limiting the civil rights of Japanese immigrants in that state. This in turn provoked the Tokyo government, which itself limited the rights of foreigners in its nation, to loud protests that carried such a strong threat of war that naval officers feared a surprise attack on the Philippines, and ordered warships to be battle-ready. There were also long-standing rumors of Japanese attempts to make some sort of diplomatic and military alliance with Mexico and thus threaten the very heart of America. Bryan was dispatched to California in an ineffectual effort to tone down the rhetoric against Japanese land ownership and integrated education. Eventually, the anger on both sides became more muted, but it did not completely disappear.

Armed interventions were ordered in Haiti, the Dominican Republic, and Nicaragua, where the navy and marines were used to establish protectorates to prevent political chaos, or so that custom duties could be collected and the money used to pay off loans that those countries had contracted with Europeans. Just as with the administration of Theodore Roosevelt, no excuse would be allowed for European intervention in the Caribbean, especially now that the Panama Canal was going to change the strategic situation, even if that required Uncle Sam to enlist as bill collector for creditor nations such as Germany.

Mexico provided much more of a test. Francisco Madero had led a successful revolution in 1911 against the corrupt geriatric regime of the dictator General José de la Cruz Porfirio Diaz, who had ruled for thirty-one years. Taft had refused to intervene, though he felt the pressure from wealthy Americans who had benefited from Diaz's policies encouraging foreign investment, development, and ownership of the country's natural riches. By 1910, American businesses had more than $500 million invested in Mexico, and masters of great fortunes such as Rockefeller, Morgan, Hearst, Guggenheim, and Harriman made sure politicians knew of their close interest.

Closing the border to the arms trade, which denied weapons to counterrevolutionaries, had strained the limited resources of the U.S. Army, but it had allowed Madero some time to write a constitution and begin to establish a democratic government. To set Mexican society on a new course meant that Madero had to weaken the powers of the hereditary landowning class from which he himself had sprung, as well as those of the church, the army, and the foreign investors who controlled much of the economy. This was a very dangerous course indeed; unfortunately, Madero was more of a gentle dreamer, as well as a teetotaler and vegetarian, than the hardheaded politician that revolutionary conditions required. As his brother and sharp-witted adviser Gustavo put it: "In a family of clever men, the only fool was President."[6] In spite of strong warnings not to do so, Presidente Madero placed the defense of his government in the hands of Victoriano Huerta, one of Diaz's former generals who had ambitions of his own. In February 1913, Huerta staged a coup, and had both Madero and his vice president murdered, while Gustavo Madero, as punishment for opposing Huerta, was tortured to death by a mob of the new dictator's supporters.

Great Britain, France, Germany, and Japan quickly established relations with Huerta when he promised not to threaten foreign ownership of companies or natural resources, but William Howard Taft left the question to his successor. Wilson refused to recognize what he called a "government of butchers,"[7] in spite of pressure from Taft-appointed American ambassador Henry Lane Wilson, who had secretly aided the coup, and business interests in the United States such as the Rockefellers and the Californian Edward Doheny, who owned oil rights in the country, and the Southern Pacific company, which controlled railroads. The British, as well, pushed Woodrow Wilson to get in line with the other powers in regard to the Mexican situation, but he pushed back. "I am going to teach the South American Republics to elect good men!" the former professor told a British diplomat.[8] At the same time, Wilson felt a "sneaking admiration" for the way Huerta exerted his will, writing his old friend and former lover Mary Peck that he found the dictator "a diverting brute . . . so false, so sly, so full of bravado, yet so courageous . . . seldom sober and always impossible yet what an indomitable fighter."[9]

At first Wilson and Bryan tried to use moral pressure to force Huerta from office, but that proved ineffective. Although few alternatives were available to them, the immediate uprising of the Constitutionalists against Huerta—led by Venustiano Carranza, governor of the northern state of Coahuila, and the former bandit Pancho Villa—offered hope to optimists that some form of democracy and social justice would eventually be established. Once the unreliability of Ambassador Henry Lane Wilson became obvious and rumors of his involvement in the coup spread, the president dismissed him, but did not appoint a replacement. Instead, he dispatched trusted though inexperienced friends to investigate conditions in Mexico and send secret reports directly to him. One was William Bayard Hale, who had written a 1912 campaign biography of Wilson, and the other was

Governor John Lind of Minnesota; neither of then spoke Spanish or had the slightest familiarity with the country. Their reports assured the president that Huerta was indeed a brute, and not to be reasoned with. When further negotiations to have Huerta resign turned fruitless, though the dictator coyly teased his American opponents along for months, Wilson went before Congress on August 27, 1913, and announced a policy of "watchful waiting."

The wait was not long, and what they saw was not pretty. Huerta finally abandoned all pretense of following constitutional norms on October 10, dissolving the legislature, throwing more than a hundred opposition members of the Chamber of Deputies into prison, and overtly ruling as a military caudillo. He was evidently encouraged to take this action by the new British minister to Mexico, Sir Lionel Carden, who had tight connections to Lord Cowdray, owner of large oil properties in the country. Wilson now realized that in order to force Huerta from power, he would have to convince the other powers to withdraw their support, and he put his strongest effort into having Great Britain take that step.

This was difficult. For one thing, the British could see no great moral difference between Huerta and any of the chieftains rebelling against him. For another, the British navy was converting from coal power to oil, and Mexico was by far its greatest supplier. Sir Edward Grey, the British foreign secretary, was caught in a dilemma. A European war was growing ever more possible, and the oil would be needed to protect the empire and the British Isles, but in the event of such a war, the friendship of the United States would also weigh in the balance. Grey decided that this friendship was the essential factor; relations with Huerta were broken.

Unfortunately, that did not end all support for the Mexican dictator. Japan immediately provided a shipment of arms, and Admiral Paul von Hintze, the German ambassador, also stepped forward and offered to supply the government with modern weapons, in return for denying the British access to oil if war between the two nations broke out. The offer, which was gratefully accepted, raised hackles in the United States.

The Constitutionalists had been enjoying some military success in their rebellion against Huerta's government, and Wilson had his agents approach their first chief, Venustiano Carranza, offering support as long as the rebels promised to keep to a democratic path and hold elections as soon as possible. Carranza had no interest in being tutored by an American president in the fine points of ruling his own country; all he wanted was the right to buy arms and ammunition north of the border, and to be left alone.

But the revolutions and counterrevolutions rending Mexico were now drawing the attention of the world.

MABEL DODGE was not happy about Jack Reed's decision to cover the revolutionary fighting in Mexico. She tearfully pleaded with her lover not to go, while the twenty-six-year-old gave the ancient male assurance: "I will take you with me in my heart," insisting that "we *must* be free to live our own lives." Mexico and its problems was the subject of a salon evening that was held the night before he departed, and Mabel remembered him "puffed up and excited, his curls tossed back, standing up and declaiming wildly." After her guests left, she wept until dawn, clasping Jack to her breast, and wanting "to drown him in myself so that he couldn't leave me."[10] But leave he did.

Mabel waited for a few hours, perhaps hoping he would reconsider and return to her bed. When he didn't, she hurriedly packed and caught up to him in Chicago, and the couple traveled together to El Paso, making love so passionately behind the locked door of their compartment that Reed referred to the trip in a letter to his friend Eddy Hunt as a "honeymoon."[11]

Reed found the border city of El Paso full of raffish characters. Spies, con men, and detectives seemed to predominate, with the latter, "conspicuous by the elaborateness of their disguises," providing comic relief as they "shadowed" important men and one another through the hot, dusty streets. Jack and Mabel were conspicuous enough themselves, with him, as he wrote Hunt, resplendent in a "bright yellow corduroy suit and Mabel in her orange hat and satin-lined tiger-skin hunting-jacket." He was excited by what he had already seen: "If I don't get a single note from the front—if I don't set foot over the frontier—I'll have material enough for six books."

Leaving Mabel in El Paso, he traveled the couple of hundred miles to Presidio, Texas, which was enjoying "metropolitan days," as other journalists, gunrunners, and spies waited there for Villa and the Constitutionalists to attack Huerta's federal troops in Ojinaga, just across the Rio Grande, tantalizingly and picturesquely within view of the mud roof of the post office. "One could see the square, gray adobe houses of Ojinaga, with here and there the Oriental cupola of an old Spanish church. It was a desolate land, without trees. You expected minarets. . . . Toward evening, when the sun went down with the flare of a blast furnace, patrols of cavalry rode sharply across the skyline to the night outposts. And after dark, mysterious fires burned in the town."[12]

Journalists were not welcome in Ojinaga, but Reed sent a letter to the military commander in the town, General Mercado, asking for an interview. The letter fell into the hands of another federal officer, a General Orozco, who returned a brief, chilling reply: "ESTEEMED AND HONORED SIR: If you set foot inside of Ojinaga, I will stand you sideways against a wall, and with my own hand take great pleasure in shooting furrows in your back."

Reed waited for a day or so, then defied the threat by wading the river and entering the town, intent on finding Mercado and gaining his interview. "Luckily, I did not meet General Orozco." Up close, Ojinaga showed the price of having been taken and retaken five times during the war: roofless houses, cannon-shattered walls, starving people. He tracked down General Mercado, "a fat, pathetic, worried, undecided little man, who blubbered and blustered" and who, lying, blamed his problems on the United States Army, claiming it had helped Pancho Villa defeat him.

A few days later, Reed returned to Mabel, who had been shopping and looking for "atmosphere" in El Paso, and took her across the border into Juárez. There he saw some of the revolutionary Constitutionalist army: "Two thousand nondescript, tattered men, on dirty little tough horses, their serapes flying out behind, their mouths one wild yell, simply flung themselves out over the plain. That's how the general reviewed them. They had very little discipline, but . . . what spirit!" And thinking back to the Paterson strike, he enthused to a friend, "what pageant material."[13] These vivid, though brief, adventures proved an irresistible draw, convincing Reed that he had to journey deeper into Mexico to really see war—and to test his manhood. He admitted to himself that he "was afraid of death, of mutilation, of a strange land and strange people whose speech and thought I did not know." But there was also the "terrible curiosity" that he shared with many other American men of his and previous generations—the need to know how they would handle themselves in combat.[14] He put Mabel on the train for New York City, then headed south to find the action.

It is difficult to know his exact itinerary, since his resulting book, *Insurgent Mexico*, plays with the actual chronology, and much else, for dramatic effect, but he seems to have traveled part of the way with an Arab peddler. Within a few days he had joined La Tropa, a band of colorful irregular cavalrymen. "About a hundred, they were, in all stages of picturesque raggedness; some wore overalls, others the *charro* jackets of peons, while one or two sported tight *vaquero* trousers. A few had shoes, most of them only cowhide sandals, and the rest were barefooted. . . . Rifles slung at their saddles, four or five cartridge belts crossed over their chests, high, flapping sombreros, immense spurs chiming as they rode, bright-colored serapes strapped on behind—this was their uniform."

Reed rode with them across the fierce desert of northern Mexico, "the most terrible desert in the world," sharing their privations and joining in their rough carousing and laughter.

" 'Come here, Meester!' " he reports the captain calling to him one evening, producing a bottle of sotol, a particularly potent form of firewater, and insisting that the Americano drink. " 'Drink it all. Show you're a man.' "

"It's too much," Reed said, laughing, but to shouts of approval he did drink it all.

" 'Good for you, *compañero*,' " cried the captain, "rolling with mirth" while the "men crowded around, amused and interested." Now he was really one of them. This feeling would make the two weeks he rode with them the "most satisfactory" of his life. "I made good with these wild fighting men and with myself."[15]

They usually rose very early and were in the saddle before dawn, riding hard from hacienda to hacienda, where they would camp, eat, and sometimes force reluctant señoritas to dance with them. These dances could become ugly, as happened when the men drank too freely from a barrel of sotol, and the *baile* grew "wilder and wilder. . . . Everybody was drunk now. Pablo was boasting horribly of killing defenseless prisoners. Occasionally, some insult would be passed, and there would be a snapping of rifle levers all over the place. Then perhaps the poor exhausted women would begin to go home, and what an ominous shout would go up: 'No vaya!' Don't go! Stop! Come back here and dance! Come back here!"

La Tropa had an airborne escort along its whole route of march. "And always the mighty Mexican vultures circled over us, as if they knew we were going to war." They found the war at La Cadena, where they were sent to guard a mountain pass against the *colorados*, federal irregulars known for their savagery. First contact, though, displayed Reed's *compañeros'* own lack of humanitarian restraint when they captured one of the enemy and tortured, then shot him; his rifle was, Reed claimed, presented to the author as a gift. "The *colorado* they left to the great Mexican buzzards, which flap lazily above the desert all day long."

But the *colorados* returned in overwhelming force, driving back the Constitutionalists and breaking their lines. As Reed loaded his camera and prepared to cover the fighting, he was struck by how unreal it all seemed; shortly thereafter he was fleeing through the chaparral, tossing aside his camera and coat so he could run faster. "I ran on—ran and ran and ran, until I could run no more. Then I walked a few steps and ran again. I was sobbing instead of breathing. . . . Everything still was so unreal, like a page out of Richard Harding Davis."

Which, given the unreliability of the book, perhaps it was; it is hard to know which parts of the exciting adventure tale of *Insurgent Mexico* actually happened and which were skillful fiction in line with the adventure stories of Davis. Everywhere Reed goes, according to his tale, he faces violent death or less extreme tests of his manhood, with enough resolution and charm to escape, often because some gringo-hating Mexican recognizes his sincerity and courage, then befriends and protects him. The most unlikely event of many takes place after he manages to escape the *colorados* and rejoin the remnants of La Tropa. A young woman whose lover was killed in the battle supposedly chooses to spend the night with him, innocently, rather than with the captain, who has assumed she has now become his woman. As Reed leads her to his bed, the young boys "followed . . . close behind, shouting the joyful indelicacies they shout behind rustic wedding parties" while an unhappy, and heavily armed, captain merely goes whining to the colonel that the "gringo has taken away my woman. It is the grossest insult!"

The goal of Reed's journey was finally reached some time around the end of December 1913 in Chihuahua City when he met the man he had been seeking all along: Pancho Villa. The rebels of Greenwich Village had heard of him, though most of America had not, a condition of ignorance that Reed was going to cure. Reed's old mentor Lincoln Steffens reports that the "reds" in New York "were on Villa's side, but the only reason they gave was that he was at least a bandit. . . . Jack Reed talked that way, and he later went in on Villa's side."[16]

Villa certainly had been a bandit, and Reed recognized quickly that, for all his good-natured banter, here was a man far rougher and untamed than even Big Bill Haywood. "He is the most natural human being I ever saw," he wrote in his notebook, "natural in the sense of being nearest a wild animal." He particularly noticed Villa's eyes, which were the eyes of a killer, "absolutely hot and steely."[17] Though recognizing that Villa was a "terrible man," Reed was drawn to him, like many middle-class radicals would be attracted to such hard, callous, strong-willed militants in the twentieth century, as men of almost primitive force and violence, authentic revolutionaries who got things done without oversensitivity to human cost. Writers, perhaps more than others, would be particularly susceptible, feeling a need for that authenticating brush with manliness and a life of action.

Reed presented his new host with gifts, he wrote Carl Hovey, the editor at *Metropolitan* who had given him the assignment: "I bought Villa a saddle and a rifle with a gold nameplate on it and a Maxim silencer. He is hugely delighted, and will do almost anything for me now."[18] Villa also must have been charmed by the naïveté and evident hero worship of the young journalist, whom he nicknamed Chatito, or "Pug-nose," and he issued him a pass that called on all officers and officials to provide him with aid, and the free use of trains and telegraph lines.[19]

In return, Villa received laudatory attention. Reed, whose observations about Villa the killer never made the leap from notebook insights to print, instead described to the American public a simple man of the people, who neither drank nor smoked, and who had the genius to devise a military strategy new to Mexico, using it to liberate poor peons. "His method of fighting is astonishingly like Napoleon's. Secrecy, quickness of movement, the adaptation of his plans to the character of the country and of his soldiers, the value of intimate relations with the rank and file, and of building up a tradition . . . that his army is invincible, and that he himself bears a charmed life, these are his characteristics."

But beyond possessing Napoleonic military skills, Villa, as Reed presented him, was a kind of Robin Hood, who fervently believed in taking the enormous estates of the rich and dividing them among the landless, yet was too humble to have greater ambitions for power. "I am a fighter," he is quoted as explaining, "not a statesman. I am not educated enough to be president. I only learned to read and write two years ago. . . . There is one thing that I will not do, and that is to take a position for which I am not fitted." He was "perfectly obstinate" in his loyalty to Carranza, and only wants, he tells the author, "to help make Mexico a happy place." Reed portrays himself as helping Villa make a start on entering the modern world by educating him, through a translator, of course, about socialism and feminism. Women deserve the vote, Reed argued to Villa, who was supposedly old-fashioned and sentimental about the need to protect and love females, because they "can be crueller and harder than men."

Reed spent weeks with Villa's Army of the North, interrupted by a quick visit to the border town of Nogales to interview Carranza, whom he thought a frail old man disconnected from the true roots of the struggle, worried more about constitutional niceties than the necessary land reform. This pale specter contrasted markedly with the ebullient, earthy revolutionary with whom Reed now rode.

The articles in *Metropolitan*, later published with some additions as *Insurgent Mexico*, were the making of Reed's national reputation. Picturesque and full of vitality and colorful descriptions of landscape, battle scenes, and people, his passionate and partisan writings gave the truest sense yet to Americans of the massive social upheaval south of the border. That he did this while overdramatizing and distorting what he had actually experienced and while patronizing and sentimentalizing the Mexicans with whom he had lived did not hurt the success of the story at all. Mexican bandits turned courageous and honorable guerrilla soldiers, an Arab merchant with whom he had traveled, Chinese cooks and gamblers, poor *pacíficos,* civilian men and women suffering from poverty and war, Villa and his lieutenants—all came alive on his pages.

Walter Lippmann wrote congratulations. "Your . . . articles are undoubtedly the finest reporting that's ever been done. It's kind of embarrassing to tell a fellow you know that he's a genius. . . . You have perfect eyes, and your power of telling leaves nothing to be desired. I want to hug you, Jack. If all history had been reported as you are doing this, Lord, I say that with Jack Reed reporting begins. Incidentally . . . the stories are literature."[20]

Reviews of the book were not as enthusiastic but were generally positive. *The Nation* caught some of the flaws, finding the book a "lurid exaggeration . . . and the frenzied manner of the whole composition aims not so much at depicting sober truths as at shocking the reader." *Outlook* had a particularly racist take, which was easy enough to find, on his "truthful delineation," while missing the humanity with which he had tried to imbue his characters. "None of the war correspondents in Mexico has got so close to the Mexicans themselves; he describes them as they are, without idealizing them or concealing their ignorance, brutality, or semi-barbarism. Emphatically his book is dramatic; his frequent use of the dialogue form of narrative gives an effect at times like that of a skilled fiction writer, while the abundance of incident and anecdote makes the book immensely readable."[21] There seemed to be no admirable Americans in all of Mexico—except himself, of course. In a private letter, a friend who knew him well, Dave Carb, pointed out, "It's so much Reed that I suspect it is very little Mexico."[22]

Metropolitan magazine had advertised his series in newspapers with drawings of the intrepid author shaded by a sombrero and decorated with a pistol, calling him an "American Kipling," and promising that what "Stephen Crane and Richard Harding Davis had done for the Spanish American war in 1898, John Reed, 26 years old, has done for Mexico." In early April 1914, feeling that his work in that country was at least temporarily completed, he returned to New York, and the arms of Mabel Dodge. He was famous now, and even more impatient for adventures worthy of a committed radical and man of action.

The right for the Constitutionalists to buy weapons and ammunition in the United States was finally granted by Wilson in February 1914, while the arms embargo against Huerta continued. Wilson had considered using American troops to aid Constitutionalist forces, but had not, partly because Carranza had warned him that he not only did not want American forces in his country, but would actually fight to expel them if they entered Mexican territory.

Wilson was also reluctant to interfere directly because he shied from the idea of committing American soldiers to the hazards of combat. In April 1914, however, an opportunity to use minimum force to bring down Huerta seemed to present itself. American warships had been sent to the two major Mexican ports, Tampico and Veracruz, to protect American and other foreign residents from the now continuous fighting between the armies of Carranza and Huerta. Tampico, on the Pánuco River, was a particular worry; large numbers of American and European engineers, technical experts, businessmen, and their families had moved there to help develop the huge oil fields nearby and to service the network of pipelines and refineries that had grown up around the port. The situation was particularly dangerous because Carranza's Constitutionalists had the city under tight siege and might begin a bombardment at any time, which meant civilians could suffer not only the direct hazards of artillery, but also the possibility of a shell setting the refineries and storage tanks afire, sparking a holocaust. The commander of the American flotilla, Admiral Henry Thomas Mayo, tried to convince U.S. citizens to come aboard his ships, but they, not believing that there was anything to worry about, refused even to have the women and children evacuated.

On the morning of April 9, 1914, a whaleboat from one of the American ships docked at a warehouse on the Pánuco River for a load of gasoline. Constitutionalist shelling had set some storage tanks ablaze and oily black smoke drifted over the water, while a Federalist gunboat noisily returned fire. The Americans were unarmed and unworried, trusting to the Stars and Stripes, prominently flying above their boat, for protection. But Federalist troops were edgy, expecting an attack, and an overly aggressive lieutenant, deciding that the gringos had no business being in the area, arrested the crew and marched them to regimental headquarters, where his horrified commander immediately released them. The commanding general of the garrison not only sent an apology to Admiral Mayo, he had the unfortunate officer arrested for negligence.

The admiral, however, was not satisfied, and he wrote the general that such an insult to Old Glory could be redressed only by severe punishment of the officer responsible. In addition, the note demanded that the Mexicans "publicly hoist the American flag in a prominent position on shore and salute it with twenty-one guns, which salute will be duly returned by this ship."[23]

Radio was a recent technology, and Mayo's transmissions were too weak to reach the United States, so messages had to be relayed through the American squadron steaming off Veracruz, and news of the incident took more than twelve hours to reach Washington. Secretary Bryan found nothing wrong with Mayo's demand: "I do not see that Mayo could have done otherwise," he advised the president.[24] Wilson evidently agreed, and saw this as an opportunity to topple Huerta. When it became clear that the Mexican government would not accede to the demand for a humiliating twenty-one-gun apology, Wilson ordered the Atlantic Fleet, consisting of seven battleships, two cruisers, and a troopship carrying a regiment of marines, to steam for Tampico.

The House of Representatives, and to an extent the public, backed the president, though some felt that the action contemplated was out of scale to the insult. The Senate, led by Henry Cabot Lodge, was a bit more reluctant, but only because of Lodge's feeling that the action should be more broadly based, not only against Huerta but against every threat to American lives and property in Mexico. But Wilson had not shared all his information. Intelligence had come through that the *Ypiranga,* a German ship owned by the Hamburg-America line carrying machine guns and tons of ammunition for Huerta, was due to dock in Veracruz in the next few days. Here, it seemed to Wilson and his advisers, was a chance to weaken Huerta both by denying him the shipment and by making a forceful show of American disapproval of his dictatorship. It was also an opportunity to discourage German maneuvering in Mexico. On the morning of April 21, 1914, twelve hundred sailors and marines landed in Veracruz to seize the customs house; as F. H. Delano, a marine captain, wrote his mother, "We do not expect much if any resistance."[25]

The president had also expected things to go smoothly. As he told a combined session of Congress the day before the landing, "our quarrel [is] with Huerta, not the Mexican people," and he claimed that the United States had been "singled out" for harassment in Tampico because it refused to recognize Huerta's dictatorship as the legitimate government of Mexico. Wilson promised that "the present situation need have none of the grave complications of interference if we deal with it promptly, firmly, and wisely."[26]

Grave complications, however, arose immediately. As soon as the com-

manding general at Veracruz learned of the American landings, he supplemented his forces by releasing and arming prisoners from the military jail,
and by having a "moving picture show" that advertised itself as "for men
only"—once the theater was full, the audience was gathered up by soldiers
and drafted into the army. The general also distributed extra rifles to civilians, but then he received orders to fall back to a small town some miles
away from the coast. He withdrew his regulars, but did not collect the
rifles: civilians, freed prisoners, and naval academy cadets began sniping at
the Americans.

Admiral Frank F. Fletcher, hoping for a bloodless and quick capture of
the customs house, had ordered his men not to fire unless fired upon. The
first killed was a navy signalman wigwagging his flags to the fleet from the
top of a building; other deaths quickly followed. Over the next few days,
the Americans extended their control over the city in difficult house-to-
house fighting, killing or driving the snipers from rooftop to rooftop. The
marines were well trained in this, but the sailors had to learn as they
fought, and there were some ugly mix-ups when Americans mistakenly
fired on Americans. Marine captain Delano thought the sailors "were all
gallant enough but had little idea of the use of the rifle and at times made
things positively dangerous by the way in which they handled their
weapons; they shot several of their own people and killed one of [ours]."[27]
When particularly difficult positions were attacked, artillery support from
the ships was called in by courageous sailors standing in full view of their
enemies, wigwagging their flags. By late morning on April 22, Veracruz was
"pacified," but 17 marines and sailors were dead and 63 wounded, while
Mexican casualties were estimated, probably too conservatively, by the
Americans at 126 dead with 195 wounded.[28] Still, Delano wrote his family,
it had been a valuable experience to have been under fire, and to have
stayed calm and done one's duty.

Wilson was shocked at the toll. At a news conference, a journalist
reported "how preternaturally pale, almost parchmenty, Mr. Wilson looked
when he stood up there and answered the questions of the newspapermen.
The death of American sailors and marines owing to an order of his seemed
to affect him like an ailment. He was positively shaken."[29] "I cannot get it
off my heart," he admitted to his secretary Joe Tumulty. "It was right. Nothing else was possible, but I cannot forget that it was I who had to order
these young men to their deaths."[30] But there was to be no turning back
now that the sacrifices had been made, and greater ones might be in store.
Mexican troops were reported to be gathering in the countryside around

the port in sufficient numbers to wipe out the occupying force. Wilson held back from calling up hundreds of thousands of reservists. Instead, the Fifth Infantry Brigade, consisting of about five thousand men, was sent under Brigadier General Frederick Funston to take over land duty from the navy; the battleships and cruisers would remain offshore in case their fire support was needed.

Funston was one of the most accomplished field commanders of the American army. An alumnus of the University of Kansas, he had fought with Cubans during their revolt against Spain and was wounded twice, once through the lung. He had then joined the United States Army, serving in the Philippines, where he had won fame, a promotion, and the Congressional Medal of Honor for leading a daring unconventional expedition that had captured the leader of the Insurrectionists, General Emilio Aguinaldo. He had, as his college fraternity brother, the journalist William Allen White, recalled, "absolutely no sense of fear, physical or spiritual."[31]

The city quickly returned to normal, Delano writing his family that "the natives . . . are beginning to realize that we are not making war on them personally and the majority of them are going about their business as if nothing had happened. . . . Stores are open and the trolley cars are again running."[32] The Americans, like good progressives, began a crusade for cleanliness: sweeping and washing the streets, scrubbing down and disinfecting the food markets, and completely reorganizing the sanitary system. Other health problems also had to be resolved. There had been a somewhat embarrassing scene when the sailors had made a farewell parade before returning to their ships. Bands played and army troops cheered the blue jackets, while the sailors cheered right back. And then some passing prostitutes recognized friends in the marching ranks and impetuously rushed forward to embrace them, calling out *"Mi dulce corazón"* so loudly as to almost drown out the bands.[33]

Funston, like most army officers, was no prig, and did not forbid prostitution, but he tried to contain the spread of venereal disease by having the local women undergo regular health inspections while expelling foreign professionals. None of these measures completely solved the problem, as illustrated by the case of a thirteen-year-old girl who had run away from home in a nearby town to see the Americans occupying Veracruz. She became a prostitute in order to survive, was treated twice for gonorrhea, then was found to have syphilis and to be pregnant. Horrified by this, Funston immediately ordered all underage and unattached girls out of the city. The overall drive for a healthier Veracruz was successful. "The death rate from disease among the Mexicans dropped by 25 percent from that of the previous three months," reports the historian John S. D. Eisenhower, "even though the yellow fever season was just beginning."[34]

Funston not only aggressively pursued a campaign for health and sanitation, he also pushed his superiors to order an advance inland, perhaps all the way to the Mexican capital. "Have just been informed," he told Washington in early May 1914, "[that] foreigners and citizens in Mexico City will unite in request that US troops occupy city to prevent massacre and pillage. . . . Under such conditions [we] can go through in a day or two. . . . Merely give the order and leave the rest to us."[35] As it was, he was not allowed even to send reconnaissance patrols beyond the limits of Veracruz.

One of the main reasons for seizing the city proved fruitless: the *Ypiranga,* intercepted by the American battle fleet and denied use of Veracruz, simply sailed farther down the coast to unload its deadly cargo at another port. The president and his advisers had also been unpleasantly surprised not only by the armed resistance to their intervention, but by the angry criticism from Carranza and other Constitutionalist opponents of Huerta. The *New York Times* printed a public letter from Carranza to Wilson and Bryan on April 23 that demanded the Americans leave Mexican soil immediately: "The invasion of our territory and the permanency of your forces in the Port of Veracruz are a violation of the rights that constitute our existence as a free and independent sovereignty, and will drag us into an unequal war which until today we desired to avoid." The only rebel leader who supported the American action was Pancho Villa, who both publicly and privately gave assurances to Wilson of his feelings of friendship toward the United States.

Demonstrations had been held against the occupation of Veracruz in many cities of Latin America, and U.S. citizens living in these places were threatened. But on April 25, the ambassadors from Argentina, Brazil, and Chile asked the State Department if it would accept their mediation in the crisis. Wilson was delighted and welcomed the offer, which surprised Latin Americans, who were not used to the Colossus of the North taking them seriously. "The transformation was amazing," wrote an American living in the region. "American flags were run up; the United States was cheered," and he was "seized and carried on the shoulders of a yelling, rejoicing mob, which had been ready to tear [me] in pieces a moment before."[36]

Most Americans also celebrated the diminishing of the threat of war, though there were some who thought that this would be the perfect opportunity to solve the Mexican problem once and for all. The journalist Paul Scott Mowrer, returning to Chicago from his post in Paris for a bit of home leave, found that his father "and some of his business friends were for licking and taking over our troublesome neighbor."[37] Idle talk over drinks in the upper Midwest, perhaps, but at least one U.S. senator agreed. "If the flag of the United States is ever run up in Mexico," roared Senator William Borah, Republican of Idaho, "it will never come down. This is the beginning of the march of the United States to the Panama Canal!"[38]

One of those who would have to make that march, an African American trooper of the Ninth Cavalry, agreed with him. While patrolling along the border, he stopped to water his horse in the Rio Grande.

"Hey, coon!" shouted a Mexican squatting on the other bank who had obviously learned his English from racist whites, "when are you damned gringos going to cross that line?"

"Chile!" was the response. "We ain't agoin' to cross that line at all. We're just goin' to pick up that line an' carry it right down to the Big Ditch!"[39]

Woodrow Wilson certainly did not want to do that much heavy lifting, but he still intensely desired to expel Victoriano Huerta from Mexico, and his quick acceptance of the mediation offer was part of his strategy to establish the Constitutionalist rebels as the governing force in the country. No matter what else was decided, he informed the Latin American ambassadors in a confidential memorandum, there would be no settlement without "the entire elimination of General Huerta."[40] Wilson had been giving a great deal of thought to the root causes of Mexico's troubles, and he also ordered the American delegates to the ABC conference, held at Niagara Falls, Canada, to urge that recommendations be made to address Mexico's problems of illiteracy, poverty, and especially land reform.[41]

In July 1914, Huerta was forced into exile by the Constitutionalist forces under Carranza and Villa, who then immediately began fighting each other. Wilson was now willing to evacuate Veracruz, but threats had been made against local people who had been helping the Americans run the city, and he demanded public assurances from Carranza that they would not be harassed. Long, difficult negotiations followed, and it was not until late November that the last U.S. troops embarked.

CHAPTER SIX

———◦———

Massacre

*[The] failures which a man makes in his life are due almost always
to some defect in his personality, some weakness of body, or mind, or
character, will, or temperament. The only way to overcome these
failings is to build up his personality from within, so that he, by
virtue of what is within him, may overcome the weakness which
was the cause of the failure.*

John D. Rockefeller[1]

*What does all this strife and turmoil growing out of the coal strike
and the Ludlow Massacre mean? It means that the workers would
rather die fighting to protect their women and children than to die
in death-trap mines producing more wealth for the Rockefellers to
use in crushing their children. . . . It means that the whole nation
is on the verge of a revolution.*

Mother Jones[2]

VIOLENT BATTLES had been taking place in the United States as well as
south of the border. Jack Reed rejoined Mabel Dodge in her white-on-
white Fifth Avenue apartment in early April 1914, working fitfully on turning his articles on Mexico into a book, and giving speeches about his
adventures in that country to a variety of groups, including students at his
prep school alma mater in Morristown, New Jersey, where Mabel's son
John was now enrolled. But when news came of the massacre of men,
women, and children in the coal-mining camp of Ludlow, Colorado, on
April 20, he and Max Eastman went west to investigate.

Such bloody confrontations had been occurring for decades. The
United Mine Workers had been founded in 1890 with the ambition of
organizing all workers in the coal industry, whether a middle-aged skilled
machinist or a ten-year-old "breaker" who picked slate out of the coal

crashing through the chutes on its way to being washed. Unions trying to organize a whole industry had to struggle against fierce resistance both from conservative unions such as the American Federation of Labor that excluded the unskilled and from businesses that controlled particular industries. The UMW was aided by growing worker frustration, and particularly by anger aroused by the 1897 Lattimer Massacre, in which deputies in Pennsylvania fired into a crowd of miners, killing nineteen. The union had won an important victory in 1898 after a violent strike in the Illinois coalfields that had resulted in the death and wounding of dozens of miners in an ambush.[3] Recognizing that the union was not going to surrender after this bloodshed, the owners signed a contract. Obviously, there was almost as much danger in organizing as there was in working underground, but the Illinois contract gave impetus to UMW efforts as the union gained confidence from this and other successes.

One of the areas of greatest contention was West Virginia, where bribery and financial trickery had resulted in absentee owners controlling 90 percent of the land in some counties. The political system was corrupt, and many state officials also served as employees of the coal companies, which contributed to West Virginia's spending less on mine safety and on enforcing fair work laws than any other state. As a result it had the worst death rate in the nation, a rate that was five times worse than that in the most hazardous European countries. In spite of the dangers, miners there averaged only $275 a year on a wage scale lower than that in any other part of the country. Even this meager amount was paid not in dollars but in company scrip that was good just in company stores and to pay rent in the company towns that provided the only housing.[4]

Years of effort were put into organizing in West Virginia, and sometimes the fight went well, but most of the time it did not. A major agent in the field was Mary "Mother" Jones, an Irish immigrant born some time around 1837 who had lost her husband and four children in a yellow-fever epidemic in 1867. She had then made the labor movement her family, using the stereotypical image of an older, gray-haired Victorian woman to free herself for a life of adventurous, and dangerous, activism. She organized mainly in textile mills and mining camps, using creativity to outmaneuver the owners, as with the Children's Crusades. Started in 1903 in the Kensington Mills of Philadelphia, child laborers, many only eleven or twelve years old, would march long distances, always preceded by a large American flag, to display their frail, deformed bodies before a sympathetic public. The tactic was effective, and variations were used over the years to gain support for workers, as during the strike at the mills of Lawrence, Massachusetts, in 1912.

Poverty drove parents to enroll their children as laborers so the family could survive, but the personal cost, in lost fingers, limbs, and lives, was great. The social cost was also large since the children were uneducated, unhealthy, and short-lived. Lewis Hine was hired by the National Child Labor Committee to document with his photography the conditions under which the youngsters worked, and this helped awaken the nation's conscience. Unfortunately, courts overturned laws to protect children on the grounds that they meddled with the child's right to make a contract, while the Supreme Court decided that such federal laws interfered with states' rights. Mill and mine owners defended the practice of child labor by arguing that it protected those of a tender age from bad influences while teaching them work habits and thrift. The poet Sarah N. Cleghorn had her own view, writing in 1913:

> The golf links lie so near the mill
> That nearly every day
> The laboring children can look out
> And see the men at play.

*Child laborer at textile mill. Photographed by Lewis Hine for the
National Child Labor Committee sometime between 1907 and 1913.*

Mother Jones was particularly drawn to organize in the coal mines, where both adults and children suffered from exploitation. Her combination of grandmotherly appearance, tough rhetoric, and undaunted courage drew thousands of miners to the cause, and kept them there through firings, blacklistings, evictions, and violent intimidation. As one miner remembered: "She would take a drink with the boys and spoke their idiom, including some pretty rough language when she was talking about the bosses. This might have been considered a little fast in ordinary women, but the miners knew and respected her. They might think her a little queer, perhaps—it *was* an odd kind of work for a woman in those days—but they knew she was a good soul and a friend of those who most lacked friends."[5]

The miners of West Virginia needed all the friends they could find during the long, bitter strike of 1912–13, when they were evicted from company housing and set up tent colonies on whatever public land they could find; often even the roads through the mountains were owned by the operators, patrolled by armed mine guards, and denied to anyone not following the company line. The Baldwin-Felts Detective Agency was the most notorious of the private guard services because of its brutal tactics, and the miners themselves, inured to hardship and death by their dangerous job, did not shrink from confrontation. Gun battles became so frequent that the governor declared martial law and sent in the militia. News reports from the military zone were embargoed while about a hundred miners and union organizers, including Mother Jones, were tried by court-martial, unconstitutionally since civilian courts continued in session. It was during this strike that the mine owner, Quinn Morton, brought a darkened armored train near enough to the tent colony at Holly Grove to pour rifle and machine-gun fire into it, killing one person and wounding another. Not one of the gunmen was even held for questioning.

Mother Jones emerged from this struggle a national figure. A settlement was imposed by the governor that gave a partial victory to the United Mine Workers, but this same politician kept Jones confined under house arrest for three months. He saw her as too dangerous a troublemaker to be allowed on the loose. Letters were sent to the White House and to Secretary of Labor William Wilson, an old friend of hers, and questions were asked in Congress that led to an official investigation of what had happened in the coal region. When she was finally released in the late spring of 1913, she was interviewed at length by the *Brooklyn Daily Eagle*, which called her "perhaps the most remarkable woman in America."[6] The *New York Times*, which editorially had no love of unions, also interviewed her.

The reporter was patronizingly "astonished" at how, after all the charges of fire-breathing, she was really quite a charming, even conventional, old lady; or at least that was how she cleverly manipulated his impression of her. "I had expected much incendiary talk in uncouth English and found an educated woman, careful of her speech and sentiments. If she had a red flag with her, she kept it in her satchel with her comb and brush and powder puff. She has a powder puff. That too astonished me."[7] Jones talked of her struggles to help the helpless, like a widow she had known in the South who, along with three young children, had been forced to work fourteen hours a day, seven days a week in the cotton mills. She solemnly assured the reporter that far from revolution, a worker, like "the average human being only wants a quiet home, a well-fed, comfortable family, so situated that its happiness is possible." Immediately after the interview she headed for the bleak coalfields of Colorado, where little such happiness seemed likely.

The UMW had abandoned the state after a failed strike in 1903–4, one that had involved mainly English-speaking miners—Americans, English, Welsh, and Irish. The Rockefeller family, whose Colorado Fuel and Iron (CFI) company controlled one-third of the state's coal production, had led the other operators in a successful battle to crush the union. "We are prepared to stand by in this fight and see the thing out, not yielding an inch," John D. Rockefeller, Jr., had instructed his agent on the scene. "Recognition of any kind of either the labor leaders or union, much more a conference such as they request, would be a sign of evident weakness on our part."[8]

The owners did not weaken. The Colorado National Guard had arrested strikers, while vigilantes and guards had kidnapped and forcibly deported the most militant unionists from the state. Mine owners then brought in immigrants from thirty-two countries that spoke twenty-seven languages as strikebreakers, believing that these recent arrivals to America would prove more docile and that language and cultural differences would make union organizing difficult. Soon, about two-thirds of the Colorado coal miners were foreign-born, with most from Italy, Mexico, Greece, and various Eastern European countries. Even with this cheap and unorganized labor, the CFI investment was proving a poor one for the Rockefeller family. Workers were pushed to labor harder, faster, and longer, which resulted in a series of deadly accidents, the worst on January 31, 1910, when an explosion in one of the CFI mines killed seventy-nine men. The junior Rockefeller paid little attention, while the company blamed the accident on the carelessness of miners; the Colorado Bureau of Labor Statistics, however, pointed the finger at the CFI, charging it with "cold-blooded barbarism" for ignoring proven safety procedures.[9] In 1913, 464 men were killed or injured working the Colorado mines; by fall of that year even the immigrant miners who had been brought in as strikebreakers were ready to strike, for the same reasons that the English speakers had in 1903 and that the West Virginian miners had in their recent action. They demanded better wages, observance by the owners of the eight-hour day (which was already a state requirement), access to noncompany housing and supplies, safer works, abolition of the company guard detachments that served as private occupying armies, and, most important, recognition of the United Mine Workers, which could then enforce the new conditions.

The Rockefellers and other mine operators, passionately antiunion, had refused to negotiate, Junior telling his man at Colorado Fuel and Iron, "Whatever the outcome, we will stand by you to the end."[10] When 11,000 of the nearly 14,000 workers struck on September 26, 1913, the owners had armed guards evict families from their houses even though early storms had already begun to pelt the area with rain, sleet, and snow. The United Mine Workers had expected this after their recent experience in West Virginia and had shipped in the same tents used there. Thousands of families made their way through the mud and icy wind to the various UMW centers, the largest one being in Ludlow. These had been placed at the mouths of the desolate canyons leading up to the mines, the better to block the passage of strikebreakers.

The owners did their own importing from West Virginia, bringing in some of the same Baldwin-Felts detectives who had tried to crush the strike there, and, just as in that state, they also had enough local political power to have their guards sworn in as deputy sheriffs. Strikers and mine guards were heavily armed, though only the guards had machine guns. The miners, some of whom were veterans of the Balkan wars, were not intimidated. Shooting began almost immediately, with men killed and wounded on both sides; on October 17, Baldwin-Felts agents used an armored automobile they had built and dubbed the Death Special to machine-gun a tent colony, killing and wounding miners. As in West Virginia, the governor called out the National Guard. Though he did not officially declare martial law, the general in command, a noteworthy incompetent named John Chase, who had a hard time keeping his seat on a horse, acted as if he had been given those powers. One of the first things the general did was try to ban Mother Jones from the strike area, claiming that she was "dangerous because she inflames the minds of the strikers."[11]

Jones and the union ably used the resulting publicity, reminding the politicians that in Colorado women had the vote, and following her usual tactic of adding seven or eight years to her age, she pointed out that arresting "an 82-year-old woman" would not be very smart. She refused to stay away, and was detained for a total of more than ninety days, mostly under primitive conditions. "I had sewer rats that long every night to fight, and all I had was a beer bottle; I would get one rat, and another would run across the cellar at me. I fought the rats inside and out just alike."[12] Meanwhile, the Rockefeller forces spread malicious, long-standing rumors of her having been a whorehouse madam at some undetermined point in her life.

Woodrow Wilson sent mediators, but the owners ignored them. To talk was to show weakness. One of the Colorado Fuel and Iron executives wrote Rockefeller about the union organizers, "When such men as these, together with the cheap college professors and still cheaper writers in muck-raking magazines, supplemented by a lot of milk and water preachers . . . are permitted to assault the businessmen who have built up the great industries . . . it is time that vigorous measures are taken."[13] Many of the vigorous measures involved the Colorado National Guard, which actively supported the owners, and some of the mine guards were sworn in to the military units. One particularly aggressive officer was Lieutenant Karl E. Linderfelt, who had fought in both the Philippines and Mexico, where a warrant had been issued for his arrest for robbery and looting. He excused his beating and harassment of strikers, whom he referred to as "wops," "dagos," and "red-necks," by explaining that "you can't go at it with kid gloves."[14] The miners themselves rejected kid gloves, and their resistance went beyond economic issues; they felt they had to prove their manhood: "Let's show them we are men," Jack Reed quotes them saying. "We'll do some real fighting."[15] Reed was of course sympathetic to the argument.

As the winter of 1913–14 grew more severe, the union families suffered in their cold, drafty tents, going on short rations as the strike fund ran low. A huge blizzard battered the camps in December, covering southeastern Colorado in several feet of snow. Even in the bad weather, miners and guards continued shooting at one another when opportunity offered, and the miners dug pits under the tent flooring so their wives and children could find protection from the bullets.

Unfortunately, Colorado was also running out of money and could no longer pay for the activated National Guard, which had been costing the state $5,000 a day.[16] Most of the regular militia units were withdrawn in early spring of 1914; the ones that stayed were paid by the coal companies, and were made up of the mine guards who had been sworn in to service.

Sunday, April 19, was Orthodox Easter, and the Greeks hosted a large

festival at Ludlow to which the whole camp was invited. "Everybody celebrated it with them, because the Greeks were loved by all the strikers,"
Jack Reed wrote later. "There were about 50 of them, all young men and all
without families. . . . It was the Greeks who had done all the hard work
around the colony."[17] They had become the strikers' police and nursing
corps, as well as the snow-removal brigade. To start the festivities, the
Greeks donned their traditional white-skirted costumes and performed
national dances. This exotic show was followed by men and women's baseball games (the women wearing sports bloomers), a simple lunch, and
music.

Then the shooting began. Who started it is unclear, but Company B of
the militia, made up of mine guards and under the direction of the aggressively antiunion Lieutenant Linderfelt, soon had the tent colony under a
cross fire from machine guns and Springfield rifles. Many of the miners ran
out of ammunition early and slipped away into the hills. An eleven-year-old
boy was killed by a bullet through the head, and mothers grabbed their
children and sought safety in the pits under the tents. That night, Linderfelt led his company into the camp and began burning the tents. Those
who could, fled, but three strikers who were caught were murdered by the
lieutenant and his men. After the fire destroyed the camp, two women and
eleven children were discovered, asphyxiated, in one of the pits where they
had sought protection.

Reed and Eastman found Ludlow a scene of desolation when they
arrived after the massacre. "The tent colony, or where the tent colony had
been, was a great square of ghastly ruins," as Reed described it for *Metropolitan* magazine. "Stoves, pots and pans still half full of food that had been
cooking that terrible morning, baby carriages, piles of half burned clothes,
children's toys all riddled with bullets, the scorched mouths of the tent cel-
lars, and the children's toys that we found at the bottom of the 'death
hole'—this was all that remained of the entire worldly possessions of 1,200
poor people."[18]

Locally, as word of the deaths of women and children spread from
encampment to encampment, the miners reacted with rage, hundreds of
them grabbing their Winchesters and taking to the hills to conduct an
impromptu guerrilla campaign against any nearby mining works, shouting
"Remember Ludlow!" as they attacked. Buildings burned, and dozens of
strikers, strikebreakers, and mine guards died. Telegrams demanding federal intervention to protect the miners and their families from further massacres poured into the White House, where Woodrow Wilson was already
depressed and exhausted from dealing with the Veracruz crisis.

The rage quickly spread nationwide, at least among those who supported the workers' right to organize. Journalists such as George Creel, Walter Lippmann, and Lincoln Steffens wrote scathing pieces on the operators, especially Rockefeller. Reed, who was pushed further along his leftward course by the tragedy, did his usual talented cheerleading for the cause by depicting noble innocents whose simple quest for a decent life had called down vicious revenge from the bosses. Activist writer Upton Sinclair not only attacked in print, he led black-clad demonstrations in front of the Rockefeller mansion on the Upper East

June 1914 cover for The Masses, *drawn by John Sloan*

Side and at the offices at 26 Broadway in New York City, before moving to the gates of their enormous estate of Pocantico Hills, just outside the city, where Junior and his wife and children sought refuge. It would have been hard not to recognize that the massacre had left a stain, and the younger Rockefeller quickly hired the pioneering public relations expert Ivy Lee to do whatever was necessary to refurbish the family image. He also made sincere, if belated, efforts to improve conditions for his miners.

But there were those who felt that street theater and the wearing of black clothes and armbands did not go far enough in protesting Rockefeller's actions in Colorado and on other fronts in the ongoing war between labor and capital. In Greenwich Village, Alexander Berkman, one of Emma Goldman's lovers and temporary editor of her *Mother Earth* magazine while she was on a nationwide speaking tour, brought together several other anarchists in a conspiracy to kill the plutocrat along with his wife and children. Berkman was no stranger to such direct action. During the Homestead Strike of 1892, the most violent labor-versus-capital battle up to that time in American history, he, aided in the planning by Emma Goldman, had tried to assassinate Henry Clay Frick, coal baron, head of the Carnegie steelworks, and breaker of unions. Frick proved tougher than expected; shot twice and stabbed three times, he managed to subdue the twenty-one-year-old Berkman with the help of a secretary. Frick rested for only an hour after having the bullets removed, then returned to his office and immediately launched a successful campaign using the attack to discredit the steelworkers' union, which had known nothing of Berkman or his plot. Berkman, would-be assassin of tyrants, spent fourteen years in prison before being released in 1905. Though Goldman had been suspected of having played a role in the attack, she was not indicted.

Now Berkman, feeling the time was ripe for another attempt at punishing a capitalist guilty of crimes against the working class, enlisted several other anarchists in a plot to blow up the Rockefellers on their estate at Pocantico Hills. Three of them met in a tenement on upper Lexington Avenue to assemble the bomb, but something went wrong, and the ensuing explosion killed not only these plotters but also a young woman who lived in the building; Berkman was not present. Emma Goldman was shocked. "Comrades, idealists, manufacturing a bomb in a congested tenement house! I was aghast at such irresponsibility." But then she remembered Sasha, as she called Alexander Berkman, experimenting with a bomb at the apartment they had shared on Fifth Street. "I had silenced my fear for the tenants, in case of an accident, by repeating to myself that the end justified the means. . . . In the zeal of fanaticism I had believed that the end justifies the means!"[19] She still believed in righteous violence used against the oppressor, but her zeal had diminished to the point where she now believed that care had to be taken not to jeopardize "innocent lives."

Berkman, who evidently lied to Goldman about his involvement in the plot, no doubt lamented the deaths of his comrades, but he also saw an opportunity to turn their funerals into a giant demonstration at Union Square. The attraction grew when authorities announced that no such public ceremony would be allowed; other radical groups, including the IWW, tried to dissuade him, but he persisted, having the bodies cremated and placed in a common urn cast in the shape of a clenched fist. Berkman evaded police, who tried to prevent him from reaching Union Square—at one point, in order to reach the speaker's stand, he used a red automobile that police mistook for that of the fire chief, officers clearing the way through the crowd.

Goldman was amused by Sasha's daring, but she was outraged by the edition of *Mother Earth* that he edited following the funeral. The speeches

given at Union Square, most of them full of violent threats involving dynamite and the use of force to overthrow the system, were admirable she
thought. However, she had always been careful to avoid such language in
her magazine, trying to reach out to the liberal element of the middle class.
"I was so furious that I wanted the entire issue thrown into the fire. But it
was too late; the magazine had gone out to the subscribers."[20]

PRESIDENT WILSON finally sent squadrons of the Fifth Cavalry to Colorado, though the small American army was being dangerously overextended; one of their first duties was arresting six soldiers of the National
Guard for looting a saloon.[21] Slowly tensions eased, a truce held, and the
strikers came down from the hills and turned in their arms. Wilson again
asked Rockefeller and the other owners to agree to mediation, but they,
knowing that the United Mine Workers union was running out of funds,
refused. In December 1914 the strike collapsed. No member of the National
Guard or of the mine owners' security forces was punished for the murders
at Ludlow, but strike and union leaders were prosecuted for violence. Many
were arrested and also blacklisted by employers, which presented them
with an ugly dilemma; they were unable to find work in Colorado, but they
couldn't leave the state while on bail.

John Reed was bitter about the massacre at Ludlow and suspicious
about American intentions in Mexico, telling friends that he would immediately rejoin Villa to help fight any Yanqui invasion. But he was surprised
when the military force was directed at Huerta instead of the Constitutionalists. It is a sign of how politically open the society was in the years before
the Great War that when this radical journalist expressed a desire to interview both Secretary Bryan and the president about their ideas, he was
immediately invited to Washington.

A sweltering June afternoon found him in William Jennings Bryan's
parlor, where the secretary sat on an old-fashioned horsehair sofa, surrounded by incongruous oil paintings of sultans and Indian rajas. Reed was
struck by the fine appearance and stately bearing of his host, and, like most
mortals, he was charmed by the voice as Bryan spoke "slowly, impressively,
with massive seriousness." But underneath all this, Reed felt he spotted a
true American provincial who did not understand the way the country was
changing. Having just toured the devastation of Ludlow and other Colorado mining camps, the reporter was astonished when Bryan told him: "I
must confess to you that there is one thing I cannot understand about the
Mexicans. Do you know, when one faction captures a soldier of another

faction, they stand him up against a wall and *shoot him down!*" It is unclear whether Reed tried to educate him about what had just happened in Bryan's own country.

The president invited him for the next afternoon, meeting him in the Oval Office, welcoming him warmly, and talking with great understanding of the power of "predatory minorities" that controlled workers' lives. Reed was impressed with the calm gravity of the man, and the power of his intellect, but he was bitterly surprised later when Wilson refused to permit him to print his article based on the interview.[22] This exchange with Reed, or perhaps his writings, may have been the cause of the president, for a short while, regarding Villa as "a sort of Robin Hood."

Provincetown, sitting at the end of the long arm of Cape Cod in Massachusetts, had become the summer refuge for increasing numbers of Greenwich Villagers. Still a picturesque working harbor for Portuguese American fishermen, rents were cheap, the company good, the weather warm but freshened by ocean breezes. Reed joined Mabel Dodge there, taking the raw material of his interviews to be worked into shape, and keeping a worried eye on the increasingly chaotic events in Mexico.

CHAPTER SEVEN

The Smash Up

A general European war is unthinkable. . . . Europe can't afford such a war, and the world can't afford it, and happily the conviction is growing that such an appalling conflict is altogether beyond the realm of possibility.

New York Times editorial, July 28, 1914

A complete smash up is inevitable. It will be the greatest war in the world's history.

Franklin Delano Roosevelt to Eleanor, August 1, 1914

I wonder if this is the end. The end of civilization as we have known it.

Myron T. Herrick, American ambassador to France, August 2, 1914[1]

EUROPE WAS BOTH lure and threat to Americans of the early twentieth century. This ambivalence had existed from their beginnings as a nation, though earlier they had sensed the risk more often than the attraction. George Washington had warned that too close an involvement in European affairs could lead to dangerous entanglements for the republic, a warning that had been constantly renewed by politicians, editorial writers, historians, and cracker-barrel philosophers. But now the dangers were no longer as distant and easily avoided as they had been. Great European empires had been established around the globe during the nineteenth century, empires that threatened American international trade and the new sense of power and confidence the country had developed after its victory over Spain in 1898.

But Europe still appealed as well as threatened. Ancestry made its claims, though many of those European ancestors had fled persecution, prejudice, or poverty to make their way to a freer and more prosperous land. Now that very prosperity was allowing large numbers of middle-class Americans to visit the old countries to marvel at castles still inhabited by kings and queens, princes and princesses, dukes and duchesses. Perhaps they were a bit medieval and ridiculous, but these old trappings of privilege offered a romantic fairy-tale charm if not taken too seriously. For recently minted millionaires whose treasuries bulged with profits from mundane enterprises such as meatpacking plants, cotton fields, oil wells, steel foundries, and railroads, the European social scene also provided a way to raise their own prestige by marrying daughters to nobles rich in lineage but poor in ready cash.

More than any other place, France, and especially Paris, fascinated Americans as a fertile mix of the old with the new, a place of beauty and tradition, but also a rich source of innovative approaches to politics, literature, art, and good living. These modern ideas often shocked American sensibilities, but even in rejection there was a certain frisson. "She was all things to all men," wrote the foreign correspondent Richard Harding Davis about everyone's favorite city.[2] Gay Paree, with its glittering boulevards, chic and sophisticated women, cynical and witty men, festive esprit, and reputation for never disappointing no matter how recondite the need or desire, drew these travelers by the thousands.

Not that most American tourists pursued obscure desires. When a journalist asked the visiting humorist George Ade just before the Great War to expound on the "secret of the gaiety of Paris," Ade mocked the idea. "It doesn't exist. It's all stage-managed for tourists. . . . They hustle into a hotel with their baggage at midnight. They hurry out before breakfast, buy a bunch of picture postcards and spend the rest of the day addressing them to envious friends back in Kokomo, from a list as long as a city payroll. Then they rush on to the next burg and buy more postals."[3] However, some of the purchased postcards could not be trusted to the mails. One young man from the Midwest said that "each time I crossed the Place de l'Opera, I was annoyed by guides trying to sell me dirty postcards or wanting to take me to the 'Crystal Palace—twenty naked women!' " He confounded them a bit by claiming that in his hometown of Chicago "we have hundreds of naked women," but they continued to pester him until he disguised himself as a Parisian, growing a small mustache, wearing spats, and carrying a cane.[4]

There was also a sizable American colony in residence, expatriates living on money from home who had found a way of life both comfortable and stimulating. Women were especially drawn to the cultural richness of the capital and the easier relations between the sexes, so different from home. An observer noted, "In the art exhibits, concerts, and operas that never ceased, in the easy association with artists, musicians, and writers, American women found, apparently, something they had craved and been unable to satisfy at home. . . . For whatever reason, lots of American women were living in Paris without their husbands."[5] Some of the wealthy, such as Anna Gould, whose father was the notorious railroad robber baron Jay Gould, married into the French aristocracy. Anna and her millions had won the heart of Prince Helie de Sagan, Duc de Talleyrand-Périgord, who put his newfound fortune to work building a pink palace, a copy of the Grand Trianon, on the Rue du Bois de Boulogne, and holding brilliant soirees there. But even for those who lived on a humbler scale, this was a seductive city. One of the expatriates wrote a song that seemed to speak for all his fellows, and would resonate through the experiences and feelings of Great War doughboys and, later, members of the Lost Generation: "Oh, when I say I'm homesick, I mean I'm sick of home."[6]

American newspapers were grateful that Paris and the French seldom disappointed in furnishing scandals that titillated their readers, while also providing the opportunity for righteous editorial disapproval. During the spring and summer of 1914, while the United States was worrying about possible war with Mexico and the domestic struggle for women's suffrage and other progressive crusades, an affair leaped onto the front pages that was particularly diverting, involving as it did political corruption, sex, and murder. The story had begun in early January, when Gaston Calmette, editor of the powerful conservative newspaper *Le Figaro,* wrote and published a series of articles accusing Joseph Caillaux—former premier, current minister of finance, and leader of the Radical Socialist Party—of high crimes and misdemeanors. Calmette charged that Caillaux, while serving as head of the government, had conducted traitorous negotiations with the German government during the Agadir crisis of 1911, and that he had later benefited from financial schemes involving public money. These charges and the offered proofs would have been shocking enough, but Calmette went on to censure Caillaux for hypocrisy and immorality in his personal life, publishing passionate love letters he had written to his present wife while they had both been married to others.

Madame Leo Raynouard Claretie Caillaux had been enraged by the attacks. Not only was her husband's career being destroyed, she was being publicly humiliated. On the morning of March 16, 1914, she went to a gun shop on the Avenue d'Autin, bought a Browning automatic pistol, had a salesman load it, then practiced shooting at a man-sized target in the basement firing range. The same salesman thoughtfully reloaded the gun for her before she left the shop.

Later that day she visited the offices of *Le Figaro* and asked for Gaston Calmette, who was out. The lady waited, and when the editor returned, he had her shown into his office.

Rising, Calmette greeted her. *"Bonjour, madame."*

"Bonjour, monsieur," Madame Caillaux replied, then, without another word, she emptied the Browning into his body. Calmette died a few hours later.[7]

The press of the world came running, and when another European act of violence took place on June 28 in Sarajevo, it only briefly distracted attention from the Caillauxs. The new victims were Archduke Francis Ferdinand, in line to be the next emperor of Austria-Hungary, and his wife, gunned down by a Serbian terrorist. It was a tragedy, but distant and mixed up somehow with the almost farcical, comic-opera affairs of the Balkans and the Austro-Hungarian Empire. A few days of headlines and front-page attention, then the story was, for a while, relegated to the back sections, near the advertisements for baldness cures and patent medicines. Perhaps the *Daily Herald* of Grand Forks, North Dakota, spoke for the larger public when it editorialized, on the first of July: "To the world, or to a nation, an archduke more or less makes little difference."[8] To the Austrians, however, it did make a difference, for reasons both of sentiment and power, and plans were set in motion to punish Serbia.

Madame Caillaux's trial began in early July, and her defense was necessarily simple. She had called on Calmette to argue that his attacks on her husband were unfounded and unfair, and that when she had pulled out the automatic to impress him with the sincerity of her feelings, it had fired itself six times.

Spectators struggled hard for the relatively few seats available, since the authorities had distributed twice as many passes as there were places in the suffocatingly hot courtroom. Rumor said that $200 was the going price for a seat. Even reporters were hard-pressed to find space, since there were more than a hundred of them vying for the lurid details at the trial. At least a good half dozen of this contingent were American. Wythe Williams, Paris correspondent of the *New York Times,* remembered that they always had a "tussle" to keep a seat. "Famous *cocottes* of the period, friends of Grand Dukes and well-known statesmen, were a picturesque feature that found prominent place in our dispatches. The spectators' rows were crowded with famous personages of the political and social world, who spread over into the press gallery at every opportunity."[9] Williams found the case a curious study because of the way the defense counsel kept twisting testimony into political questions so that the prosecutor had to constantly remind him that this was a murder trial. There were street battles, as well, that often took place between political supporters and opponents of the Leftist Caillaux.

At midday on Saturday, July 25, as the trial neared its end, a whisper ran through the press gallery that there was a panic on the French stock exchange. The terms of the Austrian ultimatum, setting humiliating conditions if Serbia wished to avoid war, had been announced the day before, and now the bankers were scared. The importance of the trial began to dim in journalists' eyes, yet when the jury returned an astonishing finding of "not guilty" a few days later, the reporters, as they made their way out of the Palais de Justice, were expecting to find frenzied crowds shouting "Down with Caillaux!" Instead, the angry citizens jamming the boulevards were chanting "*A Berlin! A Berlin! Alsace! A Berlin!*" The Austro-Hungarian Empire was readying to attack Serbia, France's ally Russia was mobilizing troops in its role as protector of the Serbs, the Germans were vowing to support Austria come what might, and French crowds were crying "On to Berlin."

PAUL SCOTT MOWRER had served as Paris correspondent of the *Chicago Daily News* for three years, covering not just events in the French capital but also the bloody Balkan War of 1912. He was unhappy about the pieces on trivial society news and scandals that his editors demanded, and had long felt that the relevance of political and military events in Europe to the United States was not fully recognized by the home office. He chafed, therefore, when assigned to accompany a band of visiting Chicago aldermen who had come to the Continent on a junket investigating the European design of railroad terminals and, in addition, vice conditions—"a corollary," Mowrer remarked, "if I knew Chicago aldermen, that could safely have been left to their initiative."[10]

He had met the politicians in Liverpool on July 21 and traveled with them to Manchester and London, keeping one eye on the fast-breaking news that was filling the papers. By the time their party reached Paris, war seemed inevitable. The aldermen had just begun to investigate Parisian brothels, but Mowrer warned them that they would probably not be able to continue on to their next destination, Vienna.

The leader of the delegation, a lawyer named Walter L. Fisher, refused to take the warnings seriously, arguing that this was only a small affair involving Serbia and Austria. Mowrer persisted, "I'm afraid the whole continent is going to war." Fisher just gave him a "look that put me in my place. In the self-confident American tone I knew so well, and with the deprecatory smile of one who has inside information, he pronounced these words: 'Oh, no. There isn't going to be any war.' " A few days later Fisher and the aldermen fled in haste for what they were certain was a safe refuge in neutral Belgium, a country unconnected to any of the Great Power alliances that were speeding to catastrophe. Mowrer believed that what finally convinced them of danger was the closing of the New York and London stock exchanges. If the moneymen were scared, then it really was no time to take chances.

Here was the evil coming to life that American wise men had warned about for more than a century. The Europeans had sought security through alliances, hoping to maintain a balance of power that would discourage war, or at least delay the struggle, according to each country's calculations, until it was strong enough to win. Thus Germany and Austria-Hungary were united in facing France and Russia, and possibly Britain. Much of the tension came from the competition for empire abroad, and nations had come close to war a number of times in the previous sixteen years through confrontations in far-off places such as Jiaozhou, Fashoda, and Agadir. Germany, particularly, felt denied its rightful place in the tropic sun, and boasted not only a large, well-trained, and well-equipped army, but was also building a modern battle fleet that would rival Great Britain's.

At the same time, there was a strong belief among intellectuals and businessmen in Europe and America that war had become impossible in the modern world. It was too expensive, for one thing, and the inevitable progress of human civilization, not just in technology but also in moral responsibility, made it an archaic way to settle differences. After all, Europeans, with occasional help from Americans, had set themselves the mission of civilizing the world, supposedly raising the standards of living and morality of millions of darker-skinned people, while benefiting economically from the resulting empires. Though Americans viewed the economic parts of this activity with suspicion, fearing exclusion from imperial markets, they had no doubt of the moral benefits being extended to native peoples and had done their own part by taking up the burden of empire in the Philippines.

But on August 1, France began to mobilize and Germany declared war on Russia, then two days later Germany declared against France. Mowrer watched as the city he loved began to change, the very pace of life speeding up. "More people than usual were hailing taxis. Men were leaving stores and offices to hurry home, make ready and say good-bye. . . . In doorways, women, young or old, stood vaguely waiting, unconscious of the tears that wet their cheeks. Here and there I saw a young man running, or some couple locked in desperate embrace. The taxis were driving faster now. A haze of dust shimmered over the city. In the pale sunlight of this August day, all Paris, all of France, the whole of Europe . . . was rushing into war."[11] Wythe Williams also realized that an age had passed when he was aggressively challenged on a city street by a sentry in one of the old-fashioned and gloriously colorful French uniforms of long blue coat, red trousers, shiny black belt, and bright brass buttons. " 'Gay Paree' had vanished," Williams understood. "The World War was on the way."[12]

BOTH BRAND WHITLOCK, the American ambassador, and Hugh Gibson, first secretary of the embassy, had sought their posts in Brussels because Belgium was a peaceful backwater in European affairs, where duties involved more of a social whirl than momentous negotiations. Whitlock had been a journalist, a successful "clean government" mayor of Toledo, Ohio, and an acclaimed novelist. His friend Woodrow Wilson had appointed him so that he might have the quiet to write while still serving his country and collecting a paycheck. Gibson had been posted to many trouble spots during his professional career in the State Department, including the Balkans. On July 4 he had written in his journal: "For the last year or two I have looked forward to just such a post as this, where nothing ever happens, where there is no earthly chance of being called out of bed in the middle of the night to see the human race brawling over its differences."[13] He admitted to being a bit bored with the easy diplomatic life in Brussels, but that was soon to change. The reason for the lack of tension in its international affairs was directly tied to Belgium's founding as a nation in 1839 when Great Britain, France, Prussia, Austria, and Russia signed a treaty guaranteeing that it would be "an independent and perpetually neutral state." This had helped defuse dangerous rivalries, and the treaty had been honored ever since as one of the bases of European peace. But Germany now was faced with what she had long dreaded: a two-front war— against Russia, with an army of more than six million hardy peasants; and France, a technologically advanced nation with a large military, an extensively fortified frontier, and a bitter grievance against Germany for having seized the Alsace-Lorraine region after defeating France in the war of 1870. Their only hope, German leaders were convinced, lay in the strategy devised by the chief of the general staff, Count Alfred von Schlieffen, in

1905. The Schlieffen Plan required German forces in the east to conduct a defensive fight, while in the west they would strike immediately against France through the neutral states of Luxembourg and Belgium. They would then take the French army by surprise from the north, first enveloping, then destroying it in a lightning campaign similar to the victorious one of 1870. With the western front thus quickly secured, the bulk of the German army would be shifted to deal with the lumbering, though powerful, Russian bear.

On Saturday, August 1, when the Germans declared war on Russia, they swiftly overran the tiny neutral principality of Luxembourg. At 7 p.m. the next day, the German minister in Brussels delivered a note demanding that German forces be allowed free passage through Belgium. If this was granted, Germany would, once victory over France was achieved, "evacuate Belgian territory," pay for any damages resulting from the troop movement, and "guarantee" the continuing sovereign rights and independence of the kingdom.[14] If this request was denied, the "eventual adjustment of the relations between the two States must be left to the decision of arms." The Belgian government was given twelve hours to respond.

Albert, king of the Belgians, refused the demand, ordered his army to secure the borders, and asked France and England, two of the other signatories of the treaty of 1839, to help defend his country's territorial integrity. On August 3, the Germans declared war on France and began their invasion of Belgium, which brought the British in: they could not allow the Belgian channel ports to fall into the hands of Germany, with its powerful army backed by a large, modern fleet capable of supporting an invasion of the home islands.

Just the week before these events, there had been hardly a tourist in Belgium, but they now came by the thousands seeking shelter as awareness of the gathering storm became unavoidable. "All sorts and conditions [of Americans]," lamented Ambassador Whitlock, and all expecting the embassy to provide solutions to their needs. At first the tourists thought that neutral Belgium would be a safe haven, but as the German threats became known, an unsettling fear set in. Many travelers became so panicked that they were helpless, though Whitlock noted that "in many instances the women are calmer, braver than the men." He had to admit that these fears stemmed from an ugly reality. Their banknotes and travelers checks were now useless; only gold and silver, the old reliables in conditions of war and other disasters, were the acceptable monies in hotels, shops, and restaurants. Shipping was at a standstill, hotels were full, local citizens were hoarding food, those Americans who were touring by automobile were having their machines seized by the Belgian government for military purposes. What was to be done? Now the disadvantages of such a quiet post became evident. There were only three people to deal with the crisis: Whitlock, Gibson, and Cruger, the clerk. American volunteers quickly came forward, here and in the other major capitals, to help deal with the crisis.

Still, the demands were overwhelming: "They all think," Whitlock complained to his journal, "that I have some supernatural power, that I can evoke ships, money, care, comfort for them; predict the course of the war, tell them where they will be safe, and how long the war will last, and so on." Little sympathy was wasted on the rich, but the ambassador could not help but be personally touched by the troubles of some of his fellow Americans. "I could weep at the plight of the American school teachers, here on their first trip to Europe, after years of pinching and saving and planning, and consulting guide books! It is pathetic. And then the young couple on a bridal tour—with their all invested in a tourist ticket. The young bridegroom drew it out of that manly pocket—the bride looking so confidently at him, as he did so!—and unfolded about four kilometers of coupons, hotels, railroads, steamships, and so on; all useless now."

On August 4, an hour after German troops launched their opening attack on his country, King Albert, booted and spurred and wearing an unadorned field uniform of a lieutenant-general, rode horseback through the sunny, flag-bedecked streets to address Parliament, a ceremony that Whitlock and Gibson attended. Belgium had been rocked by domestic social and economic crises in the preceding few years, but now all classes, ethnic groups, and political parties joined in cheering the king, and pledging to defend the country with their lives. Albert concluded his address with: "The watchword is, To Arms!"

Whitlock, profoundly moved, throat catching, eyes moist, leaned his long frame over the railing to watch, and caught sight of the young Duke de Brabant, heir to the throne, who was staring up into his father's face, enraptured, never taking his eyes off him. "What are the thoughts in that boy's mind?" the American wondered. "Will this scene come back to him in after years? And how, when, under what circumstances?" As it turned out, the boy, grown to be crowned as Leopold III, would himself be forced to surrender his nation to the Germans after their blitzkrieg campaign of 1940.

To add to their already heavy burdens, the American diplomats agreed, as neutrals, to take on the added duty of protecting British and German interests in Brussels as those diplomats withdrew in deference to the soldiers. Now they had more than four thousand German citizens to protect, as well as their own, and the Germans were panicking because a spy hysteria had developed. "The regular arrests of proven spies have been numerous enough to turn every Belgian into an amateur spy-catcher," wrote Gibson. "Yesterday afternoon [the mayor of Brussels] was chased for several blocks because somebody raised a cry of *'Espion'* based on nothing more than his blond beard and chubby face. I am just as glad not to be fat and blond these days." Angry crowds were also attacking German shops and restaurants, shots were fired through windows, beatings administered. The Belgian government was doing all it could to live up to standards of civilized behavior, but it was now the American responsibility to maneuver these enemy civilians safely out of the country.

When Whitlock and Gibson drove to the German legation to officially take charge of its contents, they found the minister and his staff perspiring heavily and chain-smoking. Gibson was struck by how the need to pack up and seal the records and end the functioning of an embassy in order to make war reflected the fantastic air of the past few days: "It was . . . like a scene in a play. The shaded room, the two nervous diplomats registering anxiety and strain, the old functionary who was to stay behind to guard the archives and refused to be moved from his calm by the approaching cataclysm. It seemed altogether unreal, and I had to keep bringing myself back to a realisation of the fact that it was only too true and too serious." That seriousness, as well as the bizarreness, was emphasized by the comments of one of the Germans, who kept repeating about the Belgians: "Oh, the poor fools! Why don't they get out of the way of the steam roller. We don't want to hurt them, but if they stand in our way they will be ground into the dirt. Oh, the poor fools!"

Both men thrived under the stress, full of energy despite lack of sleep, regular meals, recreation, or even a chance to bathe. They knew that what they did was vital and that they were witnessing history at a great turning point. "Up very late . . ." Whitlock confided to his journal, "sending despatches to Washington. The room is so hot, the night so still, the tension is so great—it reminds me somehow of those long gone days when I was a newspaper man, and sat up late at night sending other despatches, but never such a big story as this!"

AMERICAN JOURNALISTS had recognized the scale of the story before their fellow citizens, and had immediately begun moving toward the action, some from as far away as the Mexican border, where rumors of a different war had drawn them. Those already in Europe had an advantage, but were impeded by bureaucratic red tape. Wythe Williams, Paul Scott Mowrer, and others went to the proper government offices in whichever country they were based and requested formal recognition and signed passes permitting them to accompany armies to the front. Permission was always refused, and it was for this reason that a gifted amateur gained some of the best early stories about the fighting.

Granville Fortescue had enjoyed a varied career. Member of a wealthy Philadelphia family, he attended the University of Pennsylvania for a couple of years but was lured away in 1897 to deliver the gift of a sword to a Cuban general leading guerrillas in the revolt against Spain. Though this publicity stunt was performed at the instigation of the press baron William Randolph Hearst, the young adventurer was not then drawn to a newspaper career, but instead went into the army. He fought at San Juan Hill during the American campaign in Cuba in 1898, meeting and impressing Theodore Roosevelt. After further army service in the Philippines and attendance at the Staff College at Fort Leavenworth, he became one of President Roosevelt's military aides. In 1904, he served as U.S. military observer in the Russo-Japanese War, where he met most of the leading foreign correspondents of the day. In 1907, he accompanied one of them, Gerald Morgan, on an exploration of the headwaters of the Orinoco River, and in 1909 carried out some correspondent duties himself in Morocco. He decided that he liked the glamorous work.

In 1914, Fortescue was summering with his family in a small seaside village near Ostend, Belgium. When the war excitement started, he managed to get his family to England, then he went directly to the American embassy in Brussels, where he had been given a "beat" right at the door of the embassy. Fortescue had found the porter in animated discussion with a Walloon peasant. It turned out that this peasant was the porter's brother, reporting that he had talked to German officers near his farm outside Liège just that morning; these were the first reports of Germans actually on Belgian territory.

Fortescue used that exclusive to wrangle a position with the *London Daily Telegraph,* then headed for Liège, where on August 5 he learned that the German army was within six miles of the town, readying to attack its protective ring of forts. He prepared himself with the best dinner that the Grand Hotel offered, then set off just before midnight for the point to which he figured the attack would be directed. Liège having been built over coal mines, the reporter left the road to use the dumps of debris from those workings as cover from both the Belgians and their enemies as he made his way forward, becoming lost for a while but finally climbing to the high point he had sought. "Once you climb this ridge you get a splendid view of the whole country to the east and south." To the east was the Fort of Fléron, which reminded the ex-military man of "some monster Dreadnought. . . . This likeness to a battleship was heightened by the searchlights. They swept the ground before the fort, as if it were the sea full of approaching enemies; and so it was." Fortescue watched through the night as "flaring rifles," searchlights, illumination rounds, and shell fire gave some evidence of what was happening. "Above, the full moon shone down calmly on all."[15]

Later, in the predawn light, he was surprised to see a battalion of Germans attacking in close order. "This is against all modern theory of tactics. As they come on, they fall like standing corn before a hurricane. No discipline can stand before this blast of death. The line begins to waver; now it breaks. . . . So long have I been taught to think of the German infantry as invincible that I cannot believe my eyes. If, in our work at the Staff College at Leavenworth, I had advanced the statement that Belgium might smash the columns of the Kaiser, my brother officers would have ridiculed the idea." The Belgians, hampered by the piles of dead Germans on the glacis of the fort, launched a bayonet counterattack that drove the enemy off. As he watched, Fortescue was reminded of Julius Caesar's remark: "Of all the peoples I have fought, the Belgians are the most sturdy."[16]

When the fighting died away, the American tried to return to the train depot, but kept being arrested on suspicion of being a spy. Once, he was followed to the police station by a mob shouting "Lynch the German!"; another time he was rescued by a passing officer who could read the identity papers that Whitlock had provided him. The officer advised him to try to not look so German, as "it might lead to an unfortunate accident."

"That was reassuring, as the comedian would say, I don't think. This is the only face I have got, and it will have to get me through this war, even if the Belgians can't recognize its American origin." As soon as possible, Fortescue made his way to a shop where he found an American flag on a toy warship. He pinned the tiny banner to his jacket.

He rushed back to Brussels to write up his story. He had witnessed the opening slaughter of a war that would take millions of lives over the next four years, many of them through the same kind of infantry frontal attacks against defensive positions protected by machine guns and artillery. He would have experienced another historic milestone had he stayed in town just a few hours longer. After failing in their initial attacks, the Germans warned that if the forts did not immediately surrender, zeppelins, giant airships, would be sent to destroy the town of Liège from the air. The Belgians refused. On August 6, Zeppelin LZ made good on the threat. "The thirteen bombs it dropped," writes the historian Barbara Tuchman, "the nine civilians it killed, inaugurated a twentieth century practice."[17]

Not much detailed news was making its way across the Atlantic. The confusion, censorship, and most of all disbelief interfered at first with a true understanding of what was happening in Europe. Humanity had progressed too far, and modern war had become too expensive for such a return to barbarism. This inability to comprehend the crisis extended to the White House, where Woodrow Wilson told his daughters that Austria's declaration of war against Serbia was "incredible—it's incredible."[18]

Myron T. Herrick, American ambassador in Paris, cabled Wilson on July 28:

> Situation in Europe is regarded here as the gravest in history. It is apprehended that civilization is threatened by . . . a general conflagration. . . .
> It is felt that if Germany once mobilizes no backward step will be taken.
> There is faith and reliance on our high ideals and purposes, so that I believe expression from our nation would have great weight in this crisis.
> I believe that a strong plea for delay and moderation from the president of the United States would meet with the respect and approval of Europe, and urge the prompt consideration of this suggestion.[19]

Despite the urgency, Wilson, consumed by a personal tragedy, did nothing about the growing catastrophe for several days.

Ellen Axson Wilson was the pillar of strength on which Woodrow Wilson leaned. She had not only run a comfortable home that allowed him to concentrate on his work, she had also taken a role in that work, advising him on political matters and tempering his strict Presbyterian moral stands with a gentler view. Yet she had hated the public aspect that their lives had assumed with her husband's rise to the presidency; on Inauguration Day in 1913 she had broken down, weeping in her unhappiness.

Now, after months of illness, she was dying from Bright's disease, and Wilson was devastated. "I carry lead at my heart all the time," he wrote a friend on Sunday, August 2, the day that the Germans issued an ultimatum to Belgium to allow German troops to march through their country. When his daughters asked him what was going to happen, would this all result in a world war, he stared into the distance, then covered his eyes before telling them, "I can think of nothing—nothing, when my dear one is suffering. Don't tell your mother anything about it."[20] He was convinced that had he not entered politics she would have retained her health, and he wanted to spare her knowledge of how all her hopes of goodness and progress in the world were failing.

So little attention had been paid in the press to the growing crisis that when the armies began marching the American public was shocked by how the war seemed to have come from nowhere. And what were the issues at stake? Wasn't this all over a murdered aristocrat in some unheard-of city in a distant country that few Americans could even find on a map? Didn't this involve those entangled alliances that we were so wise to have avoided, and those equally entangled royal houses with their competing claims to power and prestige? And now men would die, cities would be destroyed, and prosperity and progress would be derailed for such obscure but corrupt and decadent reasons? A midwestern paper headlined the story: "Blood-mad monarchs prepare dread sacrifice. Fifteen millions facing death. Royalty forces wreck and ruin on fated lands. Stubborn rulers play subjects as pawns."[21] What was to be made of the news reports from every part of Europe that spoke of citizens parading, laughing, cheering, and singing at the declarations of war? Had they all lost their minds?

There were, to the surprise of a good number of Americans, repercussions for their country. "Our stock exchanges closed for the first time since 1873," wailed Edward S. Martin, the editor of *Life* magazine, "our values disordered, our blessed tourists by the thousand running hither and yon in Europe, their credits useless and no ships to bring them home! It is like being caught in a vast flood, an overwhelming torrent of hate and sudden death from Europe's broken dam."[22] On August 3, President Wilson held a press conference in which he asked reporters to help keep the country calm, especially important because of the millions of immigrants from the warring nations. He also set a theme that he would pursue for the next two and a half years: "I want to have the pride of feeling that America, if nobody else, has her self-possession and stands ready with calmness of thought and steadiness of purpose to help the rest of the world."[23] On the fourth, he sent an offer to the belligerent governments to mediate a peaceful solution to the crisis, but it was too late. Ellen Axson Wilson died three days later, never knowing that war had broken out. The president immediately left Washington to escort her body to the funeral in Rome, Georgia.

SPY MANIA was now everywhere in Europe, as well as anger at "foreigners." Paris, Berlin, Brussels, London all had outbreaks of violence, though these were usually quickly contained by the forces of government. In Paris, cavalry charged through the streets trying to maintain order, but still, many shops owned by Germans were destroyed and several Germans killed.[24]

In Berlin, the Russian ambassador and the women with him were beaten on their way to the train station by men wielding sticks, and an angry crowd broke all the windows in the British embassy while another mob gathered at the Hotel Adlon hoping to lynch British newspaper correspondents. Strangers were seized on the streets, and some were shot as spies; it was widely believed that the Russians had poisoned Berlin's water supply, and that their agents were being arrested all over Germany disguised as women. Rumors spread through the German countryside that automobiles full of French gold were fleeing to Russia. "Peasants and gamekeepers and others turned out on the roads with guns," reported James Gerard, the American ambassador, "and travelling by automobile became exceedingly dangerous. A German Countess was shot, an officer wounded and the Duchess of Ratibor was shot in the arm." Gerard himself was spit on by a man who assumed he was British. The ambassador chased the fellow down the street and caught him, but before anything more could happen Gerard's footman came running up to explain who he was. The spitter, to Gerard's amazement, was not a street tough but a Berlin lawyer, and he proffered his card as well as apologies, and came to the embassy the next morning to apologize once more for mistaking his target.[25]

Undergoing trials and tribulations everywhere were the more than 120,000 American tourists, 30,000 of them schoolteachers, stranded by the outbreak of war, some of them in very remote parts of the continent. A Wild West show comprised of twelve Indians and ten cowboys was caught in Poland and had all their horses confiscated by the government for military use. A mounted Texan awash in a sea of refugees and soldiers in northern France was encountered by Frances Wilson Huard, an American married to a French artist. She and her household staff had been forced to flee from her chateau by the rapid German advance, and met the cowboy in a town where he was trying to buy a straight razor. "Got a Winchester, two revolvers, a Bowie knife, a lance and a lasso. Razor's flat and easy to carry. . . . Might be useful. . . . Nothing like being properly armed. If I've got to sell my hide you bet I'll sell it dear," he promised before riding off with a troop of British cavalry.[26]

The worst place for American tourists seems to have been Germany. Here there was not only a lack of hard currency, credit, and transport, but also at times an active hostility. Some Americans were detained at their hotels until given official permission to leave, and even after that permission was granted they suffered harassment on their trips out of the country.

One couple from Ohio tried to flee to Holland and were forced from the train at four different stops; the wife was stripped naked each time before German officers. Others were merely relieved of their money and documents.[27] At least one such confiscated passport was later used by a German spy in England.[28]

But no matter where they found themselves, the world had become an unexpectedly dangerous place in just a very few days. It is no wonder that when one citizen, an African American, was given the usual form to fill in, he answered the question "Why do you desire to return to the United States?" without any hesitation: "I am very much interested in my home at the present time."[29]

Most of the distress of these Americans began to be relieved by the middle of the month when the U.S. warship *Tennessee* arrived carrying $250 million in gold to help them, and army officers arrived to augment embassy staffs. Those staffs, however, continued to be under great pressure, for they found themselves taking care of most of the belligerents' diplomatic business. Neutrals also came to the Americans for advice, and when one worried about the possibility of the Germans bombarding Brussels, Brand Whitlock tried to soothe him: "I reminded him of his diplomatic extraterritoriality," that as a neutral he was not a target.

The man just smiled, replying with perfect common sense, "But de cannons got no eyes!"

German forces had finally been able to conquer the forts of Liège by bringing up huge, specially designed artillery pieces that pulverized their thick reinforced concrete domes. Then the invading army seemed to disappear as far as reporters and the public could tell, though there were rumors of German soldiers disguised as nuns infiltrating Belgian positions.

The one place where a German presence could not be avoided was the sky. Their Taube, or "Dove," aircraft seemed to be everywhere, over countryside or city, observing and bombing. Mildred Aldrich, magazine writer and member of Gertrude Stein's "charmed circle," had retired to a hilltop villa near the Marne River just north of Paris. From the first days of the war, she was struck by the number of "aeroplanes" over her strategically located farm, and she remembered a young engineer from Boston with whom she had visited the Galerie des Machines at the Paris Exposition in 1900 saying about a model of a manned flying machine that such a device might exist someday, but that he would probably not live to see it. Now, just fourteen years later, they were present in such profusion that she was reminded of a recent science-fiction novel: "I could not help feeling as if one chapter of [H. G.] Wells's 'War in the Air' had come to pass."[30] When a group of

French soldiers in her garden fired on a Taube, the officer in charge apologized: "I am sorry we missed. . . . It is a pity you should not have seen it come down. It is a beautiful sight."

Unfortunately, the wild shooting at the planes as they soared over Paris and other cities was almost as dangerous as the explosives they dropped, though when one released a bomb at random near the American embassy, almost killing Ambassador Herrick, a young American working there saw the damage they could do: "I . . . had just turned the corner when the bomb fell, killing an old man and tearing a leg off a little girl." He reported that the psychological effects of these attacks on Parisians "has been immense."[31] The reporter Irvin Cobb, along with many others, noted an irony: "To think of calling this sinister adjunct of warfare a dove, . . . which has always symbolized peace, seemed a terrible bit of sarcasm."[32]

DOZENS OF AMERICAN reporters for newspapers and magazines were trying to make their way to the battlefields in spite of government and military interference. The best of them had honed their skills in a hard, sometimes violent domestic school, investigating, charming, and occasionally facing down uncooperative city-machine politicians, smaller-scale con men, gang leaders, U.S. senators, and industrial titans richer than Croesus. Few had any international experience, but that didn't provoke even momentary qualms. "None of them . . . speak any language but English," noted Hugh Gibson, "but they are all quite confident that they can get all the news." The biggest story of their lives was breaking, and they were not going to be stopped from covering it.

The European officials trying to impose strict news censorship were not prepared for such reporters. For one thing, few of them knew about American publications and their traditions. "The names of our papers, that now count so importantly with European officialdom, were then practically unknown," Wythe Williams wrote decades later.[33] The special importance of magazines in the United States for keeping the public informed was also not understood. When Brand Whitlock received word that many of these reporters were heading for Brussels because of the German breakthrough, he sent word at once to the Belgian Foreign Office requesting that they "prepare a cordial reception for them." He tried to explain "the exceptional position of these men in America, pointing out that they are not to be treated in that informal, cavalier manner with which journalists here are treated." In addition, publishers had tried to help with their reception in Europe by providing them with money belts full of gold coins for buying food and shelter, which were also useful, experience showed, in bribing stationmasters for permission to climb aboard troop trains or government clerks guarding secrets. They could also provide fine wines and gourmet dinners for government ministers whose friendship could be important.

No one now knew where the various armies were, but the reporters did know that at some point a great battle would be fought, a battle that would decide the victor of what all were convinced would be a short war. They spent their days driving through the beautiful sun-washed countryside, the fields laden with the promise of a bountiful harvest, searching. "Over the map of Belgium," wrote Richard Harding Davis, the most famous of American correspondents, "we threw ourselves."[34]

On their forays they were often accompanied by American embassy officials. Hugh Gibson went with Frederick Palmer, another experienced war correspondent, to check on reports of a battle at Haelen, a town several hours away from Brussels. They found that Uhlans, German cavalry of ferocious reputation, had attacked, but had been driven off with heavy losses. They walked the field, eagerly gathering souvenirs such as lances and spiked helmets, but were appalled by the thousands of casualties caused by such a brief encounter. If there were this many dead from a relatively unimportant engagement, they wondered what would happen when the major forces met. Even more disturbing was what they were told about German actions toward civilians, "that only a few hours before . . . Uhlans had appeared in a field a few hundred yards from where we were standing, had fired on two peasant women working there, and then galloped off. Everywhere we went we heard stories of peaceful peasants being fired on. It seems hard to believe, but the stories are terribly persistent."[35]

As it turned out, the German army found the correspondents. The sudden appearance of enemy troops at the approaches to Brussels was announced by hordes of panicked refugees fleeing the recently peaceful countryside. First came the blaring of horns as automobiles raced along the avenues, and that drew reporters from their hotel rooms. Streams of cars ran together: taxicabs, racing cars, and limousines, their horns and sirens sounding one long, continuous scream. These were the rich, the nobility, and the prosperous gentry, their faces white with fear and the dust of the road. The peasants who followed were in farm carts, piled high with mattresses, sacks of grain, and children, pulled by their plow horses, the bent old men weeping over the livestock they had left behind. Mixed in were family carriages of the country gentry with servants in the box who were half dressed in livery, coatless, but wearing the striped waistcoats and silver buttons that marked them as grooms and footmen. This was more than the

beginnings of a war that the Americans were witnessing. A Europe that had
enjoyed a hundred years of peace marred by only short conflicts, a society
whose stability had not been doubted, a civilization confident of rationality
and steady progress, all were disintegrating before their eyes.

Brussels was surrendered without a fight, and less than twenty-four
hours later, in early morning of August 20, Germany's gray-green columns
began marching along the grand boulevards: cavalry, infantry, artillery.
Reporters, diplomats, and stunned Belgians watched the spectacle for
hour after hour. "No longer was it regiments of men marching," Richard
Harding Davis wrote in his classic first dispatch from the occupied city,
"but something uncanny, inhuman, a force of nature. . . . It was not of this
earth, but mysterious, ghostlike. It carried all the mystery and menace of a
fog rolling toward you across the sea." Davis and other observers were particularly struck by the uniforms, which seemed to have no color, but
instead blended into any background. "It is the gray of the hour just before
daybreak, the gray of unpolished steel, of mist among green trees."[36]

Whitlock found the whole scene "weird, unreal." Adding to the unreal-
ity for everyone were the songs and rhythmic chants of the invaders. "The
scene," Whitlock noted, "had the allure of medievalism, something terrible
too, that almost savage chant, and those grey hosts pouring down out of the
middle ages into modern civilization." The ambassador was even more
shocked when he was told by the mayor of Brussels that the Germans were
extorting 50 million francs ($10 million) from the city as a *contribution de
guerre,* 450 million francs ($90 million) from the surrounding province of
Brabant, enormous supplies of food and forage, and a large number of
prominent citizens to be held as hostages to guarantee the good conduct
of the populace. That "word hostages has such a medieval sound, my hair
almost stood on end." When later that day news came that the Pope had
died in Rome, Whitlock wondered, "Is the world coming to an end?"

For three days and nights the tramp of iron-shod boots echoed in the
streets of the Belgian capital as a whole army corps poured through. In the
six wars that Richard Harding Davis had observed as a correspondent, he
had never seen such a well-prepared, intelligently equipped army. Gerald
Morgan was also impressed. He, like Davis, had covered the Russo-
Japanese War, and had always considered the Japanese army one of the
best organized in the world, but he told Whitlock that that "was a haphaz-
ard affair compared with this."[37] The flood of gray really did seem a force of
nature to these bystanders, a force too powerful to be stopped by any mere
human agency.

But flesh and blood was evidently trying to stop it, or so new rumors claimed. The French and British were believed to be making a stand nearby. Reporters set off on foot, bicycles, horse-drawn carriages, taxis, hired limousines, or trains, calling to one another more or less sincere wishes of good luck, with nothing for protection but their passports and whatever small replicas of American flags they had managed to find. For the next three weeks, they worked their way along the various lines of approach or studied the aftermath of battles, trying to take advantage of the chaos to escape censorship. When lucky, they were ignored or welcomed by the soldiers, but at other times they were threatened with execution as spies. Much depended on the mood of officers, but also helpful were widespread rumors that the United States either had joined or might join the war on the host army's side. All the belligerents wanted to believe such news, so the journalists usually just smiled graciously at the reports.[38]

The first thing that struck most of them was the pitiful condition of the refugees, Belgian and French. These old men, women, and children fled by the tens of thousands along violently contested roads. Those who stayed in their homes often had them burned down around their ears, either by artillery or as the result of a deliberate policy by the Germans, who claimed that this was done only in retaliation for hostile small-arms fire. Some civilians were used as living shields for German troops approaching risky positions.[39] Granville Fortescue came across refugees who were obviously victims of the hysteria that would later be termed *shell shock:* "At every sharp sound they would crouch and tremble." When a woman tried to describe what had happened to her family during a bombardment, her daughter burst into tears, "and she said piteously, '*Pas plus de canon, maman, pas plus de canon.*' "[40] The stench was also memorable. The reek of dead men and horses was everywhere on the battlefields, and the recently conquered villages had their own foulness.

Also striking was the efficiency and ruthless discipline of the German army. This force had been impressive enough just marching through Brussels; now that they had beheld it in action, all seemed to agree that it was the largest, best-equipped, and most proficient the world had ever seen. One lieutenant boasted to a group of Americans about equipment, élan, and effectiveness, but then expressed pity for the poorly prepared French. "*Ach,* but it was shameful that they should have been sent against us wearing those long blue coats, those red trousers, those shiny black belts and bright brass buttons! At . . . half a mile, [we] . . . in . . . dark-gray uniforms . . . fade into the background; but a Frenchman in his foolish monkey clothes is a target for as far as you can see him. . . . While they have been singing their Marseillaise Hymn, we have been thinking. While they have been talking, we have been working."[41]

But the retreating British, French, and Belgians were obviously giving punishment as well as taking it. The number and variety of the dead and wounded of all sides was astonishing. Hundreds of thousands of soldiers were losing their lives in only a few weeks of combat. Airplanes were just one of the new technologies for killing. Machine guns, accurate and powerful artillery, modern magazine-fed rifles: all were proving that here was a truly unprecedented kind of war, where the industrial system had produced mobile factories of death.

To the surprise of most observers, the British and French were able to rally before the gates of Paris and launch a counterattack at the Marne River on September 6 that drove the Germans back and saved the city. A "race to the sea" took place as the armies tried to outflank each other, then lines stabilized and men began digging in; the war of movement became one of trenches, trenches that left a jagged scar stretching across the face of Europe from the Swiss border to the English Channel.

The reporters, shaken by what they had seen and experienced, wrote and tried to cable their stories, though censorship had quickly become so well established that it was often difficult to get them to the United States. Americans were horrified by the slaughter, but there was also a certain sense of self-satisfaction that they were not involved, that in the very month that Europe had fallen into such a feast of blood, their country was opening the Panama Canal to promote international commerce. "The European ideal bears its full fruit of ruin and savagery," boasted the *New York Times,* "just at the moment when the American ideal lays before the world a great work of peace, goodwill, and fair play."[42] As if to symbolize this, on August 3, the same day that Germany declared war on France and that Belgium asked Britain for aid, an ocean liner made its way through the canal for the first time.

Even more shocking than the battlefield deaths were the reports of German atrocities, including mass executions of hostages. American correspondents and diplomats did all they could to determine whether these stories told by refugees were true. The place where evidence was most obvious was the city of Louvain, home to a great university, a library of more than 225,000 volumes that included an extensive collection of rare medieval manuscripts, and numerous Gothic architectural treasures. Richard Harding Davis, who had come very close to being executed by the Germans, was locked in a railway car on a siding in Louvain along with fellow reporters Will Irwin, Gerald Morgan, and Mary Boyle O'Reilly, all being shipped out of the country by the invaders. They had each visited the city in the previous weeks, and had remarked on its beauty. Now they bore witness as the Germans, many of them drunk, methodically destroyed it, claiming that they were doing so because civilians had fired on their soldiers. Houses, offices, and the ancient library were looted, then set afire with explosives. This went on block by block as the Americans watched, and they also watched as a long procession of Belgian civilians was led through the Place de la Station. "These are the men who are to die tonight," an excited German soldier told them. "They are being paraded as a lesson to the people of this town. There are four priests at the head of the line!"[43] Later, they heard the sound of ragged volleying. Soon after, Hugh Gibson came to inspect the destruction and was convinced that there had been no civilian resistance, that this outrage, and those massacres coming to light in other parts of Belgium and the use of aircraft to bomb cities, were deliberate attempts to terrorize the people into surrender. It was the policy of what the Germans themselves called *Schrecklichkeit,* or, as it was translated, "frightfulness."

Irvin Cobb, one of the most gifted of the journalists, had spent weeks behind the battle lines. In his wanderings, he had witnessed numerous unhappy incidents, but the one that came to symbolize for him the tragedy of August 1914 was the sight on a rainy evening of an old Belgian peasant weeping in a squalid cowshed just over the border in Holland. "He must have been all of eighty. His garments were sopping wet, and all that he owned . . . rested at his feet, tied up in the rags of an old red tablecloth. In one withered, trembling old hand he held a box of matches, and in the other a piece of chalk. With one hand he scratched match after match; and with the other, on the wall of that little cowshed, he wrote, over and over and over again, his name; and beneath it the name of the old wife from whom he was separated—doubtlessly forever."[44]

These scenes of weeping refugees, massacres, burning towns, and bloody combat shocked and horrified America, but they were not really something new in contemporary history. For a hundred years and more such events had occurred around the globe as the imperial powers extended their reach to one "barbaric" people after another as they took up the "white man's burden" of civilizing the world. Americans had been responsible in the Philippines, Germans in Africa and China, Japanese in China and Korea, French in Africa and Indochina, British on many continents, and the Belgians themselves, in one of the cruelest of conquests, in the Congo. Now the rivalries for power and the dominance of "culture" had come home to Europe. Cobb discussed this with an educated Prussian who insisted that all the suffering would soon be forgotten, and that Belgians and other "lesser peoples" would benefit from being part of the German empire. "Germany is a giant . . . and she must have breathing space; and only by the swallowing up of smaller states can she get that breathing space. . . . At first they may not want to accept our German civilization. They will have to accept—at the point of a bayonet if necessary."[45]

With all these destructive forces at work on the Old Continent, it is no wonder that one American newspaper's reaction was that the European war "suggests that maybe the white man's burden is the white man himself."[46]

CHAPTER EIGHT

———◦———

Peace and Prosperity

VICTORY!
Five hundred miles of Germans,
Five hundred miles of French,
And English, Scotch and Irish men
All fighting for a trench;
And when the trench is taken
And many thousands slain,
The losers, with more slaughter,
Retake the trench again.

Edwin Dwight, *Life* magazine, April 8, 1915

WITH AMERICAN ATTENTION so focused on Mexico, the outbreak of war in Europe in early August 1914 came as a great and terrible shock, all the more powerful because of its suddenness. Charles D. Henry, a banker in Monterey, California, and the father-in-law of the brilliantly successful mining engineer Herbert Hoover, had ventured with some friends into the high Sierra Nevada on a fishing trip in July. While making their way back down a few weeks later, they were called to from across a ravine by an ascending party: "Any news of the war?"

Thinking that they were being kidded, Henry, remembering a phrase from his boyhood during the Civil War, shouted back, "All's quiet along the Potomac." It wasn't until several days later, when they finally reached civilization, that they learned that a new and all too real war had begun.[1]

"This dreadful conflict of the nations came to most of us as lightning out of a clear sky," wrote Robert Page to his son Walter, American ambassador to the Court of St. James. "The horror of it all kept me awake for weeks, nor has the awfulness of it all deserted me."[2] Ambassador Page himself reflected on the traditional view of sea as moat—"Again and ever I thank heaven for the Atlantic Ocean"—while Theodore Roosevelt thought of a more disturbing reference to oceans, finding it "on a giant scale like the disaster to the *Titanic*."[3] Senator John Sharp Williams of Mississippi exclaimed that he was "mad all over" about the start of the war, "down to the very bottom of my shoes, and somewhat sick and irritable, too."[4]

Many Americans who had placed a sincere, though naive, reliance on the new arbitration treaties promoted by Secretary of State Bryan felt sick and irritable themselves, as well as disillusioned, when the ultimate uselessness of such devices was demonstrated in blood. This failure of well-intentioned moral diplomacy was underscored by the remarks of Theobald von Bethmann-Hollweg, the German chancellor, who, angry that the British would enter the war, at least partly because of their treaty obligations to protect the independent neutrality of Belgium, charged that it was "all for just a word—'neutrality.'" He condemned the treaty as "just . . . a scrap of paper."[5]

Walter Page was quick to recognize that, as he and many others were putting it, "The Great Smash is come." Certainly the normal routine of the embassy had gone to smash, and it was in trying to put the pieces back together that Herbert Hoover first became involved with the responsibilities of public life. Hoover, a graduate of Stanford University, had made a fortune plying his trade of mining engineer and venture capitalist around the globe. He had been based in London for years and had recently been encouraging European governments to take part in the Panama-Pacific Exposition to be held in San Francisco to celebrate the opening of the Panama Canal.

Robert P. Skinner, the American consul general in London and a friend of Hoover's, asked the engineer, who had a well-deserved reputation as a brilliant and tireless organizer, for help with the distraught travelers. Hoover was also shocked by the self-indulgent behavior of some, but he was moved by the dilemma of "American school teachers who had pinched, saved and planned for this one trip to Europe all their lives. They had come to make themselves better teachers. . . . They were the hardest hit of all these refugees. . . . They were anxious but not imperious. They were also polite."[6] And some of the wealthier tourists were generous, donating thousands of dollars to help their less-well-off compatriots. Hoover used his contacts with the American community in London to form a committee that established a million-dollar credit line with a bank. Then he arranged for the stranded tourists to be interviewed, provided with money according to their needs, and in many cases put on ships for home even before the battle cruisers *Tennessee* and *North Carolina* arrived with their cargoes of gold. Of the more than $1.5 million given in emergency loans, less than $300 went unrepaid.

The world had seemed so good, so firmly on the path to progress, that this eruption had left Americans bewildered. Hoover, who can serve as a spokesman for middle-class American attitudes on this, recognized that there were flaws in prewar society such as "squalor, privilege, slums, slum minds, greed, corruption and bad taste," but even so it was "the happiest period of all humanity in the Western World in ten centuries." The cause of human welfare was making great strides, and the "dignity of men and women and their personal liberty were everywhere receiving wider recognition. Human slavery had long since disappeared. Freedom of speech and worship, the right of men to choose their own callings, the security of justice were yearly spreading over wider and wider areas. . . . Fear had disappeared in the hearts of men. It was an era of released human spirit." And then "the world stumbled into the Great War," initiating "a period of Great Fear" that "settled like a fog upon the human race—to last, perhaps, for generations."[7]

Another source of pain and confusion, besides the fog of war and disillusion over the failure of treaties to disperse it, was horror at the actions of the German army against civilians in Belgium. Few Americans had admired the militaristic cast of the German state, and there was a history of tension between the United States and the Reich, both nations coming late to imperialist expansion and therefore forced to compete for what unattached lands remained. There had been trouble between them over Samoa in the 1890s, then during the Spanish-American War of 1898 a German flotilla had suddenly appeared in Manila Bay after the American victory there, interfering with fleet operations. Admiral George Dewey, who feared that the Germans planned to either help the Spanish or grab the Philippines for themselves, had forced them to behave by threatening to take hostile action.[8] More recently, suspected German ambitions to acquire territory in the Caribbean that would threaten the new canal had brought additional unease to American leaders.

But in spite of such anxiety over German expansionism and the military and naval might that undergirded it, there were aspects of that nation's culture that drew respect. American intellectuals admired the life of the mind in Germany, and its institutions of higher learning had provided the models for new research universities such as Johns Hopkins, which had trained Woodrow Wilson, among other scholars. Great German composers provided the foundation of American orchestras' classical music repertoire, while even inhabitants of small towns enjoyed the opportunity for a good musical education because of the thousands of German teachers, bandmasters, and musicians who had emigrated.[9] German émigré socialists provided much of the inspiration and base of the domestic party, and German immigrants as a whole were seen as solid, hardworking contributors to American life, though the more severe prohibitionists condemned their fondness for sociable drinking in beer gardens.

Now there were charges of barbarism: not only the forcing of war on a peaceful Belgium, but the deliberate destruction of an irreplaceable library, a university, and ancient cities, and, even worse, revenge killings of old men, women, and children—the policy of *Schrecklichkeit*. The editor and journalist William Allen White, summering at Estes Park in the Colorado Rockies, witnessed the dismay of an intellectual friend at the news. "I remember Professor Hodder, of the history department of the University of Kansas . . . sitting tight-lipped and grim while we discussed the invasion of Belgium, the fall of Liege, the sack of Louvain, and all the horrors that followed that gray steel wave of Germans that washed over Belgium. For two days, maybe three, Hodder declared: 'It can't be so. They aren't telling the truth. Why, there's a treaty between Belgium and Germany that would prevent it!'"

When Hodder finally had to accept the truth of the invasion and destruction of Belgium, "the foundations of his faith in modern civilization completely caved in, and he was a heartbroken man."[10]

Not everyone was willing to accept the moral dimension of these events, particularly the millions of German immigrants in the United States, and their American-born children. Joining these still-loyal Teutons were the Irish, who felt, after centuries of oppression in the home country, that any enemy of the British Empire was a friend. Jeremiah O'Leary, leader of the American Truth Society, one of the most militant of these Irish groups, argued that the kaiser's forces were innocent of the charges of evil, and insisted that his followers stand in respect when the German anthem, "The Watch on the Rhine," was played. Irish American and German American newspapers took up the defense of the German cause, and they quickly had help as the German government began an elaborate and well-financed propaganda campaign in the United States, establishing an Information Service office in New York City before the end of August. George Sylvester Viereck, who had been born in Munich but raised in the United States, started his propaganda effort with *The Fatherland*, which appeared within a week of the outbreak of war, and which would receive large subsidies from the kaiser's government. Hugo Münsterberg, a well-known professor at Harvard, also became a popular, and subsidized, spokesman for the German cause. These German agents knew at least one effective line to take, and made much of the Teutonic role in defending Western civilization against the peril posed by Slavic Russia.

For reasons of shared language, values, and political traditions, however, as well as the belief that Germany started the war and outrage over the rape of Belgium, the greatest number of Americans emotionally supported the French and the British. Charles W. Eliot, president emeritus of Harvard and therefore spokesman for the eastern Anglo-American establishment, wrote to Wilson as early as August 8 that the United States should join with the Allies "to rebuke and punish Austria-Hungary and Germany for the outrages they are now committing" by imposing a blockade on them. "The proposal would involve the taking part by our navy in the blockading process."[11]

Richard Harding Davis, still horrified by what he had witnessed in Belgium, put the case most strongly and, given his popularity, most widely: "Were the conflict in Europe a fair fight, the duty of every American would be to keep on the side-lines and preserve an open mind. But it is not a fair fight. To devastate a country you have sworn to protect, to drop bombs upon unfortified cities, to lay sunken mines, to levy blackmail by threatening hostages with death, to destroy cathedrals is not to fight fair. . . . When a mad dog runs amuck in a village it is the duty of every farmer to get his gun and destroy it, not to lock himself indoors and toward the dog and the men who face him preserve a neutral mind."[12]

It was obvious to Woodrow Wilson that having such ethnic and political divisions loose in the land could tear the United States apart, especially since the outbreak of war had made the already worrisome national recession even worse. Unemployment in the cities was high, over 300,000 in New York alone, as mills and factories laid off workers. The price of cotton, so important to Wilson's Southern supporters, dived, while wheat, which would affect the price of bread and other staples, was charging up to record levels. The stock exchange, in a sign of how international the prewar financial markets had become, was closed because of panic selling by Europeans. Secretary of the Treasury McAdoo, who had advised the closing, had been forced to issue over $350 million of "emergency currency" to keep the economy afloat until the recently approved Federal Reserve System was in place.[13]

A policy of absolute neutrality, the president recognized, was required both to keep the country from being drawn into the conflict and to preserve domestic peace. The census of 1910 had shown that out of a population of almost 92 million there were 13,515,886 who were foreign-born and

18,897,837 where one or both parents were foreigners. Of these, close to 11 million were born in either Germany or Austria-Hungary, or had a parent who had been, and there were more than 4 million Irish Americans. Many immigrant Jews had bitter memories of Russian or Eastern European pogroms, and favored the German and Austrian empires.

On August 19, after having traveled to Georgia to bury his beloved Ellen, the president issued his strongest warning yet against taking sides: "The effect of the war upon the United States will depend upon what American citizens say and do. . . . The United States must be neutral in fact as well as in name during these days that are to try men's souls. We must be impartial in thought as well as in action, must put a curb upon our sentiments as well as upon every transaction that might be construed as a preference of one party to the struggle before another. My thought is of America."[14] The plea struck a responsive chord in most of his countrymen, who, whatever their sympathies, wanted no active part in the bloodbath now drenching Europe. As the *New York Sun* editorialized, "There is nothing reasonable in such a war . . . and it would be folly for the country to sacrifice itself to the frenzy of dynastic policies and the clash of ancient hatreds which is urging the Old World to destruction."[15] Even Theodore Roosevelt, very briefly, subscribed to this position, finding excuses for Germany's unprovoked invasion of Belgium, and arguing, "We should remain entirely neutral and nothing but urgent need would warrant breaking our neutrality and taking sides one way or the other."[16]

Wilson appointed a neutrality committee to advise governmental departments on how to conduct themselves, and he ordered army and navy officers, as well as members of the State Department such as Hugh Gibson, who had investigated German atrocities in Belgium, to keep silent. Similar orders would follow when American officials tried to report on, and stop, the massacres of Armenians that took place in Turkey in 1915. Turkey was an ally of Germany, and Wilson would refuse to condemn the slaughter because he felt to do so would go against a neutral stand. In a few months he would learn from a newspaper report that the army's general staff had done some preliminary work on what to do if the United States should become involved in the war against Germany. The president exploded, not understanding that this was exactly what the general staff needed to do to meet potential threats. He warned that if such planning continued the officers involved would be scattered to remote assignments far from Washington.

William Jennings Bryan was a particularly strong supporter of neutrality, and argued successfully with Wilson that "money is the worst of all contrabands because it commands everything else," so no banks should be allowed "to loan to any belligerent."[17] Both men were sure that such a policy would lead to an early end to the war, and a restriction on loans was put in place by the middle of August. Bryan wrote to J. P. Morgan and Co.— who because of its close ties to Allied bankers was considering a French government request to borrow $100 million—saying, "In the judgment of this Government, loans by American bankers to any foreign nation which is at war are inconsistent with the true spirit of neutrality."[18] Morgan did not make the loan, but this policy would prove to be as temporary as Theodore Roosevelt's support for the United States' staying on the sidelines.

There was an immediate surge of interest in stopping the war from the gender that was seen as the moral arbiter of the country. A group of women's organizations organized a Peace Parade in New York on August 29, and two thousand women, clad in the black of mourning, silently marched down Fifth Avenue to the beat of muffled drums. Out of this would come the American Union Against Militarism and the formation of the Women's Peace Party. Wilson, distracted by his wife's illness and death, had not stepped forward to try to stop the war as aggressively as he should have. But he now hoped that his stand for complete neutrality would hasten the time when the warring powers would ask the United States to play the role of mediator, when they would come, humbly admitting, "You were right, and we were wrong. . . . Now, in your self-possession, in your coolness, in your strength, may we not turn to you for counsel and for assistance?"[19] The president also prayed for a higher assistance, proclaiming October 4 as a Peace Sunday, asking "all God-fearing persons" to repair on that day to their places of worship, there to unite their petitions to "Almighty God that . . . He vouchsafe His children healing peace and restore once more concord among men and nations." Churches and synagogues were filled to overflowing, and many were turned away from the doors. A WHOLE NATION PRAYS FOR PEACE ran the *New York Times* headline the next day.

BY SEPTEMBER 1914 it became obvious to Brand Whitlock and others that the suffering of the Belgians had reached a new stage. The Germans had forced the government to pay enormous cash indemnities, and quickly looted the conquered country of industrial equipment. Civilians were being drafted into forced labor for the war effort, and even the mildest forms of resistance were still being punished by prison or shooting. As winter approached, the populace was also facing the very real possibility of starvation and death by exposure because the invaders had seized that fall's abundant harvest and had destroyed so many houses and public buildings. A delegation of high-ranking Belgian officials from the government in exile visited the United States to ask for aid.

Negotiations started quickly. The British government, in spite of objections from its admirals, was willing to allow food for the Belgians and the people of occupied northern France to pass through the blockade they had imposed, but only if German authorities gave assurances that all such supplies would go directly to civilians and not be requisitioned for military use. By mid-October a final agreement had been reached between the hostile powers, and Americans were asked to provide food and arrange for its transportation. Here, again, Herbert Hoover stepped forward, just as he had when American tourists were stranded without funds.

It was not an easy acceptance. The disruptions of war had quickly destroyed the fortune that Hoover had labored so hard to build. "Well, I'm broke!" he told his houseguest in London, the reporter Will Irwin, a friend since their years as undergraduates at Stanford. "Flat!"[20] When Ambassador Page asked him to lead the Belgian rescue effort, Hoover agonized for days over his decision, knowing that he would have to forgo all money-making business during his tenure. "I'll have to make enemies," he told Irwin. "Too many factions on both sides of the line won't want this job done. They'll believe that I'm doing it only to make important business contacts and get concessions when the war is over." Since extraction of the base metals, such as lead, copper, iron, and zinc, used in munitions was his specialty, as a neutral he could easily recoup the money he had lost if he concentrated on business. Irwin's room was under his, and every night he would awaken to the sound of Hoover's constant pacing. The hard-driving engineer, born in poverty, orphaned at an early age, and barely forty years old, was touched by the suffering of the Belgians and ready for new challenges. Finally the decision was made, and one morning at breakfast he told Irwin, "Well, let the fortune go to hell!"

As a businessman with international contacts, he knew what had to be done. Immediately contacting grain brokers in Chicago, he bought $10 million of wheat futures, then he turned to the American community in London and organized the Commission for Relief in Belgium, or CRB. Irwin agreed that "the Chief" was "the one man in the world suited to the job. His ability and integrity spoke for themselves; behind that, he had more experience in dealing practically with Europe than any other American alive."[21]

Whitlock, with the help of Spanish diplomat the Marquis de Villalobar and others, handled the CRB's relations with the German occupiers in Brussels. Hugh Gibson, who had proved himself rather a daring sort through his visits to the battlefields during the fighting in August, traveled back and forth between the enemy zones dealing with emergencies. Private citizens in the United States, along with the Rockefeller Foundation, contributed millions of dollars to buy food, which Hoover's network of engineering friends helped administer. "The Chief" recruited American Rhodes scholars at Oxford to carry out much of the actual distribution of supplies in the occupied areas.[22]

All this had to be accomplished in the face of hardheaded resistance from the military authorities of both sides, who feared that the American humanitarian effort was weakening their respective war-fighting powers. General Arthur von Luttwitz, the German military governor of Belgium, asserted that because the British blockade denied Germany food as well as war supplies, it was the Allies who bore the responsibility for feeding the Belgians. He was frank enough to say that if they did not, and there were bread riots, "the natural thing would be for us to drive the whole civil population into some restricted area, build a barbed wire fence around them, and leave them to starve."[23] With great persistence, and the use of influential friends and allies in the press such as Irwin, Hoover used publicity and public relations to overcome these difficulties. Within months Hoover was world famous for his Herculean efforts to feed the starving millions of Belgium and occupied northern France.

Whitlock also bore a large share of the burden of feeding the starving Belgians. He was caught in the middle of a chaotic crowd in Brussels that often included the undiplomatic, subtly vain, monolingual Hoover; German generals who seemed unwilling to protect the CRB men from their brutal minions; and numerous other competing egos that were renowned and powerful, or that desired very much to become so. But Whitlock did such a superb job of handling these varied tensions that he and his country came to be bathed in a heroic light for the Belgians. This respect and affection was only increased by the arrival at Christmas 1914 of a special ship, sponsored by American schoolchildren, that was full of donated presents for suffering Belgian youngsters. As the Germans tightened their control—banning the Belgian flag, pictures of the Belgian king, and all Belgian holidays—the oppressed country responded by flying the American flag, displaying pictures of Wilson and Whitlock, and celebrating American holidays such as Washington's Birthday and the Fourth of July.

AMERICANS FELT PRIDE in Hoover and Whitlock, and in their own contributions to the Commission for Relief in Belgium: here were men who were heroes of peaceful effort instead of battlefield glory. But there were also other matters of concern in 1914. The struggling American economy and growing unemployment gripped everyone's attention as labor unrest continued to grow. A recession had begun in 1913, springing partly from the uncertainty that conservative businessmen felt after various federal and state investigations, the attacks of reformers, and new reform legislation, especially the new tariff law. The *New York Times* on February 3, 1914, ran a story with the headline 325,000 MEN NOW OUT OF WORK HERE, which reported on a study by the Bureau of Employment of the Association for Improving the Condition of the Poor.

Some in the Wilson camp, including Secretary of the Treasury McAdoo, suspected a concerted effort by elements of Wall Street to sabotage the administration, but there were worldwide forces of oversupply and meager consumption at work. Investors sold their stock positions and waited on the sidelines. By June 1914 the situation had further deteriorated, the production of coal and steel, the sinews of the economy, had declined precipitously, and hundreds of thousands of Americans were freshly unemployed. That same month, Wilson had tried to pump up the nation psychologically, announcing to a gathering of newspaper editors that he was confident that a business boom would be starting soon.

Even in relatively good times, the average worker was hard put to support him- or herself, let alone a family. Economists estimated that a single woman in the United States earning seven dollars a week in 1914 was existing at barely a subsistence level, and that more than eight dollars a week was necessary for even a modicum of comfort and health for one person.[24] Yet in New York City, over half of the workers in factories and stores, male and female, were estimated to be making less than that. The outbreak of war, with its disastrous impact on international trade and shipping, made their situation even more desperate, with hundreds of thousands of newly unemployed joining those already suffering.

The government was also suffering financially since so much of its revenue still came from the tariff on imported goods; the income tax was just coming on line. Tariff income would fall by almost $85 million in the first year of the war, as owners foreign and domestic refused to risk their ships on the suddenly hostile sea. This fear had dire effects on American exports since the country had relied heavily on foreign vessels to carry goods to world markets because American-flagged shipping was so expensive. Only 2 percent of the world's deep-water merchant ships sailed under the American flag in 1914; around 50 percent of the rest were British, and they had their own uses for them that year, and for years after. Trade stopped, and the commodities such as cotton, wheat, oats, corn, and much else began to rot on the docks. There were added complications, as when on August 6, Great Britain gave the American government a list of items that it would view as contraband if shipped to its enemies, the first version of what was to grow to be a very long list indeed. The country was learning that it was not as detached from foreign affairs as it had prided itself on being.

Cotton was particularly hard-hit by the shortage of "bottoms" to ship the bulky cargo to the world. In 1913 cotton had commanded a price of thirteen cents a pound for the standard grade; a couple of weeks into the war in 1914 the price had fallen to less than half that. Since it cost more than nine cents a pound to grow, the South, which depended, as McAdoo was well aware, "almost wholly on cotton" was "facing a gigantic disaster."[25] Emergency federal funds were rushed by McAdoo to southern banks to provide credit so the growers could hold their crop until the crisis passed and prices recovered. New England textile firms protested that the administration was hindering the law of supply and demand and infringing on their right to buy cotton at distress prices, but several Wall Street figures contributed their own capital to the rescue. Bernard Baruch, who had been born and raised in South Carolina before making a fortune in New York finance, appeared in McAdoo's office and offered $1 million, and Jacob Schiff, of Kuhn, Loeb, provided $2 million.

The cotton crisis had effects on the already weak economy outside the South. Richard Harding Davis ran into a young woman he had known as a "telephone girl," or switchboard operator, at one of the leading New York hotels. She had lost her job because, as she explained, the hotel depended on southerners as clientele. "They make their money in cotton and blow it in New York. But now they can't sell their cotton, and so they have no money, and so they can't come to New York." She had been looking for work for weeks, "but everybody gives me the same answer. They're cutting down the staff on account of the war." She requested a letter of reference, and plaintively asked, "How long do you think this war will last?"

"This telephone girl looking for work is a tiny by-product of the war," Davis pointed out. "She is only one instance of efficiency gone to waste."[26]

WILSON REQUESTED that Congress approve $100 million in new taxes to deal with the sharp drop in tariff revenue, and that they also provide legislation establishing a special war-risk insurance fund to convince owners to send their ships to sea once more. As a further emergency measure, he aggressively pursued a ship-purchase bill, with a provision enabling the government to buy German ships that had taken refuge in American ports to escape capture by the British navy. The new taxes were quickly voted, as was the War Risk Insurance bill, but plans to expand the supply of ships through government purchase was attacked ferociously in the Senate after it passed the House. Shipping companies were making enormous profits because of the shortage, and wanted no additional competition. As McAdoo observed, "Tramp steamers not infrequently cleared their entire cost or value in a single voyage. In the course of a year an ocean-going freighter would bring in a net return—clear profit above all expenses—of three hundred to five hundred per cent on the money invested in the ship."[27] But there was also sincere philosophical and diplomatic opposition. Henry Cabot Lodge and Elihu Root, leading Republican senators, argued that this was a socialistic attempt by the administration to control an American industry; the British made it very clear that they would regard passage as an unfriendly act rewarding its enemy. All the stops were pulled on the campaign against the bill, including attacks by rumor asserting that certain people in government were going to make private money on the deal.

The president took even the well-considered resistance very much to heart, personalizing criticism just as he had during his battles at Princeton. Lodge offered a compromise, but it was rejected. "You cannot know to what lengths men like Root and Lodge are going," he wrote a friend, "who I once thought had consciences but now know have none. We must not suffer ourselves to forget or twist the truth as they do, or use their insincere and contemptible methods of fighting; we must hit them and hit them straight in the face, and not mind if the blood comes."[28] But the most galling resistance came from seven "disloyal" Democratic senators who refused to cooperate; the bill was delayed for two years. It was the first major defeat his administration had suffered.

But the economic crisis that had gripped America through 1914 and grew worse during the first months of the war suddenly began to lift as a desperate rush of orders flooded in from belligerents. Steel, gunpowder, shells, and more were in demand from industry, but also wheat, tobacco, cotton, and other crops; even horses and mules were badly needed: both the manufacturing and the agricultural sectors entered a tremendous boom.

One of the firm beliefs of members of the peace movement had been that modern war, with its ferocious hunger for matériel, would prove too expensive for nations to indulge in. When fighting began in August 1914, many of even the most cynical politicians expected it to last but a few months before exhaustion forced a stop. But the failure of the Germans' Schlieffen Plan, to beat France quickly and then to turn and thrash Russia, meant that the fighting would continue, and this meant that supplying the needs of the industrial war machine became pressing.

Transportation of these goods was difficult, as we have seen, and both sides recognized the need to halt their opponents' access to the greatest neutral supplier, thus the British surface blockade and the German use of surprise submarine attack. But there was also the problem of financing these purchases, and here again the British had an advantage, part of which came from their ability to actually ship what they bought, and also from the sympathy with which they were viewed by leading American financiers. Thomas Lamont, a House of Morgan partner, later admitted, "We wanted the Allies to win, from the outset of the war. We were pro-Ally by inheritance, by instinct, by opinion."[29] Even more crucial was Britain's position as the center of prewar commerce, finance, and shipping.

True, the Wilson administration had forbidden outright bank loans with Secretary Bryan announcing that such would be "inconsistent with the true spirit of neutrality."[30] However, on October 23, 1914, the president came under pressure to allow some borrowing; as one of the Morgan partners explained to McAdoo, "To maintain our prosperity we must finance it."[31] There was also the argument that to deny such loans would itself be unneutral. Wilson decided that there was a distinction between private bank loans to the belligerent nations and interbank credits, which allowed some minor borrowing to take place.

As the war continued, however, the power of even Great Britain's enormous reserves of capital began to weaken. It was important to maintain the strength of the pound as the world's reserve currency, but as war expenditures mounted, its value began to slip. In August 1915 the pound suddenly dropped from $4.86 to $4.65; signs of a financial crisis became obvious early in 1915 to American observers such as Jack Morgan, Robert Lansing, and William Gibbs McAdoo. McAdoo went to his father-in-law, the president, and asked that permission be given for bankers to extend large loans to the Allied powers that would be floated to the public at a generous interest rate. A particularly powerful argument was made by State Department counselor Lansing that lack of such a loan policy would damage the trade so badly that it would cause "industrial depression, idle capital and idle labor, numerous failures, financial demoralization, and general unrest and suffering among the laboring classes."[32] Wilson refused to put anything in writing, but let it be known that the government would not interfere. The first bond sale for $5 million, though it paid 6 percent interest, was popular only with institutional investors. But now that the precedent was set, the credit began to flow. Eventually these private loans totaled well over $2 billion, most of it coordinated by the House of Morgan, allowing the Allies—Britain, France, and Russia—to continue to buy. The Germans faced not only the challenge of sneaking what they bought through the British blockade, but also had difficulty in raising loans. Kuhn, Loeb, ably represented by Jacob Schiff, one of the firm's best men, tried to interest investors, but very little money resulted. However, the size of Allied purchases alone was enough to allow the new prosperity to keep on rolling.

As AMERICA'S economic boom grew, so did an awareness of the country's military vulnerability. The navy, thanks to Theodore Roosevelt's efforts, had been built up to be the third or fourth largest in the world. This was the service supporting both a defensive strategy by protecting the coasts, and also projected power across the seas. But the subsequent development by Europeans of the dreadnought class of all-big-gun warships had made many of the older, smaller American warships obsolete.

The army in 1914 had roughly 90,000 men, ranking somewhere on the world list between Peru and Argentina. But this was a thoroughly professional force, all volunteer, physically tough, well trained and well equipped with the Springfield rifle and the three-inch field gun, and well led by a small officer corps that took its duties seriously, even if the rest of society did not. The historian John Patrick Finnegan described it as "a small disciplined force trained for war in a large undisciplined country which hoped for peace."[33] There were about 125,000 in the poorly equipped National Guard. The army had eleven thousand horses and mules, but fewer than a hundred motor vehicles; even more glaring shortages were in small arms and ammunition, and in the lack of heavy artillery, a dangerous deficiency made clear by the power of the artillery being used on the western front.

This was an expensive force despite its small size and low pay. Even with a private's pay at only $15 a month, the United States had to spend almost $1,500 per year for every soldier it enlisted. Germany, by contrast, because of conscription, possessed a prewar standing army of 800,000 with a huge reserve at only twice the American military budget.[34] All the major European powers except Great Britain had used the draft to build enormous armies, but the United States had weak neighbors, great oceans, and no enemy immediately at hand. The myth of the yeoman farmer, which predated the Revolution, combined with the strong pacifistic beliefs of the American middle class, meant that changing any of this would be difficult.

However, Theodore Roosevelt, Henry Cabot Lodge, and others of like mind began urging a larger and stronger army and navy on the country, a movement for what came to be called "preparedness." General Leonard Wood, who had served as commander of the Rough Riders before Roosevelt and who had stayed in the army and had become chief of staff, was very active in trying to awaken the sleeping power of the United States. Even before the outbreak of the World War, Wood had established summer training camps for high school and college students where they paid for their own room and board and in return were given five weeks of training in discipline, drill, and small arms. To serve as an inspiration for the young men, the first such encampment was held at Gettysburg, Pennsylvania, in 1913, as the fiftieth anniversary of the Civil War battle was commemorated. Grizzled veterans of the Blue and the Gray were there to tell their tales of courage and duty. Still serving in the U.S. Army was a veteran of the war—John Clem, who had joined as a drummer boy, had risen to the rank of general. The 1914 encampments drew even more students, many from the Ivy League.

Support for preparedness grew as views hardened toward Germany and its treatment of Belgium. In December 1914, the National Security League was formed by a group of influential figures described by the *New York Times* as "sober-minded citizens, many of them peace advocates, though not of the extravagant kind, merchants, financiers, professional men of all shades of political opinion."[35] Members of both political parties were involved in the founding, though Republicans were more numerous. Theodore Roosevelt, Henry Cabot Lodge, and Henry L. Stimson, who had served as Taft's secretary of war, were the league's best-known spokesmen, with Joseph Choate, a famous lawyer and former ambassador to Great Britain, being honorary president. "I don't think," Choate told the nation, "[Europeans] could find any better game than this country, so fat and so rich and so unprepared."[36]

Wilson was not interested in arming the nation at this time, believing that preparations for war would taint American neutrality and diminish her moral force; nor were his advisers or his party interested. At least two of his Cabinet members, Bryan at State and Daniels at Navy, were self-proclaimed pacifists who believed moral power superior to any physical force, and they reflected much of the sentiment of the Democratic Party. Wilson and many of his Cabinet later changed their minds, but they were slow to do so.

In the elections of November 1914, the Democrats kept both houses of Congress; they gained 5 seats in the Senate, giving them 56 of 96 senators, and though they lost 59 seats in the House, they still held 231, a clear majority. The slogan the party had used in these races was "War in the East! Peace in the West! Thank God for Wilson!"

Peace groups had also been organizing to resist what they saw as one of the primary causes of the war in Europe. They were convinced that large armies and navies equipped with modern weapons would lure nationalistic politicians into using them. The League to Limit Armaments also formed in December 1914; then Jane Addams and Carrie Chapman Catt's Women's Peace Party, the American Union Against Militarism, as well as the League to Enforce Peace, headed by ex-president William Taft, took up the banner along with other groups.

The president gave a qualified blessing to these peace movements, and in his State of the Union address on December 8 argued that the nation could not institutionally prepare for war and still retain its democratic political institutions, that those who urged such a course were "nervous and excited. This is the time above all others when we should wish and resolve to keep our strength by self-possession, our influence by preserving our ancient principles of action. . . . We are not asking our young men to spend the best years of their lives making soldiers of themselves." He was sure that the old system of relying for defense "upon a citizenry trained and accustomed to arms" was all that was needed, and he proposed that wider opportunities for such training be provided so that "every citizen who will volunteer . . . may be made familiar with the use of modern arms, the rudiments of drill and maneuver, and the maintenance and sanitation of camps."

To do any more, he continued, would mean "merely that we have been thrown off our balance by a war with which we have nothing to do, whose causes cannot touch us, whose very existence affords us opportunities of friendship and disinterested service which should make us ashamed of any thought of hostility or fearful preparations for trouble." Instead, the nation should continue to "supply our own people and the people of the world as their need arises from the abundant plenty of our fields and our marts of trade; to enrich the commerce of our own states and of the world with the products of our mines, our farms, and our factories, with the creations of our thought and the fruits of our character."

So America should continue to follow its neutral course, mind its own business, prosper, and be available as example and mediator to a world at war. To that end he would send message after message to the belligerents over the next two and a half years through Edward House and others, vainly offering his efforts to bring an end to the killing. Above all, Wilson kept in mind, as he warned friends, that all the domestic reforms they had won with such great effort would be lost if the country were drawn into the war.

IN GREENWICH VILLAGE, and its "suburb" of Provincetown, the self-styled bohemians shared America's shock at Europe's return to barbarism. Harriet Monroe, editor of *Poetry* magazine, wrote: "It was a sudden shattering of hope, a brutal denial of progress, a bloody anachronism in a civilization of peaceful industry. . . ."[37] Jack Reed was just as horrified, though some of his radical friends asserted that this sort of disaster was to be expected from capitalism, and argued that the positive side was that the revolution was now bound to follow soon. Irresistible offers came, asking him to take to the field again as a war correspondent, and he responded enthusiastically.[38] Armed with a letter from William Jennings Bryan that requested American diplomats to provide him with all "courtesies and assistance," he sailed for Naples in mid-August. Italy was not yet in the war, but it seemed obvious that the country would soon join. Reed wanted to be there when the fighting began.

Mabel Dodge, summering at her villa near Florence, traveled down to Naples to meet him. She had been missing Jack, though the outbreak of war had not affected her. "As for me, it didn't mean a thing. It didn't interest or excite me, or even reach me. I dwelt alone in a deep contempt for wars, for anxieties, for humanities." A visit to a Christian Science healer in Florence restored for the moment her connection to life, and she eagerly welcomed her lover back. "He was untidy, curls damply disordered, breathless, and evidently containing more excitement than he could conveniently hold."

They visited Pompeii and Rome, but then rushed by train to Paris as news came of the German push for the city, hoping to arrive before its capture. Along the way they passed through station after station filled with mothers, wives, sweethearts, and old men waving good-bye to the enthusiastically singing troops; they also saw the early wounded coming back from the front, maimed, bandaged, and reeking of iodoform disinfectant.

Reed was feeling ill with a cold and dysentery, but Mabel watched as he rushed about "panting with pleasurable activity, his eyes shining. . . ." And he was not the only one, especially among the American journalists: "Everybody was excited, pleased, happy." This seemed to her an important "Secret of War," and she wrote an article about the scene for *The Masses* using that title. "The cafes surged with officers in brand-new uniforms and shining eyes. The male population in Paris was as lustful as the Roman mob." The session with the healer in Florence evidently having worn off, she herself felt "lifeless," spending much of her time in the apartment they had taken at 76 Rue d'Assas on the Left Bank.

Reed claimed to find the mood of the capital apathetic in the face of German conquest, and after a few days he set out for the front in a rented chauffeured automobile with fellow journalist Robert Dunn. Like the rest of the reporters trying to cover the fighting, they used various stratagems to pass roadblocks and evade arrest as spies. They did manage to visit the villages shattered and looted by the Germans and to talk to British troops about the retreat from Mons, but even though it was September 9 and the Battle of the Marne was still raging, they did not get to the action. They were soon arrested, taken to Tours, and forced to sign a promise not to return.

"What if I refuse to swear?" asked Reed.

"You will be obliged to remain in Tours until the end of the war," replied the French official.

Reed signed and returned to Paris, where he found Mabel still feeling lifeless. "At night a fierce and melancholy love rose in me and, as we joined our bodies, tears flooded my face and dried against his cheeks."

Reed had cast a cynical eye on most of the efforts being made to fight the war. Now that the Germans had been driven from the gates of the city, he claimed that the shops that had been closed with signs in their windows stating THE PROPRIETOR AND ALL THE CLERKS HAVE JOINED THE ARMY quickly reopened with these worthies back behind the counter, a claim that showed, at the very least, little understanding of the wide reach of French conscription.

The same bitter mood was with him in London, where Mabel decided to leave "and be miserable at home where at least I could be comfortable." She made him declare again and again his love for her, and promise not to do anything to threaten "our deep and inevitable love." But as soon as she arrived in New York, she received a letter from the inconstant Reed, who had returned to the Continent, confessing that the night she had left he had gotten drunk in a waterfront dive and slept with a prostitute.

Reed again tried to reach the front, but only saw the detritus of battle before being arrested. A period of time was spent drinking and whoring, but then he wrote Mabel that he had fallen in love with Freddie Lee, the beautiful German wife of Jack and Mabel's friend, the sculptor Arthur Lee. The three of them had been sharing the apartment on the Left Bank when the bolt of lightning struck. Arthur, though a bohemian, turned out to be less than understanding, and he threatened, or at least implied, that violence could be the result of this romance. Mabel was more amicable and wrote Freddie, who responded that she was sorry for the pain that was being caused, but that so true was the love between her and Jack that they were going to visit her family in Berlin, and eventually be married. Mabel, for solace, "turned once more to Nature and Art and tried to live in them."

Reed had been suffering writer's block all through this trip to Europe. Words came, but even after numerous rewrites the articles never seemed adequate at describing even the little he had seen. He was self-consciously trying to explain what he saw as the deeper social and political meanings behind the killing, but that was not where his talents lay. Lincoln Steffens gave him words of encouragement but also gently guided him: "Your views [even in Mexico] . . . were not nearly so good as your descriptions and narrative." After arguing that New York was the best base to write about the war, he continued, "You're not wise, Jack; not yet. But you certainly can see and you certainly can write."[39] Carl Hovey, *Metropolitan's* editor, agreed with Reed's own assessment that he was producing little worthwhile, but also still had faith in his talent. They decided that his trip to Germany with Freddie could lead to a visit to the trenches from that side.

He found many other journalists in Berlin waiting for such a chance, and as the relationship with Freddie exploded into irritability, shouts, and angry accusations, Reed began to spend more and more time in their company touring the bars. While at prep school, he had often entertained friends with exaggerated stories of his sexual adventures among the prostitutes of Portland. During the weeks he spent with these men, he laughingly related the complications of his romance with Freddie, claiming that her husband had chased him down the street with a pistol while Mabel was attempting suicide. In his unhappiness he would also fall into drunken, furniture-busting rages, and his companions would have to restrain him and calm him down.

Finally, in January 1915, an expedition to the trenches was put together at the request of American senator Albert Beveridge, who at the urging of editor Mark Sullivan was writing a series of articles for *Collier's* magazine. Reed went along with Robert Dunn and Ernest Poole, who had worked on the Paterson pageant with him. As the party traveled through Belgium and then occupied France, Reed was struck by the efficiency of the occupation, its progressive nature: "Don't imagine that German soldiers are a cruel, arrogant race. They have done admirable things. I am sure that some of these little northern French towns were never so clean, so intelligently organized. Everywhere they have re-opened schools and churches; they have re-established local institutions and local charities; they have scoured the whole town, lighted every house with electricity, placed up-to-date hospitals, served by the finest doctors in the world, at the free disposal of the humblest citizen."[40] Reed reported that German officers were generous in throwing coins from their automobiles for women and children to scramble for in the streets. Here, indeed, was imperialism and the "white man's burden" come home to Europe. This was an occupying army that continued to exact war reparations and food from the local economy, and the reason for repairs and improvements was that, though Reed did not seem to consider this, they did not plan on ever leaving. Local people, some of them close to starvation, did realize this motivation, and the occupiers were hated. Sometimes the American party, in military vehicles, was thought to be German, and then "misery and hatred darkened every face that watched our passing automobiles; and those who came last caught the curses that were hurled after us, 'Cochons! Boches!' "

Dunn and Reed were able to visit the fighting trenches, thanks to the influence of Senator Beveridge, who accompanied them part of the way. And an ugly way it was, walking thirty feet apart, under a misty rain through flooded fields and into a shattered village where they became aware of "a droning in many keys, like the wind in telegraph wires." These bullets struck all around, showering them with mud and bits of fence and road so that "the air was never quiet of whispering and whining and whistling steel." But Dunn and Reed pushed on to the frontline trenches, where they gained a good sense of the ordeal that men on both sides were enduring— not just the artillery shells and machine-gun fire, but mud and slime that were omnipresent, oozing into boots, matting pants and shirts, and sliding down necks. The two men peered through armored sniper holes, Reed noting the blue-coated bodies of dead French soldiers that lay between the lines, being swallowed by earth "glistening like the slime of a sea bed."

It is unclear whether the two reporters had been drinking, but the next morning they did something so foolish that it is hard to understand unless alcohol had been mixed with their exhaustion and fear. A German officer held out a Mauser rifle and asked, "Would you like to have a shot?" Both men laughed, then each fired the weapon toward the French trenches; it would not be long before these shots fired in merriment would be widely known about and condemned.

Reed had identified with the romantic cavalcade of Villa's men and their fight for land and individual liberty; he loathed this modern war dominated by machines and machinelike discipline that seemed to him to be waged for nothing more than national pride and the hope of controlling world markets. As soon as his tour of the German front was finished, he hurried to New York, hoping that Mabel would forgive and take him back.

CHAPTER NINE

Pride and Self-Respect

This represents not merely piracy, but piracy on a vaster scale of murder than old-time pirates ever practiced. . . . It is warfare against innocent men, women, and children. . . . It seems inconceivable that we can refrain from taking action in this matter, for we owe it not only to humanity but to our own national self-respect.

Theodore Roosevelt, May 8, 1915[1]

There is such a thing as a man being too proud to fight. There is such a thing as a nation being so right that it does not need to convince others by force that it is right.

Woodrow Wilson, May 10, 1915[2]

WOODROW WILSON'S capacity and need for love was, of course, not generally recognized. Supporters admired him as a brilliant thinker with a gift for fair-minded and efficient, though eccentric, administration; his detractors, especially Theodore Roosevelt, disdained his clerkish, cautious ways as reflecting a soulless intellectual meddler. As a proper gentleman, he had hidden from the public his agony over Ellen's death, though intimates such as Edward House and Dr. Cary Grayson had seen his pain and had tried to assuage it. In March 1915, just six months after Ellen had died, a more powerful cure for melancholy than detective stories, Wordsworth poems, and companionable walks with friends came into his life.

Edith Bolling Galt was an attractive, childless, and wealthy forty-two-year-old widow who had been born to a large Virginia family financially ruined by the Civil War. She had married Norman Galt, who owned one of the most fashionable jewelry stores in the capital, and after his early death she had become a leading social light in Washington. Wilson's cousin

Helen Woodrow Bones had introduced them, and there was an immediate attraction. "That evening started a companionship which ripened quickly," Edith later remembered, though she would at the time find the quick pace disturbing.

Well-chaperoned, they went for rides, and enjoyed friendly dinners, after which he often read aloud to her or they talked about their shared southern backgrounds, and she was charmed by his melodious tenor voice. He was immediately smitten, so much so that in early May, a bare two months after meeting her, Wilson proposed. Edith Galt was shocked at this break with the proprieties. "Oh, you can't love me," she replied, "for you really don't know me—and it is less than a year since your wife died."

He responded that he had lived a lifetime of loneliness since Ellen's death. But Mrs. Galt still rejected the idea of marriage, while allowing his suit to continue. Wilson, knowing that wedded bliss is the greatest bliss, pursued; the distraction of grief was now replaced for the president by the happier, if still disturbing, distraction of wooing this independent woman with whom he had fallen in love.

THE HORRORS of the war had grown over the months, and by early 1915 it seemed to many Americans that Germany, with its deliberate, ruthless policy of terrorizing its opponents through *Schrecklichkeit,* bore the responsibility for most of them. But anger now was also being sparked by Britain's high-handed demands that American commerce with even neutral Europe be subject to its control. At the opening of the war, Britain had imposed a blockade on Germany, a seagoing form of siege warfare, but one that did not meet the established international legal requirements. This illegal blockade was then extended to neutrals such as Holland and Norway, countries that could easily transship goods and war materials to the enemy; next, the British navy mined the North Sea.

Both the blockade and the mining infringed on the long-established rights of neutral nations. The first because now all shipping was subject to interception anywhere at sea instead of near an enemy port to be searched for "contraband," the definition of which was constantly being expanded by the British. By international law and custom, a blockade regarded as legal had to be "effective," i.e., completely controlling and close in to shore. This one did not meet either requirement.

On the matter of what was called "absolute" contraband, arms, ammunition, and anything else that was directly usable in making war, there was essentially agreement between the United States and the Allies. Long-established law allowed a navy to seize such cargoes being shipped to an enemy. But thorny problems surrounded questions of "conditional" contraband and "innocent" goods, those items that perhaps in some indirect way could be used by the enemy military, but could also be used by civilians. There would be months of squabbling over what material could be shipped and what could not. The mining of the North Sea meant that ships on the way to neutral nations such as Norway or Sweden were required to stop in British ports, and, after being searched and approved, pick up a pilot to guide them through the minefields.

The American government protested these requirements, which not only violated the traditional rights of neutrals but also went against the more recent codification of rights that the London Conference of 1909 had tried to establish. The British usually paid attention to American sensibilities since Sir Edward Grey, the foreign minister, understood the danger of alienating American goodwill. He tried to soften the measures taken while arguing in the British Cabinet against even harsher tactics urged by hardliners led by Winston Churchill. Even so, in May 1915 the British seized four hundred cargoes carried by neutral ships.[3] England was dependent for its protection on possessing the world's most powerful navy, and it would not agree to any restrictions on the use of that power. The United States could protest all it wanted, and would be listened to politely; compensation for seized cargoes would usually be paid eventually. But the policy of starving Germany and Austria of war materials and then the campaign for the literal starving of their civilian populations of food were not negotiable. Wilson would continue to protest these actions since they were a threat to American interests, and also because he felt it was his duty as leader of the largest of the neutrals to protect traditional rights. Soon enough, tensions between the United States and Britain appeared to be near the breaking point.

The threat from Germany, however, became more immediate in the early part of 1915. This came as a surprise to many, since Germany, as a land power restricted to the continent of Europe, did not pose such an obvious menace to American interests as did Great Britain's control of the sealanes. That was to change drastically under a new German strategy, but there were also immediate domestic actions that offended American sensibilities: disturbing signs of illegal German activity right here in America.

Germany had possessed an extremely effective espionage network in Europe before the war, but had neglected the United States, feeling that it was not important enough militarily to merit the effort. Only a part-time agent was enlisted there, and his targets were commercial and industrial,

not governmental. Once the British blockade was imposed, it was too late
to infiltrate an extensive cadre of professional agents into the country, so
the embassy staff was called on to assume roles for which its members had
not been trained. They responded willingly and managed some successes,
particularly in sabotage, but their lack of professional tradecraft also would
result in humiliation for them and arouse great anger in Americans, especially in Wilson and members of his government.

In December 1914, Wilson was informed that the German ambassador,
Count Johann-Heinrich Andreas Hermann Albrecht von Bernstorff, was
involved in the massive production of fake American passports. These were
to be used by German reservists to slip through British controls and return
to active duty in the home country via neutral ports.

Passports had been an optional convenience for travelers before the
war began, and few had bothered with them. The British decided, however, that requiring such documents would be an effective net with which
to catch spies and German and Austro-Hungarian reservists returning to
their armies from North and South America. New York, as the major American port, became the gathering point for thousands of these reservists, and
they needed passports that would disguise their actual nationality and
purpose.

Count von Bernstorff, the imperial ambassador in Washington since
1908, was an experienced and charming diplomat from an aristocratic family who actively cultivated the large and prosperous German American
communities across the nation; he, in turn, was assiduously cultivated by
the politicians who represented those voters. Ties of sentiment were still
strong between these millions of first- and second-generation immigrants
and the fatherland, and the kaiser had done much to promote that strength
with the granting of honors recognizing their loyalty, which Bernstorff and
other embassy officials would personally present at formal ceremonies. His
own prestige and intelligence had been recognized by the ten American
universities, including Princeton, that had awarded him honorary degrees.

A handsome man with a thick, curling mustache, Bernstorff was a colorful dresser who would sometimes wear yellow shoes and a black-and-
white checkered suit with appropriately outrageous ties. He once shocked
President Taft's sense of sartorial propriety by playing golf in a pink shirt
and red suspenders. The German ambassador obviously wished to be easily distinguished from black-clad businessmen and the gray-cloaked personalities of the ordinary diplomatic corps, even to the point of pursuing
rather flamboyant love affairs. In spite of his marriage to an American, he
carried all this on in the sophisticated Continental fashion. "I think a man

is a fool who denies himself any good thing in this life," he once explained to the journalist Frank Harris, himself no crusader for self-denial. "I'm very lenient, especially towards sins of the flesh when the temptation is great and the results unimportant. . . . I try to play fair and get what I want, while causing as little pain . . . as possible."[4] After Woodrow Wilson ordered the Secret Service to keep a closer watch on German and Austrian diplomats, a tap was placed on the telephones of both embassies, and an unexpected result was that Bernstorff was captured in conversations with close women friends. One called to compare him to the title character in *The Great Lover,* a current stage hit, but he demurred, saying that he had stopped his romantic career.

"Perhaps you have taken a rest, but not stopped," his caller replied, then added sharply, "You *needed* a rest."[5]

As the war progressed and anger at German actions grew, there would be a social rest of sorts, for the leading hostesses began dropping the Germans and Austrians from their party lists. They were confined to attending those soirees given by supporters of the Central Powers, the so-called Rhine Maidens. An important conquest during the early war years would be Cissy Patterson, whose family owned the influential, and fervently isolationist, *Chicago Tribune.* Her daughter Felicia particularly liked the charming count, who always brought her thoughtfully chosen presents. "He laughed very heartily. The house was alive and noisy when he was there."[6]

This liaison, however, resulted in an embarrassing scandal when one of Cissy's other lovers, a nationally ranked polo player, chased after the couple in his fast roadster, forced Bernstorff's Packard to the side of the road, then struck Bernstorff repeatedly with a riding crop until the ambassador escaped.[7]

But though a risk-taking extrovert and bon vivant, Bernstorff was an extremely able diplomat, aided by the same qualities that made him a successful seducer. Not only a graceful dancer and charming master of small talk, he could be both sincere and devious, a coolly accomplished liar, and a patient listener who never seemed to become bored, however long the state dinner or tedious the speeches or conversation might seem to the less forbearing. The ambassador also understood better than most Europeans the importance of the press in American life, and he was always willing to talk, seemingly with candor, to reporters or editors.

Bernstorff had quickly realized that the assassination of Archduke Francis Ferdinand in June 1914 could mean a European war, and immediately returned to Germany for instructions. When he came back to Washington later that summer he carried with him millions of dollars with which to buy munitions for Germany or, if that proved impossible, to prevent munitions from reaching the enemy. In addition, the funds could be expended for propaganda, sabotage, or any other tactic that could help the German war effort. The count cooperated with these campaigns, but reluctantly, and he would spend the next two and a half years trying to convince his government of the foolishness of deliberately alienating American goodwill.

There were only three additional members of the embassy staff of high rank. Dr. Heinrich Albert was the commercial attaché, and much of his time was spent at his office in New York, where he was well respected by the bankers and industrialists of the city. He and the ambassador had joint control over an account at the Chase National Bank, from which over the next couple of years he would pay out about $30 million in expenditures for propaganda, espionage, and sabotage.

The field agents in charge of much of the dirty work were Franz von Papen and Karl Boy-Ed, the military and naval attachés, respectively. Both were alert, active, and dedicated, and, like Dr. Albert, they also established offices in New York City. Their first task was to deal with the thousands of reservists who wished to return to service in the fatherland, and who therefore needed fake passports showing them as neutrals. They recruited Hans von Wedell, himself a German reserve officer, who was also an American citizen and a well-connected lawyer in New York City. Wedell was able to purchase passports for from ten to twenty-five dollars from sailors from various neutral countries such as Spain, Sweden, and Norway, and also from German Americans who requested them from their own government, then turned them over to be altered and used by the reservists. The technology behind these documents was so primitive that there was no great difficulty in changing them. The photograph of a reserve officer who matched the written description would be wetted and glue would be applied to the back. Then it was placed over the dampened original photograph already on the document. This was then put facedown on a soft cloth, and a bone knitting needle would be used to trace the lettering of the seal.

This scheme worked for only a few months before Department of Justice agents discovered the operation and broke the ring in January 1915, prosecuting and convicting several of the lower-ranking forgers.

The president was kept informed of these activities, and of Bernstorff's participation, but he was worried less by the forgeries than by the chance that the crime might become public and cause a confrontation with Germany. Wilson ordered T. W. Gregory, the attorney general, to be discreet since the "matter is . . . of the most sensational kind. I hope that you will have it looked into thoroughly, but that, at the same time, you will have all possible precautions taken that no hint of it may become public until it materializes into something upon which we have no choice but to act."[8] A secret agreement was made with Bernstorff that he would end his involvement in the plot.[9]

Increased surveillance of the Germans would soon lead to a comic-opera street chase and widespread revelations about their activities in the United States, but in the early part of 1915, the actions of Germany elicited more cries of horror than laughter.

As we have seen, the German aerial bombing of civilians began in Belgian cities and Paris in the very first days of the war. Attacks on England by zeppelins commenced on January 20, 1915, in a raid that killed four civilians and prompted the *New York Times* to call such targeting a "disgrace to civilization" and "savage warfare." There would be almost two thousand civilians killed and more than four thousand wounded by bombs in France and Britain, with 1,413 killed in Britain alone.[10] No one had forgotten that just a few months before, at least five thousand Belgian civilians had been killed during the unprovoked invasion of their country, many massacred after being held as hostages. Now British propaganda experts took the opportunity to remind Americans that at the turn of the century the kaiser had given special orders to his troops being sent to put down the Boxer Rebellion in China: "Just as the Huns a thousand years ago . . . made a name for themselves . . . so may the name German be established by you . . . in such a manner that never again shall a Chinese even dare to look at a German askance."[11] The Allies, and some Americans, began using *Hun* as a descriptive term for the Germans. This sense of outrage over German barbarism would grow in the next few months as the kaiser's forces introduced new forms of warfare such as flamethrowers and poison gas, used first against the Allies near Ypres in April 1915, and widely condemned in the American press. But it was a different revolutionary weapon that would most outrage Americans.

Germany, or at least the kaiser, did not wish to risk its large, modern surface fleet of dreadnoughts and battle cruisers in challenging the British navy's blockade; they had a far more innovative force in the *Unterseeboot,* or submarine. Though most navies possessed at least a few, there had been disagreement in naval staffs about the effectiveness of this complex and fragile new technology. But in the first weeks of the war, on September 22, 1914, seeming proof of its potency was given by the astounding success of a U-boat in sinking three British cruisers, the *Cressy,* the *Aboukir,* and the

Hogue, with the resultant loss of thousands of lives. Here, it now could be argued by Grand Admiral Alfred von Tirpitz, the head of the German navy, was a weapon that could win a war that had ground to a bloody stalemate on land.

There were, however, problems. The Germans had very few U-boats—no where near enough to maintain a legally recognized blockade as traditionally defined. Further, international law required that a blockading vessel, or "cruiser," give the crew and passengers of an intercepted ship safe escort to port or, failing that, take them on board before sinking the vessel or at least give them warning enough so that they could take to their lifeboats. But such humanitarian consideration was nearly impossible for submarines, which were extremely vulnerable on the surface. In the first days of the war, the Germans had tried these techniques before destroying commercial ships, but the British had then armed their merchant vessels, and in fact had set traps with ships disguised as freighters but carrying heavy cannon. An example of what could happen was the fate of U-27, which was caught on the surface while allowing the crew of a freighter to take to lifeboats. The innocent-looking *Baralong,* one of the British decoy tramp steamers, falsely flying the American flag and masked by the captured ship, came right up on the submarine and sank it with cannon fire. Men who survived the sinking tried to surrender, but were massacred by Royal Marines on board the *Baralong,* an atrocity, reported by American sailors serving on the genuine freighter, that shocked Woodrow Wilson. "Horrible," he said, "one of the most unspeakable performances."[12] But no official protest was lodged.

On February 4, 1915, the German admiralty announced that it would torpedo without warning all ships, including neutrals, found near the British Isles. Recognizing that this was against the requirements of international law, the Germans claimed that it was in retaliation for the illegal British methods of blockade. Wilson replied within a week that the United States would hold Germany to a "strict accountability" if American ships or lives were lost, and added that the United States would "take any steps it might be necessary to take to safeguard American lives and property."[13] The tone of this response was serious enough that the threat against neutrals was withdrawn, but this did not resolve the problem of Americans traveling or working on Allied passenger ships. When a U-boat sank the British liner *Falaba* in the Irish Sea on March 28, 111 people died, including an American. Wilson considered protesting this sinking, and was encouraged to do so by Robert Lansing, the State Department counselor, who argued that a stand had to be made to protect against further incursions against neutral rights. The president was talked out of making a formal complaint by Secretary of State Bryan, whose pacifist fervor had not dimmed during his tenure in office.

Then, further incidents added to the tension. Ships of other, smaller neutral nations were sunk, and on April 29, 1915, the *Cushing,* an American vessel, was bombed by a German airplane in British waters. A few days later the American tanker *Gulflight* was torpedoed. Several lives were lost, though the badly damaged tanker did not sink. Again the counselor and the secretary gave the president their conflicting views. Wilson was still mulling over a response when an even greater tragedy took place.

By 1914 the great North Atlantic liners had reached a previously unparalleled level of luxury, speed, and prestige. German, French, and British companies dominated the Atlantic run, competing to build the fastest, most extravagant, and most beautiful ships possible. Americans, though lacking their own, loved these graceful and elegantly designed seagoing

Passengers and crew of a ship torpedoed by a German submarine
try to save themselves

palaces, as a description by the novelist Sinclair Lewis makes clear. His character Sam Dodsworth is overwhelmed by the sophistication of the liner he is taking to Europe, and the sense of freedom he has once at sea:

> He explored the steamer. It was to him, the mechanic, the most sure and impressive mechanism he had ever seen; more satisfying than a Rolls . . . which to him had been the equivalent of a Velasquez. He marveled at the authoritative steadiness with which the bow mastered the waves; at the powerful sweep of the lines of the deck and the trim stowage of cordage. He admired the first officers, casually pacing the bridge. He wondered that in this craft which was, after all, but a floating iron egg-shell, there should be the roseate music room, the smoking room with its Tudor fireplace—solid and terrestrial as a castle—and the swimming pool, green-lighted water washing beneath Roman pillars. He climbed to the boat deck, and some never realized desire for sea-faring was satisfied as he looked along the sweep of gangways, past the huge lifeboats, the ventilators like giant saxophones, past the lofty funnels serenely dribbling black wooly smoke, to the forward mast. The snow-gusts along the deck, the mysteriousness of this new world but half seen in the frosty lights, only stimulated him . . . "I'm at sea!"[14]

To all this mechanical perfection and artistic interior design with paintings, marble columns flanking baronial fireplaces lit by huge crystal chandeliers, can be added exquisite meals. Sometimes fifteen courses were on the carte du jour, prepared by some of the best European chefs; a myriad of staff often came close to matching the number of passengers. On the great Cunard liner *Lusitania*, for instance, there were 702 crew for 1,257 passengers on its final voyage. And this was service that was unobtrusive and professional. Another novelist, Theodore Dreiser, experienced it just before the Great War.

> On shipboard, I noticed for the first time in my life there was an aloofness about the service rendered . . . which was entirely different from that which we know in America. They did not look at one so brutally and critically as does the American menial; their eyes did not seem to say, "I am your equal or better," and their motions did not indicate that they were doing anything unwillingly. In America—and I am a good American—I have always had the feeling that the American hotel or house servant or store clerk . . . was doing me a great favor if he did anything at all for me. However . . . when I went aboard the English ship . . . I felt this burden

of a serfdom to the American servant lifted. These people . . . were actually civil. . . . They are nice. They are willing. "Yes, sir! Thank you, sir! . . . No trouble about that, sir!" . . . I heard these things on all sides and they were like balm to a fevered brain.[15]

And Dreiser also loved the decor and the meals.

It was a beautiful thing all told—its long cherry-wood, panelled halls . . . its heavy porcelain baths, its dainty staterooms fitted with lamps, bureaus, writing-desks, wash-stands, closets and the like. I liked the idea of dressing for dinner and seeing everything quite stately and formal. . . . And the bugler who bugled for dinner! That was a most musical sound he made, trilling the various quarters gaily, as much as to say, "This is a very joyous event, ladies and gentlemen; we are all happy; come, come; it is a delightful feast." One can understand how easy it was to forget, in spite of recent disastrous examples like the *Titanic,* that all this comfort and beauty was being carried by a mere "floating iron egg-shell."

On May 1, 1915, a reminder of this vulnerability was offered by the German government. Advertisements were run in a number of New York newspapers under the large black headline

NOTICE!:

TRAVELLERS intending to embark on the Atlantic voyage are reminded that a state of war exists between Germany and her allies and Great Britain and her allies; that the zone of war includes the waters adjacent to the British Isles; that in accordance with formal notice given by the Imperial German Government, vessels flying the flag of Great Britain, or of any of her allies, are liable to destruction in those waters, and that travellers sailing in the war zone on ships of Great Britain or her allies do so at their own risk.

This warning, signed by the German embassy, appeared next to the Cunard announcement of the sailing of the *Lusitania,* which was advertised as the "Fastest and Largest Steamer now in Atlantic Service," and it did make an impression, though not a significant one.[16] Reporters were all around the departure dock, interviewing passengers and crew because of the notice, and everyone's luggage was thoroughly checked at boarding. All seem to have been reassured by the great speed of the ship, its excellent safety features—including many watertight bulkheads—and the skill of an experienced captain. They probably also hoped there would be some added protection in that both the German and the British navies knew that its first-class section would be populated with rich and famous Americans. Only one passenger, a cautious minister from New England, seems to have changed his mind about making the trip.

It was a pleasant voyage, with mild weather, smooth seas, the usual good food, and good company. Notables in first class included the fabulously wealthy Alfred Gwynne Vanderbilt, on his way to visit his English estate; Charles Frohman, the most successful of Broadway producers; Charles Klein, a popular playwright; Parry Jones, a famous Welch tenor; and Elbert Hubbard, an eccentric American philosopher who had written "A Message to Garcia," widely memorized by American schoolchildren to instill a dedication to duty and following orders. A more recent Hubbard effort was a criticism of the kaiser entitled "Who Lifted the Lid Off Hell." Most of those on board, though, were of more common clay, and filled the second- and third-class sections. Among them were a number of Irish and English maids returning to their homelands.

As they drew close to the southern Irish coast, none of the passengers were aware that ships had been sunk in the area since they had sailed from New York. However, some had been concerned enough by the German embassy's printed warning to ask Captain William Thomas Turner to conduct some serious boat drills that would inform passengers where to report and how to conduct themselves. Turner, however, declined, evidently feeling it would be a bother, and that the true safety of his ship lay in her speed. Submarines could manage only 9 knots underwater, and 15 on the surface, while the *Lusitania,* with revolutionary turbine engines, had reached a speed of 25 knots on her sea trials, had won the blue riband as fastest liner on the Atlantic run.

But that had been in 1907. What the passengers did not know was that the owners had ordered that six of the twenty-six boilers were to be shut down to save on fuel and labor costs, so speed had been compromised. Nor were they told that Turner had received several wireless messages warning him that submarines were active in the Irish Sea, so he should avoid headlands, where they often lurked, and take evasive action. Unfortunately, for all his skill and long peaceful years of ordinary service in running such a leviathan, the captain was evidently ignorant about proper wartime tactics, believing that one should begin to zigzag only after a submarine was sighted, rather than pursue such an erratic course whenever the predators were reported nearby. Full of unfounded confidence, on Friday, May 7,

1915, he reduced his speed even further so as not to arrive off Liverpool before full tide.

It was just nine minutes past two when the torpedo, packed with 290 pounds of the explosive trotyl, ripped a hole about forty feet by fifteen feet in the starboard side of the ship. Now the lack of drills and specific instructions for the passengers led to bewildered men and women on the edge of panic hunting desperately for life jackets and boats, only to find in many cases that these could not be lowered because of the angle of the list. Gentlemen aboard tried to maintain an example of calmness. Alfred Vanderbilt was seen easily chatting with a friend and holding in his right hand a purple leather jewelry case. "In my eyes," reported a survivor, "he was the figure of a gentleman waiting for a train."[17] Vanderbilt was later reported helping children find their way to possible safety, and giving up his life jacket to a woman; he was not the only one who lived up to the gentleman's code, holding back while others rushed for the boats. One amiable Missourian, who seems to have spent the whole voyage playing poker and quaffing beer, stepped up to the bar when everybody else fled and ordered another bottle, saying to the bartender, "Let's die game, anyway."

However, that worthy replied, "You go to hell," and ran. The Missourian finished his beer.[18]

There must have been some general sense that things would sort themselves out soon enough. They were not far from the port of Queenstown, British navy ships were nearby, and even the *Titanic*, hull ripped open for hundreds of feet by an iceberg, had managed to stay afloat for two and a half hours.

But there was not much time for panic or calm indifference or sorting out. In spite of her modern design and numerous watertight compartments, the ship floated for only eighteen minutes before she slid, hissing and groaning, into the deep. So fast had she sunk that hundreds of screaming passengers were trapped belowdecks while hundreds more were pulled down into the vortex of water that churned around her descent. So fickle is fate that the beer drinker was still in the bar when the ship capsized, and came back to consciousness as he was being hauled into a small boat. *Kapitänleutnant* Walter Schwieger, commander of *Unterseeboot*-20, watched through a periscope as his latest victim rolled over and began its plunge, the name *Lusitania* glowing in gold letters on its stern.

Soon the bodies gathered from the sea were being stacked on the docks of Queenstown like cordwood. In all, 1,198 men, women, and children were lost, of which 128 were Americans. Included among the dead were Vanderbilt, Frohman, Mr. and Mrs. Hubbard, Klein, and Mr. and

Mrs. Paul Crompton of Philadelphia and their six children, though only three of these small corpses were ever recovered. One survivor reported that the women acted stoically, "except for occasional screams of 'Where is my husband?' 'Where is my child?' "[19]

The outrage in America was immediate, enormous, and widespread, notwithstanding a couple of newspapers in St. Louis and Milwaukee, German American strongholds, that actually defended the action. Most followed the *New York Times* in condemning the Germans for making "war like savages drunk with blood."[20] Many references were made to the *Maine,* the U.S. Navy warship whose sinking in Havana harbor in 1898 had brought on the Spanish-American War; the *Literary Digest* pointed out that "condemnation of the act seems to be limited only by the restrictions of the English language."[21]

Edward House, Wilson's close adviser, was in London on one of the peace missions that the president hoped would lead to an American-mediated end to the war. At a formal dinner given by the embassy that night, he assured the British guests that the United States would be at war with Germany within a month. Ambassador Page agreed, and cabled the president: "The United States must declare war or forfeit European respect. So far as I know, this opinion is universal."[22] That Sunday, ministers across the land condemned the sinking of a passenger liner as no different from murder, while other previously unconvinced citizens added their voices to the call for war. Theodore Roosevelt, in the middle of a trial for libel brought by a corrupt Republican political boss, was advised not to comment, because there were German Americans on the jury who seemed to be supporters of the German war effort. Nevertheless, he told a *New York Times* reporter that it was an act of murderous piracy, and wrote an angry article for *Metropolitan* magazine entitled "Murder on the High Seas." Former president William Howard Taft wrote Wilson that he was sure that the nation and Congress would support a presidential demand for war.[23]

Count von Bernstorff was traveling to New York with the pro-German financier Paul Warburg to attend a fund-raising gala for the German Red Cross at the Metropolitan Opera House, and was met on the quay by Warburg's partner, Jacob Schiff, who gave them news of the disaster. It did not take long for reporters to lay siege to the count at the Ritz Carlton, while the Met asked that the fund-raiser, a performance of *Lohengrin,* by German composer Richard Wagner, be canceled. That request was refused, but Bernstorff stayed away, sending the attachés Papen and Boy-Ed in his place. "While the performance aroused scenes of great enthusiasm in the auditorium," Papen later remembered, "Boy-Ed and I were publicly insulted during the interval by a group of British and American journalists, and the violence of the street demonstrations outside left us in no doubt about the rift that had been caused between the two countries."[24]

Nor did Bernstorff have any doubt as he was chased about New York by packs of reporters before finally escaping by train to the District of Columbia and the refuge of his embassy. All his previous work at cultivating the press had now gone for naught, and as he read newspapers from across the country he became convinced, like many others, that war with the United States was likely. He later wrote that if Wilson had pushed for war he would "have had American public opinion more decidedly behind him than it was later, at the time of the final breach. Not a voice would have been raised in opposition, except that of the Secretary of State, Mr. Bryan."[25]

But perhaps this is a misreading. Though emotions and rhetoric ran hot across the country, in the West and Midwest they cooled rather rapidly. Secretary of Agriculture David Houston, in Los Angeles for a meeting with businessmen, was surprised that they only "talked for a few minutes about the tragedy without excitement," then dropped the subject. "Nor did any reporter of any local newspaper seek to interview me on the matter. No citizen brought it up during the remainder of my stay in the West, which lasted several weeks."[26] Theodore Roosevelt, to his frustration, was informed by a friend that the sense of outrage in the Midwest had "died down as suddenly as it had risen."[27] Perhaps the Detroit industrialist Henry Ford reflected the views of many in the region when he opined, "Well, they were fools to go on that boat, because they were warned."[28] For most Americans the sinking was a barbarous act, and could not be tolerated, but as to what actions should be taken—none of that was clear.

Woodrow Wilson deliberately kept an air of secluded calm. On Sunday, the ninth, he attended church, then played a round of golf and went for a drive in the country. That night he sat at his old typewriter to write a draft of a letter of protest to the German government that he would discuss with his Cabinet, and also to work on a speech he was to give in Philadelphia the next day. Far better than most other politicians, he understood that his country, though angry, was not ready to relinquish its pacifist stand. Unfortunately, he was in a highly emotional state himself, because of not just the tragedy at sea but also his own turbulent relationship with Edith Bolling Galt, who just days before had refused to accept his proposal. The result was that he did not pay as close attention to the Philadelphia speech as he later wished that he had.

Almost five thousand new citizens were being sworn in that Monday evening in the Quaker City's Convention Hall; to them and their thousands of relatives and friends he praised the special nature of America that came from diverse peoples living peacefully with one another and with other countries of the world. "America must have the consciousness that on all sides it touches elbows and touches heart with all the nations of mankind. The example of America must be a special example, and must be an example not merely of peace because it will not fight, but because peace is a healing and elevating influence of the world and strife is not." And then he went on to sound a note rather like a schoolmarm arguing for order in a playground or a mother lecturing her son: "There is such a thing as a man being too proud to fight. There is such a thing as a nation being so right that it does not need to convince others by force that it is right."[29]

The crowd applauded, of course, waving the little American flags that were even then being handed out on such occasions. More broadly, many in the nation, especially in the South and West, also applauded the argument for peace, if not the prissy language, but there were others, abroad and at home, who condemned the backing away from taking a stand on an atrocity that had killed so many innocents. A young army lieutenant named George Patton wrote to his father: "I think that we ought to declare war. . . . If Wilson had as much blood in him as the liver of a louse is commonly thought to contain he would do this."[30] And a superior officer, General John J. Pershing, shared his outrage, though discreetly. The most outspoken of all critics, as might be expected, was Theodore Roosevelt, still bitter after the defeat in 1912, who thought Wilson's response reflected cowardice, and who sarcastically argued that such a philosophy would cost the United States "the position won for it by the men who fought under Washington and by the men who, in the days of Lincoln, wore the blue under Grant and the gray under Lee."[31] The *New York Herald* ran a giant headline:

WHAT A PITY THEODORE ROOSEVELT
IS NOT PRESIDENT

Wilson himself belatedly recognized his error, and at a press conference the next day tried to explain that he was not speaking to the *Lusitania* disaster or any connected policy. "I was expressing a personal attitude, that was all. . . . I did not regard that as a proper occasion to give any intimation of policy on any special matter."[32] To the woman who now dominated his emotions, he wrote, "I do not know just what I said in Philadelphia . . . because my heart was in such a whirl."[33]

Certainly the note that the president presented for discussion to his Cabinet on Tuesday was not a meek turning of the cheek, or a return to remembered motherly strictures about genteel behavior. There was a lively discussion on the proper response to the murder of 128 Americans who had peaceably been going about their business when attacked. Again it was Secretary of State Bryan who stood for moderation, while other members of the Cabinet argued for strong language. At one point during the three-hour meeting Bryan became angry, and made clear that he thought that some present were not neutral, but were willing to risk war against Germany. At this the president himself grew steely, and said, "Mr. Bryan, you are not warranted in making such an assertion."[34]

The secretary apologized, but continued to argue for a softening of tone. That softening did not appear in the official note of May 13, which essentially demanded that the attacks on unarmed merchantmen and liners stop, but Wilson did make his points like a gentleman, politely and without threats. The note pointed out, among other things, that American citizens had the right to travel the ocean in "confidence that their lives will not be endangered by acts done in clear violation of universally acknowledged international obligations." The unlawfulness of submarine warfare was also noted because they "cannot be used against merchantmen . . . without an inevitable violation of many sacred principles of justice and humanity." And the last sentence made a particularly strong statement: "The Imperial German Government will not expect the Government of the United States to omit any word or any act necessary to the performance of its sacred duty of maintaining the rights of the United States and its citizens and safeguarding their free exercise and enjoyment."[35]

Wilson had taken these positions assuming that the German government and people would be as horrified as the rest of the world by the scale of the *Lusitania* tragedy, by the number of women and children that had been killed if nothing else. In this he was wrong. The German press and public supported the sinking of the passenger liner, much newspaper commentary sounding like the *Hamburg Correspondent,* which emphasized the *Schrecklichkeit* effect: "Now the sinking of their proudest ship has reminded them [the British] in a terrible way of the seriousness of the situation, and it will fill the entire nation with horror."[36]

German officials made various charges about the *Lusitania* being a munitions carrier and an auxiliary ship of the British navy, but none of that was relevant to the question of its appropriateness as a target. The liner had carried four or five thousand cases of small-arms cartridges, but that was not illegal, nor was there a danger of secondary explosions from such a cargo.[37] There were also charges that she had been secretly outfitted with large cannon that were somehow disguised behind false bulkheads. A German American dockworker named Gustav Stahler came forward to testify, perhaps at the instigation of the German embassy, that he had seen these clever emplacements, but he turned out to be lying, later confessed to perjury, and ended up in federal prison.

The German government does not seem to have taken the president's first note very seriously, feeling perhaps that Wilson's earlier hesitations had come from weakness rather than a patient hope that some peaceful resolution could be found. They also may have believed a rumor making the rounds in Berlin that Count Constantin Dumba, the Austrian ambassador to the United States, had been told by William Jennings Bryan that the Lusitania note was not seriously meant, but sent only as a sop to American public opinion.

From Berlin, Ambassador James Gerard reported this rumor to Washington on May 22.[38] Bryan denied ever saying it, as did Count Dumba, but the controversy further weakened the secretary of state's position. When the official German reply finally came and was found unsatisfactory, Wilson decided that he had to send a second, even more strongly worded note to make his position absolutely clear. "The sinking of passenger ships involves principles of humanity which throw into the background any special circumstances of detail that may be thought to affect the cases, principles which lift it . . . out of the class of ordinary subjects of diplomatic discussion or of international controversy." And the president argued that his government was "contending for nothing less high and sacred than the rights of humanity."[39]

William Jennings Bryan had again argued for a milder tone, but was ignored. The president had over the months lost faith in his secretary's judgment, and Bryan, recognizing this, resigned rather than agree to what he saw as a path toward war. From now on he would be outside the governmental tent, and using his still considerable prestige with the party faithful to fight what he saw as forces desiring to take America into the conflict. To add to his anguish, he was replaced by a man he saw as contributing to those forces, the State Department counselor Robert Lansing.

A fierce debate began within the German government over the proper course of action regarding American demands. One of the Kaiser's many flaws was indecisiveness, and he wavered now when faced with contradictory advice. Grand Admiral von Tirpitz and the navy demanded free use of their undersea weapon; Chancellor von Bethmann-Hollweg and civilian officials, supported by Ambassador von Bernstorff, recognized the enormous potential power of the United States, and resisted. The army, for the time being, supported the civilians. Ambassador Gerard in Berlin wrote Wilson that "it is the German hope to keep the Lusitania matter 'jollied along' until the American people get excited about baseball or a new scandal and forget. Meanwhile the hate of America grows daily."[40] The purpose of the "jollying along" was to provide time to build up the German submarine fleet to a size where it could resist any American protests with impunity.

But the *Lusitania* had been a watershed. Count von Bernstorff later said that during the first part of the war "the Belgian question was the one which interested Americans most and which was most effective in working up American public opinion against us."[41] After the sinking of the liner, he recognized that no German propaganda could be effective.

Many influential Americans had their viewpoints changed by the sinking. Robert Lansing, the new secretary of state, became convinced that German ruthlessness threatened, as he recorded in his personal diary in that month of May, "the overthrow of democracy in the world, the suppression of individual liberty, the setting up of evil ambitions, the subordination of the principles of right and justice to physical might directed by arbitrary will, and the turning back of the hands of human progress two centuries."[42]

Jacob Schiff, the brilliant German Jewish American financier who had felt bonds of loyalty to Germany—the country "of my birth, the country in which my ancestors lived for many centuries"—now experienced a change of heart.[43] "But ever since the sinking of the Lusitania and the subsequent ruthless and inhuman acts of the German Government, my attitude has undergone a thorough change, and I now only hope that before very long Great Britain and France will be able to force a peace which shall prevent the return of conditions that have brought upon the world the present ghastly situation."[44]

The crisis muted, for a time, the wrangling with Great Britain over the illegal Allied restrictions on American overseas trade. "The first German U-boat campaign," Winston Churchill wrote after the war, "gave us our greatest assistance. It altered the whole position of our controversies with America. A great relief became immediately apparent."[45]

Wilson would spend the next year trying to convince the Germans to give up "unrestricted" submarine warfare, to cease sinking noncombatant ships without warning, and would have temporary success after another British liner, the *Arabic,* was sunk in August 1915 with the loss of American lives. So strong was the president's message at that time that the German government issued the so-called *Arabic* pledge. As Ambassador von Bernstorff then publicly announced: "Liners will not be sunk by our submarines without warning and without safety of the lives of noncombatants, provided that the liners do not try to escape or offer resistance."[46] But this seeming resolution would be only temporary.

WHILE THE UNITED STATES was still raging at the loss of civilian lives on the *Lusitania,* the Bryce Commission, which had been charged by the British government to investigate the reports of German atrocities in Belgium, issued its findings. Viscount James Bryce was a historian and diplomat with unusual prominence in the United States, for he had not only served as ambassador to Washington between 1907 and 1913, but had also written *The American Commonwealth,* a brilliant exploration of this country and its system of government that had borrowed liberally from the work of Woodrow Wilson.[47] In addition, Bryce could not be automatically discounted as a "Hun-hater," because he had been awarded honorary degrees from German universities, and also received a decoration from the kaiser before the war.

His committee had been made up of men of reputation as fair-minded scholars and editors, but most of the collection of evidence had been left to staffers without rigorous standards of proof. They had interviewed Belgian refugees in England, as well as British and Belgian soldiers, and taken depositions from 1,200 people. They had also studied diaries taken from dead or captured German soldiers.

Printed in the *Report of the Committee on the Alleged German Atrocities,* released in America on May 12, 1915, was tale after tale of torture, rapes, murders, hideous mutilations of men, women, children, and even babes in arms. "The soldier," asserted one refugee who claimed to be a witness, "drove his bayonet with both hands into the child's stomach, lifting the child into the air on his bayonet, he and his comrades still singing." That the most extreme of these stories were made up is hard to doubt at this date, and some neutral voices pointed that out at the time. But there was no denying the cold-blooded invasion of a country that Germany was bound by treaty to protect, the burning of Louvain, and the execution of hundreds of civilians. There could be no denying the German introduction of poison gas and the flamethrower to the battlefields of Europe or the quietly murderous submarine to the struggle for control of the Atlantic.

Americans particularly, with their respect for women and children, their ideal of fair play, and their patriotic certitude that their soldiers would never behave like such beasts, built on their earlier revulsion over the destruction and death the Germans had committed in Belgium. Outrage leaped even higher since the report came so close on the terrible event in the Irish Sea, where unquestionably defenseless women and children were killed, including dozens of infants under the age of two. American belief in even the most unlikely atrocities was widespread, and deeply felt.

Brand Whitlock, who had already witnessed so much German ruthlessness in Brussels, was horrified by the sinking of the *Lusitania*. "To think of it," he wrote in his journal, "all those innocent non-combatants, women, children! Oh, what glorious martial courage to steal up, armoured, safe, and deal that murderous blow! Why, it is more than piracy! . . . The cowards!" When another member of the American embassy staff told a high-ranking German official that the United States would not stand for such despicable actions, the German, spreading his arms out wide, said dramatically, "If we have to fight the whole world we will do it."[48]

CHAPTER TEN

The War Comes Home

To narrate, to stimulate, to perpetuate.

D. W. Griffith on the purpose of motion pictures[1]

Blackton's film has done more for the Allied cause than twenty battalions of soldiers.

Theodore Roosevelt[2]

THOUGH COUNT VON BERNSTORFF had more or less promised to behave, there were events occurring in the early part of 1915 that raised suspicions in the government that German agents had continued to violate American laws even after the exposure of the passport fraud. There were, for example, a series of mysterious fires on ships carrying cargo to the Allies, and a number of unexploded time bombs that were found aboard others, while sabotage and wildcat strikes were occurring in munitions plants. In May 1915 the president had the Treasury Department's Secret Service broaden its investigation of German embassy activities directed against the United States. This increased surveillance led to a chase scene in New York City that resulted in an important counterintelligence coup, but it was unable to prevent several other tragedies.

Much of the prosperity that had come to America with the war orders was rolling through the doors of the House of Morgan. The firm became not only broker for Allied bond sales but, even more important, their major purchasing agent for war matériel, an arrangement that increased efficiency for the British and French by reducing the profiteering of middlemen. Rewards for Morgan were not only the tens of millions of dollars in commissions, but also political and business contacts that would continue to pay dividends through the next several decades. Edward R. Stettinius, a man dedicated to work and the exploitation of details, was recruited to head the operation, and he did it so well that threats by German agents were made against his family and his life; he ended up living on a secure ship in New York harbor.[3]

J. P. Morgan, Jr., known as Jack to his friends, became the lightning rod for criticism about the munitions trade. Seen as a merchant of death by pacifists, and recognized as an active enemy by Germans and German Americans, there had been threats against him and other Morgan partners besides Stettinius, but very little had been done to protect them.

Jack Morgan was even more of an Anglophile than most members of the eastern establishment. Much of the family fortune had come through close alliances with British finance, and he owned a large estate in England where he usually spent six months of the year; he donated his grandfather's English country house to be used for British officers recovering from their wounds. He was friends with a number of British politicians, and particularly close with Sir Cecil Spring-Rice, the ambassador to Washington.

Sir Cecil and his wife were visiting the Morgans at their mansion on the North Shore of Long Island, on the Saturday morning of July 3, 1915. The two couples were enjoying breakfast and discussing a mysterious bombing that had taken place the day before at the Capitol building in Washington, when a visitor came to the front door. He offered a card to the butler that read SUMMER SOCIETY DIRECTORY, REPRESENTED BY THOMAS C. LESTER, and insisted that he had to see Mr. Morgan immediately. When the butler, Henry Physick, tried to direct him to a waiting room, the stranger pushed past him, causing the surprised Physick to call out a warning, "Upstairs!"[4]

Jack Morgan and his wife, Jessie, wondering what Physick could have meant, left their guests, hurried up the back stairs, and searched the second floor, trying to understand his cry. After a few minutes of confusion, they spotted the intruder leading their two daughters up the main stairway, a pistol in each hand. Luckily, his position in front of the girls made him vulnerable; Jessie charged, followed by the heavyweight and somewhat slower reacting Jack, who, though shot twice in the groin, knocked the fellow down. Servants arrived to pile on, the guns were wrested away, and a stick of dynamite found in the gunman's pocket was drowned in a bucket of water.

Over the next few days it was learned that the man, who first gave his name as Frank Holt, was really Erich Muenter, a former teacher of German at Harvard. Muenter had disappeared in 1906 after having been indicted for poisoning his wife. The attack on the Morgans was the second blow against America he had performed in as many days. On the second of July he had placed a time bomb in the U.S. Capitol, then boarded a night train to New York so he could appear at the Morgan house the next morning.

It is probably too late now to determine whether Muenter had been inspired in his act by German agents, but given the other criminal activities they were instigating, it is possible. The news of the shooting, writes a Morgan biographer, was celebrated in Vienna "by fireworks, speeches, and jubilant crowds."[5] Certainly Jack Morgan, who recovered more quickly from his physical wounds than the psychological ones, believed that there had been a plot. He fired all German and Austrian employees at his Adirondack estate, hired a team of ex-marines as bodyguards, and when he traveled kept his name off hotel registers, "owing to the fact that . . . the Germans are still after me."[6]

Less than a month later, on Saturday, July 24, 1915, a Secret Service agent named W. H. Houghton followed George Sylvester Viereck, publisher of the pro-German—and, as it turned out, heavily German subsidized—newspaper *The Fatherland,* to the offices of the Hamburg-American steamship line at 45 Broadway in New York. Suspecting that Viereck would be leaving with someone important, Houghton telephoned another agent, Frank Burke, to join him.

At three o'clock Viereck exited the building with a tall, middle-aged man carrying a thick briefcase, whose face was marked with the saber scars that upper-class Germans made a point of collecting during their student dueling days. The agents later discovered that this imposing figure was Dr. Heinrich Albert, commercial attaché to the German embassy. Viereck and Albert walked through the hot city streets to the Sixth Avenue elevated, trailed by the Secret Service men, and took seats on the train. Burke sat close enough to hear them conversing in German; when Viereck got off at Twenty-third Street, he was followed by Houghton.

Dr. Albert lost himself in a book as the train rattled up to Fiftieth Street, then suddenly recognizing his stop, jumped to his feet and ran to the rear exit, leaving his stuffed briefcase behind.

Burke, seeing his chance, quickly grabbed the bag and rushed to the front exit, while Dr. Albert, now realizing his mistake, reentered and tried to make his own dash to his old seat, but was blocked by a large older woman in the aisle. Several minutes of hide-and-seek ensued on the platform as Burke clutched the case to his chest, used passersby as cover, and, turning to a wall as if seeking protection from the wind, pretended to be trying to light a cigar while instead gently blowing out each match until Albert left the station.

However, the German had waited outside and spotted Burke as he descended the stairs with his briefcase. He chased the younger Secret Service agent down the block in the humid heat of the afternoon until Burke jumped onto the running board of a moving streetcar, and told the conductor that he was being pursued by a crazy man who had just caused trouble on the elevated. The conductor, looking up and seeing the wild-eyed, angrily contorted scarred face of Dr. Albert, signaled the motorman to keep going and not to stop for several blocks.

Burke called William J. Flynn, head of the Secret Service, and Flynn telegraphed his boss, William McAdoo, who was vacationing on the island of North Haven, Maine. McAdoo had Flynn bring the purloined briefcase to the island, where they went carefully through the contents. What they found was so shocking that McAdoo immediately took the material to his father-in-law, who, exhausted and feeling ill, was summering in Cornish, New Hampshire. Most of the documents were disguised and indirect enough to prevent legal action, McAdoo later wrote, "yet they showed plainly enough that illegitimate activities were going on; that our neutrality laws were being grossly violated."[7]

The president, however, was still not interested in directly confronting the German government, so he had Colonel House, McAdoo, and Secretary of State Lansing decide how the papers should be handled. These three leaked some of the documents to Frank Cobb, a Wilson ally and editor of the *New York World*, and the story was picked up nationwide. The public uproar was of the volume that McAdoo had hoped for: "It was a startling disclosure of what was going on under the surface of events."[8] Among those revelations were proofs of German attempts to buy American newspapers to spread their propaganda, and the payment of large subsidies to periodicals such as Viereck's *The Fatherland*, which was receiving $1,500 a month. They were also publishing books and financing motion pictures that supported their point of view, and trying to buy the Wright Aeroplane Company in order to control its patents. Even worse were payments to corrupt union leaders to promote strikes in munition factories, and attempts to "influence," or bribe, American legislators to embargo shipments of munitions. One of the cleverer schemes involved Franz von Papen, the German military attaché, who had bought a large munitions factory, the Bridgeport Projectile Company, in Connecticut, using American citizen George Hoadley as a front. The plant took orders for shells from the British and Russians but, of course, never planned to make delivery, and it also, Papen later bragged, tied up the "Aetna Powder Company's whole capacity for the production of gunpowder until the end of 1915, with an order for five million lbs."[9]

The same propaganda techniques of subsidy and influence were also being used by the Allies, but more subtly and without careless disclosures. Now almost all pro-German writing or speech-giving was quickly discounted as bought and paid for, but the other revelations seemed far more sinister, striking at the integrity of American society, its very productivity and prosperity, through attempts to corrupt politicians, businessmen, and unions. After the war, Viereck admitted, "The publication of the Albert papers was a German catastrophe. . . . It was a veritable nest of intrigue, conspiracy, and propaganda that reposed placidly in Dr. Albert's brief-case. The inner workings of the propaganda machine were laid bare."[10] And he compared the loss of the portfolio to the loss of the Battle of the Marne, which had cost Germany the capture of Paris and an early victory.

House, Lansing, and McAdoo had hoped that such wide exposure would cause the Germans to reconsider their actions. It did not. These discoveries, however shocking, were not complete, for there was much more going on "under the surface of events."

German sabotage and interference with American life became even more intense after the capture of the Albert briefcase. American counter-intelligence, often helped by the British, was closely following some of the agents. One of the most active of these men was Franz Rintelen, who attached an aristocratic "von" to his name for cachet. Rintelen was a secret operative in charge of setting up sabotage and espionage nets, but he was possessed by such a grandiose ego that working secretly was beyond him. He had presented himself at Papen's New York office in April 1915 and told him that he was going to be carrying out acts of sabotage, organizing strikes of longshoremen, and placing bombs aboard ships. Papen was shocked not by the plans, but by the man's openness in showing up at his office. "And with these plans in your head," he said, "you pay your first visit in the United States to the German military attaché! Don't you realize that everyone who comes to this office is photographed and shadowed by the British or American Secret Service?"

"That does not matter in the least," Rintelen said. "I have no intention of hiding. As a matter of fact, what I would really like is an interview with President Wilson. I would like to have a really long talk with him, and I thought you might be able to arrange it."[11]

Such a grandiose ambition could not, of course, be arranged. His lack of discretion led to more trouble for him and his compatriots. Rintelen had been a banker in the United States before the war, with a wide circle of friends, and when he happened to run into Anne Seward at several dinner parties during the summer of 1915, he evidently bragged to her of his importance and made threats against the country. Miss Seward, a niece of Abraham Lincoln's secretary of state, with some hesitation wrote to President Wilson of her suspicions, asking that he probe "a sinister situation or one which points to organized antagonism."[12] The probing began quickly, and it discovered the organized antagonism.

In this the Americans had help. Emanuel Victor Voska was a Czech who as a youth had been forced into exile because of his association with socialists and because he was working for Czech independence from the Austro-Hungarian Empire. He had made a fortune in the United States, then used his money to support Tomás Masaryk's struggle for for a Czech state. One avenue to that independence was through the defeat of the Austrians and their ally Germany in the war, and to that end Voska organized an extremely effective network of Czechs to spy for the Allies. He had agents in both the German and Austrian embassies, in their missions and consulates, and even in their boudoirs—the maid of Ambassador Bernstorff's wife was one of his people.[13]

Rintelen, for all his poor tradecraft, was intelligent, effective, and motivated. From his long experience in the United States, he, like Bernsdorff, realized the latent power the country possessed to decide the war.

Rintelen had met with General Victoriano Huerta in Spain in February 1915, promising him help in reestablishing his dictatorship in Mexico because the German government was sure that he could cause the United States enough trouble to distract them from the European war. Huerta then traveled to New York, where he proudly told American newsmen that he would soon be back in charge south of the border. More secret were his conferences with Rintelen, attended as well by the German naval and military attachés Papen and Boy-Ed, regarding weapon shipments and money—evidently the German government was willing to commit $12 million to the attempted coup. Emanuel Voska had managed to place one of his Czech operatives at a high level in the German embassy, and this man had personally been given the assignment by Bernstorff to rent the New York suite in which the meetings were held. Voska's people wired the room, using the best equipment available, which happened to have been made in Germany, and kept close track of the negotiations. Huerta then traveled on to the border, where his timely death under obscure circumstances put an end to this German plot, though not to others.

Among Rintelen's failings was his inability to work well with the embassy staff. Demands from Papen and Boy-Ed, combined with the growing American attention being paid to his activities, resulted in his being recalled by Berlin in July 1915. The British intercepted him on the way home, having been informed by Voska of the alias on his fake Swiss passport. Rintelen ended up cooperating with British intelligence, then being prosecuted by the Americans and spending four years at the federal prison in Atlanta. After the war he wrote a book about his exploits, some of them true, that he titled, with his usual self-dramatizing flair, *The Dark Invader.*

Emanuel Voska's efficient organization, aided by the British officer Guy Gaunt, was distributing much of what it learned to the press, and by the end of 1915 hundreds of stories, editorials, and cartoons were appearing in American newspapers about German sabotage, spying, and conspiracies. These plots were often connected in print to members of the German American community, but one of Voska's greatest coups was exposing an Anglo-American courier for the Germans, a journalist named James F. J. Archibald. When Archibald's ship was stopped by the British in late August 1915, his papers were seized, and they were immediately published, publicly revealing all sorts of secrets. Austrian ambassador Baron Dumba had written reports on strikes that had been organized among Hungarian workers in American factories; there were records of sabotage activities, including reports by Papen and Boy-Ed; the connection of these attachés with the dangerous Mexican unrest was also detailed. As a bonus, there was a personal letter from Papen to his wife in which he expressed contempt for his hosts, and their attitude toward German war practices: "I always say to these idiotic Yankees that they should shut their mouths, and better still be full of admiration."[14]

These revelations led to Dumba being expelled in September. Consideration was given to asking that Bernstorff be recalled, but Wilson feared that this would be seen as too close a step to the breaking of relations and, perhaps, war. He also hoped that Bernstorff could be helpful in his continuing plans to bring peace between the belligerents through mediation.

Papen and Boy-Ed lasted a couple more months, but then they began to be named by arrested German agents. Secretary of State Lansing announced on December 1, 1915, that they were personae non grata. The two men were expelled, but the efficient sabotage rings they and Rintelen had established remained and continued to do their work.

Papen, perhaps following in the footsteps of his ambassador, fancied himself something of a Lothario, and as his personal effects and professional records were being crated for shipment back to Germany, he allowed his attention to wander to a young secretary in the office. He charmed her so quickly that right then and there she took a heavy red crayon pencil and drew two large red hearts on the top of the crate, then Papen took the pencil and put an arrow through the hearts.[15] It is unclear what romantic events, if any, followed these sweet gestures, but she was one of Voska's operatives making sure that the British would be able to easily identify the box in the crowded hold of the ship when they stopped it. Papen had been given a safe conduct through the blockade and had naively assumed it extended to his papers, so he had left behind nothing. In these were notes and check stubs that proved he had been paymaster to saboteurs, and this evidence, which the British were quick to publicize, reignited the firestorm of anger against Germans and German Americans. Papen himself returned to Germany, where in 1933 he would help Adolf Hitler rise to power.

Woodrow Wilson, whose attitude toward military preparedness had been changed at least partly through what he saw as the danger of German American disloyalty, referred to this fear in his State of the Union address on December 7, 1915, while at the same time asking for a strengthening of American military and naval forces: "There are citizens of the United States, . . . born under other flags but welcomed under our generous naturalization laws to the full freedom and opportunity of America, who have poured the poison of disloyalty into the very arteries of our national life; who have sought to bring the authority and good name of our Government into contempt, to destroy our industries wherever they thought it effective for their vindictive purposes to strike at them, and to debase our politics to the uses of foreign intrigue. . . . [They] must be crushed out. . . . The hand of our power should close over them at once."

THE PREPAREDNESS movement gathered strength after the sinking of the *Lusitania* and the increasing exposures of illicit German activity in the United States. More and more people began to believe in a German—often referred to as a Prussian—conspiracy to dominate the world. They were aided in this by skillful British propaganda, but also by the sincere efforts of Americans who fully accepted the Allied argument that they were defending civilization against a barbaric militarism, and who feared that the United States would be the next victim of aggression.

American women, as we have noted before, felt a particular affection and responsibility for France. Frances Wilson Huard, who fled from the German advance with her servants and belongings, had returned to her chateau in the village of Villiers-Saint-Denis to find that the American flag she had draped over her personal belongings had not protected them, and had, in fact, been foully desecrated. She wrote several books during the war, including *My Home in the Field of Honor,* illustrated by her French artist husband, Charles, relating the stories of French civilian suffering and heroism. Mildred Aldrich, whom we also met earlier watching German airplanes from her house on the Marne, continued to reside at her hilltop villa, La Creste, observing and writing about the close-by fighting, and the lives of her villagers in a series of magazine articles and books that reached a large audience in the United States.

Alice B. Toklas and Gertrude Stein drove ambulances, while the California novelist Gertrude Atherton reported sympathetically from France. Edith Wharton, one of the most respected and successful of American writers, established workshops to help French women earn their living in the early days of the war, before it became obvious that munition factories would be hiring all the labor that could be found. She, even more effectively, wrote books supporting the French cause, then helped found an ambulance corps, a number of which were financed and staffed by Americans.

One of the most famous of these humanitarian efforts was the American Ambulance Field Service, which was manned, like its brother organization the Norton-Harjes Ambulance Service, mostly by idealistic and adventuresome graduates of elite colleges, such as Jack Reed's artist friend Waldo Peirce of Harvard and Carleton Pike of Bowdoin.[16] Several volunteers were killed or wounded in the line of duty, as were other Americans who took an even more active role in the fighting.

These volunteers fought in both British and French units, and as the war ground on several wrote best-selling books of their experiences. The most famous of all these warriors for the Allied cause in the early years was another Harvard friend of Reed's, the romantic poet Alan Seeger, who had joined the French Foreign Legion in September 1914. Seeger continued to write poetry that glorified war and the French cause, and also contributed articles along the same lines to the *New York Sun,* and to the *New Republic* magazine, where his Harvard classmate Walter Lippmann was a founding editor. One of Seeger's most quoted lines, "I have a rendezvous with Death at some disputed barricade," proved all too prophetic; he was killed at Verdun in the summer of 1916. Reed, though even more passionately against the war than he had been earlier, joined with other friends to organize a memorial edition of his work. The growing number of Allied partisans in the press also celebrated the fallen soldier-poet.

Another poet-volunteer with a similar rendezvous received a hero's accolades. Victor Chapman, son of the eccentric New England intellectual and political activist John Jay Chapman, also joined the Foreign Legion, then transferred to the Lafayette Escadrille, a fighter-plane squadron financed and piloted by American citizens. He, too, wrote home of his feelings of battling to save civilization from a barbarous militarism, and he, too, made the ultimate sacrifice for the cause, being shot down over Verdun, and in his death becoming famous.

VAUDEVILLE was the great public entertainer, but a younger, more technological sister art was gaining in popularity. Motion pictures were a European invention, and by 1895 the Lumière brothers were showing films to paying audiences in Paris. But many of the most important refinements and innovations were American, and America's greatest inventor and public hero, Thomas Edison, early put his stamp on the technology, demonstrating his Vitascope at Koster and Bial's Music Hall in New York in April 1896.

Very quickly, as was the American way in any new endeavor, numerous competitors jostled onto the field. Also in the American tradition, numerous lawsuits were filed as each distributor and exhibitor sought to inhibit as many of these competitors as possible, hoping to drive the weaker into bankruptcy and the stronger into weakness. Such a bloodletting could not last long, and the American solution was then struck: in 1908 a "trust," the Motion Picture Patent Company, was formed by Edison and American Biograph and others to consolidate power, control patents, and limit newcomers.

The earliest films were only a minute or two in length, showing farm scenes, locomotives pulling into a station, firemen responding to an alarm—just curiosities to draw the idle, take their nickels, show off the technology. Then the human need for narrative came into play, and story films were developed. The first real artistic and financial success was *The Great Train Robber*, directed in 1903 by the pioneer Edwin S. Porter, who cut back and forth between parallel scenes of action involving bandits, wearing black hats, and the sheriff's posse, wearing white hats, in order to build tension leading to an exciting climax. Many of these early dramas involved moral themes to reform or uplift their audiences, hoping to instill Victorian values in native sons and daughters, as well as the millions of new immigrants. But the risqué, even at this early date, was recognized as a moneymaker, resulting in titles such as *The Indiscretions of Betty* starring Mabel Normand, who later became the "Keystone Girl."

Documentaries, of a sort, were also popular. Cameramen did accompany the troops in the Spanish-American War of 1898, though in order to quickly satisfy an impatient public at home "reenactments" were often resorted to. Thomas Edison, for example, improved on history by showing Theodore Roosevelt's mounted Rough Riders attacking Spanish troops, even though the Rough Riders had not been allowed to take horses to Cuba; the film was actually shot in New Jersey using actors. A young innovator named J. Stuart Blackton also used the Spanish-American War; his short entitled *Tearing Down the . . . Flag* was the first propaganda film ever made. He had managed to produce footage of the Battle of Manila Bay by mounting photographs of Spanish and American ships on blocks of wood floating in a tub, setting off pinches of gunpowder every once in a while, and filming the action frame by frame.

By 1914 such crude studio fakery was unnecessary, and fakery in the field could be used. Arthur Sweetser was one of the American reporters who had rushed to the front in the first days of the war, traveling with German, Belgian, and French troops, and almost being shot as a spy by the latter. At one point he joined up with Phil Rader, a cameraman from Philadelphia, and they visited the closest town to Paris that the Germans had taken. "Somehow we . . . felt like ghouls as we moved about taking moving pictures. The earth seemed hallowed by the passions and struggles which had passed over it. The dead alone seemed to have title to it." But those dead were buried in graves so shallow that "in spots nests of maggots as big as one's fist were visible at their filthy work." Rather than film such disgusting reality, Sweetser posed as a more presentable German corpse, then he and Rader "worked other dodges of the movie game," before rushing back to the security and pleasures of Paris.[17]

Nickelodeons were the venue for early "flickers," and there were eight thousand of these crowded, noisy working-class theaters in the United States by 1908. The fact that the movies were silent, though often accompanied by live music, meant that everyone, no matter what their cultural background, could understand and enjoy the action. Louis B. Mayer, an immigrant from Russia, like a number of other ambitious young men, opened a nickelodeon in Haverhill, Massachusetts, then built on its success to start a chain of them throughout New England. "He had noticed," as the critic David Thomson puts it, "that people liked going into the dark to see the light."[18] Most of the story films shown were one-reelers, only ten minutes or so long, the same duration as a vaudeville act, but as people's expectations rose, and the middle class was increasingly drawn to theaters, the movies grew longer, tackling more complex themes.

The great breakthrough film, one that for the first time displayed the true power of the medium, was David Wark Griffith's *Birth of a Nation*, released in 1915. Griffith, a mediocre actor and failed playwright, had found his art in film. Starting in 1908 he directed a series of one-reel melodramas for the nickelodeons while learning his craft, turning it into narrative art by developing the close-up, backlighting, fade-ins, fade-outs, location shooting, night photography, parallel editing, and the moving camera. Born in 1875 in a Kentucky that was suffering from the aftereffects of the Civil War, and the son of an impoverished Confederate colonel of cavalry, he responded enthusiastically to Thomas Dixon's odious novel and play *The Clansman,* a celebration of the Ku Klux Klan's suppression of African Americans during the postwar years. Griffith supplemented this racist screed with memories of the stories his father had told him of service with General Joe Wheeler and material from another Dixon novel, *The Leopard's Spots,* as he assembled his ideas.

Shooting was difficult since few others believed the scale he envisioned for this epic, the first one ever filmed, was possible or profitable. In spite of his desperately tapping every source available to him, there was not enough money, but also there were not enough horses, because the British and French were buying all they could for the war. The same war shortage was true for "white goods," the thousands of yards of cotton sheets in which to robe the Ku Klux Klan. Griffith, enthralled by his vision, persisted through all the challenges, improvising and adapting until he had twelve reels completed—far more than any other American film made up to that time. He also commissioned an orchestral score to complement the action.

The unprecedented length worked against him, as few distributors wished to risk the booking; predictions were made of financial disaster, but the film proved an immediate, enormous success on its opening in New York in March 1915. The whole struggle—from peaceful plantation idyll, to spectacular battles, to the disorder of Reconstruction—swept in fluid dramatic rhythm across the screen, sweeping its audience along with it. The climax was the fight between blacks, depicted as subhuman, trying, among other outrages, to sully the purity of Anglo-Saxon womanhood. The Klan, riding hard, stops them just in time. Tens of thousands of people lined up, willing to pay the unprecedented price of two dollars to see such an extravagant romantic depiction of the war that had torn America apart and that still dominated its imagination. Woodrow Wilson watched it at the White House, but never publicly commented on it; the quote so often ascribed to him, that the film was "like writing history with lightning," was probably made up by a Hollywood press agent years later.[19]

The feeding of white America's racial prejudices did not diminish the film's appeal to a mass audience, but aroused great anger among African Americans and their allies. The National Association for the Advancement of Colored People published a pamphlet condemning *The Birth of a Nation,* theaters were picketed, and in Boston and other cities there were riots protesting its showing. White southerners had a different reaction; that summer of 1915 a group gathered at Stone Mountain, Georgia, to burn crosses to mark the twentieth-century rebirth of the Ku Klux Klan. But this was a Klan with a broader commandment of hate. No longer were blacks alone seen as the threat, included now were Roman Catholics and Jews. In 1915, there would be more than a hundred lynchings, but the most notorious was that of Leo Frank, a Jewish factory manager in Atlanta, who had been convicted, on questionable evidence, of raping a fourteen-year-old girl. When his death sentence was commuted, an armed group seized him from the state prison and lynched him. Through the next ten years the Klan would grow to be a political, and financial, power even outside the South.

Controversy brought publicity and, combined with the powerful narrative energy that supported long-held fantasies, helped make the film the greatest moneymaker of the silent era. Griffith gained a fortune, but so did numerous others, including film distributors such as Louis B. Mayer, who had been daring enough to buy New England rights to the film, and then discerning enough to realize how easily box-office revenues could be "adjusted" so extra profits could be skimmed. Such a great achievement served as the spur of ambition to others, who desired not just the financial and artistic rewards, but also the power to move the public's emotions that it had demonstrated.

J. Stuart Blackton had been an illustrator for Joseph Pulitzer's *New York World* when he met Thomas Edison, who liked his drawings so much that in 1896 he made a film called *Blackton, the Evening World Cartoonist.* The cartoonist decided to become a filmmaker himself, and with two other English immigrants started the Vitagraph Company in 1897, a couple of their earliest movies being the ones about the Spanish-American War mentioned above. Blackton directed and acted in many of their early productions, and developed single-frame cartoon animation as well as other technical innovations; he also helped start the first publication for movie fans in the United States, *Motion Picture Magazine.* As Englishmen, he and his partners proudly brought a number of Shakespeare's plays to the screen. Vitagraph became one of the most prosperous of the pioneer movie outfits. Blackton, nouveau riche and desiring to give himself a touch of class, spent $300,000 building an enormous Italianate mansion at Oyster Bay on the North Shore of Long Island, joined the Atlantic Yacht Club, became its "Commodore," and adopted that title as an honorific for the rest of his life.

Blackton supported the Allies in the war, and was a friend of Sir Gilbert Parker's, a popular Canadian novelist who was in charge of British propaganda for America. He was also close with members of the American preparedness movement, one of whom was Hudson Maxim, brother of Hiram Maxim, inventor of a particularly effective machine gun. Hudson Maxim was also a firearms inventor, losing his left hand while developing an explosive for use in torpedoes, and a type of smokeless powder that was being manufactured by the E. I. DuPont de Nemours Company. Blackton read a book Maxim had written entitled *Defenseless America,* which argued that it was time that the country enlarged its army and navy and prepared to defend itself against the aggressive powers of the world, such as Germany, who envied its riches, and that the United States could stay out of war only by becoming strong militarily.

Here, Blackton was convinced, was a perfect vehicle not only to awaken America to its need to prepare for war, but also to serve his personal ambitions. Film historian Kevin Brownlow believes that Blackton "saw a heaven-sent opportunity to garner some of the praise lavished on Griffith, and to cap the financial success of *The Birth of a Nation* with an even more profitable sensation."[20] It took Blackton only a few days to write a screenplay for *The Battle Cry of Peace,* which he then read to a neighbor at Oyster Bay, Theodore Roosevelt, who immediately recognized its potential for winning support for his own preparedness efforts. Roosevelt called a meeting of his allies, including Major General Leonard Wood; former secretary of war Elihu Root; the editor of *Outlook* magazine, Lyman Abbott; and the hero of Manila Bay, Admiral George Dewey. Each spoke strongly for preparedness, and when each fell silent, Roosevelt would add his own coda, barking, "Put *that* in your picture." Lyman Abbott, mild-mannered doctor of divinity and highly cultivated, spoke last. "I cannot think that all war is wrong. If I did I should not want to look upon a Bunker Hill monument—it would be a monument to our shame! I should never want to speak the name of Gettysburg. I should want to bury in the grave of oblivion the names of Washington and Grant." And Roosevelt crowed, "Get every word of that in your picture. Drive it home to the peace-at-any-price *creatures!*"[21]

The film certainly drove home the horror of brutal and unprovoked invasion. Only bits and pieces of *The Battle Cry of Peace* survive, but from reviews and contemporary accounts the narrative can be reconstructed. It opened with Hudson Maxim delivering a lecture in Carnegie Hall, flanked by maps of the New York area, ship models, high-explosive shells, and with his one hand resting on one of his brother's Maxim machine guns, which in his book he called "the greatest life-saving instrument ever invented." A young man who attends the lecture is convinced enough to work for preparedness, but his fiancée's millionaire father is a proponent of "peace at any price." The father is supported in this position by a close friend, a foreigner, who is a peace activist, but really, it is revealed, a spy and agent who bribes or otherwise influences American politicians not to build America's defensive strength. The invasion comes, New York and Washington are bombarded into ruins; soldiers of an unidentified country, whose acts echo those reported of the invaders of Belgium, indulge in rape, drunken looting, the burning of homes, and the murder of helpless civilians. All the principal characters are killed (the fiancée and her sister are shot by their mother when it becomes obvious that they are to be raped by the invaders), and the lessons of preparedness are learned too late.

Blackton spared no effort in the nine-reeler. Wood and Dewey appeared as themselves, while George Washington, Abraham Lincoln, and U. S. Grant are all presented by actors as also being on the side of the righteous. There was a cast of thousands, some of whom were soldiers provided without charge by Wood.[22] Veterans of the Civil War were on the screen representing a more heroic age; these included Captain Jack Crawford, a soldier and showman who billed himself as the "Poet-Scout," and whose major point was how much he hated the anti-preparedness song "I Didn't Raise My Boy to Be a Soldier." The main actors were skilled, attractive professionals; the fiancée who meets such a tragic end was played by Norma Talmadge, who was made a star by the role.

The *New York Times* reviewer found that the film displayed, besides too many shots of Hiram Maxim, "a slender plot, a modicum of heart interest, and a great deal of flag waving."[23] The critic for *Variety* had some criticisms, but thought the cast marvelous, and pointed out that "from a pictorial standpoint the picture is a revelation. There are a score of panorama scenes, some of which have been taken from hydroplanes flying over New York, which are little short of wonderful. The picturing of the bombardment of the city has been worked out in a manner which will win universal admiration, and the fleets and forts in action add much to the stirring value."[24] Both reviewers recognized the political purpose of the picture, and though Blackton had made some effort, for political reasons, at disguising who was being depicted, the *Variety* writer said that as the invaders "swarm our streets, . . . one can recall R. H. Davis' description of the great grey cloud that marched for hours through the streets of Brussels on to fade like a mist in the distance." The *New York Times* man also noted the deliberate blurring of identity, "but it is difficult to escape the impression that you are expected to recognize the nationality. They are certainly not Portuguese, for instance." He thought the film had been "done on a large scale but it represents no advance in the motion picture art, nor indeed, does it pretend to do so. That is not what it is for." What it was for required no deep thought: "It is designed to make many a person in each audience resolve to join the National Guard, the American Legion, the National Security League, and the Navy League, forthwith, and to write his Congressman by the next mail."

That many acted on at least some of these impulses there can be no doubt. Certainly people turned out to view the epic; police in several cities had to be called to control unruly crowds, which, of course, helped bring publicity. And publicity was actively sought: one extreme stunt involved having airplanes drop paper "bombs" on a city's streets, parks, and residential neighborhoods; printed on the devices was "This might have been a real bomb. Prepare. *The Battle Cry of Peace* . . . shows us what might happen if we don't prepare."[25] Attendance has been estimated at fifty million people, and gross profits at over a million dollars, such a great success that Blackton immediately began work on a sequel, *The Battle Cry of War,* and competitors rushed to make their own versions. Thomas Dixon, whose novel *The Clansman* had been used by Griffith for *The Birth of a Nation,* was reported to be at work on a script for a film entitled *The Fall of a Nation.*[26]

No doubt Blackton found additional pleasure in the great anger he aroused in the pacifist and anti-preparedness communities, who, except for one man, lacked the resources to immediately do much about their feelings. Automobile manufacturer Henry Ford was opposed to the preparedness movement and believed that the war raging in Europe was a disgrace to civilization. He vowed that he would bring it to an end; as part of his personal crusade he would deal with this piece of filmed prowar propaganda. In response to *The Battle Cry of Peace,* and particularly the paper bombing of Detroit, which he seemed to take as a deliberate insult against himself, he launched an advertising campaign that ran in newspapers across the nation. At a cost of $500 to $5,000 each, Ford ran full-page ads under the title "Humanity—and Sanity."

"Have you seen that awful moving picture *The Battle Cry of Peace?*" Ford asked. "Did you shake with fear and tremble for your country's safety? Did you know that others were shaking at the same time, but with laughter at your fear, and with joy at the fat contracts your fear might bring them?" This great fear, the automobile manufacturer stated, was not based on a realistic assessment of danger. "All the wild cry for the spending of billions, the piling up of armament and the saddling of the country with a military caste has been based on nothing but *fiction*." He did not hesitate to name the profiteer behind the fearmongering: Hudson Maxim, whose corporation, Maxim Munitions, stood to gain from increased military spending.[27]

The result was a lawsuit brought by Vitagraph, charging that "the printed statement that munitions manufacturers were back of [*Battle Cry*] prejudiced many people and damaged business of many theatres in many cities."[28] But, of course, Blackton, like his inspiration David Wark Griffith, was actually delighted by the controversy and the resulting free publicity.

CHAPTER ELEVEN

Henry Ford and the Peace Ship

I will build a motor car for the great multitude. It will be large enough for the family but small enough for the individual to run and care for. It will be constructed of the best materials, by the best men to be hired, after the simplest designs that modern engineering can devise. But it will be so low in price that no man making a good salary will be unable to own one—and enjoy with his family the blessing of hours of pleasure in God's great open spaces.

Henry Ford in 1909[1]

If I can make automobiles run, why can't I steer those people clear of war?

Henry Ford in 1915[2]

GREAT WAR ENDS

CHRISTMAS DAY

FORD TO STOP IT

Headline in the *New York Tribune,* November 25, 1915

AMERICANS have always been on the move, and the faster that motion, the better; it was one way to keep ahead of danger, real or imagined. Whether the threat was a grizzly bear or a mortgage, a death in the family, a domineering mother, an angry boss, or a boring job, the hope was that everything would be fine if you could just move away at breakneck speed. As Theodore Roosevelt believed, and acted on, "Black care never sits long behind a rider who rides fast enough."

The development of the safety bicycle during the 1890s had increased freedom, speed, and individual mobility for Americans, especially after wheelmen and -women successfully lobbied local, state, and national governments for hard-surface roads. The technological needs of bicycles sparked improvements in ball bearings, gears, tubular steel for frames, and spoked wheels with pneumatic tires, all of which were easily adapted for automobiles. At the same time the younger generation of American males was trained in the broader mechanical arts and in the making of precision machine tools, which became the best in the world. This training led not only to the development of motorcycles and automobiles, but also to airplanes; the Wright brothers made their living as bicycle mechanics.

It was difficult at first for many to recognize the automobile's potential, as when the *Literary Digest* asserted in 1899: "The ordinary 'horseless carriage' is at present a luxury for the wealthy; and altho its price will probably fall in the future, it will never, of course, come into as common use as the bicycle."[3] The novelist Edith Wharton, who certainly qualified as wealthy, owned several expensive early "motors" but found them unreliable: "I remember in particular one summer night when Henry James, Walter Berry, my husband and I sat by the roadside till near dawn while our chauffeur tried to persuade [our automobile] to carry us back to the Mount. . . . In those epic days roads and motors were an equally unknown quantity, and one set out on a ten-mile run with more apprehension than would now attend a journey across Africa."[4] Young William Allen White, who was becoming a national journalistic figure though his base was the small town of Emporia, Kansas, recalled standing with sophisticated friends watching a parade that contained "a buggy drawn by two mules, with a great sign over it 'Horseless Carriage,' and we laughed with the others." He admitted that they were "as blind as anyone. How could we know that the syncopated puff-puff of the gasoline engine in Kincaid's cabinet shop and at the mill . . . was the machine gun of an impending revolution?"[5]

Ignorance and inability to see into the future were not the only sources of resistance: as the *Literary Digest* pointed out, the automobile was first viewed with good reason as a toy for the rich. So Woodrow Wilson felt in 1906, arguing that "nothing has spread socialistic feeling in this country more than the automobile. To the countryman they are a picture of the arrogance of wealth, with all its independence and carelessness."[6] He was right. Farmers and country folk detested the expensive, noisy, smelly machines that ran down free-ranging chickens and stampeded horses. One young woman who was traveling with her husband through the West in 1911 in a covered wagon remembered that their horses "were more upset by automobiles than by anything else in the world. . . . Given plenty of room, they would bow their necks and, snorting and prancing, circle around an automobile; but in close quarters they were truthfully full of fear and panic

Covered wagon encounters an automobile in 1912

and had one idea—to turn around, regardless of space, and go in the opposite direction as quickly as possible."[7]

Ambitious young politicians saw a chance to reach more of their country voters, but they had to be as wily and adaptable as Franklin Delano
Roosevelt proved to be in 1910, when he hired a big red Maxwell touring
car to roam a sprawling rural district during his first campaign. He would
always stop some distance before an oncoming wagon, then dismount and
stand peaceably smiling and ready to talk when the farmer arrived, a farmer
grateful to the youth for not having spooked his horses.[8] Working-class
neighborhoods in cities also hated the arrogant and careless motorized
intruders, especially as the pedestrian death toll began to mount. By 1917
more than a thousand children had been killed by automobiles in Manhattan alone.

Adventurers began risking their primitive machines, open to wind-
blown dust and rain, on the even more primitive cross-country roads. In
1903, Horatio Nelson Jackson and a professional mechanic, Sewall Crocker,
traveled from the East to the West coast in sixty-four days; Alice Ramsey
was the first woman to make the trek, entitling her resulting book, *Veil,
Duster and Tire Iron,* after the absolute, if minimum, necessities in 1909.

Some progress was made when the private Lincoln Highway Commission was founded in 1913 with the goal of establishing a modern road linking the coasts. That dream road became even more likely after Congress voted in 1916 to make $75 million available to states that would match federal grants for modern highways.

Writer Emily Post, who would soon win fame and fortune advising Americans on how to be socially correct in a rapidly changing world, was looking for a project in 1915. She had driven European roads, "In fact I had in 1898 gone from the Baltic to the Adriatic in one of the few first motor-cars ever sold to a private individual."[9] In 1915, with her favorite places in Europe cut off by the war, she decided it was time to see the United States, and proposed, much to the shock of her friends, to drive from New York to San Francisco. Neither the Automobile Club nor the Lincoln Highway Commission was able to help with even rudimentary information, and when she mentioned the Lincoln road to an acquaintance, she was told that it didn't exist yet, but was "an imaginary line like the equator!" Nevertheless, she persevered, with a friend along for company and her son as chauffeur and mechanic of their big European touring car. The difficulties were all too real, roads of sand or dirt, few good places to stay or eat, and parts for their exotic automobile hard to find. They became experts on varieties of mud: "Illinois mud is slippery and slyly eager to push unstable tourists into the ditch, but in Iowa it lurks in unfathomable treachery, loath to let anything ever get out again that once ventures into it." There was also an appalling lack of road signs to help find the way; local people knew where they lived, and they knew where Aunt Em lived. Who else needed to know? But her book *By Motor to the Golden Gate,* displayed a zest for the trip and its challenges that must have lured others to take to the road, or at least make the search for it.

Many brave entrepreneurial souls had foreseen that there would be a demand for these machines. Between 1898 and 1910 more than five hundred companies were founded to manufacture horseless carriages powered by steam, electricity, or gasoline. Just as with the new film companies, and bicycles earlier, most of these ambitious enterprises would quickly collapse into bankruptcy. Detroit, with nearby beds of iron and copper, skilled machinists, carpenters, and leather craftsmen, early became a center for automobile production, helped as well by its reputation as a militantly antiunion town.

There was resistance to gasoline engines at first: they were messy, smelly, required fiddling and adjusting, and were also dangerous. Colonel A. A. Pope, who had made a fortune in bicycle manufacturing before turning to electric vehicles, warned, "You'll never get people to sit over an explosion."[10] But the colonel was wrong; the strengths of the internal combustion engine were too evident to be resisted—they were light for the power produced, relatively cheap to make and run, and very efficient.

Henry Ford investigated all three power sources before deciding that gasoline was the one to use on his experimental "quadricycle" in the 1890s. The machine ran well, and such was the average American male's confidence in his own abilities to handle anything mechanical that Ford found that whenever he parked it on the street some passing lout would jump in to give it a try. "Finally, I had to carry a chain and chain it to a lamp post whenever I left it anywhere."[11] An irritation, perhaps, but also proof that the fiddling requirements of the gasoline engine would not be a barrier to sales. Ford was eccentric, provincial, moody, restless, self-taught, and a brilliant practical engineer. After several failures at starting companies—failures mainly resulting from Ford's resentment over not being given either a large enough economic share of the enterprises and in not having his way in designing the cars he wanted to make—he recovered his reputation, and the interest of investors, by developing two race cars, the Arrow and the 999, named after crack trains of the time. Ford drove these primitive oil-slinging speedsters in early races, but their improvisations, like the iron bar used for steering, made them so dangerous that he hired Barney Oldfield to take over, though this former bicycle racer had never driven a car before, let alone raced one. But Oldfield was a speed-loving daredevil, telling Ford before his first race, "Well, this chariot may kill me, but they will say afterward that I was going like hell when she took me over the bank."[12] He won that race, and went on to become, with Eddie Rickenbacker, one of the most famous of this new breed of American hero, the master of machines.

In 1903, Ford started his new Ford Motor Company, backed by a number of Detroit businessmen, including the two redheaded Dodge brothers, owners of one of the best local machine shops, who would later start their own automobile brand. After a rocky beginning, when it seemed that the firm would follow its predecessors into bankruptcy, a Ford automobile was sold, and then a dozen, and then scores. Investors made a 100 percent return on their investment within the first year. But in spite of the sales success, Henry Ford was not satisfied with the designs of these early models, which were given the letters A, B, C, F, and N. He kept his team working until he came up with one that satisfied his desire for a vehicle that would liberate country folk, that would be simple, inexpensive, powerful, and tough: the Model T.

Ford had a genius for attracting talented young men to work with him, not just in industrial design, but also administrators such as James Couzens, one of the company's few shareholders and an active participant in forming the business. Couzens was a severe, methodically precise manager who, among other important contributions, put together a nationwide network of Ford dealers. Ford, however, was the great creative force behind the company's success. He drove an American foundry to develop a new lighter, stronger steel; he pressed his engineers to perfect his idea for a cast engine block with a bolt-on head for ease of manufacture and service; he found a way to insulate a magneto so that for the first time an inexpensive car didn't have to rely, or try to rely, on heavy dry batteries for an engine spark. All these innovations and more Ford contributed to, constantly improvising while resolutely immune to failure, tirelessly roaming through his engineering laboratories and factory floor, pushing his team to labor with very little rest. Hard work was expected in early twentieth-century America—ten hours a day, six days a week being the norm—but that hard schedule was seen as the bare minimum at the Ford enterprise. "Thinking men know," he believed, "that work is the salvation of the race, morally, physically, socially. Work does more than get us our living; it gets us our life."[13] The T went on sale in October 1908 at a price of $850 for the large open touring car, which, though low compared to the cost of most automobiles of the time, was still roughly half again the average annual family income. What purchasers owned was a simple, light, reliable automobile that was flexible and high enough to ride the rutted country roads without shaking to pieces. It was powered by four cylinders that produced twenty horsepower harnessed by a two-speed semiautomatic planetary transmission that not only made it easy to drive but also allowed the driver to shift quickly from forward to reverse, to and fro again and again to rock the car out of even the deepest hole or ditch. Emily Post enviously pointed out the great advantages of the Model T in her book, noticing, as her low-slung European machine slipped and slid along the rural roads, "in every barn, a Ford."[14]

For the response had been immediate: more than 10,000 sold the first full year of production, 18,664 the next, and almost double that number the following year.[15] Here were early signs of how successful such vehicles would be in America, with its huge national market that, although of continental size, had no trade barriers between states. Farmers had quickly recognized the Model T's value, not only as dependable transportation on bad roads but also as a hard worker on the land. There were attachments to fit the drive wheel that allowed it to saw wood, grind feed corn, pump water, and in other ways serve as an inexpensive hired hand. There was a great and immediate upwelling of affection for the "tin lizzie" or "flivver" that inspired a flood of jokes, stories, and reminiscences in praise of this mechanical beast of burden.

All this success led to a crisis in production, and the company purchased an old horse-racing track in Highland Park on the outskirts of Detroit. Ford hired the innovative architect Albert Kahn, German-born son of a rabbi, to design a modern factory using the new technique of reinforced concrete. It was literally a brilliant success, as the strength of the material allowed fifty thousand square feet of glass to be in the walls, thus flooding the work spaces with light, and giving it the nickname "Crystal Palace." This new plant opened in 1910 and improved production efficiency, but Ford was still not satisfied. He pushed a team of talented production engineers on a design for a moving assembly line, made possible by the new electric motors powering belts and chains, which could bring the work to the worker.

There were other challenges. George Selden, something of a mechanical innovator, though his real talent was as a patent lawyer, claimed to have "invented" the automobile. It was a ridiculous assertion, but in 1899, he convinced a gang of Wall Street moneymen to back him in using his patents—issued by the often careless U.S. Office of Patents—to put the squeeze on other automobile manufacturers by establishing a monopoly. Most of these early companies were short on funding, and when bullied by such large capital they surrendered meekly. In 1903, Selden and these captives formed the Association of Licensed Automobile Manufacturers, a motor trust, and when the early Ford models began hauling in barrels of money, the association demanded royalties. Ford, recognizing the technological invalidity of the patents, not only refused but taunted the trust, publishing newspaper advertisements assuring his suppliers, dealers, and customers that the company would protect them against any lawsuits, reminding everyone that he and Oldfield had driven his cars to early victories over other makes, and had set the world speed record: "We have always been winners."[16] Ford was willing to take on the Wall Street Goliath, and protect the rights of innovative entrepreneurs.

An early judgment against him led almost all of the independent companies to seek accommodation with the trust, including William Durant's General Motors, which had been founded in the same year that the Model T began production—1908. But Ford's stubbornness and sense of being in the right made him fight on, which called forth an enthusiastic editorial in the *Detroit Free Press* headlined FORD THE FIGHTER, which described the automaker as "equal to his weight in wildcats. . . . As a human figure he presents a spectacle to win the applause of all men with red blood; for this world dearly loves the fighting man, and needs him, too, if we are to go forward."[17] In 1911 he won his case on appeal. Again, the pioneer's stubborn insistence on his own way had paid off.

Also continuing to pay off in amazing fashion was the T. Every time the company increased production capacity, new orders flooded in, necessitating even greater efficiency. Finally, in 1913, the electric motors, the rubber conveyor belts, and the moving chains came together in revolutionary form: "Every piece of work in the shops moves," as Ford later described the system; "it may move on hooks, on overhead chains; . . . it may travel on a moving platform, or it may go by gravity, but the point is that there is no lifting or trucking. . . . No workman has anything to do with moving or lifting anything. Save ten steps a day for each of 12,000 employees, and you will have saved fifty miles of wasted motion and mis-spent energy."[18] Production immediately jumped from around 168,000 Model Ts of various configurations in 1912–13 to 248,000 in 1913–14, then picked up even more, so that by 1919–20 more than 635,000 were built and sold. Along with rising efficiency, prices fell; the touring car that had cost $850 in 1908 would be offered for only $360 in 1916.[19]

These new, very expensive methods of mass production meant that no longer could a couple of bicycle mechanics or a tinkerer like Henry Ford start a company with the backing of a few local businessmen. But there was an even greater human price to be paid for this efficient use of electric power—men could not easily bear the clangorous noise, the machinelike pace, and the unending routine. The old traditions of individual craftsmanship and skill achieved after long apprenticeship were ending. "The man who places a part does not fasten it," bragged Henry Ford about the new assembly process. "The man who puts in a bolt does not put on the nut; the man who puts on the nut does not tighten it."[20] The man instead just stood there, repeating each simple motion thousands of times a day as the assembling Model T rapidly slid by his station on the line, the speed of that line set by the company and determining his own pace. The era of the "speed up" had begun.

In January 1914, the Ford Company announced a revolutionary change in factory conditions and wages for workers. Henceforth there would be three shifts of eight hours each per day, and pay, when combined with profit-sharing, would be effectively doubled, to five dollars per shift. There were several reasons for what many other industrialists saw as a dangerous pandering to labor: Ford's personnel director had convinced him that sub-sistence wages that forced workers and their families to live in slum condi-tions were not only immoral, but inefficient for productivity—satisfied workers put out satisfactory products, and this level of pay would help attract and retain the best men. The most radical union of all, Bill Hay-wood's Industrial Workers of the World, had been making attempts to enlist Detroit workers, and Ford would later tell one of his associates that he "would lick the I.W.W. by paying the men $5 a day."[21] Another major change that Ford, along with Couzens and other managers, had decided upon was that employees should share in the enormous financial gains pouring into the company. "This is neither charity nor wages," Ford explained to the press, "but profit sharing and efficiency engineering."[22]

For the next five or six years, Ford and his company would personify many of the beliefs of the progressive movement, for there was a sincere desire to directly improve the lives of his workers, over 70 percent of whom were new immigrants who could not speak English or read in their native languages. Ford recognized that there was misery even among his men, and much worse in the country at large. This was especially true during the winter of 1913–14, when the severe recession had forced mil-lions out of work. Now thousands of those unemployed traveled to Detroit, standing outside the gates of the Ford factory in freezing weather, hoping to be hired and make a living wage to support their families. Only a relatively few jobs were available, and rioting broke out, bringing even more condemnation of Ford and his progressive ideas from other industri-alists. The *Wall Street Journal* predicted ruin for the capitalist for bringing "biblical or spiritual principles into a field where they do not belong," because those would "get riddance to Henry Ford of his troublesome mil-lions" and result in "material, financial, and factory disorganization."[23] The *New York Times* also condemned the change as "distinctly Utopian and dead against all experience." But Ford, as usual when he was seized by an idea, persisted against all criticism, not only paying a decent wage but, also in the progressive way, overseeing how it would be spent. A "Sociolog-ical Department" was started at the company, and its agents energetically visited workers' homes to ensure cleanliness, good morals, and the proper environment for raising children. "There are thousands of men . . . who are not living as they should," Ford told the Reverend Doctor Samuel S. Marquis, dean of Detroit's Episcopal Cathedral, who later came to run the Sociological Department. "Their homes are crowded and unsanitary. Wives are going out to work because their husbands are unable to earn enough to support the family. They fill up their homes with roomers and boarders . . . to swell the income. It's all wrong—all wrong. It's especially bad for the children."[24] Ford promised that he would do something about these conditions, and he did. As a worker named Woljeck Manijklisjiski told a Detroit reporter: "My boy don't sell no more papers. My girl don't work in the house of another and see mother but once in the week no more. Again we are a family."[25]

In addition, African Americans were hired on an equal basis with whites, and successful efforts were made to employ at full pay the physically and mentally handicapped—including some who were blind or lacking hands or feet—and convicted criminals who seemed like they honestly wanted a new start. Since such a large percentage of Ford workers were immigrants, from twenty-two different ethnic or national groups, there were mandatory courses at the company's English School, including "Americanism." Graduation from the school was celebrated with an elaborate ritual where the students wore their native costumes as they filed down the stage-set gangway of a symbolic ship supposedly docked at Ellis Island, then entered, as one witness wrote, "an immense caldron across which was painted the sign *Ford English School Melting Pot*," only to emerge "dressed in American clothes, faces eager with the stimulus of new opportunities. . . . Each man carried a small American flag in his hand."[26]

The reforming of "drunkards" was also undertaken. "Blindfold me and lead me down there into the street and let me lay my hands by chance on the most shiftless and worthless fellow in the crowd," Ford assured the Reverend Marquis, "and I'll bring him in here, give him a job with a wage that offers him some hope for the future, some prospect of living a decent, comfortable, and self-respecting life, and I'll guarantee that I'll make a man out of him."[27]

For all the social good Ford and his advisers were trying to accomplish, the innovations were also good business. A huge amount of free advertising was one benefit, and so was increased productivity; the company had a cash surplus at the end of 1915 of almost $50 million. "The payment of five dollars a day for an eight hour day," Ford later boasted, "was one of the finest cost-cutting moves we ever made."[28] Perhaps, but, as the wife of a worker wrote Ford in January 1914, "The chain system you have is a *slave driver! My God!* Mr. Ford. My husband has come home & thrown himself down & won't eat . . . so done out! Can't it be remedied? . . . That $5 a day is a blessing—a bigger one than you know but *oh* they earn it."[29]

Henry Ford, who had recently turned fifty, had already become something of a folk hero among midwestern farming families for having made millions of dollars through providing, inexpensively, a valuable tool that bettered their lives, while at the same time remaining a man of the people, free of pretension or airs. This shocking doubling of wages while reducing working hours now blazed his reputation across the nation, though much of the business commentary, as in the *New York Times* and the *Wall Street Journal*, condemned the move. Henry Ford didn't care; money, at this time, meant little to him, but he understood that it did allow him to be his own man, and to sponsor causes he believed in, no matter how unpopular or eccentric they might seem to others. Hating alcohol and tobacco, Ford early on published an anticigarette pamphlet, entitled *The Case of the Little White Slaver,* to try to convince young boys not to start the nasty habit. He was a lover of nature, taking long walks alone in the woods and being particularly fond of birds; he had played a role in Congress's passing of the Weekes-McLean Migratory Birds Bill in 1912–13, and had become a friend of the naturalist John Burroughs, giving him driving lessons and a new automobile every year.

Ford was capable of deviousness, petty cruelty, and impetuous, overwhelming acts of generosity. He felt, with good reason, that he had proven the correctness of his own intuitive vision over and over again, and could be stubborn to the point of perverseness when convinced he was right.

It was, of course, not unusual for successful American businessmen to make authoritative statements about great and small events outside their experience based on nothing more than the habitual sureness of their own judgment, reinforced by the deference of others. Thus Chicago lawyer Walter L. Fisher told journalist Paul Scott Mowrer in Paris in August 1914. That Mowrer, in spite of all his experience in Europe, was wrong about the political situation, giving him a "look that put me in my place. In the self-confident American tone I knew so well, and with the deprecatory smile of one who has inside information, he pronounced these words: 'Oh, no. There isn't going to be any war.' "[30] Another man of affairs made his pronouncement when Emily Post declared her plans to drive to California: " 'They'll never get there!' said the banker, with a successful man's finality of tone," predicting that they would retreat to a Pullman car soon after leaving New York.

Henry Ford now shared this confidence that success in business had given him invaluable expertise in all other fields of human endeavor. This certainty was accompanied with a sense of moral urgency that his worldly expertise had to be applied immediately to end the great tragedy taking place in Europe. Ford felt, along with millions of his fellow citizens, that all that was needed was for the right person to travel to that benighted continent bearing some old-fashioned American common sense.

Early in 1915, he began making public attacks on the preparedness movement, as well as expressing his general hatred of war and his willingness to spend his fortune to end it for all time, telling the *New York Times* that "the word 'murderer' should be embroidered in red letters across the breast of every soldier."[31] Wars, he assured the public, occurred only because capitalists and Wall Street profited from them. These pronouncements, some reprinted in company publications, caused Canadian-born and pro-British James Couzens, who had organized the business side of the company, to resign in protest.

The outspokenness also drew two peace campaigners to Detroit to talk to him. Louis Lochner was a balding, sensitive American youth of twenty-eight who had been active in peace organizations as well as ghostwriting the newspaper articles of social worker Jane Addams; the flamboyant Hungarian Rosika Schwimmer was widely known as a strong-minded journalist, a robust and charismatic lecturer, and an activist for peace and women's suffrage who had long been searching for "a millionaire to finance her peace ambitions."[32] In her late thirties, she had taken a leading role in the International Congress of Women at The Hague in April 1915, where she had won support for a plan devised by Julia Grace Wales to set up a commission of neutrals to conduct "continuous mediation" between the belligerents.[33]

Schwimmer claimed to have secret documents proving that the warring nations were open to mediation, though she would not show them to anyone. She and Lochner, who managed to see Ford only through a fluke, asked Henry and his wife, Clara, to sponsor a peace campaign, and they enthusiastically agreed. Schwimmer, as a Jew, must have been taken aback by the automaker's casually patting his pocket and claiming that he had proof that the war had been started by German Jewish bankers, but she suppressed her doubts for the greater cause.[34]

Clara Ford, as the mother of a soldier-aged only child, Edsel, agreed immediately to donate $10,000 to pay for citizens to flood the White House with telegrams demanding that President Wilson officially support continuous mediation. Ford and Lochner quickly followed these subsidized pleas with a visit to the president, arranged by Edward House. Ford, sitting with his leg dangling over the chair's arm, tried to charm Wilson with compliments on his trim physique, and by telling a joke about seeing a grave digger excavating an extra large hole in a cemetery. Asked if a whole family was going to be buried there, the grave digger answered no, saying that the deceased had wanted to be buried in his Model T because it had pulled him out of every hole he'd ever been stuck in, and he was sure that it would pull him out of this one.

Wilson laughed and replied with his favorite self-mocking limerick:

> *For beauty I am not a star,*
> *There are others more handsome by far,*
> *But my face, I don't mind it,*
> *For I am behind it—*
> *It's the fellow in front that I jar.*

Then the serious discussion began—and went nowhere. Wilson, involved in his own secret strategies to stop the war, was reluctant to complicate them by appointing an amateur commission, though Ford offered to finance it himself. When it became obvious that the president would not cooperate, Ford startled him by saying, "If you feel you can't act, I will." As they left the White House, Ford told Lochner that Wilson was "a small man" because Wilson could not see the potential in Ford's scheme.[35]

The industrialist had impressed young Lochner with his understanding of publicity, advising him early that "whatever we decide to do, New York is the place for starting it." Ford established headquarters at the Biltmore Hotel, summoned the "biggest and most influential peace advocates," as he put it, including Jane Addams, and gave press conference after press conference in late November.

At first the tone of news reports and editorials was more or less respectful. The *New York Times,* reflecting the views of many politically sophisticated Americans, feared that an immediate armistice would leave Germany in possession of Belgium and northern France, but pointed out that Ford's project would do "as little harm as good," and would perhaps show that "immediate peace, enormously desirable as it is, . . . might be attained at costs in comparison to which those of continuing the struggle would be negligible."[36]

But then the self-righteous naïveté of Ford and Lochner, the manipulative egotism of Schwimmer, and the gathering collection of eccentrics and self-seekers among the sincere pacifists began to affect the hard-bitten editors and reporters of the old school, who always welcomed cranks flaunting naive idealism the way they would aged whiskey—as an excuse for an uproarious good time. Ford was not skilled at handling the large, jostling crowds of reporters, yet he would not listen to those he had asked for guidance, such as the liberal editor and publisher Oswald Garrison Villard, who tried to tame some of the impetuosity out of the automaker.

Instead, Ford continued to say whatever popped into his head, assuring reporters in late November that he had chartered a ship to Europe. "We're going to stop the war," he said.

"Going to stop the war?"

"Yes, we're going to get the boys out of the trenches by Christmas."

"But how are you going to do it?"

"Oh, you'll see."

"Where are you going?"

"I don't know."

"What country will you head for?"

"I don't know."

"But what makes you think you can put it over?"

"Oh, we have had assurances."[37]

And the mocking and satirical page-one extravaganza began, including headlines about Ford single-handedly stopping the war.

The *Oscar II,* also dubbed the "Peace Ark" and the "Ship of Fools" by the press, was to depart almost immediately, on Saturday, December 4, 1915, leaving very little time for planning the European phase of the campaign or for assembling the "biggest and most influential peace advocates" before the voyage. Ford sent wireless messages to political, business, and peace leaders around the world, but most of the more responsible figures begged off, discouraged by the air of circus ballyhoo. Jane Addams, who had argued against the whole idea of the voyage, thinking it was too flamboyant and would be ineffective, was too ill to go; department-store mogul John Wanamaker refused to sign up; Thomas Edison, who had in October become head of a committee to advise the navy on preparing for war, declined, though his good friend Henry offered him a million dollars for his time; another friend, the naturalist John Burroughs, also said no, telling Ford that his heart in this matter was bigger than his head. Rabbi Stephen Wise and Washington Gladden, leading Social Gospel progressives, declined, as did Dr. Felix Adler, founder of the Ethical Culture Society. Few politicians accepted, though William Jennings Bryan at first teased Ford with promises to go, but then withdrew.

However, considering the short time available, a number of well-known social activists did enlist, among them: Ben Lindsey, a judge from Denver who had made a national name for himself through progressive proposals to solve juvenile delinquency; feminist firebrand Inez Milholland Boissevain, who was famous for her beauty and intelligence, as well as for leading suffragette demonstrations mounted on a spirited white charger; and publisher S. S. McClure, who had started the muckraking journalism that had helped inspire the progressive movement. A number of Protestant and Jewish religious leaders agreed to come, as did several dozen idealistic students. Some forty-five reporters were also eager to enjoy the hospitality.

Henry Ford was footing the entire bill for the venture. Not just the chartering of the ship and all other costs of the voyage, but also the hotel and restaurant bills of his gathering band of saints. Some of these took full advantage of the millionaire's largesse by outfitting themselves with new clothes appropriate for such an important diplomatic mission. Rosika Schwimmer was a leader here as she was in so many aspects of this campaign. She had a luxurious suite in the Biltmore, from which she dispatched $1,000 worth of telegrams a day while also choosing a "peace wardrobe" of evening clothes and furs. "All I have to do is wave my wand for what I think is necessary for our Peace Mission," she bragged to Louis Lochner about the Ford resources at her disposal, "and lo! it appears."[38]

Schwimmer was disliked by the press and some of the peace campaigners for her autocratic ways, and was held in suspicion because she was a subject of the Austro-Hungarian Empire. Lochner also grated on people. Unequipped with the slightest shading of a sense of humor, they were both overarmored with self-righteousness, and Schwimmer suffered from her inability to respect any opinion other than her own.

Clara Ford had certainly had enough of Schwimmer, Lochner, and the whole idea of "continuous mediation." She was sensitive to the mockery surrounding the Peace Ship, even if her husband was not, and she was appalled at the extravagance of the Biltmore operation, blaming Schwimmer in particular. Weeping, she begged her husband to withdraw; he resisted her tears, but agreed at her insistence to take the Reverend Marquis along as an adviser in common sense. Schwimmer had the gall to send Clara a necklace, evidently unknowingly paid for by Henry, as an appreciation of her early support, then later wrote wondering why she had never received a thank-you note, which gave the aggrieved wife an opportunity to blast back: "The way Mr. Ford's name and money was used was shameful, and you were the leader. . . . I shudder when I think what might have happened had I not begged Dr. Marquis . . . to go along to protect him. You and your followers cared not if he died, just so long as he went along to lend his name and provide money to be squandered."[39]

The departure from Hoboken on a bright, bitterly cold day was chaotic, with thousands of people jamming the dock area while a brass band on board competed with one on the pier to see who could play "I Didn't Raise

My Boy to Be a Soldier" the loudest. Pacifists unfurled a banner showing
St. George trampling the dragon of war. German sympathizers broke in
with a lusty rendition of "Deutschland, Deutschland Über Alles," which
was countered by French and British supporters singing "La Marseillaise"
and "God Save the King."[40] A brawl churned through the audience while
impatient voyagers struggled to identify their luggage stacked on the dock,
then wrest it from under the bystanders, reporters, and photographers who
were using it as a grandstand. An onlooker created a stir by having a grand
mal epileptic seizure; a reporter was at the last minute married to his
sweetheart by one of the on-board legion of ministers; while another
romantic, Dr. Charles Giffin Pease, was explaining to a circle of reporters
that he had been forced to withdraw from the voyage because of his suddenly ill mother, but under close questioning this social evangelist, president of the Anti-Smoking League among other worthy causes, was forced
to admit that he had been ejected from the ship for trying to have his girlfriend, Annette Hazelton, share his cabin. Ford had been "shocked to the
marrow" by this, especially since Pease, director of many aggressive campaigns for public health, was just the sort of eccentric do-gooder that usually attracted his support.[41]

Speeches were shouted at the crowd from various parts of the ship,
and every time a dignitary arrived tremendous cheers would echo off its
steel hull. As William Jennings Bryan pushed his way through the mass to
express his good wishes, somebody handed him a cage containing a squirrel, and he, not catching the reference to squirrels and nuts, carried it the
whole time he was there. The squirrel later became a mascot of the peace
crusaders. A large crate of white doves was released as the ship finally left
the dock, and Ford stood at the rail throwing red roses to Clara, who was
perhaps still weeping; only fifty yards into the stream a final indignity
arrived to mock the seriousness of the voyage. A small muscular man energetically pushed his way through the waving, cheering crowd. He posed at
the pier's edge for a dramatic moment, then plunged into the icy water and
began swimming frantically after the *Oscar II*. When rescued by harbor
police, he identified himself as Mr. Zero, "swimming," he explained, "to
reach public opinion."[42]

Things grew no calmer on board as stormy seas battered the peace ship
and factions among the delegates formed, broke apart, and reformed,
though seasickness during the first few days muted confrontations. The
sketchy plan of action was for the group to stop in Norway to gather delegates, then do the same in Sweden and Denmark before ending up at The
Hague and making themselves available to conduct negotiations. Those

able to tolerate the ship's exaggerated motion prepared for the task ahead by discussing such issues as "excessive military history in textbooks and children playing with toy guns," while one woman "suggested schoolhouses should not be painted the incendiary color red."[43]

A crisis occurred when a wireless report arrived describing President Wilson's December 7 address to Congress, in which he argued that the "whole face of international affairs has changed" and asked that the nation prepare to defend itself by increasing substantially the army and navy.[44] Meetings were held aboard the *Oscar II* to determine the proper message to radio to the American media, with Lochner and others arguing that they should unanimously support immediate and unilateral disarmament. Less radical delegates demurred, and were self-righteously lectured by Lochner: "Any one who accepted the invitation of Mr. Ford, and now refuses to sign this resolution, came for a free ride!"[45]

The patron of the mission spent his first days below in the engine room, studying the complex machinery, and it was probably the best place for him to be. The North Atlantic in December was rambunctious, and Ford, almost washed overboard by a wave while taking his exercise on deck, came down with a severe cold and retired to his cabin, though that peace and quiet was broken when a mob of reporters forced their way in to check on a rumor that he had died.

The contingent of more than forty representatives of the press seems to have taken a liking to Ford, whom they saw as an innocent being exploited by charlatans and faddists, though some of their mellowness toward the patron came from the fact that the most expensive drink at the bar cost only fourteen cents. The prime focus of their ridicule became Schwimmer, Lochner, and other such worthies; Schwimmer retaliated by locking them out of the wireless room, and letting them know that she, informed by her spies, was keeping careful note of every negative comment. William C. Bullitt, reporter and scion of a prominent Philadelphia family, wrote: "This did not tend to produce any undue amount of good feeling."[46]

Many of the delegates also became upset with Schwimmer because of her dictorial style and continued refusal to share the contents of her black bag with them. It was on these supposed documents that Ford had based his statements to the press about "assurances" that the warring powers really were ready for negotiations, and that therefore the voyage did have a legitimate hope of stopping the war. As it became obvious that Schwimmer had lied about having such diplomatic guarantees, the Reverend Marquis worked on convincing Henry that the trip was not going to bring about the desired peace, arguing that he should abandon the enterprise and return home as soon as possible.

When the *Oscar II* finally docked at Oslo, on Sunday, December 19, delayed by bad weather and the British navy, Henry Ford walked to his hotel and, except for a brief excursion for a park visit and a snowball fight, stayed in his room. He still suffered from his cold, and now he listened as the Reverend Marquis argued that he had personally done all he could to promote peace. Ford finally allowed himself to be convinced, on the grounds of his ill health if nothing else; on Thursday, at 4 a.m., he had his trunks sent down, preparing to sneak away from Schwimmer, Lochner, and the whole expedition. However, they were spotted, and a brief melee ensued as Ford and Marquis entered their taxi—a peace campaigner attacking one of Ford's attendants. "A lot of fists were flying," remembered a witness, but they got safely away.[47] The rest of the party, though disappointed and recognizing that they had lost their major source of credibility, continued on their quest, the automaker still paying all the expenses.

CHAPTER TWELVE

Unprepared

We have a traditional prejudice against armies, which makes us stop thinking calmly the minute we begin talking about them. We suppose that all armies are alike and that there can not be an American Army system, that it must be a European system, and that is what I for one am trying to divest my own mind of.

Woodrow, Wilson January 1916[1]

The true traitor, the real traitor today, is the American who clamors for a larger Army and Navy and who would make us faithless to our belief in Jesus and to our belief in everything Godlike in man.

Oswald Garrison Villard[2]

Tell the people to cry peace and fight preparedness.

Henry Ford[3]

WOODROW WILSON'S romance with Edith Bolling Galt had proceeded apace, in spite of machinations by friends and advisers such as House, McAdoo, and Postmaster General Burleson to prevent it. Burleson told Secretary of the Navy Daniels that some "pretty big men in the Democratic Party" had decided that he should urge the president to postpone his marriage. The level-headed Daniels declined, remarking that he did not want "the difficult and, perhaps, dangerous high and exalted position of Minister Plenipotentiary to the Court of Cupid on a mission in which neither my heart nor my head was enlisted and in the performance of which my official head might suffer decapitation."[4] All these men, very aware that 1916 was a presidential election year, feared a negative public reaction to what, for the times, was a hasty romance. The couple were married on

December 18, 1915, and since she was Episcopalian and he, of course, Presbyterian, in this time of strong tribal distinctions two clergymen were required to do the honors. His subsequent happiness can be measured by the observation of his Secret Service bodyguard who came upon him the morning after the ceremony as their flower-filled private railcar pulled into the siding at Hot Springs, Virginia, where the couple would take a two-week honeymoon. "I entered quietly down the narrow corridor flanking the bedrooms. Suddenly my ear caught the notes of a familiar melody. Emerging into the sitting room I saw a figure in a top hat, tailcoat, and gray morning trousers, standing with his back to me, hands in his pockets, happily dancing a jig. As I watched him he clicked his heels in the air, and from whistling the tune he changed to singing the words, 'Oh, you beautiful doll! You great big beautiful doll!'"[5] The president wrote friends that they did not do "anything that needs to be described."[6]

Unfortunately this bliss was interrupted by crisis when the British steamer *Persia* was torpedoed with two Americans killed, one of them a consular official, and the couple returned to Washington on the fourth of January. The advisers proved wrong about general popular reaction to the marriage, for the couple was greeted by cheering crowds whenever they attended public events. Even so, malicious rumors circulated that the White House doctor had poisoned Ellen or that she had died of a beating so the president could wed Edith. These traveled so far and fast that Anita Patton, visiting her brother George at a remote army post, was disturbed by them.[7]

At least one bawdy joke made the rounds:

"What did Mrs. Galt do when Woodrow Wilson asked her to marry him?"
"She fell out of bed."

A more serious problem was that the challenges of courtship and the satisfactions of marriage had so distracted Wilson that he lost control of the Democratic House of Representatives. That body tried to take control of foreign policy by threatening to pass a resolution banning Americans from traveling on armed foreign merchant ships. Wilson was barely able to have the resolution tabled, and he then faced powerful resistance to his new attitude toward preparing the nation for war. His change of mind regarding "preparedness" had come from the sinking of the *Lusitania,* and the continued frustration with Germany's submarine policy, but also because of his growing fear that the American army was not strong enough even to repress a German American uprising, which he was beginning to believe, might take place if war broke out with Germany.

To make matters even more difficult, the main resistance to his program for improving the nation's defenses came not from Republicans but from antimilitary Democratic politicians. William Jennings Bryan argued, as he crisscrossed the nation speaking fervently against "preparation," that "this nation does not need burglars' tools unless it intends to make burglary its business."[8] William J. Stone of Missouri, chairman of the Senate Foreign Relations Committee, and Claude Kitchin of North Carolina, chairman of the powerful House Ways and Means Committee, were also agriculturalists who were convinced that the money spent for a military buildup would benefit only big industry and Wall Street. "When this measure becomes law," Kitchin argued, "thereby putting the arms of the munitions makers into the Treasury up to their elbows, with . . . heretofore undreamed of profits at stake, we can hardly conceive of a power in the nation strong enough to extract them."[9] Whispers began that perhaps Wilson should not be renominated. To counter this opposition, Wilson, confident of his rhetorical skills and the openness of citizens to his ideas, decided to use a favorite tactic from his days as university president and governor of New Jersey—take the fight directly to the people with a speaking tour.

The campaign opened in New York on January 27, 1916, where he reminded his audience of just how amateurish their feat of arms in 1898 had been. "It is discreditable to this country, gentlemen . . . that we should have exhibited to the world the example . . . of stupid and brutal waste of force. Think of asking men who can be easily trained to come into the field, crude, ignorant, inexperienced, and merely furnishing the stuff for camp fever and the bullets of the enemy. The sanitary experience of our Army in the Spanish-American War was merely an indictment of America's indifference to the manifest lessons of experience in the matter of ordinary, careful preparation."[10] He wanted to increase the small Regular Army, and to have a federally directed 400,000-man reserve force that he called the Continental Army to be well trained enough for an immediate call to duty in emergencies. The navy did not require his arguments. "The Navy is obvious and easily understood; the Army apparently is very difficult to comprehend and understand," and this was because of the traditional American suspicion that a large standing army would inevitably lead to European-style militarism.[11]

The president, accompanied by his bride, traveled on to the Midwest, drawing large, responsive crowds that cheered his arguments, or at least his speeches, in which he pointed out the dangerous fact that "the world is on fire, and there is tinder everywhere."[12] Returning in triumph to the capital in February, he reasserted his control of his fractious party both through this evidence of his popularity and by the political art of compromise. To ensure passage of his preparedness bill, which would enlarge the active-duty army from 125,000 to 140,000, Wilson had to give up his Continental Army reserve plan. Resistance had come from governors, the National Guard establishment, and their congressional allies, because there was so much patronage involved, plus some southern politicians rebelled because African Americans would have been allowed to join. Wilson extracted in return stronger federal control of the Guard. But the agriculturalists were determined to use the issue to promote economic democracy by making the income tax even more progressive. In cooperation with Senate progressives such as Robert La Follette, they raised taxes on incomes over $20,000 a year to pay for the new military, hoping that this would have the added benefit of discouraging the enthusiasm of rich industrialists for an even larger buildup.

In reaction to the rejection of his redesign of the reserves, Secretary of War Lindley Garrison resigned. Wilson appointed in his stead a self-proclaimed pacifist, Newton Baker, progressive former mayor of Cleveland who had turned down a Cabinet post in 1913. "It would greatly strengthen my hand,"[13] the president had told him, and it was a good political stroke, since Baker's lack of martial expertise and fervor complemented the lack of such traits in Secretary of the Navy Daniels, to reassure many of the anti-preparedness activists. The *New York Times* headline

BAKER TO BE NEW SECRETARY OF WAR; HE IS KNOWN AS AN ARDENT PACIFIST

must have put some uneasy hearts at rest, as did his mild manner and boyish appearance. Wilson also met with representatives of the Women's Peace Party and the American Union Against Militarism, a group that included radicals such as Max Eastman and his sister Crystal, to give them his personal guarantees that he was "just as much opposed to militarism as any man living."[14]

But pacifism was growing fast out of favor as a violent world kept intruding on the United States. As the president had emphasized on his speaking tour, "America cannot shut itself out from the rest of the world,

[just] because all the dangers at this present moment, and they are many, come from her contacts with the rest of the world."[15]

FIGHTING IN MEXICO had grown more widespread and bloody during 1915 and early 1916, some of it spilling over the border into Texas, Arizona, and New Mexico. Carranza had continued to extend his control of the government and armed forces, sometimes with American help, though Wilson did not like the man, finding him arrogant, overproud, and, for some unfathomable reason, resistant to his advice. "I think I have never known of a man more impossible to deal with on human principles than this man Carranza," Wilson wrote to a friend.[16]

But problems with this new Mexican dictator came from more than just personal incompatibility. Carranza had taken over the Plan of San Diego, a plot to promote a Mexican American rebellion in the lower Rio Grande Valley. This had been devised and used by Victoriano Huerta to put pressure on the U.S. government when it seemed too threatening. Now Carranza, probably with German guidance, had his own agents revive the plan to pressure the Wilson administration to recognize his government as the sole legitimate authority in Mexico. During the summer and early fall of 1915, a guerrilla force that included some Mexican Americans was launched from the safe haven of northeastern Mexico to burn bridges, cut telegraph and telephone lines, snipe at passing trains, and murder any unfortunate Anglos who strayed across their path.[17] A number fell victim; one of the worst outrages took place on September 24, when eighty raiders led by one of Carranza's officers attacked a store near Progresso, Texas, killing a soldier, wounding two, and capturing another. After looting the store, they set it afire, then retreated across the Rio Grande under covering fire from Carranza's forces. The captured American soldier was dragged along and killed, then his head was cut off and displayed on a pike. When Washington "demanded an explanation," Carranza falsely pleaded his own ignorance and lack of control over some units of his extended army.[18]

Full specific details of the plan were unknown to American officials, but they knew that something more than just bandit border raids were taking place. "Your army and our rangers," the Texas governor wrote to the president in October 1915, "find great difficulty in apprehending these invading bands."[19] As often is the case when legitimate forces of order cannot do their job, vigilantes organized; in August 1915 a Law and Order League was established in the border region of Texas. A number of Mexican

American leaders took part in fighting the guerrillas; José Tomas Canales, a prominent political figure in Brownsville, organized the Canales Scouts, which provided intelligence for the U.S. Army, and Deodoro Guerra, a local political boss, led armed posses in the field.[20] But, even with this, Mexican Americans, the great majority of them innocent of any involvement in the Plan of San Diego, began to pay the price for the manipulation of their legitimate grievances by Mexican politicians. Many, perhaps several hundred, were murdered by vigilantes and, it was rumored, Texas Rangers. In 1918, José Tomas Canales, then serving in the Texas legislature, would launch a campaign to investigate Ranger atrocities, and demand both higher levels of pay and higher recruiting standards for the force to make sure nothing similar ever happened again.

In spite of its dislike and legitimate distrust of Carranza, the Wilson administration had solid reasons for favoring him; it was becoming obvious that the Germans were happily promoting the Mexican chaos. As Ambassador von Bernstorff had written to his government in 1915: "During the next months something will have to happen in regard to Mexico, and every step in this direction must necessarily be to our advantage." If renewed fighting broke out between Mexican and American forces, Bernstorff was sure that "under the prevailing circumstances, this for us would be a favorable solution, because the deliveries of arms and ammunition to our enemies [the Allies] would be cut back considerably."[21]

Secretary of State Robert Lansing noted in his diary:

Germany desires to keep up the turmoil in Mexico until the United States is forced to intervene; *therefore, we must not intervene.*

Germany does not wish to have any one faction dominant in Mexico; *therefore, we must recognize one faction as dominant in Mexico.*[22]

The strongest faction was Carranza's, therefore in October 1915 Wilson gave him de facto recognition as the legitimate ruler of the country. Carranza, satisfied for the moment, stopped the anti-American guerrilla warfare.

Recognition of his enemy did not please Pancho Villa, who had earlier taken the risk of supporting the American occupation of Veracruz. Forced by successive defeats to fall back to his home region of Chihuahua, he now took revenge on any American citizens his fighters could reach. The earliest of these deliberate atrocities occurred on January 9, 1916, at Santa

Isabella in northwest Mexico when Villa's men, shouting "Death to the *gringos*," pulled seventeen American mining engineers off a train, shot them, then stripped and mutilated their bodies. Several tried to run, but only one, shot and left for dead in some distant brush, survived to tell the tale. There was worse to come.

So great was the rage of Texans when they learned of the massacre and what had been done to the bodies that martial law had to be declared in El Paso to keep vigilantes from crossing the border and killing Mexicans wholesale. Carranza apologized, and had his men search for the culprits; at least two leaders of the murderous band were then executed. This more or less satisfied Wilson, but people living on the border not unreasonably demanded that more be done to protect American lives, especially since Villa's men had also been making quick incursions across the line, rustling cattle, robbing, and killing.

COLUMBUS, New Mexico, was a sandy border town that normally sheltered a population of about 350 men, women, and children within its adobe walls; that number had doubled by March 1916 as troopers of the Thirteenth Cavalry Regiment were stationed there to conduct patrol and guard duty.

In the early morning darkness of March 9, the peace of the town was broken as hundreds of Villa's soldiers rode in shooting; if the gringos wouldn't come to Chihuahua to be killed, they would bring the killing to the gringos. The initial attack went well, for the garrison was caught by surprise, but Villa, who stayed a safe distance away, mistakenly thought there were only twenty or thirty soldiers stationed there. His men were surprised in turn by the fierce resistance. Severely wounded sentries shot back, cooks poured boiling water on invaders of their kitchens, and a stable boy beat one intruder to death with a baseball bat. Officers recovered from their shock, organized their men, and led a counterattack. Still, the Villistas were able to murder eighteen Americans, soldiers and civilians, including a young newlywed torn from his bride's arms, and burn the town's few wooden buildings before fleeing. Setting the fires was foolish, for they illuminated the moonless night and backlit the raiders; they left dozens of their own dead and dying in the streets. "The Mexicans were poor shots . . . ," noted Lieutenant John P. Lucas. "One of them fired at me with a rifle. . . . He missed me even though he was so close that I easily killed him with a revolver."[23] A troop of cavalry led by Major Frank Tompkins pursued the band, carrying on a running fight across the border and through the desert, leaving dozens more bodies strewn among the chaparral, and recovering much of the booty they had taken.

Villa's reasons for attacking Columbus were more than mere banditry. He held a grudge against a town merchant who had taken money from him to buy machine guns, but who had never delivered them or returned the money; desire for revenge and plunder also played roles. But his real hope was that by killing Americans in their homes he would provoke a reaction that would embarrass his enemy Carranza and bring the Mexican people to his side, and in this he possibly had German help. At least one German agent, Felix Sommerfeld, was close to Villa and willing to spur him to acts that would bring intervention.[24]

The whole nation was now in an uproar, and Wilson, who had been trying to avoid any further interference in Mexican affairs after Veracruz, was faced with an irresistible demand for action. March 10 was Secretary of War Baker's first day in office, and he, recognizing his amateur status, asked Major General Hugh L. Scott for guidance: "I know nothing," Baker said. "You must treat me as a father would his son."[25]

It was the opinion of commanders on the border that unless Villa was driven away and his forces scattered, he would continue to raid American towns and kill U.S. citizens. The White House was listening to them and to the rage of the public, and quickly issued orders that "an armed force be sent into Mexico with the sole object of capturing Villa and preventing any further raids by his band, and with scrupulous regard for sovereignty of Mexico."[26] This was refined by a directive from Secretary Baker's office that the mission could be considered concluded "as soon as Villa's band or bands are known to be broken up."[27] Unfortunately, not enough attention would be paid to the difference in these two sets of orders.

Detailed directives required that the military expedition be small enough so that it would not give rise to suspicions of any desire to grab territory from Mexico; at the same time, assurances along the same line were given to President Carranza, who was not convinced. He insisted that his forces were capable of capturing Villa and dispersing his band, ignoring the fact that they had already been trying to do that for months. Within twenty-four hours of the Columbus raid, Brigadier General John J. Pershing was organizing his "armed force"; just past midnight on March, 16, 1916, he led his men across the Mexican border on the last campaign of the old horse cavalry.

The fifty-five-year-old Pershing, with a gift for diplomacy as well as skill in arms, was the perfect choice for the job. At West Point he had won the distinction of being cadet first captain. Robert Lee Bullard, who was a fellow cadet and later a general under Pershing, gave a good description of him at the academy:

> Of regular but not handsome features and of robust, strong body, broad-shouldered and well developed; almost or quite six feet tall . . . with keen searching gray eyes and intent look, Pershing inspired confidence but not affection. Personal magnetism seemed lacking. He won followers and admirers, but not . . . worshipers. Plain in word, sane and direct in action, he applied himself to all duty and all work with a manifest purpose, not only of succeeding in what he attempted, but of surpassing, guiding, and directing his fellows in what was before them. His exercise of authority, was then and always has been since, of a nature peculiarly impersonal, dispassionate, hard and firm. This quality did not in him . . . give offence; the man was too impersonal, too given over to pure business and duty. His manner carried to the mind of those under him the suggestion, nay, the conviction, of unquestioned right to obedience.[28]

After graduation in 1886, Pershing had ridden with the cavalry in the Indian campaigns on the western frontier before earning a law degree. He was teaching at the military academy when the Spanish-American War erupted in 1898, and gone on to lead African American troops in Cuba, winning the Silver Star for bravery. He valued these men, writing, "We officers of the Tenth Cavalry could have taken our black heroes in our arms. They had again fought their way into our affections, as they here had fought their way into the hearts of the American people."[29] Because of this affection fellow officers nicknamed him "Nigger Jack," though newspapers gentled that to "Black Jack."

Pershing had then served with great distinction in the conquest of the Philippines in both administrative and combat roles, winning the respect of the insurgent Moros, as well as that of American authorities. After being an official observer during the Russo-Japanese War, Pershing had been promoted by Theodore Roosevelt—who had fought beside him in Cuba—from captain to general, passing over 862 senior officers.

Luck, courage, and unusual ability had helped Pershing advance, but his late marriage had not hurt either. In 1905, when forty-five years old, he had wooed and won Frances Warren, daughter of Senator Francis E. Warren of Wyoming, who as an enlisted man had won the Medal of Honor during the Civil War. The couple's four children had been born in various parts of the world as Pershing moved from assignment to assignment, but then tragedy struck. Pershing had reported to a new post in Texas while leaving his family in the presidio of San Francisco until their new quarters were ready. On the very day they were to leave to join him, August 27, 1915, a fire broke out in their presidio residence that killed Frances Pershing and their three daughters. Only his six-year-old son, Warren, survived.

The general retreated into his work, an already hard man becoming harder; Warren was turned over to an aunt to be raised.

MEXICAN RAIDS were not the only threat to American peace and safety in 1916, but these other dangers could not be met by mere expeditions.

The loss of the *Persia,* which had forced the president to curtail his blissful honeymoon, was just one of a series of new sinkings of passenger ships, in spite of the German promise in September 1915 to desist from torpedoing without warning. American government protests grew even more heated after the *Sussex,* a Channel ferry with more than four hundred passengers, was torpedoed in March, with eighty people killed or wounded, several of the injured being Americans. The German government at first claimed the *Sussex* had struck a mine, but since the ship was able to limp into the port of Boulogne, it was not difficult to determine the real cause of the damage. It seemed to many Americans, including Wilson, that the Germans were proving their untrustworthiness by lying about their actions after reneging on their *Arabic* Pledge of the year before. After much hesitation and consultation with his advisers, who argued for an immediate break in relations, the president decided on a firm warning. On April 18, 1916, an official notice was sent demanding that Germany follow the "cruiser" rules of "visit and search" or the United States would sever diplomatic relations "because . . . the very character of the vessels employed and the very methods of attack . . . [are] utterly incompatible with the principles of humanity, the . . . rights of neutrals, and the sacred immunities of non-combatants."[30]

As soon as the note was dispatched, Wilson called and addressed a special session of Congress, explaining in a brief sixteen-minute speech that the question of a break in relations with Germany was now up to that government. The general expectation was that Kaiser Wilhelm II would reject the note, and the president quietly ordered Daniels to prepare the navy for possible hostilities.

German chancellor Bethmann-Hollweg again had to struggle with elements in his navy that wanted to let the break take place and return to unrestricted submarine warfare, and again he was supported by Bernstorff, who recognized the power an aroused United States could bring to the struggle against his country. The chancellor prevailed, but just barely, helped by the fact that Germany still had only around fifty submarines, and not even twenty of those could be on patrol at any one time. Kaiser Wilhelm resented Wilson's note for what he felt was its "impertinence." The arrogant but ambiguous response that Wilhelm finally approved on May 4 seemed to reflect all the confusingly different German positions, as well as the kaiser's personal resentment of the professorial president, whom he referred to in private conversations as a *Rechthabers,* or "Know-it-all."[31]

This "*Sussex* Pledge" of early May indicated that Germany would cease attacking merchant vessels without warning, but made that contingent on American efforts to force the British to raise some of the restrictions of their blockade and to follow the long-established rules of traditional blockade. Few Americans found it satisfactory, but Wilson recognized within the rhetoric of threat and compromise the kernel of what he wanted: a promise to limit submarine targets. He seized on that and, working through Bernstorff in Washington and Ambassador Gerard in Berlin, managed to have his way, at least temporarily.

Actually, the British during these same months of 1916 were also trying the patience of Woodrow Wilson. Edward House had negotiated a bizarre plan with Lord Grey, the British foreign minister, which called for American mediation to end the war; if Germany refused, then, the memorandum read, "it would be necessary for [the United States] to join Allies and force the issue." Wilson had the sense to add the qualifier "probably" before "be necessary," and it all came to naught anyway.[32]

The Irish Easter rebellion, aided by the Germans, erupted in April and was so brutally repressed, with artillery firing into civilian neighborhoods in Dublin among other measures, that even Anglophiles such as Theodore Roosevelt publicly voiced their protests. These protests grew even more heated when the rebel leaders were executed. Increased anger also resulted from the peremptory way the British were tightening their blockade, ignoring months of American protests about the already onerous restrictions. The Royal Navy began seizing American mail from neutral ships, and at the end of June 1916 the British reinstated their prohibition against the export of tobacco to Germany through neutral countries. This was particularly painful for southern growers, an important part of Wilson's political base, who had planted larger crops because an earlier decision had said that the trade would be allowed. But the British then recognized, perhaps from their own experience, that smoking helped German soldiers endure the privations of war.

In July a commercial blacklist was established that included eighty-five

American firms with which British subjects were forbidden to do business because they were under suspicion of having traded, on some level, with Germany. This infuriated Americans, who saw it as a strategy designed to ensure the empire's postwar domination of trade.[33] By July, Woodrow Wilson was writing House: "I am . . . about at the end of my patience with Great Britain and the Allies. This blacklist business is the last straw. . . . I am seriously considering asking Congress to authorize me to prohibit loans and restrict exportations to the Allies. It is becoming clear to me that there lies latent in this policy the wish to prevent our merchants getting a foothold in markets which Great Britain has hitherto controlled and all but dominated. . . . I may feel obliged to make it as sharp and final as the one to Germany on the submarines."[34] He also had Walter Hines Page, his excessively pro-British ambassador in London, return for "consultations," hoping, as Wilson put it, that he might be brought "a little way at least to the American point of view."[35] In early September, Congress did vote funds to enlarge the American navy to be a rival to Britain's, which irritated the British, but Wilson didn't care, writing to House: "Let us build a navy bigger than hers, and do what we please."[36]

Wilson's frustration with both sides began to be visible in his speeches, in one of which he seemed to turn his back on his efforts to resolve the war, remarking about "the present quarrel" that "with its causes and objects we are not concerned. The obscure fountains from which its stupendous flood has burst forth we are not interested to search for or explore."[37] This disdain for the warring nations certainly did not hurt him as the presidential election campaign began to warm, and he was advised particularly to twist the British lion's tail in order to encourage the electorate.

But for all the oratory against the British, it was the Germans who again posed the greater threat to American interest. It was they who were killing American citizens and destroying their property, not just on the high seas, or through proxies in Mexico or on the border, but right in the industrial heart of the country.

◄○►

CHAPTER THIRTEEN

War Abroad and War at Home

It's like trying to catch a rat in a cornfield.

John J. Pershing on chasing Villa.[1]

Russia is all it is cracked up to be . . . an amazing and most interesting land.

Jack Reed to a friend, June 1915[2]

THE GREAT EXPANSE of northern Mexico, especially the rugged wilderness of the Chihuahua Mountains, provided Pancho Villa and his men plenty of places to hide, while the lack of good roads or major cities meant that the American expedition would be at the end of a long, fragile logistics trail. It had been hoped that some of the practical difficulties would be overcome with the help of Carranza's forces and by using Mexican rail lines, but Carranza had no intention of cooperating with the Americans, though he hid that for a while.

Two columns comprising almost seven thousand men advanced into Mexico. One consisted of cavalry and infantry; the other, which General John Pershing led from a rented Dodge touring car, was a "flying column," all cavalry.[3] Word had reached the Americans that local Carranzistas would resist their entry, but by the time they crossed the border on March 16, the Mexican troops had disappeared.

Cavalry elements moved quickly, with the infantry trailing and providing security to the dozens of supply wagons and the few trucks that had been so quickly collected. Major Frank Tompkins, who had led the immediate pursuit of Villa from Columbus, commanded the advance guard of the Thirteenth Cavalry, and they paused only by necessity, as when they found "the body of a white man. . . . He was dressed in drawers and an olive drab shirt, was blindfolded, and been shot in the head. Dead about a week. We paused long enough to bury the poor fellow and murmur a prayer for the repose of his soul."[4]

Speed was of the essence if there was any hope of keeping Villa from escaping deep into the mountains, so Pershing pushed on relentlessly across the broken, freezing, five-thousand-foot-high plain. Men and horses suffered, but arrived at Casas Grandes–Colonia Dublan in the evening of March 17, thereby setting an endurance record for the U.S. Cavalry. There was no time for rest and recuperation; a base was established, then Pershing sent three columns of cavalry south, chasing rumors.

The local population was unfriendly from the start; this was Villa's home territory, there was fear of his retaliation, and, anyway, few were willing to cooperate with an invading force of gringos. The very daring American scouts, many of them cowboys and Apaches as well as drafted Mexicans who knew sections of the country, provided some intelligence, though the drafted guides were suspected of deception at times. As it was, the Seventh Cavalry came very close to catching Villa at Guerrero, but he was wounded in the leg by one of his own men, either accidentally or in an attempt to assassinate him, and was evacuated just before the troopers fought their way into the town on March 29.

Pershing had remained at Colonia Dublan organizing the base and keeping in touch with his cavalry units by airplane. He was already concerned about his logistics problem. There were few supplies to purchase in this barren high desert, and certainly not nearly enough food, water, and forage for thousands of men and their horses and mules. Carranza still blocked use of the railroad, and the U.S. Army had very few trucks. The latter problem was expeditiously, if illegally, handled by Chief of Staff Hugh Scott, who took it on himself to order $450,000 worth of such equipment and supporting mechanics, even though the money had not yet been appropriated by Congress. Secretary of War Baker immediately backed his actions, an example of quick, necessary decision making that would later be lacking in his department during the first year of America's entry in the Great War. The result was that mechanized "truck trains," or convoys, were soon carrying heavy loads of supplies along the few and very sketchy roads, totaling ten thousand tons over the course of the campaign. Wagons pulled by mules, burdened with their own forage, continued to serve also, especially in wet weather that turned the roads into quagmires.

Starts were also made on other aspects of modernization for the army, which had been held back by the nation's unwillingness to pay for anything beyond traditional basic equipment. The airplanes—JN-3s, or Jennies—accompanying the expedition were fragile, primitive machines that lacked

American soldiers with captured Villistas in 1916

almost every improvement that the Europeans had made after the pioneering work of Americans such as the Wright brothers. Captain Benjamin Foulois and his men did their best to keep these eight outdated craft flying, a job that required not only mechanical and flying skills but also great stores of courage. On the original flight from Columbus, New Mexico, to join Pershing at Colonia Dublan, two crashed and were destroyed, and all the rest had to either turn back or make emergency landings. Foulois had no illusions about the craft, informing his superiors:

> The aeroplanes are not capable of meeting the present military needs incident to this expedition. Their low power motors and limited climbing ability with the necessary military load makes it impossible to safely operate any one of these machines in the vicinity of the mountains which cover the present theatre of operations. . . . Even the united efforts of the entire technical ability in this command cannot make these aeroplanes suitable to meet present military needs.[5]

Pershing supported Foulois's request to the War Department for ten new and different models of airplane, but this time Baker was not per-

suaded, and refused to buy them. Still, in spite of dangerous winds and the
high altitude, the surviving Jennies were able to provide intelligence and
communication links, often via parachute drops, that showed the commanding general how important the air service could be.

After the near miss of capturing Villa, Pershing felt that he needed to
be closer to his cavalry. He left the base at Colonia Dublan in a subordinate's hands, and taking only a few members of his staff, among them
Lieutenant George Patton, and four riflemen as bodyguards, he drove farther south in his Dodge. A contingent of newsmen, including Floyd Gibbons and John Reed's old friend Robert Dunn, trailed along in their own
motley assortment of motor vehicles.

The next few weeks were spent by his cold and hungry but eager troopers crisscrossing the higher elevations of the Chihuahuan plateaus and
mountains, often encountering weirdly combined snow and sandstorms.
Major Tompkins gives a brief but telling description, reminiscent of Jack
Reed, of the hardships that were endured over and over again in his book
on the campaign: "Three or four horses died this date, the victims of short
forage, hard marches and freezing nights. The poor beasts drop by the trail,
the equipment is removed, the column goes on, and the circling buzzards
are eloquent of the end of long and faithful service."[6] But some of the
young men who had access to motor power were impressed by the newer
technology. George Patton enthused to his sister, who then passed on to
the rest of the family that "Georgie" had written, "They travel so fast by
auto. [sic] that they haven't had their own horses at all."[7]

A couple of brushes with Villistas took place, one led by Major Charles
Young, an unusually gifted officer who had graduated from West Point in
1889 in spite of undergoing vicious harassment because he was African
American. He had later served on military and diplomatic missions to Haiti
and Liberia, the only posts available to blacks, and was now commanding
F and G troops of the Tenth Cavalry, the famous Buffalo Soldiers, and a
favorite with Black Jack Pershing. As this great gathering of American military units proceeded, more white officers encountered Young and his men
for the first time and were impressed by their professionalism. One noted
in his diary: "Rode up to the Cavalry camp and saw Major Young. He seems
to be a very decent Negro and a capable officer." But he was also struck by
Young's self-segregation: "He had his tent over on the flank of camp away
from white officers."[8]

Another officer who drew the fascinated, if not always positive, attention of peers was Patton. Though not originally assigned to the expedition,
he had used the commanding general's friendship with his sister Anne

plus, as one jealous fellow officer thought, "outrageous persistence" to convince Pershing not only that he, Patton, should go but that he should also be part of the general's staff.[9] Pershing obviously enjoyed the aggressive, cheeky young man enough to tolerate what others might see as behavior bordering on insubordination. Patton lived up to his promises, not only in doing good intelligence work on the staff, but also in seeking out the enemy. In May 1916, he took ten men and three automobiles to try to buy some supplies, but after that duty was fulfilled, he then laid an ambush at a hacienda a Villista officer was known to frequent. The trap was sprung, and in the resulting gunfight three Mexicans were killed and the other forty horsemen were forced to flee. The bodies of the dead were tied across the hood of one of the cars, and Patton "skidood back to the post," as another officer, Major Richard McMaster, put it. McMaster went on to report to his family, "One of the Mexicans killed was Capitan Cardenas who belonged to Villas 'dorados.' Patton got a fine silver mounted saddle from Cardenas' horse and a pair of leather chaps (riding trousers)."[10] He also received the grateful approval of his general, who took to calling him "my bandit."

Not much else good was happening at the time with Pershing's expedition. A series of unpleasant encounters with Carranzista forces had led to a running gun battle near Parral, four hundred miles deep into Mexico, between an element of Tompkins's Thirteenth Cavalry and local civilians as well as Mexican army units who pursued them for miles. Tompkins was convinced that the cause of the trouble was a German agent in the town of Parral. "I noticed a small, compactly built man, with a Van Dyke beard, riding a fine looking Mexican pony, who seemed to be trying to stir the people to violence. He was well dressed in grey clothes and looked like a German." The consequence was four dead and five wounded Americans, and a far greater number of Mexican casualties.[11]

Worse results were avoided only by the timely arrival of the Tenth Cavalry, whose African American troopers had ridden hard to the rescue. Tompkins, wounded in the fight, was so happy to see them that he called out as they arrived, "I could kiss every one of you!"

Charles Young replied, "Hello, Tompkins! You can start with me."[12]

This was probably the point when the expedition should have been called a success and withdrawn. Though Pershing's men had not killed or captured Villa, they had killed a number of his lieutenants, dispersed his bands and driven them away from the border. From now on, their trouble was going to be not with Villistas but with the Mexican army of Venustiano Carranza, who, never happy with the entry of American troops into his country, grew angrier, and his people more alarmed, as those soldiers journeyed deeper south. Memories of the Mexican-American War of 1846–47 were still very much alive, as was a burning resentment of the resulting loss of Texas, Arizona, New Mexico, and California. Fear of what might be lost this time was intensified by renewed calls in the American press for annexation of additional parts of Mexico, a campaign led by William Randolph Hearst, who owned an enormous ranch in Chihuahua over parts of which the Punitive Expedition was already galloping. The Hearst press empire, which consisted of large-circulation dailies in most major cities in the United States, ran stories advising that "the way to IMPRESS the Mexicans is to REPRESS the Mexicans. . . . The way to begin is to say to them: 'We are no longer planning to catch this bandit or that. We are GOING INTO MEXICO. And as far as we GO, we'll stay."[13]

Carranza had a strategy of his own to deal with the *Americanos*. Troops were massed near Pershing's forces, and the Plan of San Diego was revived, leading to renewed guerrilla raids into Texas, raids that were sometimes blamed on Pancho Villa. On the night of May 5, forty Mexicans, joined perhaps by some Mexican Americans, attacked the small settlements of Glenn Spring and Boquillas, Texas, killing three soldiers and a young boy, while wounding others.[14] Colonel George T. Langhorne led a pursuit of about eighty cavalrymen from his chauffeur-driven Cadillac that chased the raiders back into Mexico and rescued two hostages that had been taken.[15]

Chief of Staff Hugh Scott had been asking the president to call up a limited number of National Guard troops to help defend the border, thus releasing regulars for more aggressive duty. After this attack, Wilson immediately called 4,500 from Arizona, New Mexico, and Texas to federal duty, but others soon followed as the raids continued. By the end of July, about a hundred thousand federalized Guardsmen were summoned; some would man the frontier that stretched from California to Texas, but such was the disorganization, and the poor state of their training and equipment, that almost half would never leave their home states.[16]

Pershing withdrew his men to the north to better protect them and the border, but Carranza wanted them out of the country completely, and increasingly he was voicing these demands publicly, while making direct threats privately. All of Foulois's fragile aircraft were unusable by June due to crashes and maintenance problems, which meant that Pershing had to rely on his cavalry for intelligence. There were reports that Carranza was assembling a huge force not too far from Colonia Dublan, so patrols were sent to check, but with orders from Pershing "to avoid a fight if possible."[17]

Captain Charles Boyd of the Tenth Cavalry, however, did not pay close attention to this part of his orders. American units were undermanned, so Boyd was leading fewer than eighty men when he encountered a Mexican commander at the town of Carrizal who ordered him to turn back. There were four hundred Mexican troops armed with machine guns and modern rifles blocking the way, and most were well protected in the bulletproof adobe houses of a small town. Boyd's scouts and junior officers advised that they go around, but the aggressive captain ordered an interpreter, "Tell the son-of-a-bitch that we're going through."

The Mexican officer responded, "You might pass through the town. But you'll have to walk over my dead body."[18]

Boyd led his African American troopers in a charge. In the ensuing battle on June 21 both commanders died. The Mexicans lost forty-five men, and more than fifty were wounded. American losses were twelve dead— including a particularly brave lieutenant, Hank Adair, who later had a town named after him in his native Oregon—eleven wounded, and more than thirty taken prisoner. The surviving soldiers, realizing that all their officers were dead or wounded, became demoralized and scattered into the brush. After they finally made their way back to the base, "for weeks afterward," reported an officer, "they crooned all night a song about that affair to the music of 'You were a tulip and I was a red red rose.' "[19]

Wilson already had his hands full dealing with American anger against Germany, Great Britain, and Mexico; of the three, Mexico was by far the weakest as well as the nearest and thus roused the most enthusiasm for blood. Pressure mounted so high after the clash at Carrizal, which early newspaper reports had wrongly claimed was an ambush by the Mexicans, that the president had a hard time resisting war. The pressure mounted even higher when Carranza at first refused to release the prisoners, and Wilson came very close to issuing orders for the occupation of northern Mexico.

But the organized peace community was also busy. The American Union Against Militarism and the Women's Peace Party paid for space in leading American newspapers in which to publish an eyewitness account that showed the battle had been one the American commander had sought.[20] The resulting mass of telegrams to the White House helped Wilson resist the call to full hostilities, and after Carranza finally agreed to release the prisoners the worst was past. "The easiest thing is to strike," he said in a speech in New York. "The brutal thing is the impulsive thing."[21]

It is unclear why Captain Boyd had charged so aggressively at Carrizal, but straight-ahead action was something cavalry officers were bred for. An

army engineer on the expedition described the Old Cavalry as "hard drinking, hard riding, afraid of nothing."[22] Another reason might relate to a
half-overheard remark Boyd made to a fellow officer before the battle,
something about "making history."[23] As it was, most higher-ranking officers, including the commander, were unhappy with the limits placed on
them by Washington, wanting to really go to work and finish what had been
started. Colonel John Parker had won fame and the nickname Gatling Gun
Parker in the Spanish-American War when he had brought his guns up
under heavy fire to give essential support for the charge at San Juan Hill.
While visiting one of the camps of the Punitive Expedition, he remarked at
a campfire bull session with younger officers, "If I were in command here I
would go to Chihuahua tomorrow and then on to Mexico City. Next fall I
would go to the Republican convention and on to the White House!"[24] No
doubt Woodrow Wilson now appreciated more than ever the politically
sophisticated, diplomatic, self-restrained qualities in Pershing, himself an
old cavalry officer.

As things stood, it is no wonder that German ambassador Bernstorff
confidently wrote his government during the *Sussex* crisis that "as long as
the Mexican question remains at this level, we are, I believe, rather safe
from aggressive actions by the American Government."[25] And it is also no
wonder that German agents were doing all they could to keep the pot in
Mexico at a boil.

JACK REED had kept to his traveling ways. After visiting the western front,
he had spent a couple of months in the United States working at journalism while writing poetry. But then, in April 1915, he had journeyed to Eastern Europe on assignment for *Metropolitan* magazine, accompanied by the
Canadian artist Boardman Robinson, also a *Masses* contributor, to provide
illustrations. *Metropolitan* was paying Reed very well, and he bragged to his
mother from the transatlantic liner, "I find that I am a celebrated figure
already, as all the people on the boat have read my 'works.' Am treated with
amusing marked deference by all."[26]

In Eastern Europe, far from the industrially organized slaughter of the
western front, he found cultures close to the barbaric color and dash he
had loved in Mexico. There was slaughter enough, God knows, but it
seemed an old-fashioned welter of blood, more on a human scale.

The Serbs were particularly attractive, brave, and resolute, assuring
him that their English and French allies only had to follow the Serb example to win victory on the western front. "What they need there are a few

Serbians to show them how to make war. We Serbians know that all that is needed is the willingness to die, and the war would soon be over!"[27] They were a generous people, like the Mexicans, willing to share all they owned, if they accepted you, but their overwhelming desire for a Greater Serbia was disturbing, an imperialistic ambition to reconquer all the lands lost to others over the centuries. Mothers greeted their children: "Hail, little avenger of Kossovo!" Similar ambitions were later found festering in the other Balkan states.

Russia was the most fascinating to Reed, "Holy Russia, somber, magnificent, immense, incoherent, unknown even to herself." He found here an even greater contrast to the deadly efficiency of the Germans. Chaos, savagery, corruption on an astonishing scale, but also the old-fashioned martial splendor of swaggering Cossacks, and high-cheeked Tartar cavalry that brought to mind the Golden Horde of Genghis Khan, flamboyant and colorful uniforms carrying mysterious meanings, uproarious meals, "gargantuan hospitality" shared with glamorous warriors who accepted you as a brother—a vivid mix of Occident and Orient that was a romantic's dream.

At first the adventures in Russia went well, and Reed certainly did not avoid the ugly realism of prejudice, poverty, disease, and war. He and Robinson had gained entrance to the country by convincing an American foreign service officer to issue an official letter empowering them to check on the condition of listed Jewish Americans living near the battle fronts in Bukovina and Galicia. What they found was horrifying. Evidently not only had all the American citizens on their list been killed, but thousands of other Jews as well, all massacred by the Russians. As they traveled deeper into Russia, they were appalled by the sordid condition of the Jews in the ghettos, their desperate cringing from any uniformed authority. At the beginning of the war, the czar had issued a proclamation that discrimination against Jews was to cease, that these long-suffering but talented people would no longer be denied civil rights or forbidden from reaching the highest levels of government or the military. But when Reed asked an officer if this was being enforced, the response was a laughing denial: "Of course not. All Jews are traitors."[28]

For weeks they successfully bluffed their way past suspicious officials— "What's the use of regulations when Americans are about?" one sighed—as they tried to cover the story of Russia's defeat at Gorlice-Tarnow, which had resulted in nearly a million soldiers dead, wounded, or missing, and a headlong retreat. But under such testing their luck ran out; they were arrested, came close to being shot as German spies, then were held in various forms of confinement or under restriction until their fate was decided.

The American embassy was deliberately not much help, having their own suspicions of the two, especially since the ambassador, David R. Francis, knew of the incident where Reed had so stupidly fired at the French trenches, and was probably informed about his radical politics. Because Robinson was a Canadian, British officials helped them finally win permission to leave the country.

Several more months were spent rather aimlessly wandering about Eastern Europe trying to satisfy the needs of their magazine for frontline stories. At some point a running argument began between the illustrator and the reporter over just how highly colored, or distorted, were the stories that Reed was writing.

"It didn't happen this way; it happened that way," Robinson complained.

"What the hell difference does it make?" Reed exploded. Grabbing one of the artist's sketches, he said, "She didn't have a bundle as big as that," and of another he remarked, "He didn't have a full beard." Robinson replied that he was trying for the artistic impression, not to re-create a photograph.

"Exactly," Reed shouted, "that's exactly what I am trying to do."[29]

Well, perhaps. But of course, just as in Mexico, he was also deliberately presenting a political point of view, not just local color, as when he would meet, or at least write of, selfish bourgeoisie or people who could be used as mouthpieces for unattractive positions—people such as Frank, an ugly American all too reminiscent of some characters who had appeared in *Insurgent Mexico.* Reed encountered Frank at the railroad station in Bucharest as the man was bidding farewell to a young, weeping Romanian girl. Every man working in the oil fields, he later explained on the train, took in such a girl as both maid of all work and concubine. As reward they received only food, a place to stay, and perhaps some clothing. Now he was going to England to enlist because "England is fighting for the rights of small nations and I don't see how anybody can keep out of it that's got any guts." But after that, say in five years, it would make sense for him to settle down and marry some pretty girl in the States with a good reputation and some helpful social standing.

This gave Reed a chance to indignantly respond: "If I lived with a girl, whether we were married or not, I'd make her my equal, financially and every other way. And as for your plans for marriage, how can you marry any one you don't love?"

"Hell," Frank replied, "if you're going to get sentimental . . ."[30]

Robinson and Reed returned to the United States in October 1915, seven months after they had left instead of the three expected. The various magazine pieces were quickly combined with some other material and published by Scribner's in early 1916 as *The War in Eastern Europe*. Reed's fascination with the czar's Russia shone through the book even more than it had in the articles. It was an empire, like the United States, but while Americans lived narrow, congested lives, in Russia "the people live as if they knew it were one." He found that the

> vast chaotic agglomeration of barbarian races, brutalized and tyrannized . . . for centuries, with only the barest means of intercommunication, without consciousness of any one ideal, has developed a profound national unity of feeling and thought and an original civilization that spreads by its own power. . . . Russian ideas are the most exhilarating, Russian thought the freest, Russian art the most exuberant; Russian food and drink are to me the best, and the Russians themselves are, perhaps, the most interesting human beings that exist. . . . There are no particular times for getting up or going to bed or eating dinner, and there is no conventional way of murdering a man, or of making love.

One aspect of this sprawling barbaric empire that most intrigued Reed was its revolutionary potential: "Is there a powerful and destructive fire working in the bowels of Russia?"

Reed was delighted to be home, though his on-again, off-again romance with Mabel Dodge was now off as she had taken up with the painter Maurice Sterne. Nevertheless he tried to reawaken her interest, even moving into the house she shared with Sterne, until it became obvious that she was no longer stirred by his presence. He poured some of his energy into public speaking, giving talks at the Harvard Club and Sing Sing prison about his adventures in Russia; he found members of the first more skeptical of his tales than those of the latter.

His mother and brother still lived in Portland, and were dependent on his income as well as his moral support. Responding to these needs, he immediately sent several hundred dollars to Oregon, then followed in early December by train. He chafed at being back in his provincial hometown, and frustrated by his mother's helplessness, writing to a friend that "I have been here one day. It is awful beyond words. . . . It seems to me very wrong to have to undergo another long period of suspended animation after the seven months' one I've just gone through."[31] But very quickly the trip was turned worthwhile, and he soon wrote to the same friend: "This is to say . . . that I think I've found her at last. . . . She's . . . wild and brave and straight, and graceful and lovely to look at. A lover of all adventure of spirit and mind. . . . In this spiritual vacuum, this unfertilized soil, she has grown (how, I can't imagine) into an artist, a rampant, joyous individualist, a poet and a revolutionary."[32]

Louise Bryant was indeed an individualist, a poet, and a beauty with ambitions to be known outside the narrow confines of Portland's small bohemian community. She was also married, but that does not seem to have delayed for even an hour the consummation of their sudden passion. When he returned to New York, she quickly followed, moving into his apartment at 43 Washington Square South, and joining enthusiastically in his rounds of Village life, the bars, restaurants, and dance halls. She was charmed by it all, and charming to all, and most of Reed's friends responded warmly. But Boardman Robinson and his wife, Sally, were not so enthusiastic, finding Bryant "basically shallow" while worrying "that she was a climber, willing to use Reed to advance her own career."[33] And Max Eastman told Floyd Dell that he found her "hard to take."[34] The painter Andrew Dasburg, however, thought her easygoing, and responded quickly to her desire for a casual but clandestine affair that was limited to afternoons and weekends when Jack was out of town. Just why she felt the need for this adventure soon after arriving in New York is unclear, but it may have been in reaction to Jack's own peccadilloes.[35]

It was an exciting, challenging time in the Village, even more so than usual. Both Margaret Sanger and Emma Goldman were fighting government attempts to stop their teaching of birth control. Reed joined with others to defend them, believing that, since rich women already knew the techniques, this censorship was really an attempt to keep the working class producing large families, "so that there may be a great hungry flood of unemployed to regulate the labor market . . . [and] soldiers to fill the armies of the world."[36]

Offers came from important newspapers and magazines for Reed to cover Pershing's pursuit of Villa, but he refused. Though regarding the atrocities at Santa Isabella and Columbus as "hideous crimes," he refused to believe that Villa was responsible for them. He was afraid that he would be required to celebrate the American soldier in his reports, which he certainly did not want to do. In fact, privately Reed told friends that he would be happy to join the Villistas in their fight against the expedition.[37]

Reed saw all this as related to the aggressive drive for American militarism. The bohemian radicals of Greenwich Village campaigned even more fiercely than William Jennings Bryan and his agriculturalists against the United States' preparing its army or navy for eventual hostilities, whether against Germany, Britain, or Mexico. They, like the Bryanites, felt that the only purpose of such a program was to further load the already overflowing coffers of the rich industrialists, but they also, of course, distrusted capitalists of any persuasion or scale.

This became the great issue for Reed in early 1916. Here again was the class struggle writ large. The leading proponents of improving the American military were the titans of finance and heavy industry, men of the caliber of Hiram Maxim of Maxim Munitions Corporation and Edward Stotesbury of Baldwin Locomotive Works, who was also an important figure at the J. P. Morgan bank. Jack Morgan, Jr., was active himself, as were leaders of other financial houses such as Jacob Schiff, as well as the chiefs of U.S. Steel, Bethlehem Steel, and the Guggenheim copper companies.

The Masses was one of the organizers of the resistance, printing numerous articles and cartoons against what its staff saw as militarism run amok. "The country," warned Reed in the pages of the magazine's "Preparedness Number" in July 1916, "is rapidly being scared into a heroic mood. The workingman will do well to realize that his enemy is not Germany, nor Japan; his enemy is that 2% of the people of the United States who own 60% of the national wealth, and are now planning to make a soldier out of him to defend their loot. We advocate that the workingman prepare himself against that enemy. This is our Preparedness."[38]

Emma Goldman, after she had spent fifteen days in jail for birth-control advocacy, also dedicated her time to resisting the buildup; she traveled the nation to tell audiences that expanding the military would inevitably lead to war, which she, like Reed and other friends, opposed not because of any rejection of violence, but because the violence was misdirected; this would be a war to enrich the "privileged few and help them to subdue, to enslave and crush labor." She argued that war would lead to a betrayal of "the fundamental principles of real Americanism, of the kind of Americanism that Jefferson had in mind when he said that the best government is that which governs least; the kind of America that David Thoreau worked for when he proclaimed that the best government is one that doesn't govern at all."[39]

Cities had begun mounting Preparedness Day parades during 1916 complete with bands, waving flags, and thousands of marchers to show Congress that the American people supported the buildup. Goldman would time her arrival in a city to coincide with these festivities, the better to counter their appeal. She arrived in San Francisco several days before that city's scheduled parade, but postponed her talk out of consideration for the local radicals' own anti-preparedness mass meeting.

Saturday, July 22, 1916, was sunny and mild, a perfect day for a parade, though some unease must have been felt by those who knew that a couple of hundred letters had been received by civic leaders and newspapers threatening "direct action" if the festivities took place. Flags were snapping from buildings and light poles along Market Street and being waved in the hands of the tens of thousands of bystanders and marchers as they listened to the fifty-two bands participating. The start was a bit delayed; the first section set off at 1:30, led by Republican mayor "Sunny Jim" Rolph. Further back was seventy-four-year-old Phoebe Apperson Hearst, mother of the publisher, who, dressed in white and holding an American flag, headed the women's contingent. All went well until, at exactly 2:06, a large bomb hidden in a suitcase exploded near the corner of Market and Steuart streets, indiscriminately shredding the bodies of men, women, and children, marchers and viewers alike. Ten were killed, and forty badly wounded.

Suspicion immediately fell on radical union organizers since San Francisco had been the site of a series of unsuccessful strikes, the most recent having been broken just the week before. Five people were arrested, and two convicted, Tom Mooney and Warren K. Billings, both of whom had long histories as militant labor activists. Mooney, thirty-three years old, had been arrested for possession of explosives years earlier, but after three trials he had been acquitted; Billings, only twenty-two, had been convicted in a separate case. Mooney was sentenced to death, and Billings, because of his youth, to life in prison. Later it became clear that perjured testimony had aided in the convictions, and Mooney's death sentence was commuted to life. Their innocence became an international cause, both seen as martyrs for radical labor. They would be finally released in 1939.

Goldman and her former lover Alexander Berkman, who had been lunching together in the Mission District when the suitcase bomb went off, were also under suspicion for a while. Berkman had recently moved to San Francisco to begin publishing an anarchist magazine with a title, *The Blast,* that celebrated the power of dynamite; he had close associations with the accused. At this late date it is unlikely that the case will ever be definitively solved, but Goldman had no doubt as to who was responsible. This usually fearless defender of free speech denied the promoters of Preparedness Day the same right to the courage of their convictions that she enjoyed, blaming them for the attack because militant labor had boycotted the parade, and threats of violence had been made: "Yet the 'patriots' had permitted the parade to take place, deliberately exposing the participants to danger. The indifference to human life on the part of those who had staged the spectacle gave a foretaste of how cheaply life would be considered should America enter the war."[40]

Just over a week after the San Francisco Preparedness Day massacre, another, much larger though somewhat less deadly explosion took place three thousand miles away, and here there is less doubt about responsibility.

Under pressure to stop the flow of armaments to the Allies, German spies and saboteurs were becoming more brazenly active in 1916. Even after all the revelations resulting from the seizure of Dr. Albert's briefcase, the expulsion of Austro-Hungarian ambassador Dumba and of the German naval and military attachés, and the anger about German agents having organized strikes, sabotaged ships, and fomented border violence, they felt the risks were worth taking. The administration began, with good reason, to worry that there were more secret, and more deadly, German networks that had gone underground.

Of course the very nature of the beast makes it impossible to be absolutely sure of all that these operatives did or attempted to do. However, enough counterintelligence was gathered early in 1916 to cause Baker of the War Department and Lansing of State to fear that it might be necessary to withdraw Pershing's force from Mexico to protect American cities from subversives, while the police commissioner of New York City requested that his men be equipped with Springfield rifles in case of attack by German agents, meaning German Americans. Growing in many people's minds was the same fear that Edward House confided to his diary: "There are more German reservists here than I thought."[41] This was a danger that the president began referring to frequently in his speeches. On Flag Day in June 1916, he took part in a five-hour-long march for preparedness in the District of Columbia, for which all stores and government offices were closed. "There is disloyalty active in the United States," he warned in his address, "and it must be absolutely crushed."[42]

BLACK TOM ISLAND, which had been turned into a New Jersey promontory by fill, lies just opposite Bedloe's Island and the Statue of Liberty.[43] In spite of its closeness to Manhattan, the Lehigh Valley Railroad had turned the tongue of land into a giant munitions dump, storing tons of TNT, artillery shells, dynamite, and fuses there while awaiting shipment to the Allies. Security was provided both by the Lehigh Valley's watchmen and by operatives of the Dougherty Detective Agency, but there was no gate or fence sealing off the property, and the risks of collecting such volatile cargo in one place were taken rather casually. At 12:45 a.m. on Sunday, July 30, 1916, a guard spotted a fire in one of the railroad cars loaded with munitions. He sounded the alarm, then, knowing full well the dan-

gers, fled. But there was also a second fire set around the same time, which
was spotted by a witness on nearby Bedloe's Island. This was on a barge
that was three hundred yards distant from the railroad car, a barge, as one
writer pointed out, "loaded with 100,000 pounds of T.N.T. and 417 cases of
detonating fuses, a veritable floating bomb."[44]

The first tremendous explosion came at 2:08 a.m., "like the discharge
of a great cannon," as the *New York Times* described it, a cannon heard as
far south as Philadelphia and Camden. The whole city of New York shook
as munitions shot into the sky, lighting up streets, buildings, and the Statue
of Liberty, which was peppered with shrapnel. Windows shattered all over
the region, raining shards of glass on terrorized citizens fleeing their homes
and hotels into the streets. The *Times* reported that "women rushed out
scantily clad, and men . . . wore pajamas covered with overcoats. . . . Many
women became hysterical. . . . Police whistles were blown frantically, but
the police themselves did not know what it was all about."[45] Confusion and
panic only increased when the second tremendous blast came at 2:40.

Buildings on Ellis Island were damaged, and frightened immigrants
awaiting entrance into the United States had to be evacuated. Even more
terrified were the jolted passengers on trains passing under the river in the
Hudson tubes, who must have feared that they would be sharing a watery
grave. But, as it happened, the fatalities were limited: three men died at
the scene—one of them, Captain Johnson, perhaps a hero trying to guide
his burning barge away from the greater store of munitions—and a child
who was thrown from the security of his crib.

Outrage at first was directed at the managers of the Lehigh Valley Railroad for their careless handling of the more than two million pounds of
explosives that blew up. There certainly had been a cavalier disregard for
public safety, but as investigators began studying the mysterious fires that
had started separately three hundred yards apart, more and more evidence
was uncovered that tied German saboteurs to the disaster. The same group
was also connected to another prodigious explosion the next January at an
artillery-shell manufacturing plant in Kingsland, New Jersey, about ten
miles from New York. Here again a fire of mysterious origin led to utter
destruction, though there were no casualties, because the shells lacked
detonator fuses. Financial losses at Black Tom were around $14 million
and at Kingsland $17 million, serious amounts at the time that spurred the
Lehigh Valley Railroad to great efforts to determine the causes, and that
led to unquestioned truth of German government involvement. After
decades of litigation, the records of which provide excellent though under-

used proof of the sabotage campaign, full recovery of the losses would be achieved.[46]

But in 1916, as the evidence mounted that Germany was fighting a secret, undeclared war against the United States, anger that had begun among the Anglophilic elite of the Northeast was now spreading across the nation. The rage against German Americans would burn fiercely over the years ahead, and would have long reaching consequences for another group of Americans. Franklin Delano Roosevelt, as assistant secretary of the Navy, was deeply involved in the antisabotage campaign, and he did not forget its dangers while serving as president in a later war. When military leaders, after the Pearl Harbor attack in 1941, wanted to sequester both first-generation Japanese immigrants and their citizen children in camps far from industrial centers, he had no hesitation in agreeing. "We don't want any more Black Toms," he told John J. McCloy, who was in charge of the relocation.[47]

CHAPTER FOURTEEN

———◁◦▷———

Progress and Peace

*He has dulled the national conscience and relaxed the spring of
lofty, national motives by teaching our people to accept high sounding words as the offset and atonement for shabby deeds.*

TR attacking Woodrow Wilson in 1916[1]

He Kept Us Out of War!

Democratic presidential campaign slogan, 1916

*I can't keep the country out of war. . . . Any little German lieu-
tenant can put us into war at any time by some calculated outrage.*

Woodrow Wilson to Josephus Daniels

WOODROW WILSON may have hesitated a bit about seeking reelection
in 1916, especially given the strains of the previous few years and his
guilt over how unhappy his first wife had been with the exposed life of politics. But Edith Galt Wilson was a different personality from Ellen Wilson,
in fact "startlingly different," according to one witness;[2] she enjoyed the
excitement of public gatherings, the insights and sense of importance
gained when her husband shared state papers with her. In February he
made clear his intention to run in the Ohio primary; in March he beat back
an attempt by Bryan and his allies to pass a resolution critical of his submarine policy. After that, there could no longer be any doubt as to who was
head of the party. He also quickly made clear his determination, in spite of
the war and troubles with Mexico, to extend his domestic program in new
directions.

The successful legislative campaigns of his first term focused on establishing economic equality, dealing with difficult issues including the tariff
and establishing the Federal Reserve to take, at least to some extent, con-

trol of credit and the money supply out of the hands of private bankers; he had wanted to defend the "small unit," that is, start-up entrepreneurs and small businessmen, against their stifling by the great monopoly corporations. Now, as the next step, he threw himself into battles for progressive social programs that included the outlawing of child labor in interstate commerce, workmen's compensation for those under government contract, and rural credits to provide low-cost government loans for farmers. This new emphasis first became evident in judicial appointments. In January he nominated Louis Dembitz Brandeis for the Supreme Court, a daring move because not only was Brandeis the first Jew ever nominated, he was also an outspoken progressive activist who had led successful legal battles against monopolies and for organized labor, which had won him the nickname "the People's Lawyer."[3] Conservative reaction against the nomination was immediate and fierce. Leading Republicans such as William Howard Taft, who wanted the seat himself, Harvard president A. Lawrence Lowell, and statesman-of-all-work Elihu Root, along with five other former heads of the American Bar Association, organized a national campaign attacking Brandeis as a radical who was "unfit" for the Court. They hoped to sway the Senate, which had to approve the appointment. Anti-Semitism played a role in the fight (Lowell would later argue for a quota on Jews at Harvard), but the strongest passion was aroused by Brandeis's "radicalism" and his belief in a "living law" that would respond to social conditions.

Wilson seems to have held no religious prejudices, or at least no anti-Semitism (as a Presbyterian his feelings about Catholicism were more complex). Many of his most valuable and respected advisers were Jews: Walter Lippmann, Bernard Baruch, Louis Brandeis. The president very publicly entered the struggle for the appointment, writing in support of Brandeis: "He is a friend of all just men and lover of the right; and he knows more than how to talk about the right—he knows how to set it forward in the face of its enemies."[4] Wilson won this fight in the Senate, 47 to 22, losing only one Democratic vote. A few months later, he took on another such contest when a second vacancy allowed him to nominate John Hessin Clarke for the Supreme Court. Clarke, a federal district judge from Ohio, was also a progressive who had supported organized labor, and who drew more charges of radicalism, charges that real radicals more or less supported. *The Call,* the New York Socialist daily, editorialized, "There will be another radical on the bench. Not as radical as Justice Brandeis, but something of a near radical."[5] Again Wilson stood by his man, fought hard, and won the seat.

The president, in good health and energized by the relationship with

Edith, took on all the political battles of 1916 with a confident spirit. After an appearance before Congress, the *New York Times* reported that he looked "especially strong and vigorous and quite youthful."[6] Wilson had hesitated about proposing social legislation in previous years because he sensed that the country was not ready for it, but now seemed the time to strike. Masterfully, and aided by the party's need to be unified before the election, he maneuvered his progressive social agenda through Congress. This included perhaps the most radical change of all, a federally mandated eight-hour day for railroad workers, the successful passing of which ended a looming nationwide rail strike that seemed to promise battles as bitter as those around Ludlow, Colorado, just two years before. It "threatens to be the greatest industrial battle in the history of the country," warned the *Times,* but the president's success brought virulent attacks from Republicans, who called the new laws "class legislation."[7] Wilson had managed to reform his party, forcing it to evolve from a narrow provincial agglomeration of agricultural interests and city machine politicians into a force for progressivism while Theodore Roosevelt was deliberately destroying his own Progressive Party in quest of reconciliation with the Republicans.

Roosevelt knew that his splitting of the Republicans in 1912 doomed any chance he had of winning the party's nomination in 1916, but he did make himself available, while warning, "It would be a mistake to nominate me unless the country has in its mood something of the heroic."[8] He felt that the GOP was now "completely under the control of the reactionaries," but Roosevelt had also grown disenchanted with the Progressive Party, which he had done so much to create.[9] When the Progressives nominated him in 1916, he stunned them by refusing the honor. William Allen White thought that TR had lost his interest in "social and industrial justice" because he "had a war, a war greater than even he realized it would be, to engage his talents."[10] But the still-ambitious former president really had lost interest in a minor party. Quit "spurring a dead horse," he told White and other Progressive Party members. "I did not desert the Progressives," he later claimed. "The Progressives deserted me."[11]

The Republicans, successfully avoiding the heroic, nominated Charles Evans Hughes, a dignified, gray-bearded lawyer-politician who had twice been a successful reform governor of New York, and was currently a U.S. Supreme Court justice. In spite of having challenged the power of the big insurance companies while governor, he had managed to remain close to the conservative big-business wing of the Republican Party. TR was not fond of the man, partly because of his lack of true progressive instincts but also because he reminded Roosevelt, in his coldness and excessive intellectuality, of the bookish demagogue ensconced at the White House; "the bearded iceberg," he called Hughes in private.[12] Roosevelt, however, recognized that if he went along with the party, and if Hughes failed to win the contest, he would be the logical choice in 1920. Besides, his hatred and jealousy of Wilson had grown so that he would have campaigned for anyone who might defeat him.

The Democratic convention, held in St. Louis, ran smoothly on the rails laid for it, but there was one surprise that immediately established the theme of the party's campaign. As the keynote speaker, Martin Glynn, former governor of New York, orated on previous great crises in American history that had not resulted in hostilities, the crowd began to cheer, and at each specific example of turning the other cheek, the chant came: "We didn't go to war! We didn't go to war!" The astonished campaign managers were listening. "The impression created," thought a *New York Times* reporter, "was that the delegates had been strongly in favor of peace under provocation, but that they were not sure this was an heroic attitude. When Glynn told them that it was . . . true Americanism to bear with provocation and to settle disputes without war . . . the effect was simply electric. He identified in their own minds the cause of pacifism with that of Americanism, and made the two identical."[13] Shortly after that speech, another, given by Senator Ollie M. James of Kentucky, sparked a twenty-minute ovation when he said, "Without orphaning a single American child, without widowing a single American mother, without firing a single gun or shedding a drop of blood, he [Wilson] wrung from the most militant spirit that ever brooded over a battlefield [Kaiser Wilhelm II] the concession of American demands and American rights."[14] These outpourings set the tone of the whole campaign of 1916, and while the president privately demurred, recognizing that the forces of war and peace were only partly under his control, he did not try to educate the public to these dangers, but concentrated, as a good politician would, on winning reelection. However, he did point out an important new development in a campaign speech: "This is the last war . . . of its kind or of any kind that involves the world that the United States can keep out of. I say that because I believe that the business of neutrality is over; not because I want it to be over, but I mean this, that war now has such a scale that the position of neutrals sooner or later becomes intolerable."[15]

Wilson's campaign was helped by the legislation he had just maneuvered through Congress. Many of TR's former enthusiasts recognized how much of the progressive agenda he had accomplished and supported him in the presidential race of 1916. Walter Lippmann, after a visit to the White

House, wrote in *The New Republic* of his respect for "the Wilson who is temporarily at least creating, out of the reactionary, parochial fragments of the Democracy, the only party which at this moment is national in scope, liberal in purpose, and effective in action."[16]

Lippman was not the only one to be convinced. Former Bull Moose progressives, including Jane Addams, Amos Pinchot, and philosopher John Dewey, climbed on board, as did more radical activists such as the socialists Jack London, Charles Edward Russell, Upton Sinclair, and Helen Keller. Even Mother Jones was impressed by the legislation that Wilson and the Democratic Party had passed to aid children, workers, and farmers. "I am a Socialist. But I admire Wilson for the things he has done. . . . And when a man or woman does something for humanity I say go to him and shake him by the hand . . . and say, 'I'm for you.' "[17] Many rank-and-file workers agreed with the activist intellectuals. The Socialist Party was unusually strong in Ohio, but a machinists' union official reported: "Everywhere . . . the machine-shop workers give Wilson credit for doing more than any other President has done. . . . The shopmen seem to think Wilson is the best President we ever had."[18]

Max Eastman, still editor of *The Masses,* along with many of the magazine's writers publicly argued for Wilson. They saw him as the best hope for national progress not just in legislation to aid workers, but because he seemed determined to avoid the extremes of militarism and eliminate war through some instrument similar to the League to Enforce Peace. "Wilson aggressively believes not only in keeping out of war, but in organizing the nations of the world to prevent war. His official endorsement of . . . international federation in the interest of peace is the most important step that any President . . . has taken toward civilizing the world since Lincoln."[19] The fervent muckraking journalist George Creel authored a campaign tract, *Wilson and the Issues,* lauding his struggle to keep America neutral. An even more surprising supporter was Henry Ford, who still hoped that some way could be found to keep the country out of Europe's war. He continued to fund his peace crusade as it made its futile and expensive way from capital to capital on the Continent, and now he gave the immense sum of $50,000 to reelect Woodrow Wilson, most of it spent in the swing state of California.[20]

In May 1916, Wilson had addressed the League to Enforce Peace, and agreed with the general idea of a league of nations that would prevent war, an idea that would loom larger and larger in his mind over the next two years. During the campaign, he made several references to new ways to ensure that war would not dominate the future of mankind. "The world is linked together in a common life and interest such as humanity never saw before, and the starting of wars can never again be a private and individual matter for the nations. What disturbs the life of the whole world is the concern of the whole world. And it is our duty to lend the full force of this nation—moral and physical—to a league of nations."[21]

John Reed was busy that summer of 1916, covering the political conventions on assignment by *Metropolitan,* for high wages, and *The Masses,* for the satisfaction of free expression. He also traveled to Detroit to meet with Henry Ford, whom he seems to have misread as "a genuine revolutionary" who might underwrite a daily antiwar newspaper. "I have had two glorious interviews with Ford," he wrote excitedly to Louise Bryant to prepare her to move to Detroit, "and am putting up to him the most magnificent scheme ever conceived. . . . It would cost Ford more than a million dollars."[22] But the industrialist, though sincerely interested in peace, recognized that more than just an end to the war was involved here, and refused to sign on.

The romance with Bryant had developed into a full and deeply rewarding love, though of the "modern," bohemian kind, and when Jack was not on the road that summer the couple spent their time in Provincetown, Massachusetts, at the end of the Cape Cod peninsula. They and their friends from Greenwich Village had discovered that the old whaling village offered a stimulating refuge from the heat and noise of New York, a refuge that offered full play to their creativity. In the summer of 1916, the richest form of that creativity was theater. All these bohemians looked with disdain on the commercial products of Broadway, believing that true theater would allow unfettered exploration of the human condition without worrying about "uplift" or profitability. Reed helped form the Provincetown Players, while he and Louise wrote and acted in some of the early productions that were mounted in an old fish house on the wharf across from the rented cabin of Mary Heaton Vorse. The great discovery of the summer, both for the Players and Louise Bryant, would be Eugene O'Neill, son of one of the most famous actors in the country. He had spent his time alternating between Princeton and Harvard, and working as a reporter, merchant seaman, and gold prospector. Though an alcoholic and suffering from tuberculosis, he had written a trunkful of plays, and the first he offered to the Provincetown Players, the one-act *Bound East for Cardiff,* was quickly recognized as the real thing. Reed along with several others insisted that they should organize, in order to, as the resulting constitution put it, "encourage the writing of American plays of real artistic, literary and dramatic—as opposed to Broadway—merit. That such plays be considered without reference to their commercial value, since this theater is not to be run for pecuniary profit."[23] When they all moved back to New York that fall, the O'Neill play was one of the first staged, thus launching the career of the greatest American dramatist.

Reed kept suffering from kidney pain, but that did not slow him much. While taking part in all the creative ferment of the Village and Provincetown, he continued both his necessary moneymaking journalism, though he turned down offer after offer to cover fighting either in Mexico or Europe, and his equally necessary writing of political pieces. He and Louise also bought a cottage in Croton, New York, which led to them casually, but practically as property owners, marrying. It is unclear how much Reed knew of his bride's relationship with Eugene O'Neill, which, at least at the beginning, she had tried to keep secret. She, like many other women, had been drawn to the handsome young playwright. "Women loved Gene," remembered a friend. "There was something apparently irresistible in his strange combination of cruelty (around the mouth), intelligence (in his eyes), and sympathy (in his voice). It made him seem hardboiled and whimsical, brutal and tender."[24] O'Neill liked Reed, and felt grateful to him, but evidently Louise got around his hesitations by telling him, lying to him, that since Reed was unable to perform sexually because of his kidney problems they lived like brother and sister. The play-

Louise Bryant in the dunes near Provincetown, Massachusetts

wright needed little encouragement; the affair began sometime that summer of 1916 while Jack was off covering the conventions and trying to woo
Henry Ford.

The presidential campaign absorbed most of Reed's energy that fall.
Since he considered the Socialist candidate, a journalist named Allan Benson, "too small to be spoken about with seriousness," and as the Republicans seemed the war party, he supported Woodrow Wilson.[25] He joined
with others to issue a public appeal for all on the Left to vote Democratic
instead of Socialist because "every protest vote is a luxury dearly bought.
Its price is the risk of losing much social justice already gained and blocking much immediate progress."[26] George Creel, a journalist who often took
radical stances, had organized fellow writers to support Wilson, and Reed
contributed an article to a series that Creel made sure was distributed
widely:

> I am for Wilson because, in the most difficult situation any American
> president since Lincoln has had to face, he has dared to stand for the
> rights of weak nations in refusing to invade Mexico; he has unflinchingly
> advocated the settlement of international disputes by peaceful means; he
> has opposed the doctrines of militarism and has warned the American
> people against sinister influences at work to plunge them into war; and in
> this dark day for liberalism in the United States, he has declared himself
> a liberal and proved it by the nominations of Louis D. Brandeis and John
> H. Clarke to the Supreme Court, by . . . the child labor bill, and the
> workmen's compensation act, and by the labor planks in the St. Louis
> platform.[27]

Such support from radicals, liberals, and former Progressive Party
members helped Wilson in a very close election. Money, as usual for the
Democrats, was scarce; donations had dramatically dried up after the passage of the law that gave railroad workers an eight-hour day—it was just too
radical for most businessmen, no matter what scale they operated on. To
counter scurrilous rumors attacking his sexual morality, campaign managers had Stockton Axson, brother of Wilson's first wife, Ellen, write an
article about their happy home life that was published in the Sunday supplement of the *New York Times*. Mrs. Malcolm Forbes of Boston paid for
printing a million copies that were distributed as a pamphlet.[28] Along the
same line, Edith took an active part in the campaign, which gave Woodrow
opportunities to make jokes as he introduced her, about her being easier to
look at than he. While visiting Omaha, the couple attended a historical

pageant where Edith was introduced to the Indians taking part as a descendant of Pocahontas. Whether these tribesmen of the Great Plains were impressed was not noted by the accompanying journalists.

A boon to the campaign had come from one of the president's most vociferous enemies. Jeremiah O'Leary, head of the German-subsidized American Truth Society, sent a telegram attacking Wilson for his pro-British stands, which gave Wilson the chance to respond strongly and publicly: "Your telegram received. I would feel deeply mortified to have you or anybody like you vote for me. Since you have access to many disloyal Americans and I have not I will ask you to convey this message to them."[29] Charles Evans Hughes, the Republican candidate who was courting the German American and Irish American vote, was caught flat-footed.

Some help was given by the Republicans themselves. Hughes was an inept campaigner, who lacked any platform charm, human skills, or political instincts. These flaws became evident during a visit to the Golden State when he snubbed California's popular former governor Hiram Johnson, who had run with TR on the Progressive ticket but, like TR, had now returned to the Republican fold. Just as detrimental was the shrill tone that Roosevelt himself took in supporting Hughes, delivering hectoring monologues about preparedness and patriotism that scared or put off many voters, particularly the German Americans, whose support was vital.

Daily bulletins from the war front in Europe telling of horrendous slaughters at Verdun and Flanders underscored the Wilsonian diplomatic achievements. He had stood up for American rights, confronting Germany over its crimes on the high seas, and made the kaiser retreat. In Mexico, American troops were chastising miscreants, and protecting the border; and now the first steps were being taken to better prepare America to defend itself in a very dangerous world. The country, in other words, was acting honorably yet had managed to stay out of full-scale conflict.

Lessons about the value of peace also had a timely illustration on the silver screen when Thomas Ince released his epic antiwar film *Civilization* in the spring of 1916. Partly a pacifist response to J. Stuart Blackton's call to arms in *The Battle Cry of Peace,* Ince also hoped to achieve the money-making success of that film and of David Wark Griffith's *The Birth of a Nation.* In Ince's film, two nations begin a disastrous war that is stopped only because of the intervention of Jesus Christ, who takes over the body of a wounded officer and shows a king the true horror of war. Christ is aided by the women of the country, who organize, march on the palace, and demand peace. The king ends the fighting, proclaiming, via dialogue card: "During my reign it is my command that my subjects enjoy peace and goodwill."

Civilization was ineptly made—poor acting combined with a sentimental, simpleminded plot—but well marketed. "It was a further victory for hokum," writes the film historian Kevin Brownlow, and not surprisingly it was hokum that made a healthy profit, combining as it did favorite American beliefs—the power of Christ joining with the innate goodness of women to morally save the world.[30] It also, according to one of the Democratic National Committee operatives, helped appreciably in Wilson's reelection, perhaps by capturing the female vote in the twelve states that now allowed women's suffrage.[31]

He needed all the help available, as the reunited Republicans poured great amounts of money into the campaign. Wilson was doubtful about his chances, and felt that the times were too perilous to allow him to serve as a lame-duck president, unable to truly speak for the United States, during the four months between the vote and the inauguration in March. He discussed an elaborate plan with his advisers by which Hughes would be appointed secretary of state, then Wilson and Vice President Marshall would resign, thus allowing Hughes to take possession of the presidency with little delay.

When the election results began coming in on the evening of November 7, it appeared that the plan would have to be followed. All the major eastern states, including his home state of New Jersey, were going for Hughes, though by modest totals. Newspapers, even the strongly pro-Wilson *New York World,* began running headlines announcing the Hughes victory. The president impressed those around him with his composure as the bad news came in, the *New York Times* reporter noting that "outwardly . . . he was as calm and unruffled as if he had nothing personal at stake."[32] But, of course, that was only outwardly.

The next morning showed that the celebration of Republican victory was premature, as results from the West made it more of a contest. Utah, Kansas, North Dakota, New Mexico, and, most important, California leaned to Wilson, though in many states the results were so close that it would take days for the final vote to be tallied. Minnesota, for example, went for Hughes by only 392 votes; California, which usually voted two to one for Republican presidential candidates, finally put Wilson over the top—though his victory margin there was fewer than 4,000 ballots while Hiram Johnson, the Republican candidate for the Senate, had a margin of 300,000; Henry Ford's money must have helped greatly. Kansas, too, had split its vote, electing a Republican governor, but also giving a large major-ity to Wilson because of his progressive program.[33] The South, of course, was solidly Democratic, and Ohio, alone of the major industrial states, also went for Wilson, perhaps helped by the appointment of the popular politi-cian and native son John H. Clarke to the Supreme Court. Allan Benson, the Socialist Party candidate, managed only 586,000 votes, and the shift by Socialists to Wilson was a major factor in his victory.[34] Wilson ended up with 277 electoral votes to his opponent's 254, and a surplus of almost 600,000 popular votes, but it took Hughes more than two weeks to send a telegram conceding defeat. "It was a little moth-eaten when it got here," Wilson joked to a friend.[35] The broader election had not gone as well for the Democrats. Their Senate majority was reduced, and the House was now essentially evenly divided: 216 Democrats, 210 Republicans, and 6 independents.

The president was determined, now that he had his mandate, to move forcefully to end the European conflict. The war had reached new degrees of horror during the butcheries of 1916 around Verdun, and Woodrow Wil-son noted how different this new industrial type of warfare was from the old. "Deprived of glory, war loses all its charm. . . . The mechanical slaugh-ter of today has not the same fascination as the zest of intimate combat of former days; and trench warfare and poisonous gases are elements which detract alike from the excitement and the tolerance of modern conflict. With maneuver almost a thing of the past any given point can admittedly be carried by the sacrifice of enough men and ammunition. Where is any longer the glory commensurate with the sacrifice of the millions of men required in modern warfare to carry and defend Verdun?"[36] There were also growing signs that Germany would not restrain itself much longer: "The situation is developing very fast," Wilson wrote House after the elec-tion. It was urgent that peace be arranged soon, or "we must inevitably drift into war with Germany on the submarine issue."[37]

In December he made a public call for the warring nations to propose their terms for ending the fighting. Britain and France could not accept the idea of negotiations while Germany still controlled Belgium and northern France, and Germany's own proposals, even with the worst sections kept secret, displayed such arrogance that they were obviously unacceptable.[38] This was made especially clear since they came just after the imperial gov-ernment brutally drafted 300,000 Belgian civilians into forced labor in Ger-many, an action that was denounced in the American press as virtual slavery and aroused enormous anger in this country. There was also trouble with Robert Lansing, Wilson's secretary of state, who had decided that the

United States should enter the war as soon as possible on the Allied side and did everything he could to sabotage the president's peace proposals.[39] Wilson was confident that war could be avoided, assuring House, "This country does not intend to become involved in this war. . . . It would be a crime against civilization for us to go into it."[40] Instead, the duty of the United States was to bring sanity back to the world.

But he had little cooperation in that effort. Frustrated that the belligerents would not make reasonable efforts to end hostilities, Wilson went before the U.S. Senate on January 22, 1917, to express his own ideas about how peace could be achieved. One thing was evident: a league of nations was necessary to provide the grounds for a lasting peace. "Is the present war a struggle for a just and secure peace, or only for a new balance of power? If it be only a struggle for a new balance of power . . . who can guarantee the stable equilibrium of the new arrangement? Only a tranquil Europe can be a stable Europe. There must be, not a balance of power, but a community of power: not organized rivalries, but an organized common peace." That peace must be "a peace without victory." He knew that was a difficult truth to accept, but it must be accepted: "Victory would mean peace forced upon the loser, a victor's terms imposed upon the vanquished. It would be accepted in humiliation, under duress, at an intolerable sacrifice, and would leave a sting, a resentment, a bitter memory upon which terms of peace would rest, not permanently, but only as upon quicksand. Only a peace between equals can last."

Wilson then summarized the three conditions he thought necessary: "I am proposing government by the consent of the governed; that freedom of the seas which in international conference after conference representatives of the United States have urged with the eloquence of those who are the convinced disciples of liberty; and that moderation of armaments which makes of armies and navies a power for order merely, not an instrument of aggression or of selfish violence."

And he concluded, after pointing out that there would be no "entangling alliances" in such a community of nations: "These are American principles, American policies. We could stand for no others. And they are also the principles and policies of forward-looking men and women everywhere, of every modern nation, of every enlightened community. They are the principles of mankind and must prevail."[41]

Wilson knew that the governments, so caught up in the Darwinian struggle for dominance that had cost so many lives, would not be immediately swayed by this "Peace Without Victory" speech, but, as he explained to a friend, he was not really speaking to either the Senate or foreign governments, "but the *people* of the countries now at war."[42] In this goal of bypassing the established authorities he had at least some success: the French Socialists and the British Labour Party cheered his words, and the Russian foreign ministry also expressed support.[43] The Germans, who had already decided to resume unrestricted submarine warfare, were silent.

Not silent was Theodore Roosevelt, who announced to the *New York Times* that "peace without victory is the natural ideal of the man who is too proud to fight."[44] It was a view shared by his good friend Henry Cabot Lodge and a number of other Republicans, who also found great fault with the league of nations proposal.

PERSHING had withdrawn his troops to Colonia Dublan while a joint commission was established to try to smooth the tensions between Mexico and the United States; a hold was put on the Punitive Expedition's activities until they were resolved. This meant that Pancho Villa could now resume his raiding, though only in Mexico, a safe distance from American cavalry. Villa led a sensational foray into the city of Chihuahua, where he released more than two hundred prisoners in the penitentiary, then drafted them into his forces. He also grabbed sixteen automobile loads of arms and ammunition, carried off much of the garrison's artillery, convinced hundreds of Carranza's troops to join him, and then, as a grand finale, addressed the populace from the balcony of the Governor's Palace about his ambition to liberate them from Carranza.[45] It is no wonder that American commanders and troops chafed at Wilson's forbearance; Pershing asked for permission, which was denied, to occupy Chihuahua.

Just as in Veracruz, living conditions for the Americans were dreadful. There was tropical heat and clouds of flies in the summer months, then the freezing cold of winter, while the wind blew constantly, filling tents, blankets, and mess tins with sand and debris; food was less than plentiful, and not very appetizing even without the grit. The huge Hearst ranch sprawled all about them, but they were forbidden to kill any of the cattle that had survived Villa's depredations. However, "slow deer," as the soldiers called the tough old steers, would occasionally find its way into their stew pots. In spite of all the misery, Major Tompkins, who seemed to be everywhere during the expedition, found that discipline held strong: "The men were cheerful, well behaved, and ready at all times to respond to any demand their General might make upon them."[46]

Intense training helped take their minds off discomfort, as Pershing used the opportunity to have his troops prepare for what he, and other officers, expected was coming. A number of the instructors had served as observers in Europe and they implemented the lessons learned there. Lieutenant George Patton was impressed with the live-fire training and with Pershing:

> Under the personal supervision of the General every unit went through a complete course in range and combat firing, marches, maneuvers, entrenching, and combating exercises with ball ammunition. Every horse and man was fit; weaklings had gone; baggage was still at a minimum, and discipline was perfect. When I speak of supervision I do not mean that nebulous staff control so frequently connected with the work. By constant study General Pershing knew to the minutest detail each of the subjects in which he demanded practice, and by his physical presence and personal example and explanation, insured himself that they were correctly carried out.[47]

Pershing was a demon for discipline, and another lieutenant found some of that rigor misplaced. At an inspection the general was unhappy with the ragged uniform of one of the men, saying in a disgusted tone, "You are a fine-looking specimen for a corporal!"

Lieutenant Bradford Chynoweth stepped forward in defense of his woebegone NCO. "It isn't his fault, General."

"Then whose fault is it?" Pershing snapped.

"If it is anybody's fault, General," Chynoweth claimed to have replied, "it is the fault of the Commanding General for not having our requisitions filled."

Furious, Pershing roared, "When I want you to take command of this expedition, I'll tell you."[48] But, typically for this open-minded general, he didn't inflict any revenge on the young officer.

Tensions were relieved and boredom kept at bay in what free time existed by sports. Hunting was popular, as were boxing matches and baseball. Chynoweth remembered how good the Tenth Cavalry's team was: "But could those negro troopers play baseball! We had a league. I played 1st base on our local engineer team, and they had a tall negro pitcher who mowed us down. I can still remember his fast ball whistling past my ears." There were Carranzista soldiers about searching for treasure rumored to have been buried by Villa, and it is likely that a few Yankees also sneaked off with picks and shovels. Chynoweth while on a hunting trip came across an old mine, where someone had made a last stand. He found a skeleton with a rifle and a lot of empty shell casings scattered about.

Fear of typhus kept soldiers out of local houses, but Pershing, as an old frontier cavalryman, was not a puritan. A number of prostitutes had followed the troops down from El Paso, and the commanding general detailed an officer to make sure they were well housed and healthy, thus keeping his troops happy and—since each woman was required to take a prophylactic after a visit—the rate of venereal disease low.

Farther north, along the American side of the border, National Guard troops were also enduring boredom, discomfort, and a somewhat less rigorous, but still valuable training. The call-up had not gone smoothly, and these citizen soldiers needed all the discipline and field experience that could be provided. Former secretary of war Henry Stimson felt that even China, the example that seemed to leap to every American official's mind of military incompetence, could have done as well.[49] Almost every unit had been undermanned and poorly equipped, some lacking even weapons and uniforms. One cavalry troop when summoned to the colors was unable to be inspected because, a Regular officer observed, it was "an agglomeration of men, three of whom wear shoulder straps, some of whom wear chevrons, and some are privates. In that the command was without horses, its efficiency in connection with mounted work was not able to be observed."[50] Some companies still voted to select their junior officers, and even those that did not had a rather casual attitude toward military leadership. One Pennsylvania Guardsman remembered "the benign command of First Lieutenant Harry E. Robb, a much-loved . . . teacher who'd taught some of us at the William Smith school. Commanding officer though he was, we called him Uncle Harry as a mark of our love and respect."[51]

Most found their experience on the border just as uncomfortable a duty as the Regulars farther south. Some complained, especially as the weeks turned into months, but most settled into learning their new trade of soldiering, becoming excellent shots and expert at that other necessary military skill—making do with what was at hand. The National Guard also found ways to relax. Talent shows, boxing, and baseball were favorites, as were bar fights with locals. Some spent their free time in entrepreneurial pursuits such as drawing comic sketches of their comrades being terrorized by the ever present rattlesnakes and tarantulas, having a local engraver run them off as cards, then selling them to be sent home. One skilled private caught and stuffed hundreds of the little prehistoric-looking horny toads and sold them for several dollars apiece. California wine was available for thirty-five cents a gallon, and though most of these soldiers did not have close access to whorehouses on the American side, and were forbidden to cross into Mexico, the Rio Grande runs shallow and was easily waded.

But some really suffered financially as Congress debated and delayed paying family support, then finally agreed to a fifty dollar a month supplement. Others were away too long from fiancées and careers. One wrote of his comrades: "They were sent down into a wilderness too wild for maneuvers, they were kept in dismal boredom while their jobs were lost, their opportunities missed, their rivals established."[52] Hundreds of Guard officers resigned and thousands of enlisted men promised that when their terms of service ended they too would leave. This attitude was also reflected in the lack of men coming forward to sign up for the newly authorized expansion of the Regular Army. As a journalist noted, "Forty thousand post masters, acting as recruiting agents, and all the drum-play of modern advertising at the service of the War Department, were failing to bring recruits for the Regulars or the National Guard."[53]

By early 1917 the crisis with Mexico had cooled. The binational commission did not accomplish much, but Carranza seemed to be less uncooperative and to be moving toward a more democratic government. However, the most important factor was the disintegrating relationship with Germany. The Punitive Expedition was ordered back to the United States, and most elements of the Guard were sent home, but only for a little while.

Mexico remained in turmoil for years after the expedition was withdrawn. Carranza continued to resist attempts by Villa and Emiliano Zapata to overthrow him. In April 1919, Carranza managed to have Zapata assassinated, and in 1920 the first chief himself was murdered. Villa's luck lasted until July 1923, when he was killed in an ambush while driving his own Dodge touring car into Parral. These violent deaths and thousands more did not end the fighting, and it was not until almost a decade later that some peace returned to the unhappy country.

CHAPTER FIFTEEN

The Web of War

From the military point of view, the assistance which will result from the entrance of the United States into the war will amount to nothing.

Admiral von Capelle of the German Navy[1]

As usual [the kaiser's government has been] more stupid than ourselves in our dealing with the U.S.

British diplomat to his government, February 1917[2]

If the United States, on any excuse, is forced by the flag-wavers, the munitions-makers, into that chaotic stupidity, I for one will not fight.

Jack Reed, January 1917[3]

THERE HAD BEEN a constant struggle in the German government over how to respond to the American demands that submarines follow the traditional rules of cruiser warfare. Ambassador von Bernstorff and Chancellor von Bethmann-Hollweg, aided by the army, had managed to resist the navy's arguments for an unrestricted submarine campaign by convincing the kaiser that there were insufficient numbers of the undersea craft to be decisive. It would therefore not be worth the risk of awakening the potential military strength of the United States.

But in early 1917, conditions were both more desperate and more encouraging for the Germans. The British blockade of food, as well as war matériel, was causing great distress among the civilian population; in spite of impressive victories in Eastern Europe the fronts were still in bloody deadlock; both of Germany's major allies, Turkey and Austria-Hungary, were losing their enthusiasm. But a number of U-boats had been built in the past year, and the imperial navy now possessed around 130 of the silent ship killers. Something had to be done, so on January 9, 1917, a meeting of the Crown Council was held in the headquarters of the Supreme High Command amid the barbaric but luxurious splendor of the castle of Pless, on the marches of Poland. Though it was couched as a debate, the decision had essentially already been made.

The Supreme High Command, or OHL (Oberste Heeresleitung), was now headed by Field Marshal Paul von Hindenburg and General Erich Ludendorff, whose stunning victories of 1916 against the Russians had made them revered figures in the Reich. These powerful men had finally been convinced that the only way to break the stalemate on land was through use of the undersea weapon.

Bethmann-Hollweg was now in a much weaker position, having lost the support of the Reichstag, so his advice was discounted in advance. He had also lost an ally in November 1916 when Foreign Minister Gottlieb von Jagow, who had great respect for Bernstorff's understanding of the United States, had been replaced by the comparatively unsophisticated Arthur Zimmermann, a change that many American officials mistakenly thought was an improvement. But as Reinhard R. Doerries, one of the best German scholars of the period, notes, "Complete recklessness and an underestimation of the United States bordering on stupidity . . . only became the rule of the day when Arthur Zimmermann . . . took office."[4]

Hindenburg and Ludendorff had already convinced the kaiser to suppress his usual indecisiveness and support them, arguing that there were now a sufficient number of submarines to strike hard and cut Great Britain's seaborne lifeline of food and munitions. Generals and admirals assured the kaiser and his civilian advisers that "we will have England on her knees by the next harvest."[5] Britain would then be willing to negotiate on German terms, and if the Americans decided to interfere, their present state of unpreparedness meant that there was nothing they could do militarily for months, if not years. America's small, primitively equipped army was already overextended in Mexico, and its navy was burdened with the need to counter the growing power of Japan in the Pacific. Besides, if the distant sleeping giant roused itself and attempted to send an expedition to Europe, Germany's invincible submarines would block the passage. "I guarantee on my word as a naval officer that no American will set foot on the Continent," swore Admiral Henning von Holtzendorff, chief of the Naval General Staff.

The chancellor, nervously chain-smoking, listened to the arguments and managed only token resistance. The U-boat was the "last card," he said, so this was a very serious decision: "But if the military authorities consider the U-boat war essential, I am not in a position to contradict them."

Field Marshal von Hindenburg stressed, repetitively, that pitiless resolve was essential: "We need the most energetic, ruthless methods which can be adopted. For this reason we need the ruthless U-boat war to start from February 1, 1917. The war must be brought to an end rapidly, although we would be able to hold out still longer, but haste is needed on account of our allies."

The chancellor was finally convinced to join the chorus, or at least he was beaten down to the point where he could resist no longer. "Yes, when success beckons, we must act."

And Hindenburg reassured him: "We would reproach ourselves later if we let the opportunity pass by."

Bernstorff from his post in Washington could do nothing to resist this decision. He had argued from the beginning of the war about the foolishness of spurring the United States to anger. The latest warnings had been in the summer of 1916, when the military and naval leaders were pushing for a resumption of the unrestricted submarine campaign. He had said then that such repudiation of the *Sussex* Pledge would certainly "lead to the break and to [America's] entry into the war."[6] On January 19, 1917, when he learned of the Pless decision, he forcefully repeated his admonishments, cabling, "War unavoidable with intended action, . . . [would] have effect of declaration of war here."[7] Bernstorff's was the sophisticated understanding of American economic and potential military strength, the only imperial adviser who had seen for himself the bustling energy, the immense productivity of the country that spanned a whole resource-rich continent. His opponents, now in control, were essentially Prussian provincials, more at home on battlefields or tending their country estates than in dealing with the subtleties of diplomatic power or profiting from a knowledge of other cultures. For example, it should not have taken a great depth of worldly knowledge to understand that Great Britain, proud exploiter of a globe-spanning empire, would fight to the death before surrendering its necessary command of the sea. Also obvious to those who considered such nonmaterial factors important was the rise in Allied morale that would follow U.S. entry on their side. Even if the ill-prepared Americans required a year or more to contribute, that contribution would be worth the sacrifices involved in continuing to fight, and die, until they arrived.

For now this decision was withheld from the president and the world. The submarines were secretly ordered to take up positions, while Wilson continued his efforts to stop the fighting, on January 24 writing to House that if "Germany wants peace she can get it soon, *if she will but confide in me and let me have a chance.* . . . Feelings, exasperations are neither here nor there. Do they want me to help? I am entitled to know because I genuinely want to help without favour to either side."[8] And House passed these sentiments on to Bernstorff. The president was now willing to put intense pressure on the Allies, using his fiscal power since it was becoming obvious that the British treasury was exhausted. If Germany would only moderate the terms she was demanding for negotiations, Wilson was convinced he could get those negotiations started. But Zimmermann, the new German minister for foreign affairs, had already cabled Bernstorff on January 7, "For your personal information. American mediation for *genuine* peace negotiations is undesirable to us if for no other reason than public opinion. . . . We are convinced that we can bring the war militarily and economically to a victorious end. The question of communicating our terms of peace should therefore be handled dilatorily by Your Excellency."[9]

Wilson soon realized that he had spoken truer than he knew during the presidential campaign when he had explained the increasing impossibility of the United States or any other large nation preserving its neutrality during a world war. On January 31, Joseph Tumulty brought the president an Associated Press news bulletin announcing that Germany was going to resume unrestricted submarine warfare starting the next day. The presidential secretary watched "the expressions that raced across his strong features: first, blank amazement; then incredulity; . . . then gravity and sternness, a sudden grayness of colour, a compression of the lips and the familiar locking of the jaw which always characterized him in moments of supreme resolution."[10] Obvious to Wilson at this moment was that this decision had been made weeks ago, yet the Germans had strung him along on his quest for peace.

Bernstorff delivered the formal notification of the policy to Lansing that afternoon; in spite of his anger, Lansing sympathetically noted that the ambassador's eyes were tearful as he took his leave. Wilson himself had little sympathy for Bernstorff once he realized that the count had known of the policy even while talking with him, seemingly sincerely, of new peace proposals.

All ships were to be sunk, neutral and Allied alike, that were encountered by German submarines within zones around Great Britain, France, Italy, and in the eastern Mediterranean. The United States would be allowed passage of one ship weekly, but under humiliating conditions that included the ship's hull being marked with red and white "zebra stripes."

These provisos were so galling to national pride that they were widely denounced in newspaper editorials. Secretary of the Treasury McAdoo reflected the indignant resentment of many Americans when he wrote later, "This was practically ordering the United States off the Atlantic."[11] He, like many others, was now convinced that if the country backed down, the Germans would beat the Allies, then both North and South America would be next. Walter Lippmann began a series of articles in *The New Republic* in February that made clear that he and his fellow editors felt the same way: Germany had become a threat to America and the nonmilitaristic mercantile civilization that it prized. More immediately, Senator John Sharp Williams of Mississippi wrote Wilson that he saw the ultimatum as "an insolent threat of ferocious terrorism," and promised the president that no matter what course of action he chose, "I am with you hand, heart, & soul."[12]

Wilson, though, seemed uncertain of what course of action to choose. When he talked to House the next day, he was "sad and depressed." Unable to rest, he roamed his office, nervously rearranging books, telling his friend that he felt as if the world had reversed the direction of its rotation so that he could not get his balance, and condemning Germany as "a madman that should be curbed." House asked if the Allies should have to do the curbing alone. Wilson winced, but said that the country should still stay out of the war.[13]

The question Wilson was trying to decide was whether to sever diplomatic relations immediately, in hopes of bringing Germany to its senses, or to wait until there was an overt act. House advised an immediate break, as did Lansing, a group of Democratic senators, and, unanimously, the Cabinet. But the decision had already been made when during the *Sussex* crisis of spring 1916 Wilson had told the Germans that if they did not follow the traditional rules of cruiser warfare, the United States would break with them.

On February 3, Bernstorff was called to the State Department, given his passports and ordered home, and James W. Gerard, the American ambassador in Berlin, was recalled. Later that day, Wilson went before Congress to announce that diplomatic relations with Germany had been broken, though, he said, "I refuse to believe that it is the intention of the German authorities to do in fact what they have warned us they will feel at liberty to do. . . . and destroy American ships and take the lives of American citizens in the willful prosecution of the ruthless naval programme they have announced their intention to adopt. Only actual overt acts on their part can make me believe it even now." And, the president insisted, "We are

*Woodrow Wilson announcing to Congress the break in relations
with Germany*

the sincere friends of the German people and earnestly desire to remain at peace with the Government which speaks for them. We shall not believe that they are hostile to us unless and until we are obliged to believe it; and we propose nothing more than the reasonable defense of the undoubted rights of our people."[14]

In fact, during the month of February, no American ships were attacked, but then relatively few had taken to sea because the German offensive proved spectacularly successful; in the first three months of the campaign, U-boats sank 844 ships of all sorts, including hospital ships. Just the warning that they were at such risk cowed many American shippers into holding their vessels in safe harbors, storing wheat, cotton, munitions, and other cargo in secure if unprofitable warehouses. As a dramatic illustration of what fate might await American sailors, on February 25 the British passenger liner *Laconia* was torpedoed off the coast of Ireland on its passage from New York to Liverpool, killing an American mother and her daughter. Also aboard was the *Chicago Tribune*'s adventurous reporter Floyd Gibbons, who had chosen to travel on the *Laconia* for the very reason that it was in danger; he had hoped for the opportunity to describe such a deadly experience, which he did in prose that gave a vivid sense of what a sinking meant in human fear and suffering, a scene of tangled ropes, poorly handled lifeboats, panicked people jumping into the frigid waves, violent seasickness: "It was bedlam and nightmare." Immediately cabled home after his rescue, the story appeared in newspapers across the United States on the twenty-sixth, and shortly thereafter was read from the floor of both houses of Congress.

On the same day as the *Laconia* sinking, Wilson went before Congress to ask for the authority to arm merchant ships, seeing this as an important step toward "armed neutrality."[15] He hoped that having navy-supplied cannon and gun crews aboard would intimidate the Germans and give enough confidence to owners that they would return to the sea-lanes, releasing the freight that was so burdening the wharves. But legislators at first were afraid that such arming would only invite attack and draw the country closer to war. In this fear they were supported by a number of peace groups.

Pacifists had been as shocked as everyone else when Germany had rescinded the *Sussex* Pledge and reopened its unrestricted submarine campaign. Louis Lochner, who had temporarily returned from Ford's Peace Ship crusade to deal with organizational problems, met with Wilson just hours after the official notification had been received. Lochner found him looking "haggard and worried," but interested in and supportive of the Ford group's efforts for the immediate end to fighting, and a postwar league of nations. Wilson also assured the young man that he would continue to do all he could to keep the nation out of war.[16]

From the beginning of February, peace activists were organizing for the new challenge: a National Pacifist Congress met in New York City, and the Association of German American Pastors called for a day of prayer to overcome "all evil counsel and base machinations which are at work to plunge our nation into war," while the American Union Against Militarism, the Women's Peace Party, and the Socialist Party organized petition drives, marches, and rallies in major cities, including Washington.[17] William Jennings Bryan was also actively campaigning against any action that might bring war. Emboldened by these developments, members of both houses began to organize against the Armed Ship bill.

The German government, too, was preparing for the future, though that country's leaders held few doubts about the direction of their relations with the United States. When American diplomats secretly attempted to continue negotiations with the imperial government even after the formal break in relations, Kaiser Wilhelm made clear that he was not interested, writing in the margin of a diplomatic note: "*Negotiations* with America are *finished* now once and for all! If Wilson wants war, then he shall bring it about, and then have it!"[18] What illusionary hopes the Germans held concerned Mexico and Japan.

As a particular mark of courtesy, Wilson, at House's urging and over the objections of Secretary of State Lansing, had secretly allowed the Germans to use the American government's telegraph lines for the transmission of coded messages without demanding a key to the code. House, who in spite of his pose as man of the world was rather naive, was easily convinced by Bernstorff that this privilege would only be used for discussions of peace proposals. Wilson, spurred on by Lansing, became increasingly uncomfortable with the arrangement, writing to House on January 24 that Bernstorff had "sent a long message to his government the other day, but I do not know what it was about. . . . If we are to continue to send messages for him, we should . . . in each instance receive his official assurance that there is at least nothing in his dispatches which would be unneutral for us to transmit." And he went on to admit that with all his burdens, "I feel very lonely sometimes and sometimes very low in my mind, in spite of myself."[19]

The British, whose counterintelligence activities during this war were brilliant and unceasing, as a matter of clandestine routine intercepted American diplomatic traffic. They quickly recognized that a German code was occasionally appearing among the American messages, and after intense, patient work, aided by a captured codebook, broke it. So it was that when in January another German message was intercepted on the American wire, the British were able, after weeks of complex decoding, to read much of the content, though they had trouble believing what they read: Germany was proposing an alliance with Mexico and Japan, which was at the time a British ally, against the United States. "MAKE WAR TOGETHER," it read in part, "GENEROUS FINANCIAL SUPPORT, AND . . . MEXICO IS TO RECONQUER THE LOST TERRITORY IN TEXAS, NEW MEXICO, AND ARIZONA." It was hoped that Carranza, as president of Mexico, would be inspired by the unrestricted submarine campaign's guarantee of victory to "ON HIS OWN INITIATIVE, INVITE JAPAN TO IMMEDIATE ADHERENCE AND AT THE SAME TIME MEDIATE BETWEEN JAPAN AND OURSELVES."[20]

The British faced a dilemma. They recognized the power of what they held, evidence of the "overt act" Woodrow Wilson had said he didn't believe was coming. But they also had to conceal from the Germans the

breaking of their code, and from the Americans the British reading of their
governmental communications. These problems were eventually solved
through elaborate maneuvering involving sources and agents in Mexico
and London, including Ambassador Walter Page; on Saturday, February 24,
the telegram and a new dilemma landed on the desk of Woodrow Wilson.[21]

The president was still trying to steer a middle course between armed
neutrality and war, but he was feeling the strain. Tensions had erupted in a
Cabinet meeting just the day before, on the twenty-third, when he had felt
that several members were taking too hard a line against Germany. "[He]
turned on them bitterly," wrote Franklin Lane, the secretary of the interior,
"especially on McAdoo, and reproached all of us. . . . We couldn't get the
idea out of his head that we were bent on pushing the country into war."[22]
He now held this explosive telegram at the same time he was asking a
rebellious Congress for permission to arm merchant ships, a move that he
thought would show Germany that the United States would not allow itself
to be pushed off the Atlantic. At first, he did not want to use the Zimmermann plot as a tactic in the legislative battle, especially since the anger
produced might overwhelm his control of the question of war or peace, but
then, as opposition to his bill mounted, he felt that it might give just
enough impetus to force passage. Wilson, without consulting the Cabinet,
had the Zimmermann telegram released to the Associated Press on the
evening of February 28, and by the next morning headlines were blazing
across the nation, as in the *New York Times*:

GERMANY SEEKS ALLIANCE AGAINST U.S.
ASKS JAPAN AND MEXICO TO JOIN HER;
FULL TEXT OF HER PROPOSAL MADE PUBLIC

Outrage was intensified by the fact that this revelation came fast on
the heels of Floyd Gibbons's graphic account of the tragedy of the *Laconia*,
and because many news stories recapitulated the recent involvement of
German agents in Mexico. Headlines began referring to the "Prussian
Invasion Plot." Here was evidence of anti-American hostility so crude and
overt that even the most oblivious man in the street was aroused. Overnight
the mood of the country changed, and the political institution designed to
reflect any such moods changed with it. The House of Representatives
quickly passed the Armed Ships bill by a vote of 403–13, but Robert La Follette of Wisconsin led a filibuster in the Senate that blocked its passage
until the end of the session, on March 4, which also blocked the army and
various other appropriation bills. This meant that soldiers serving on the

Mexican border would not be paid. The president had known all along that he already possessed the power to arm merchant ships under an old antipiracy statute, but had wanted the support of the legislature in making such an escalation. Now he bitterly, and publicly, condemned the eleven senators responsible as a "little group of willful men" who had "rendered the great government of the United States helpless and contemptible."[23]

Wilson's second inaugural came in the midst of these struggles. March 4 fell on a stormy Sunday in 1917, so, because of the holy day, his swearing-in by Chief Justice Edward White was held in the small presidential office at the Capitol. It was supposed to be private, and it is a sign of the stress he was feeling that he was greatly irritated by the various Cabinet members, legislators, and members of their families who tried to crowd into the space to witness the historic occasion. Some of that irritation may have come from his also trying to sign end-of-session bills immediately before and after the ceremony, including one establishing Prohibition in the District of Columbia. This he signed in spite of numerous arguments from union leader Samuel Gompers and important local politicians that he veto it, one of whom pleaded, "We beg you, Mr. President, to show mercy."[24]

Another group also asked for consideration. Hundreds of women braved the elements to march for suffrage. "The rain beat in their faces," noted one onlooker, "and the wind played havoc with the banners. They presented a sorry sight, but they went through with their program as well as they could." The favorite banner slogan was: "Mr. President, how long must women wait for liberty?" When the march finally arrived at the White House and the leaders asked to see the president, they were politely told, "This is Sunday and the White House grounds are closed to all visitors."[25]

The rain and high winds continued as the president gave his formal speech on Monday. All the recent controversies had brought such a number of threats against his life that an anxious Secret Service had marksmen guarding the procession from rooftops along the route. Events went smoothly enough, but with no sense of celebration or satisfaction. Assistant Secretary of the Navy Franklin Delano Roosevelt was seated too far away to hear the president's address, which was blown hither and yon by the wind, but he noted in his diary that there was "little enthusiasm in the crowd." And when he did join the more important politicians on the reviewing stand as soldiers, sailors, and marines marched by, the young man was critical of the overprotection, thinking it an "awful mistake to review troops from [a] glass cage."[26]

But the glass cage was to be extended. The very real possibility of German action, and a paranoid fear of pacifists, led Congress to pass the

Threats Against the President Act in February 1917, to be used against those who "knowingly and willfully" threatened the president in writing or speech. This would result in sixty prosecutions by June 1918, and at least thirty-five convictions.[27] Also introduced was legislation attempting to define and outlaw espionage, but it did not complete passage before Congress adjourned. These were early signs that war would bring a toughening of American attitudes toward traditional civil liberties.

The Zimmermann message was such an anti-German bombshell that many people doubted its authenticity, assuming that it was a British forgery. This was immediately charged by the German American press, especially by paid agents such as George Sylvester Viereck, editor of *The Fatherland,* but such suspicions were held even by those who favored the Allies, such as the eastern social and intellectual elite who made up the Round Table Dining Club. Joseph Choate, former ambassador to Britain, along with Nicholas Murray Butler, president of Columbia University, and Elihu Root, former secretary of war, were among the members present one evening when they surprised Captain Guy Gaunt, a very effective British agent, by challenging him to prove the telegram's authenticity.[28]

So secret was the real source that Lansing and other members of the Cabinet were worried about how to answer the growing demands for an explanation, but this crisis was resolved by the German foreign minister himself. Astonishingly and inexplicably, Zimmermann, on March 3, acknowledged that the message was genuine, and attempted to justify sending it.[29] A relieved Lansing wrote that this "was a surprising example of incompetency and showed him a man of little ability. . . . The admission suppressed all the clamor of the German-American press about the message being faked and the unexpressed suspicion that it was fraudulent held by many other people." Lansing also noted that as a result "the people all over the country are extremely enraged at the perfidy of the German Government in talking peace and friendship with this country and at the same time plotting a hostile coalition against it."[30]

People all over the country certainly were now taking notice: westerners, who were particularly sensitive to the troubles with Mexico and nearest the threat posed by Japan, as well as easterners, who had most resented the losses from earlier submarine campaigns. What had seemed a remote quarrel between Europeans, who were notoriously quarrelsome, now had an immediate bearing on every American's life. Disagreements over shipping rights had been a bit abstract, although the sinking of ships with Americans on board had been real enough, but the numbers of these incidents were small and involved citizens willing to risk their lives on a passage that most people could not afford. A vague consciousness of German involvement in deadly sabotage in the United States, and of subversion along the border, had been growing, but the German American press and German sympathizers, not least the millions of German American citizens, had actively denied the reports. Now, after Zimmermann had admitted the truth of the plot, there was no one to defend German actions. As Barbara Tuchman put it, "The German-Americans . . . retreated across their hyphen to take their stand, somewhat sullenly, on the American side."[31]

Wilson agonized during the month of March over the question of war or peace. He recognized that entry would mean the end of his progressive program, probably recalling what he had said in 1914: "Every reform we have won will be lost if we go into this war," and now saying to his secretary of the navy, "Daniels, if this country goes into war, you and I will live to see the day when the big interests will be in the saddle."[32]

Undoubtedly remembering Veracruz, he also felt personal responsibility for the deaths that would follow a decision for war, as he would soon tell the French philosopher Henri Bergson. And he recognized the dangers not only to progressivism but democracy itself. At a particularly intense point of his turmoil, Wilson unburdened himself to the liberal newspaper editor Frank Cobb of some of his fears about declaring war: "Once lead this people into war, and they'll forget there ever was such a thing as tolerance. To fight you must be brutal and ruthless, and a spirit of ruthless brutality will enter the fibre of our national life, infecting Congress, the courts, and the policeman on the beat, the man in the streets. . . . A nation could not put its strength into a war and keep its head level; it has never been done. If there is any alternative, for God's sake let's take it."[33]

And yet, he could find no alternative. The renunciation of the *Sussex* pledge, and the Zimmermann telegram, combined with the domestic sabotage and spying that had already taken place, had convinced Wilson that the Germans could not be trusted, that the military leaders were now in control and obsessed with conquering on the battlefield, which meant there was no hope for a neutral nation to broker a peace. Another set of "overt acts" drove home the point, as three American ships were sunk in the middle of March, killing fifteen Americans, and leading to prowar demonstrations in major cities. The Kerensky revolution in Russia that same month drove the autocratic Czar Nicholas II from his throne, removing a moral taint from the Allied cause. Leaning back in his chair, leg up on his desk, Secretary of War Baker crowed to Lincoln Steffens: "Well, I guess this king business is pretty near over." Wilson was also delighted with what seemed the promising birth of a new democracy, and rushed to recognize

it, making the United States the first government to do so. This overthrow
of an anti-Semitic regime also brought many American Jews into the Allied
camp, and allowed Wilson and others to see the fight now as one between
democracy and aggressive autocracy.

On March 20, the president met with his Cabinet to discuss the possibility of war. Lansing perhaps best summed up the general feeling, arguing
that there was a greater reason for war than just having ships sunk and citizens killed: "The sounder basis was the duty of this and every other democratic nation to suppress an autocratic government like the German
because of its atrocious character and because it was a menace to the
national safety of this country and of all other countries with liberal systems of government."[34] Wilson found that even former pacifists such as
Daniels and Baker now agreed that there was no other course open but
war, Daniels's eyes filling with tears as he admitted this. The advice was
given, but the president made up his own mind. At the end of the meeting,
Lansing directly asked what he now intended to do. Wilson gave what
must have been a sad smile, saying, "Oh, I think I will sleep on it." And the
decision was then reluctantly made: Germany seemed determined to make
war on the United States, so it could not be avoided any longer. Just as
important was his belief that Germany would be beaten, and to ensure that
there would be a just peace enforced by a league of nations, the United
States had to lead the way to victory, so he would have influence in the
negotiations. The morning after the Cabinet meeting, Wilson called for a
special session of the newly elected Sixty-fifth Congress to be assembled
on April 2 "to receive a communication concerning grave matters of national
policy." He then set to work on his rackety old typewriter, not sharing his
thoughts as he wrote his message, but sharing his bad mood; after a few
outbursts of anger, everyone walked on tiptoes around the White House.

JACK REED spent the last few months of 1916 hobbled by his kidney problems, now so bad that he finally was confined to the hospital at Johns Hopkins for a month to have his left kidney removed. It was perhaps this whiff
of mortality that moved him to reflect on the course his life had taken, to

> stop a minute, and look back, and get my bearings. . . . I am twenty-
> nine . . . and I know this is . . . the end of youth. Sometimes it seems to
> be the end of the world's youth, too; certainly the Great War has done
> something to us all. But it is also the beginning of a new phase of life; and
> the world we live in is so full of swift change and color and meaning that

I can hardly keep from imagining the splendid and terrible possibilities of the time to come. The last ten years I've gone up and down the earth drinking in experience, fighting and loving, seeing and hearing and tasting things. I've traveled all over . . . having adventures; seeing men killed and broken, victorious and laughing, men with visions and men with a sense of humor. I've watched civilization change and broaden and sweeten in my lifetime, and tried to help; and I've watched it wither and crumble in the red blast of war. . . . I'm not quite sick of seeing yet, but I will be—I know that. My future life will not be what it has been.[35]

And yet, it was, and would so remain for the brief time left to him. For all his fantasies and desires to be a poet, playwright, and novelist, these were not where his talents lay. He loved action, as he also noted: "A furious energy drove me to all kinds of bodily and mental exercise, without any particular direction. . . . I was increasingly active and restless, more ambitious of place and power. . . . Life became a beloved motion picture, thought about only in flashes, conceived as emotion and sensation." Emotion and sensation, not the contemplation and discipline necessary to refine these for creative work.

Jack had been alone in the hospital at Baltimore, Louise writing him regularly, but visiting just briefly. She was very ill herself, with an ovarian abscess, and at one point let him think his own kidney problems led to her infection.[36] A more likely source, though, would have come through Eugene O'Neill's vagabond life, with his intimate contact with waterfront whores as depicted in *The Iceman Cometh*. Gonorrhea can develop into tubo-ovarian abscess, as can a postabortion infection. When O'Neill ten years later wrote *Strange Interlude*, a play based on this triangle, about a man who betrays his best friend by having an affair with his wife, the wife claims that she is ill in order to hide the fact that she has had an abortion.[37]

Ambitious new plans were devised after Reed had more or less recovered from the operation in January 1917. Jack and Louise would travel to China to drink in the experience of the revolutionary changes there, he writing about them for *Metropolitan* magazine and she for other national publications. "He will hold up the mirror to this mysterious and romantic country," advertised *Metropolitan*, "and we shall see its teeming millions and the big forces at work there. Imagine Reed in this rich 'copy' empire."[38] But Germany's renunciation of the *Sussex* Pledge made editors pull back from such exotic assignments, waiting instead to see what President Wilson and the United States would do. What Jack soon realized was that this profitable connection with a prosperous and once open-minded magazine was now over, and he angrily told H. J. Whigham, the publisher of *Metropolitan,* "You and I call ourselves friends, but we are not really friends because we don't believe in the same things, and the time will come when we won't speak to each other." He then spoke of his vision of future revolution in a way that must have seemed like a threat: "You are going to see great things happen in this country pretty soon. It may kill me and it may kill you and all your friends, but it's going to be great."[39]

Peace activists as well as editors were concerned with what the president might do, but they weren't passively waiting for a decision. James Hudson Maurer, president of the Pennsylvania State Federation of Labor, called for a general strike if war was declared. Meetings were held, demonstrations mounted, men and women were summoned to Washington to lobby politicians, many of these travelers clutching white tulips as a symbol of their resistance. Reed joined in the effort with all his energy—writing articles and letters, and joining those journeying to the District of Columbia to speak against the war.

Some tried to do more than speak, but a parade permit was denied, and they were also denied permission to see the president. One group did manage to speak briefly with Senator Henry Cabot Lodge outside his office, but that free exchange of ideas between the self-righteous ended in fisticuffs when the senator told them that "national degeneracy and cowardice are worse than war."

Alexander Bannwart, a thirty-six-year-old former professional baseball player of Swiss-German extraction, then said, "You are a damned coward."

The sixty-seven-year-old Lodge responded, "You are a damned liar." Blows were exchanged. A passing Western Union messenger rushed in, explaining to reporters later: "I saw an old man in a fight, and I thought it my duty to help him." The senator's secretaries also helped; the result was a severe thrashing and jail for Mr. Bannwart, much being made of his German American heritage, and a great deal of heroic press coverage for Henry Cabot Lodge.[40]

April 2 was another day of rain, but this "a soft, fragrant rain of early spring," as William McAdoo remembered. "The illuminated dome of the Capitol stood in solemn splendor against the dark, wet sky."[41] Just before eight-thirty that evening, the president was driven in an automobile toward that glowing dome protected by a troop of cavalry, hooves clattering along wet streets lined with flag-waving citizens. Standing on the podium before an overflow audience, also flag-bedecked, of senators, representatives, Cabinet members, Supreme Court justices, ambassadors, every worthy who could wrangle entry, Woodrow Wilson eloquently laid out the case for war, though he had to wait five minutes for the standing ovation to subside.

Dispassionately, in that winning, musical voice that had been noted by so many, he went over the recent history of German aggression: "Even hospital ships and ships carrying relief to the sorely bereaved and stricken people of Belgium . . . have been sunk with the same reckless lack of compassion or of principle." Over the centuries, with great difficulty, a minimum of law had been established to protect the lives and property of innocent travelers upon the sea. That had now been swept aside. "Property can be paid for; the lives of peaceful and innocent people cannot be. The present German submarine warfare against commerce is a warfare against mankind. It is a war against all nations. . . . The challenge is to all mankind."

Armed neutrality had turned out to be "impracticable" and "ineffectual," so "with a profound sense of the solemn and even tragical character of the step I am taking . . . I advise that the Congress declare the recent course of the Imperial German Government to be in fact nothing less than war against . . . the United States; that it formally accept the status of belligerent which has thus been thrust upon it." The hall exploded with cheers and shouts as people jumped to their feet, the cheering led by Chief Justice White, himself a Confederate Army veteran and enthusiastic supporter of the Allies.

Wilson went on to emphasize that war had been thrust upon the country not by the German people themselves—"We have no feeling towards them but one of sympathy and friendship"—but by the "Prussian autocracy." He then discussed at some length the sabotage and other unlawful acts that had been directed against the country, pointing out: "Prussian autocracy . . . from the very outset of the present war . . . filled our unsuspecting communities and even our offices of government with spies and set criminal intrigues everywhere afoot against our national unity of counsel, our peace within and without, our industries and our commerce." Such threatening despotism had to be countered by a free people: "The world must be made safe for democracy. Its peace must be planted upon the tested foundations of political liberty. We have no selfish ends to serve." And since the United States did not desire conquest or dominion, it would "observe with proud punctilio the principles of right and of fair play we profess to be fighting for."

"We shall fight for the things we have always carried nearest our hearts," he said at the close, "for democracy, for the right of those who submit to authority to have a voice in their own governments, for the rights and liberties of small nations, for a universal dominion of right."

Now the great hall shook again with cheers and clapping, just as over the next few days presidential mail would reach flood proportions with more huzzahs and congratulations. Even his once and future enemy Henry Cabot Lodge pushed through the crowd to congratulate him, little the worse for his recent fistfight. Wilson had labored long, hard, and in seclusion on the speech, but it was obvious from his drawn face that none of this patriotic enthusiasm gave him pleasure. As he said to his secretary Joe Tumulty later that night: "My message today was a message of death for our young men. How strange it seems to applaud that!"[42]

Some definitely were not applauding. Though Jack Reed had been given a Senate pass by Robert La Follette, he refused to attend the historic session, instead taking part in a mass antiwar meeting. Partway through, word came that the president had just asked for war to be declared. Several of the speakers—including the chairman, David Starr Jordan, head of Stanford University and longtime peace activist—then announced that they saw no choice but to support the country, but Reed disagreed, announcing from the platform: "This is not my war, and I will not support it. This is not my war, and I will have nothing to do with it."[43]

The United States had entered among the powers of the world when it successfully went to war with Spain in 1898. Theodore Roosevelt, Leonard Wood, and Elihu Root had learned from the near disasters of that year of the urgent need to modernize the nation's armed forces, and when in power they had worked for that improvement with mixed success. Others, who had learned from that same conflict that even brief wars are fought at a great price in both lives and treasure, had resolutely set about limiting the chances of the United States ever entering another. They were confident that the world's disputes could not threaten a peace-loving democracy isolated by two great oceans. Now, however, those quarrels no longer seemed quite so distant or their outcomes so unimportant. A foreign power had sunk American ships, then reached out to a neighboring country to propose they make war together against the United States.

Even so, there was resistance to changing centuries of habit and desire. Robert La Follette tried to organize the forces of peace, and Senator George Norris of Nebraska gave a passionate speech arguing that "we are going into war upon the command of gold. . . . I would like to say to this war god: You shall not coin into gold the lifeblood of my brethren. . . . I feel that we are about to put the dollar sign upon the American flag."[44] Others proposed, such was their faith in democracy, that the issue of war or peace be put to the people in the form of a national referendum. The effort was futile. The nation was now aroused, and, though still reluctant, ready to follow the president into the conflict. An Indiana newspaper wrote on the day of Wilson's speech that midwesterners would not welcome "a declaration of war joyously and with a smile on their lips. Rather will they meet it with a deep feeling of responsibility, a feeling that if the test has come they must meet it and be men."[45] On April 4 the Senate held a daylong debate, then voted 82 to 6, with 8 abstentions, for war. The House voted 373 to 50 on April 6, Good Friday, one of the dissenting votes being cast by the first woman ever to sit as a representative, Jeannette Rankin of Montana. She would serve to vote against a second world war some twenty-four years later.

The joint war resolution was rushed to the White House; Woodrow Wilson interrupted his lunch, and came to the office of the usher, Ike Hoover. "Stand by me, Edith," he said to his wife. She handed him a gold fountain pen, a gift he had given her, to sign the document.

A signal was passed to a junior naval officer, who had been instructed by Assistant Secretary Franklin Delano Roosevelt to stand in readiness. Now the young man rushed outside and with his arms semaphored to a figure standing in a window of the adjacent State, War and Navy building, who then ordered that wireless messages be sent to all the ships at sea: the United States was at war. Just what that meant was yet to be determined.

—◄◦►—

CHAPTER SIXTEEN

Crusade

This is our opportunity to demonstrate the efficiency of a great Democracy and we shall not fall short of it!

Woodrow Wilson in his war address

[The war is] . . . a high adventure, a crusade with a compelling purpose.

Raymond Fosdick[1]

There is a lofty idealism about it which puts this war on the plane of a crusade.

James W. Gerard to Woodrow Wilson[2]

WOODROW WILSON had stated in his war speech that "what this will involve is clear." It was anything but. He had asked for financial credits to be extended to the Allies, that 500,000 men be conscripted, and urged that the war be paid for by taxation rather than borrowing. But these requests did not establish a program for putting the nation on a war footing, and the first months after the United States entered the conflict were filled with confusion and chaos.[3]

Some of the most important questions of strategy had not yet been resolved. When Major Palmer R. Pierce, aide to Secretary of War Baker, was testifying before the Senate Finance Committee on April 6, the day war was declared, he was sharply questioned by Committee Chair Thomas Martin of Virginia about the War Department's needs. Especially upsetting was its request for the unprecedented sum of $3 billion. The major explained that the budget would have to cover expanded expenses for "clothing, cots, camps, food, pay. . . . And we may have to have an army in France."

"Good Lord!" cried the shocked senator. "You're not going to send soldiers over there, are you?"[4]

The answer to that question wasn't yet clear to the president or his advisers. Baker made vague comments about the likelihood of eventually sending thoroughly trained soldiers, and McAdoo testified to Congress that "the most effective aid we could extend to Great Britain, France, Italy, and Russia was money." He believed that "the dollars that we sent through these loans to Europe were . . . substitutes for American soldiers, and the extent to which we were able to save the lives of the young men of America would be measured by the extent to which we could make operative, quickly and effectively, the credits the Allies needed to purchase supplies in the American markets."[5] Nor did the president seem eager to propose sending an army to Europe. The urgent need on everyone's mind was defense of the homeland, especially after the Zimmermann proposal that encouraged attacks by Mexico and Japan, attacks that Mexicans at German instigation had already made the previous year, killing and maiming American citizens. Intelligence reports were showing that German agents, and some German Americans, who feared what would happen now that hostilities had become official, were gathering in Mexico, but as McAdoo laconically noted: "At that time the Mexicans did not love us too well, but they were possessed of common-sense."[6] This probably gives Carranza too much credit, since he was not overly burdened with common sense when it came to relations with the United States. He willingly cooperated with the kaiser's agents but not to the point of invasion.

There was a plentitude of experts willing to offer advice on what the United States should do, and they began arriving just after the declaration. The British first, followed closely by the French, then, over the next few months, all the rest of the Allies: Italians, Serbs, Japanese, Russians, Belgians, and Romanians. It is a sign of the Allies' own lack of coordinated planning that these missions had not held discussions among themselves about what course of action to recommend to their powerful but untried new associate; instead each followed a separate agenda, the common denominator being the request for money. These delegations were usually headed by well-known political figures such as Arthur Balfour, former British prime minister and current foreign secretary, and René Viviani, former French premier and current minister of justice. They were accompanied by leading financial and military professionals. France enjoyed a public relations coup by bringing along the Marquis Jacques Adelbert de Chambrun, member of the Chamber of Deputies and direct descendant of the Marquis de Lafayette, French hero of the American Revolution, and thus an honorary American citizen.[7]

Everyone, American and foreign, was on their best, most cooperative behavior but, even so, cultural differences soon became evident. Both the British and the French were undoubtedly surprised when they attended a banquet on the presidential yacht, the *Mayflower*, and discovered that no wine or other alcohol could be served because the vessel was officially part of Josephus Daniels's navy, where temperance was enforced without exception for officers, enlisted men, and visiting dignitaries. But they were not as startled as Americans were at the Frenchman Viviani kissing politicians, as he did with the mayors of Philadelphia and Kansas City. Then there were problems of business style: "Before long I discovered that it was utterly impossible for me to conduct negotiations in person with these diplomats," remembered William McAdoo, who as treasury secretary was of great importance to the needy visitors. "It took too much time. They were . . . loquacious and accustomed to leisurely conversation." He found that with the many demands of his office he had to be "snappy." Americans understood the signals and would quickly conduct their business and leave, but the foreigners could not interpret the hints. "I had to listen for a long time to things that had no relation to the immediate problems in hand when important people were champing at the bit in my outer room and sometimes raging because of my seeming lack of consideration."[8] Assistant secretaries were appointed to suffer such wastes of time, but the real business at hand, the loans, was accomplished. Years later, when repayment was a contentious issue, McAdoo bitterly remembered "their profound and eternal (and almost obsequious) gratitude when I, as Secretary of the Treasury, handed to their representatives checks for one or two hundred million dollars apiece."[9]

Marshal Joseph-Jacques Joffre, until recently chief of the French army and the victor of the Marne, who had saved Paris in the early days of the war, was even more famous in America than Viviani, rivaling the Marquis de Chambrun in popularity. He shocked American leaders when he spoke privately to them about the real situation on the ground in Europe. Wilson and his advisers had known of the dire economic situation of the Allies, and in fact just a few months before were willing to use it to force them to the negotiating table if Germany had cooperated, but now came more bleak news of their naval and military situations. A recent offensive by the French army from which great victories had been expected had resulted instead in bloody disaster. After the even worse slaughters of 1916 both France and Britain were desperate for men to replace their millions of dead and wounded, though there were different ideas about how these soldiers should be used. The British, along with some French officials, were surprised at the lack of American military equipment and training. They proposed that U.S. troops be integrated with their decimated veteran units, which would provide immediate structure and experienced officers and noncoms. Joffre had his own doubts about the practicality of such an unprepared nation being able to raise and train the army necessary, and to provide enough high-level officers who had a sense of the strategies and, especially, the logistics of modern war. But he was intelligent and diplomatic enough to realize that such a plan as the British proposed would not be acceptable, especially in a democracy. It would be impossible, he noted, for the United States to "allow its citizens to be incorporated like poor relations in the ranks of some other army and fight under a foreign flag."[10] Resistance to such integration would be particularly strong from anyone who had paid the slightest attention to how the unimaginative tactics and strategies of Allied generals had resulted in catastrophic losses without any advance toward victory.

But before decisions could be made about how to deploy troops, they first had to be raised. Little matériel but some moral support was given by old stalwarts such as the pacifistic William Jennings Bryan, who immediately after the declaration wired Wilson asking to be enrolled as a private in the army, promising that until enlisted he would aid "in safeguarding the morals of the men in camp."[11] Theodore Roosevelt, who held higher ambitions, stepped forward more aggressively in spite of being in poor health and blind in one eye. Swallowing his pride, and his jealousy, he visited his great rival in the White House on April 10, requesting that he be allowed to raise a division of volunteers and lead them into battle, just as he had done with the Rough Riders in Cuba in 1898. Full of compliments about the majesty of Wilson's war speech, he implied that his attacks on the administration would then cease: "Mr. President, what I have said and thought, and what others have said and thought is all dust in a windy street, if now we can make your message good."[12] They managed to speak amiably for close to half an hour, then the colonel, as the ex-president preferred to be called, went outside and was interviewed and filmed by the horde of reporters and newsreel cameramen waiting for him.

Wilson would have been less than human if some resentment at Roosevelt's fierce attacks over the years didn't still smart, but he was seemingly able to enjoy his time with the man, telling his secretary Tumulty afterward that Roosevelt was like "a great big boy. I was, as formerly, charmed by his personality. There is a sweetness about him that is very compelling. You can't resist the man. I can easily understand why his followers are so fond of him."[13]

But he did resist him. This was not to be, at least deliberately, a war fought by crowds of amateurs like the Spanish-American War; luck and courage would not be enough to allow survival, let alone victory, against an enemy as skilled and experienced as the German army. The War Department urged rejection of the request, and Wilson concurred, bringing down on his head criticism from those very followers that he claimed he so easily understood. Writing decades later, William Allen White still could not forgive what he saw as a deliberate humiliation of his hero, recalling "in my mind's eye the picture that I had from the day's press reports when Roosevelt, who more than any other thing on earth desired to fight for his country, walked up the curved pathway to the White House. . . . The frigid malevolence with which Wilson denied this strong man's plea, made in what Wilson, being sensitive and wise, knew was excruciating abasement."[14] So passionate were the feelings aroused in the colonel's fans that Wilson probably should have tried to make some kind of accommodation to bring the old warrior into the fold, but he could not bring himself to do so.

Also criticized by Republican partisans was the administration's selection of commander in chief of the armies to be raised. On the evening of February 19, 1917, General Frederick Funston, overweight and out of shape, died of a heart attack while listening to an orchestra in the lobby of a hotel in San Antonio play "On the Beautiful Blue Danube," leaving the top post vacant. General Leonard Wood, former chief of staff and hero of both the Apache campaign, where he won a Medal of Honor, and the Spanish-American War, was a possible choice. He and his close friend Roosevelt certainly felt he should have been *the* choice, but as a politically ambitious Republican he had been a difficult subordinate for a Democratic administration. The choice went instead to John J. Pershing, who had proven himself to Wilson and Baker by the intelligent, calm, and discreet way he had conducted the Punitive Expedition.[15] Through this adventure he also gained the most experience handling troops in the field of any American officer, though only ten thousand or so instead of the millions that would soon be under his command.

The president had reluctantly, and only after strong urging from his military and civilian advisers, decided that the most efficient way to raise those millions would be through conscription. He had resisted this imposition of governmental power that was so radical a change from tradition. But it would allow the troops to be raised selectively, instead of relying on a rush of patriotic volunteers who might be more useful staying at their trades; it was also hailed by others as an instrument of "Americanism," a way of

A blindfolded Secretary of War Baker draws a draft number in 1917

bringing the full range of white males together, irrespective of class, creed, religion, or ethnicity, and bonding them through shared sacrifice, though this would essentially create a democratic army through undemocratic means. The very thought of conscription gave shivers of alarm to those politicians who knew of the draft riots of 1863, when Irish immigrant mobs had burned sections of New York City, hunting down and killing African Americans, police, and Union officers. Smaller-scale disturbances occurred in other cities including Albany, Boston, and some rural regions of the country. One senator charged: "You will have the streets of our American cities running red with blood on Registration day."[16]

There was also the question of honor. "I protest with all my heart and mind and soul against having the slur of being a conscript placed upon the men of Missouri," argued Speaker of the House Champ Clark. "In the estimation of Missourians there is precious little difference between a conscript and a convict."[17] General Pershing, now stationed with his troops in Texas, was an effective arguer against this point of view, visiting the state's governor and persuading him not only to support the draft, but also to use his influence with the Texas delegation in Congress to ensure they came on board.[18]

Hearings were quickly held; Jack Reed appeared before the House Committee on Military Affairs arguing that drafting citizens was undemocratic in general, but going further in specifics. "I am not a peace-at-any-price man, or a thorough pacifist, but I would not serve in this war. You can shoot me if you want and try to draft me to fight—and I know there are ten thousand other people." Two congressmen interrupted, arguing that this witness should be dismissed, but the chairman of the committee, himself opposed to conscription, allowed him to continue his argument that this was a commercial war, not one being fought for anything of value to the people.[19]

Amos Pinchot, a militant progressive, shared these feelings along with many other liberals who saw the draft as a European-type system of state coercion. Pinchot published a letter in the *New York Times* on March 13, arguing, "Conscription is a great commercial policy; a carefully devised weapon that the exploiters are forging for their own protection at home, and in the interest of American financial imperialism abroad." The rich and powerful were demanding compulsory service as "a clearly thought-out and heavily backed project to mould the United States into an efficient, orderly nation, economically and politically controlled by those who know what is good for the people. In this country so ordered and so governed, there will be no strikes, no surly revolt against authority, and no popular discontent. . . . This, if we cut through the patriotic pretext and flag-waving propaganda, is the real vision of the conscriptionist."

Southerners and westerners spoke against the new system from a less radical position, though they had their own suspicions of big business, praising the tradition of volunteerism that had sufficed in all previous conflicts except the last two desperate years of the Civil War. Much of the Democratic congressional leadership was from rural districts, and opposed the draft, which complicated passage of the act. Even Secretary of the Navy Daniels, of North Carolina, asked, "Why introduce Prussianism to fight Prussianism?"[20] Claude Kitchin of North Carolina, majority leader of the House, who had voted against the war, argued as well against the draft. This opposition was based partly on philosophical grounds, but also on fear that the South could lose its cheap black laborers to the army, where, even more alarming, they might gain ideas above their station, and with military training they would be able to defend these ideas. After the necessary compromises were reached, Kitchin wrote reassuringly to an employer: "Few of them [the blacks], if any, will be taken."[21] He was wrong: one in four eligible whites would be drafted, while the ratio for blacks would be one in three.

The Selective Service Act was finally passed 397 to 24 in the House and 81 to 8 in the Senate. Efforts had been made by Republicans to include in the bill express permission for Roosevelt to raise and lead his volunteer force, but these had been rejected at the urging of Wilson. Aside from his personal feelings against TR, he had, as we saw earlier, changed his own attitude toward war. What had once seemed romantic and chivalrous was now viewed as an unpleasant job of work to be dispatched as quickly and efficiently as possible. "Deprived of glory, war loses all its charm," he had written in 1916 during the horrific battle for Verdun, which had taken 500,000 lives. He had gone on to condemn "the mechanical slaughter . . . of modern conflict."[22] Wilson expressed similar sentiments when signing the draft law, making clear that "the business now at hand is undramatic, practical, and of scientific definiteness and precision."[23] Still welcoming volunteers would be the Regular Army, the navy, and marines, and the National Guard; eventually there would be more than a million of them serving. Draftees would be organized into their own units in what would be called the National Army.

Much thought had gone into designing the conscription system to be as palatable as possible to Americans. Young men aged twenty-one through thirty were to register at polling places, not the post offices, where the Regular Army did its recruiting, thus tying the draft to the civic duty and privilege of voting rather than the traditional military. The Selective Service boards would be made up of local citizens rather than military or governmental officers, and there was to be no "substitution," or paying for someone to take a draftee's place, which had been the most odious feature of Civil War conscription. On June 5 ten million young men showed up at four thousand polling centers to register, and were assigned group numbers to be used in a lottery selection. The first drawing was held on July 10 when Secretary of War Baker, blindfolded, pulled the lucky numbers out of a very large glass bowl that set the order in which the men would go before their local civilian boards. The civilians would then decide who was to be drafted, depending on the individual's health and the importance of his occupation to the war effort.

The process moved smoothly; by the end of the conflict almost 24 million men were registered, though perhaps as many as 3 million deliberately avoided registering, and more than 2.7 million would be drafted. Despite the warnings, there was no blood in the streets, but there were isolated protests. Families making a hard-scrabble living as tenant farmers in the hills of southern and border states sometimes resisted, and it is estimated that twenty to twenty-five people, lawmen and evaders, were killed in attempts to enforce the law.[24] The largest organized refusal came in eastern Oklahoma from the "Green Corn Rebellion," when five hundred or so poverty-stricken tenant farmers decided to rebel against the war, the draft, and their economic condition.

Probably the most telling resistance came from the 337,649, or 12 percent of those called, who just refused to show up when inducted, or who fled soon after arriving at an army base. Either failure was regarded, and punished, as desertion in this war, and would result the next year in "slacker" raids to try to round up and prosecute them, just as there would be vigorous prosecution of antidraft agitators such as Eugene Debs, leader of the Socialist Party, and Emma Goldman. Conscientious objectors who refused the uniform on moral or religious grounds also faced punishment, though the degree often depended on the specific military institution to which they were ordered.

But conscription was accepted by most citizens, the system worked efficiently, and by summer of 1917 the first tens of thousands of the millions of young men began to flow to the training camps. General Peyton March, who served as an outstanding chief of staff of the army during the struggle, thought "the draft was the most important piece of legislation enacted by Congress during the . . . war, and it is a most striking tribute to the common sense of the American people that without apparent opposition and practically overnight they accepted a system which had been hitherto opposed by the nation ever since its organization. Voluntary service gave way to a system which had been stigmatized as Prussian, militaristic, foreign, and opposed to American institutions."[25]

Though the system was to be "selective" in the sense of not taking those necessary to the efficient running of the war economy, this large-scale drafting of men at the same time that immigration had been cut off by the fighting opened many jobs to women that had always been denied to them. Women would find new opportunities, though still limited, as war workers in management, advertising, journalism, and even manual labor. Thousands would serve overseas, and some very near the combat zones, as nurses, Red Cross entertainers, YMCA attendants, and telephone operators. The singer Elsie Janis spent months trying to bring some relaxation and happiness into the lives of doughboys. Janis felt very much a part of the war effort when she was allowed to pull the lanyard on a howitzer, proud she had "personally killed a German and maybe three or four. . . . They told me I was the only woman who had fired regular hundred and fifty-five power hate into Germany."[26]

The problem of how to pay for this massive mobilization and the wider expenses of war involved long, bitter fights in Congress. The president had stated his desire that borrowing be kept to a minimum and taxes be used to pay for the war, but the first piece of financial legislation passed was for a Liberty Loan designed to raise several billion dollars through bonds paying a tax-free 3.5 percent, which could be raised if later bonds paid more. There was some controversy, as Claude Kitchin pointed out, because it was "the largest authorization of bond issues ever contained in any bill presented to any legislative body in the history of the world" and that much of the money raised would go as loans to the Allies. But the immediate need was recognized, and it sped through Congress in just a few weeks.[27] The Revenue Act of 1917 had a much harder slog.

One of the tactics used by congressional opponents of preparedness led by La Follette and Claude Kitchin during the struggles of 1916 had been to raise the income tax of the rich to pay for increased military costs. They had figured that this would bring a kind of economic democracy to the movement, as well as dampen the perceived enthusiasm of industrialists for war. They had been so successful that those with annual incomes over $20,000 paid around 95 percent of the income tax by 1917. The same allies now decided that a similar plan should help pay for this war that they had opposed.

Preliminary estimates of the needs of the army alone were for $3 billion, an amount that shocked the fiscally conservative politicians of the time who little dreamed that governmental expenditures for all operations would dwarf that figure by tens of billions. The man faced with the "prodigious problem of war financing" was William Gibbs McAdoo, who worked and reworked the figures and found that with "each fresh calculation the sum had grown larger, and the figures were appalling."[28] Appalling but still nowhere near what the final amount would be; it would take awhile before the nation understood that it had signed a blank check. Since even these early estimates were far too large to be entirely supported by taxation, McAdoo aimed at first for 50 percent, while the rest would come from bond sales to the public. As it turned out, the Liberty Loans would provide about two-thirds of the total cost of the war.

McAdoo was a student of history, and had carefully studied the problems that his predecessor Salmon P. Chase had faced during the Civil War. Part of Chase's solution had come through private banker Jay Cooke's organization of a "selling campaign" for Union bonds, but McAdoo decided that he would rely on patriotic instincts rather than the money market to promote the bonds: "Any great war must necessarily be a popular movement. It is a kind of crusade; and, like all crusades, it sweeps along on a powerful stream of romanticism."[29] McAdoo and others would provide the stream of romanticism without stint, and the people would voluntarily provide the stream of money.

Liberty Bond rallies, parades, and assemblies using the drawing power of celebrity, just in its beginning phase, would raise millions of dollars. The greatest draw of all was the pioneer movie star Douglas Fairbanks. Up to this point in American history, the great heroes had been men and women who had accomplished something important: politicians blazing with the charisma of William Jennings Bryan, warriors as stalwart as U. S. Grant, inventors as doggedly creative as Thomas Edison, humanitarians with the sympathetic heart of Clara Barton. Few actors or sports figures had been viewed in a heroic light. Now the connection between renown and achievement was changing, and fame was becoming easier to manufacture. Public relations and advertising were directing the way, but the greatest engine of celebrity was the movie industry, which was ironic since producers had done all they could to keep actors anonymous, to better retain power for themselves. Though the 1920s would see the full flowering of celebrity in sports and film, Douglas Fairbanks was raised to the firmament in the teens of the century.[30] It was a mark of how perceptive McAdoo and his advisers were that they called on Fairbanks, his bride to be, Mary Pickford, and other stars including Charlie Chaplin to "bring the powerful stream of romanticism" to the selling of Liberty Bonds.

But, as noted, the thirst was so great that involuntary streams must also be tapped, and so came the battle for the Revenue Act of 1917. La Follette and Kitchin and their political allies pushed for taxation as responsible fiscal policy, but they also had social ends in view. Excise taxes were imposed on such mundane items as chewing gum, movie admissions, and soft drinks, but really were aimed at luxury goods such as automobiles, fur coats, and those even more sinful items: alcohol and tobacco. These men were also determined that since conscription would be taking young men from their homes and sending them abroad to risk their lives, those remaining at home and reaping huge profits from industry should make their own sacrifices. High incomes should be conscripted, if men could be. Though the Revenue Act reduced the income exemption to $1,000, that was still well above the average annual wage of $830 that year. Incomes between $1,000 and $4,999 were taxed at 4 percent, and those higher were subject to surtaxes that went to 63 percent.

The part that drew the loudest screams, however, involved the excess profits tax. As Senator Hiram Johnson wrote to his old friend and Progressive Party running mate Theodore Roosevelt, "Our endeavors to impose

Douglas Fairbanks using his celebrity to sell Liberty Bonds, 1918

heavy war profit taxes have brought into sharp relief the skin-deep dollar patriotism of some of those who have been loudest in declamations on war and in their demands for blood."[31] The struggle was especially bitter since the progressives hoped to make such a feature a permanent base for the taxation of corporations. Henry Cabot Lodge led the conservative pro-business Republicans in fighting such an idea, calling it "perfectly exorbitant taxation."[32] In this contest he was aided by the taint given Kitchins and La Follette by their original opposition to the war. Republican newspapers charged that they were out now to hamper the war effort through excessive taxation on patriotic industry. The progressive version of the bill made it through the House, but the Senate's was far weaker. The compromise that the president signed in October included steeply graduated income taxes, but only a moderate excess-profits provision. There was one big loophole that allowed corporations to distribute untaxed new stock in place of dividends; creative accountants searched diligently and found oth-

ers. Soon, however, the costs of the war rocketed higher, astonishing everyone, in spite of the examples for years before of Allied and German expenditures. The politicians had to go back to the well; the Revenue Act of 1918
would more than double these rates, around 80 percent of the money coming from wealthy individuals and corporations. These revenue acts were
victories for progressives, but a price would be paid. "Kitchinism" entered
the political vocabulary to indicate the recalcitrant antiwar provincialism of
Democrats, and would be used by Republicans to great effect in the elections of 1918.

The president decided that the public mind, which he was so skilled at
reading, needed direction at this time of crisis; those fifty House votes
against war were disturbing, as would be the numbers of young men avoiding the draft. So diverse was the country, so divided by factions, parties,
regions, classes, and ethnic tensions that he and his advisers believed that
the call of traditional patriotism by itself would not be enough to bring consensus or the voluntary effort desired. In time of war, the government
wanted sole control of storytelling and mythmaking, and as McAdoo had
noted, this struggle had to be enlarged to a call for a crusade. The man put
in charge of the Committee on Public Information was George Creel,
longtime Wilson supporter and a former "muckraker" journalist radical
enough that Jack Reed in *The Masses* had admiringly called attention to his
actions during the Ludlow troubles in Colorado. There was no precedent
or guideline for the task, nor even office space or staff, but Creel had
among his many attributes enormous reserves of energy. With the help of
Douglas MacArthur, "then a handsome young major" loaned by Newton
Baker, Creel quickly found some brick town houses near the White House
to use as headquarters, and began gathering recruits such as Ernest Poole,
Will Irwin, Ray Stannard Baker, and Ida Tarbell, all progressive journalists
themselves.[33] Also volunteering were artists of the fame of Charles Dana
Gibson—whose Gibson Girl had been the turn-of-the-century feminine
ideal—Joseph Pennell, and James Montgomery Flagg. And there were
filmmakers, with the greatest of their many hits being a documentary entitled *Pershing's Crusaders,* which opened with a scene of a medieval crusader standing between two modern American soldiers while the subtitle
announced:

> The world conflict takes upon itself the nature of a Crusade. . . . We go
> forth in the same spirit in which the knights of old went forth to do battle
> with the Saracens. Notwithstanding the sacrifices, we shall gain from it
> a nobler manhood and a deeper sense of America's mission in the

world. . . . The young men of America are going out to rescue Civilization. They are going to fight for one definite thing, to save Democracy
from death. They are marching on to give America's freedom to the
oppressed multitudes of the earth. The mighty exodus of America's manhood to the plains of Europe may well be called "The Eighth Crusade."

With this core, soon to be greatly expanded, Creel began what he described as "the world's greatest adventure in advertising," using pictures
and words to reinforce what he saw as the ideals of America, first around
the country, then the world.[34]

Fears that those ideals might have trouble holding their own was also
evident in the congressional hearings on the Espionage Act. In his speech
asking for a declaration of war, the president had made a point of referring
to German espionage and sabotage that had taken place in the United
States even during the years when the two countries were officially at
peace: "From the outset of the present war [Prussian autocracy] has filled
our unsuspecting communities and even our offices of government with
spies and set criminal intrigues everywhere afoot against our national unity
of counsel, our peace within and without, our industries and our commerce." And he went on to make specific mention of

the millions of men and women of German birth and native sympathy
who live amongst us and share our life. . . . They are, most of them, as
true and loyal Americans as if they had never known any other fealty or
allegiance. They will be prompt to stand with us in rebuking and restraining the few who may be of different mind and purpose. If there should be
disloyalty, it will be dealt with with a firm hand of stern repression; but, if
it lifts its head at all, it will lift it only here and there and without countenance except from a lawless and malignant few.[35]

It was to restrain these "lawless and malignant few" that two congressmen introduced, on the same day as the war speech, legislation that would
come to be called the Espionage Act. The administration, when first
alarmed by German domestic sabotage and spying aided by some German
Americans, had earlier proposed bills directly outlawing such actions, but
they had not made it through before the term of the Sixty-fourth Congress
ended. Now in the Sixty-fifth, broadly drawn legislation that would allow
the government to censor news stories and to prosecute those suspected of
aiding the enemy or obstructing recruitment or conscription into the
armed services received close and immediate attention.

The president's proposal to censor the press brought together those opposed to the war with strong supporters of war to the hilt because both groups feared having their criticisms suppressed. Newspapers across the nation led the opposition, and they found willing allies among the politicians. Senators Johnson and Lodge, who agreed on very little, managed to put aside their other differences to fight the bill, Johnson charging that it would "render impossible legitimate criticism . . . of those who may lead during this war, and lead in incompetence and inefficiency."[36] Lodge supported this: "To attempt to deny to the press all legitimate criticism either of Congress or the Executive is going very dangerously too far."[37] Jack Reed also joined the range of voices testifying against the bill. Victory for freedom of the press seemed attained on May 31, when the House turned down the censorship sections by a vote of 184 to 144, and the Senate went along. This and assurances from the president helped defuse criticism of the bill. Wilson promised Arthur Brisbane, the top Hearst editor, that "I shall not expect or permit any part of this law to apply to me or any of my official acts, or in any way to be used as a shield against criticism."[38]

The Espionage Act, signed by the president on June 15, 1917, was followed by the Trading with the Enemy Act in October, and the Sedition Act of May 1918. Together these provided federal officials with an array of weapons to use against what they perceived as threats to the war effort; state and local authorities had their own legislation with equivalent powers. All these would be used, though often more in haste than in wisdom, for both federal and local officials would exceed the intentions behind this and similar state legislation. This would also be true of the many volunteer organizations formed by those far from the front lines but eager to prove their patriotism. There was plenty of room in these loose and baggy laws, in spite of some care given to framing the legislation to limit transgressions, to work off personal prejudices or eliminate what was seen as a threat to a favorable status quo.

Very important to the president and his administration, as well as the majority of middle-class Americans, was the concern expressed by Bryan in his note to Wilson about "safeguarding the morals" of the men now entering the military services in such numbers. Prohibition was quickly established around bases, then, under the guise of "conservation," through the whole nation. Newton Baker had been upset by the widespread stories and resulting scandal about whorehouses along the Mexican border, and perhaps rumors about Pershing's overly tolerant views about the physical needs of his troops. Soldiers, the secretary was convinced, "were easily led

aside into unwholesome diversions and recreations, patronizing cheap picture shows, saloons, dance halls and houses of prostitution."[39] Raymond
Fosdick, brother of the fervent Prohibitionist minister Harry Emerson Fosdick and though only thirty-three already well-known himself as a social
reformer through his work for the Rockefellers, was called to duty by Baker
to direct these erring military souls in "the regular provision of wholesome
recreation." He would help young American warriors don what he called
"invisible armor" that would protect their innocent purity. Aided by the
YMCA, National Catholic War Council, Jewish Welfare Board, Salvation
Army, and American Library Association, Fosdick organized programs of
sports, singing, and reading while being responsible, as he later bragged,
for the closing of more than one hundred red-light districts, which then
"had practically ceased to be a feature of American life."[40]

Secretary of the Navy Daniels as a fervent "dry" had mandated Prohibition aboard ships as soon as he was in office; now he made sure that
chances for whiskey, wine, or beer were difficult ashore as well. He supported congressional passage of a war act outlawing the use of grain for dis-
tilling that took effect in September 1917, and hoped for more such
legislation. Not only drinking was restricted. The sprawling Storyville section of New Orleans had the reputation of being the best as well as the
largest red-light district in the country. Started in 1897 on the European
theory and model that since no matter what society's moral desires were
there was going to be prostitution, especially in a seaport, it would be less
disruptive if limited to just one area of town. The idea had proved a success
from the beginning, with local guidebooks celebrating the charms of the
various brothels and individual prostitutes. The houses were segregated
both by price and race, just like the rest of southern society, but at a minimum each had a "professor" playing the piano, while the more deluxe
establishments boasted black "jazz" bands with players as talented as Jelly
Roll Morton and King Oliver.

The houses had been booming since the European war started the
money rolling into this greatest of cotton shipping ports, but 1917 saw business pick up even more as the number of young men at the nearby naval
station doubled and tripled. Daniels was not having any of this. He had
stopped the issuance of condoms when he became navy secretary; now,
using a new regulation that whorehouses would not be allowed within five
miles of naval or army bases, he ordered that local authorities shut down
Storyville. The entrepreneurs resisted, but stood no chance against the
new power of the federal government. The whorehouses closed, the prosti-

tutes scattered to more discreet places of business, and the musicians moved up the great highway of the Mississippi River to Kansas City, St. Louis, and Chicago, taking their new music with them.

Daniels also worked quickly to have the navy determine what its duties would be. He ordered Admiral William Sims, president of the Naval War College and an expert on destroyers, to Britain just before the United States officially entered the war.[41] Again there was shockingly bad news as the British revealed the true number of ships being lost to the U-boat campaign: 870,000 tons of cargo in April alone. Stores of wheat had fallen to less than a two-month supply, and shortages of coal threatened not only domestic comfort but the very mobility of the Grand Fleet. Sims was warned by First Sea Lord Sir John Jellicoe that at this rate Britain could suffer irreparable damage by November. Just as worrying to the Americans was the question of how, in the face of such losses, they could transport an army to the Continent and keep it supplied.

The British navy had resisted the convoy system—which would take advantage of the immensity of the ocean by having ships cluster together much like a school of fish—for a number of practical reasons: there was a shortage of destroyers and small craft to provide protection; a convoy might provide an even more attractive target than individual ships; the group would have to keep to the speed of the slowest vessel; civilian captains lacked the skill to stay in tight formation and those tight formations meant the ships could not zigzag. But also responsible was an old-fashioned romantic desire for "glory," which was only to be found in aggressively hunting and destroying submarines at sea, not in the mere escorting of oil tankers and freighters.

Both British prime minister David Lloyd George and President Wilson were skeptical of the Admiralty's reluctance. As early as February, Wilson had been puzzled by the unwillingness to convoy, but as a civilian amateur was hesitant to criticize. This reluctance would soon dissipate under growing doubts about British competence. By summer he would also be prompting that the British attack the U-boat bases in Belgium. "We have got to throw tradition to the wind," he told the officers of the American Atlantic Fleet in an off-the-record address that August. "We are hunting hornets all over the farm and letting the nest alone." Particularly frustrating was that "every time we have suggested anything to the British Admiralty, the reply has come back . . . that it had never been done that way." He insisted that American officers take risks, wanting them to do "the thing that is audacious to the utmost point of risk and daring. . . . You will win by the audacity of method when you cannot win by circumspection and prudence."[42]

After much urging, the British tried convoying in April 1917 and discovered that it worked. Sims requested quick support, and by early May the first contingent of American destroyers had arrived in British waters and set to patrolling; others soon followed, and the improvement was dramatic. The 870,000 tons lost in April dropped to 600,000 tons the next month, and though the figures would fluctuate for a few months, sinkings would soon average less than 350,000 tons. As these losses declined, U-boat losses mounted; only 20 were lost in the first six months of 1917, but 43 in the second six.[43]

AND SO, with hesitation and confusion, the foundation was laid for what newspapers, politicians, and particularly the Committee on Public Information were calling the Great Crusade. Some citizens were already disturbed by the extended reach of the federal government, though others rejoiced. Even Bernard Baruch, who would be one of the most powerful of the new governmental brokers, was chilled when the diminutive Edward House, Woodrow Wilson's closest adviser, stretched out his arms and exclaimed, "Isn't it a thrilling thing to deal with the forces that affect the destiny of the world!"[44]

———◄◉►———

CHAPTER SEVENTEEN

Preparing

As a final complication . . . we had to contend with the French ignorance of the characteristics of the American as an individual . . . of his methods of getting results. A Frenchman does not readily adapt himself to new ways. . . . He feels the French method is the only method. We are adaptable, and it was this trait alone that made it possible for us to survive the difficulties of this period.

Major George C. Marshall[1]

I suddenly realized that the devout Russian people no longer needed priests to pray them into heaven. On earth they were build-ing a kingdom more bright than any heaven had to offer.

Jack Reed[2]

MARSHAL JOSEPH JOFFRE urged the United States to quickly send even a token force to France to lift that country's morale. After meeting with the high command of the army, he visited the White House on May 2, and during a long conversation convinced Woodrow Wilson that a combat division along with thousands of specialists including railway men, truck drivers, machinists, medics, and communications troops should be dis-patched as soon as possible. Pershing was issued orders; actually, because of the lack of coordinated planning at the War Department, he was issued two somewhat contradictory sets of orders. He then organized his advance staff with veterans he had known from the Indian campaigns, the Boxer Rebellion, the Spanish-American War, the Philippine Insurrection, and his recent expedition into Mexico. The general also chose some Regular Army regiments to be sent to form the First Infantry Division of what was to be called the American Expeditionary Force, or AEF. After a delay caused by submarine worries, he sailed in late May 1917.

In spite of Joffre's warnings, Pershing and his officers were surprised on their arrival in France by the low morale of French society and the French army, which had suffered mutinies even in elite units after the butchery of the failed Nivelle offensive in April and May. "Pacifist sentiment was prevalent in France and in many quarters there was talk of a peace parley," Pershing recorded. "Old political feuds were revived and the influence of defeatism was openly charged against the ministry. This pessimistic and despondent mood of the people further depressed the morale of their armies as men at the front contemplated another winter of suffering and distress for their families."[3] Major George C. Marshall, who would serve in later wars as chief of staff and then secretary of state, arrived in June with the bulk of the First Division and was struck by his initial view of a French town: "Most of the women were in mourning. Very few men were in evidence."[4]

In the interest of raising morale, the French asked that the Fourth of July be celebrated in Paris by a grand review of elements of the First Division. Pershing resisted the idea because so many of his troops were raw recruits who did not march, handle their arms, or even salute very impressively. But he was finally convinced to send a battalion of the Sixteenth Infantry Regiment to parade from Napoleon's tomb in Les Invalides through the leafy, crowded boulevards of Paris to Lafayette's tomb in Picpus Cemetery. As it turned out, the recruits' lack of marching skills did not matter because of "many women forcing their way into the ranks and swinging along arm in arm with the men." Pershing went on to observe, "With wreaths about their necks and bouquets in their hats and rifles, the column looked like a moving flower garden with only a semblance of military formation, the animated throng pushed its way through avenues of people to the martial strains of the French band and the still more thrilling music of cheering voices."[5] At Lafayette's tomb, there were speeches by Brand Whitlock, ambassador to the Belgian government in exile, and other worthies. Pershing hated public speaking, in fact he wasn't too fond even of private conversation. Under duress he uttered a few platitudes, but turned the major task over to Colonel C. E. Stanton, who came up with one of the most memorable phrases of the war when he assured the deceased count and his people, "Lafayette, we are here!" And then he went on to promise that the American army would stay until victory.

But such victory looked far in the future. An old veteran of the trenches remarked to an American reporter as he watched the marching soldiers: "As human beings and raw material, they're the very best. . . . But they need a deal of training. The hardest thing to teach them is not to be too brave. They must learn . . . to hide. That's the first essential in this war."[6] Similar ideas were expressed by Frederick Palmer, a war correspondent of wide experience who, at great financial cost to himself, enlisted for the duration on Pershing's staff. He felt that he had to warn the swaggering young soldiers, so sure of American physical superiority, that the fact that an American was heavyweight boxing champion of the world would be no help against machine guns.

French instructors were assigned as each American unit arrived, but there was much training to be done. Most of these men were Regulars in name only; all the experienced noncommissioned sergeants had

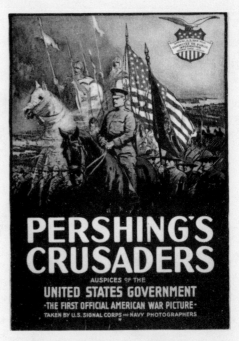

Pershing's Crusaders lead the charge in a film poster from 1917

been promoted to officers, while the best Regular Army privates had been made noncoms, then had been dispersed among all the new units being formed to give them some rigor. Even the most elementary sense of professionalism was lacking in the green recruits, as Marshall noted when he came across a "tall, rangy" sentinel standing guard in front of the commander of the First Division's office. "His blouse was unbuttoned and a watch chain extended across the front, between the pockets. A French General . . . approached the sentinel and exhibited an interest in his gun. The sentry obligingly handed the General his weapon and retired to the door of the office and sat down on the sill. I personally got him up, got his blouse buttoned and his rifle back." An embarrassment, but as Marshall went on to say: "This man was probably one of those remarkably gallant fellows who fought so hard and died so cheerfully not many months later."[7] One particular point on discipline was made very clear. When a local girl accused an American soldier of attempted rape, he was tried within twenty-four hours, convicted, and sentenced to thirty years in prison.

The same cultural misunderstandings that had caused Secretary of the Treasury McAdoo so much trouble in Washington were even more in evidence in France. Pershing and his officers chafed at the long, discursive conversations that were necessary to have the French do anything. Since few of the Americans spoke French, or their counterparts English, much of this time-wasting was prolonged by the need for translation, which brought another problem. "Don't any of these people speak American?" was a frequently asked question given extra force by the lack of enough qualified translators. Italian Americans were sometimes brought in to do such service, evidently on the theory that one Romance language is much like another. Some French phrases, like *vin rouge* and *vin blanc,* were quickly picked up by the soldiers.

George Marshall had decided to speak the language at every opportunity in order to refine his elementary knowledge of the tongue, but found that his attempts brought wry looks from the natives, especially after remarking to one officer about the beauty of the day, *"Je suis tres beau aujourd-hui."*[8] In spite of such faux pas, he and other ambitious officers persisted through trial and error in trying to bridge these language gaps, dealing with conundrums such as the French use of the wonderfully vague expression *en principe,* meaning "as a rule," or "theoretically." After having been misled into thinking that he was to be provided with trucks for an American troop movement, only to discover that these were "theoretical" trucks, he became much more careful. "This was my first meeting with that mysterious expression . . . whose dark and devious meanings stood revealed only to a native-born Frenchman." After that, whenever a French staff officer would use the expression *en principe,* "I always brought him to a prompt halt and requested that he commit to writing whatever he had to say."[9]

Even more aggravating was the slow pace that French officials and stevedores set for unloading the ships bringing increasing amounts of supplies and troops. Part of this was due to aged equipment, but also to aged noncombatant men who, it seemed to American officers, did not understand the urgency. Doughboys, often African American, soon took over the heavy labor, and expeditionary force engineers redesigned and modernized the ports. Local customs also surprised the Americans, especially the casual way men, and sometimes women, would urinate in public. They were astonished, too, by the huge manure piles in barnyards that French peasants used to fertilize their fields, the city boys finding them too odiferous. Since the troops were often quartered in nearby barns, they would sometimes band together and move the pile farther away. On the other hand, frugal French peasants who had for generations used every scrap of whatever came to hand were shocked at the profligacy of their visitors, as when a work party of African American soldiers cut down some trees but left stumps more than a foot high; the French would have used every inch of the timber. A Russian Jewish immigrant who, after long service as a Regular Army noncom, was awarded a commission, explained the problem clearly and concisely to his men: "Their vays are not our vays."[10]

The ethnic and racial diversity of the American forces also shocked the French. One soldier who had been assigned to train an American regiment wrote to his family: "There is a bit of everything, some Greeks, some Italians, some Turks, some Chinese, some Indians, some Spanish, and even a reasonable number of Huns. . . . This does not seem to bother them. But doesn't this seem to you a strange outlook? . . . Did I tell you the story of the soldier from [this] regiment who was debarking . . . and saw his German brother as a prisoner working at the port? . . . There are among the Americans the sons of French emigrants and the sons of Hun emigrants. I asked the French son if the Germans could be trusted to fight against their brothers or cousins, and he said without hesitation, 'yes!' "[11]

American soldiers had their own way of describing their ethnic mix, singing to an Irving Berlin tune:

> Oh, the army, the army, the democratic army,
> They clothe you and feed you because the army needs you
> Hash for breakfast, beans for dinner, stew for suppertime,
> Thirty dollars every month, deducting twenty-nine.
> Oh, the army, the army, the democratic army,
> The Jews, the Wops, and the Dutch and Irish cops,
> They're all in the army now![12]

In one area, at least, there was easy communication across cultural lines. American soldiers during these first months in the country admired their French counterparts for the courage with which they had fought in previous years, and were more than happy to share their relatively bountiful pay of twenty-one dollars a month with these comrades and the local girls. "On Sunday," George Marshall observed, "the roads and lanes were dotted with quartets consisting of an American soldier, a French Chasseur, and two girls, with large paper bags filled with provender, bound for an outing at the expense of the prodigal American. This first payment fully confirmed the French in their belief that we were rotten with money and ripe fruit for the French shopkeepers," a belief that would later lead to no little bitterness.[13] One technique used to solve this problem was to require the soldiers to buy war bonds and make other allotments to reduce their ready cash. Pershing was also determined to not lose any men to venereal disease, which had decimated some British and French units. Chastity was preached, perhaps as a sop to stateside puritans, but prophylaxes were also provided for those who strayed. Georges Clemenceau, who did not appreciate the charms of abstinence, offered to help by providing licensed houses of prostitution for American troops. Pershing forwarded the letter to Raymond Fosdick, who brought it to the secretary of war. Baker, eyes undoubtedly popping, read it twice before crying out, "For God's sake, Raymond, don't show this to the President or he'll stop the war."[14]

There were two things the French did at a speed that brought protests from the Americans. The careless esprit with which they drove terrified some of the senior officers; even that hard-charging cavalryman John J. Pershing was on occasion taken aback.[15] And they were pushing the training hard, wanting to get the Americans into the trenches quickly to relieve the burden on their own men. But Pershing was insistent, thorough, and methodical; no one wanted an embarrassing defeat on the battlefield due to poorly prepared troops, and the men needed to be not only trained, but also equipped and familiarized with all the modern weapons of war, from pistols through artillery and airplanes. Very few of these did the Americans even possess, and when they did obtain them it would be from the British and French, not American, manufacturers.

Far more annoying were the increasingly insistent voices of British and French generals and politicians to have American troops immediately integrated with their formations. Only Joffre had been wise enough to understand the American need for its own army, led by its own officers; these other Allied leaders felt only the moral and physical exhaustion of their soldiers and civilians and their need for fresh blood. It was a struggle that would go on through almost the entire remainder of the war, until the American units were given the opportunity to prove themselves in battle. This uneasiness about Yankee fighting spirit was somewhat assuaged for the French politician Georges Clemenceau, soon to be premier, when he visited a field day that a battalion of the Twenty-sixth Infantry was holding. George Marshall reported that Clemenceau "was much pleased over the various competitions, particularly those between the machine-gun crews, but it was not until he was literally spattered with blood in his ringside seat during a particularly vicious boxing match that he registered enthusiastic appreciation of the American soldier."[16]

Before leaving the States, Pershing had spent some time at the War Department, and been appalled by what he saw. "I was really more chagrined than astonished to realize that so little had been done in the way of preparation when there were so many things that might have been done long before. It had been apparent . . . for months that we were likely to be forced into the war, and a state of war had actually existed for several weeks, yet scarcely a start had been made. . . . The War Department seemed to be suffering from a kind of inertia."[17] Others noted the lack of organization or sense of effort, officers and civilian officials keeping normal business hours instead of working into the night and on weekends. The rather relaxed executive manner of the secretary of war was partly to blame. Newton Baker told his biographer Frederick Palmer that his father, a Confederate veteran, had always insisted "that the reason the South seemed to prevail for so long from a military point of view was that President Davis let Lee alone," and he was going to follow the same style. There is some sense to this, since the commander of his expeditionary force was several thousand miles away and facing new challenges every day, but closer to home his generals and bureaucrats needed stronger guidance.

The confusing and archaic design of army administration was an important case in point. After the near disasters of the Spanish-American War, Elihu Root and Theodore Roosevelt had tried to reform the bureau system under which individual chiefs spent most of their time defending their prerogatives rather than coordinating their efforts under a chief of staff. The idea of a general staff to oversee military efforts had run into stiff resistance from both Congress, with its traditional fear of militarism, and the bureau chiefs, who feared giving up power. Nevertheless, some immediate improvement had been made, but over the years the balance of power had shifted back toward the bureaus. Now, under the sudden huge demands for men, uniforms, barracks, guns, and all the other constantly changing needs of large-scale modern war, the system came close to breaking down.

An example of how competitive bureau chiefs interfered with the common effort came when Baker visited the basement of the State, War and Navy building in the hope of finding some desperately needed space for offices. What he found, instead, was a mountain of typewriters, all packed in their wooden boxes and fresh from the factories. A quick-thinking officer on the adjutant general's staff, recognizing that war on this scale would demand elaborate record keeping, had cornered the market. Similar discoveries were made in other bureaus, as when the Ordnance Department, which needed canvas duck cloth for cartridge belts, mess kits, haversacks, and other such equipment, found that the Medical Department and the quartermaster had already purchased all available supplies to make cots and stretchers.[18]

Colonel E. Requin, an aide to Joffre on his visit in May 1917, recognized the lack of a strong general staff to coordinate all war efforts as one of the many problems resulting from the American suspicion of a large and efficient army. "The American General Staff was composed of officers of high distinction, possessing a solid military knowledge . . . but ridiculously few in number and distributed between the War College and the War Department, with no rational organization into divisions or effective specialization. . . . Considered as a General Staff, it did not exist."[19] A properly operating general staff would have prevented the problems that were continuing to hamper Pershing: "The Washington bureaus oftentimes followed blindly some out-of-date supply table perhaps drawn up . . . by an antiquated desk soldier long since retired and forgotten." This misuse of vital shipping space required that he send sharp cables asking that they send no more "bath bricks, book cases, bath tubs, . . . cuspidors, office desks, floor wax, . . . step ladders, lawn mowers, refrigerators, . . . settees, sickles, stools, window shades."[20] Instead they should at least be giving priority to the basic necessities such as shirts, pants, shoes, and boots for men of all sizes and shapes in this democratic army, and then rifles, bullets, grenades, trucks, and so on. One lack particularly felt by many of the soldiers was of American tobacco, and it made them feel waspish. Poor logistical and other planning would remain a problem until early in 1918 when Baker, under heavy criticism, called General Peyton March to Washington, making him a full general and chief of staff. Decisive, sharp-tongued, and a longtime crusader for army efficiency, March would then quickly bring order to the chaos hindering the army's efforts.

The War Department was, of course, just one large part of an even greater endeavor. Nearly five thousand government agencies were established to deal with the mobilization, many of them headed or staffed by volunteer women and dollar-a-year men, businessmen who had given up their private positions to work for their country. In 1916, during the preparedness battles, Congress had allowed the establishment of the Council of National Defense consisting of six Cabinet members advised by a commission of representatives from business, industry, transportation, and labor, which would coordinate mobilization if war came. Unfortunately, when the war did arrive, the council, with its very limited powers, proved inadequate to the task. One of its most important subordinate agencies, the War Industries Board, suffered in its early version from a similar lack of power, and so disorder and confusion lasted through much of 1917. The first director, Frank A. Scott, suffered a nervous breakdown from all the frustrations

Women rivet heaters and passers at the Puget Sound Navy Yard

encountered in trying to make it work. Here again things would not improve until 1918, when conditions became so bad that strong enforcement provisions had to be provided. Bernard Baruch was put in charge, and the War Industries Board became the central organizing force of the wartime economy.

More immediately successful was Herbert Hoover, who had become a hero to the American and Belgian peoples for his tireless efforts to feed the civilian victims of German aggression in Belgium and northern France. Now, with the United States in the war, the Spanish and other neutral nations took up that task, while Hoover was called to Washington in May 1917 to coordinate food rationing. Again he showed the focus, energy, and organizational skills that had made him a millionaire before he turned forty. The president seems to have been intimidated by newspaper headlines warning that Hoover was to be made a "Food Dictator" or "Food Czar" and so was ready to deflect fear of such one-man rule by his usual method of creating a board or commission, just as he had for the other war agencies. Hoover strenuously objected, arguing that it was on just such "an old rock

of divided responsibility" that efficiency was wrecked, pointing to the confusion already evident in other American and Allied departments. "I felt
there must be a single head to the food problem and that his authority
must cover every phase of food administration from the soil to the stomach. That included direct or indirect control over production, farm policies, conservation, exports, imports, buying for our military forces and
those of the Allies, prices, rationing, processors, distributors and consumers." He felt he could avoid "dictatorship" charges by using volunteers,
"and that in this voluntary action lay our guard against Prussianizing the
country."[21] A reluctant Wilson finally agreed, perhaps partly because
Hoover also came up with a new term, *administrator*, to describe his position: "I urged that this term itself would connote not dictatorship but the
ideas both of coordination and executive leadership. This was . . . the first
time this title had been used for a public function."[22] As a result of
Hoover's insistence on control, the Food Administration was one of the few
agencies that from the beginning was effectively managed.

Hoover went all out to stimulate farm production through incentives
while also reducing consumption by convincing citizens to take voluntary
action. He did not believe in rationing for Americans: "We knew that,
although Americans can be led to make great sacrifices, they do not like to
be driven."[23] Conservation would be effected through self-denial and self-
sacrifice, promoted as a national duty for the civilian population over here
as American soldiers did their duty over there. He had to work fast, for
already food prices were rocketing higher, partly due to poor grain crops in
1916 and 1917. "Wheatless" and "Meatless" days were urged on households,
with a gratifying response. At the same time, he established guaranteed
high prices for important crops and called forth greater effort from farm
families which, unfortunately, caused tens of thousands of semiarid prairie
grasslands to go under the plow; as so often in war, important short-term
results brought long-term environmental disaster.[24] The need for grains
was seized on by both the Women's Christian Temperance Union and the
Anti-Saloon League to press for the prohibition of alcohol as a wartime
conservation measure, and after such legislation was passed both organizations worked to make it permanent. On everyone's mind were the scandals
involving badly canned meat, or "embalmed beef," of the Spanish-
American War, but food in both quantity and quality was not going to be a
problem for the Allies or Americans at home or abroad. "We never had a
complaint," remembered Hoover. "The American soldiers and sailors were
the best fed fighting men in the world."[25] The campaign was so well-

managed that to "Hooverize" came to mean "to save or economize." And during these war years farmers would enjoy a double-digit growth in real income.

WOODROW WILSON, Herbert Hoover, William McAdoo, and the rest of the leadership of the administration were sure that, conscription aside, volunteerism was the most American way to direct the war, but the call of old-fashioned patriotism did not resound through the whole society. Socialist Party leaders held an emergency convention in St. Louis when it seemed sure that war would be declared. They argued over what course to pursue, some wanting all-out opposition no matter what the cost, others saying that the party should support the war effort. "Now that the war is an accomplished fact," argued John Spargo, "we hold that it is our Socialist duty to make whatever sacrifices may be necessary to enable our nation and its allies to win the war as speedily as possible."[26] Those Socialists from the Southwest, remembered Louis B. Boudin, were against the European conflict, but warned that the Zimmermann proposal could cause them to change their minds. "If those damn greasers come across the line, we'll get our guns and shoot."[27] A referendum called the St. Louis Proclamation overwhelmingly passed, promising "continuous, active, and public opposition to the war [and to military conscription, sales of war bonds, and taxes on the necessities of life], through demonstrations, mass petitions, and all other means within our power."[28] One result was an immediate resignation from the party of "conservative" and well-known members such as Charles Edward Russell, William English Walling, Upton Sinclair, Allan Benson, the party's presidential candidate in 1916, and Spargo. Spargo then publicly argued that the Socialist Party, whose membership included many German and Jewish Americans, now was "essentially un-neutral, un-American, and pro-German."[29] A much greater diminution of Socialist ranks would follow quick and severe government repression.

Oklahoma was one of the states where the Socialist Party had strong roots, and this led to some members having a connection to the Green Corn Rebellion, which burst out in the South Canadian River Valley. "The poverty of the people there approached that of Asia," wrote one historian about these rebellious tenant farmers, mostly old-stock white Americans, but including African Americans and Snake Indians.[30] Oscar Ameringer, a Socialist Party activist who knew them well, was sure that "many of these people's family names are emblazoned on the regimental lists of George Washington's army at Valley Forge; that the great bulk of them could barely read and write, and a very large percent of them could do neither; that the ninety and nine of them had never eaten a well-balanced meal, slept in a decent bed, or taken a bath in a bathtub; and I know that they lived in shacks no European peasant would keep his cows in."[31] There were two secret societies that really organized the rebellion: the Working Class Union, which had connections to the Industrial Workers of the World, and the Jones Family. One of the most radical of the local Socialists, Tad Cumbie, who was called, in the romantic fashion of the time, "the Gray Horse of the Prairie," served as "Commander in Chief" of the effort. Their action was named the Green Corn Rebellion because roasting ears were about all the makeshift force had to eat, and if their plan to march on Washington was successful, they would live off the land, off corn and the stray steer killed along the way.

But the Socialist Party organization refused to support them, and most individual Socialists counseled discretion rather than valor, for which they were labeled "yellow" by the believers in direct action. When Oscar Ameringer asked what they were planning, he was told that they were going to stop "this damned war the gang out East has foisted on us" by slamming "the bankers, county officials, and newspaper owners in jail. . . . Then we'll burn railroad trestles, bridges and blow up pipe lines." Then they would continue across the country to Washington, D.C., gathering strength along the way.

Ameringer tried to talk sense to them, pointing out that they lacked the numbers to achieve any such grasp for power, even in Oklahoma, but they claimed that their revolutionary organization had spread to every state of the union. "There are seventy thousand of us in Colorado. More than twice that many in Texas. One hundred and ninety thousand I.W.W.s in Chicago alone are waiting for the signal to break loose. What's more, we are fully armed with high-powered Marlins and ammunition. Out in the coal fields there is enough dynamite to blow up the whole country." And they assured him that all this would catch the government by surprise because they were a revolutionary organization bound to secrecy by solemn oath.

"Passwords?" Ameringer asked.

"Sure."

"High sign?"

"Why, certainly."

"Well, then . . . if all that is true, then let me say, scatter, and scatter right now. If there is only one thousand instead of hundreds of thousands of you, then at least a hundred of that thousand would be informers, planted among you . . . to inform the authorities of every move you make."[32] And he warned them that Dictaphone recording devices were probably hidden wherever they held a meeting.

But they didn't scatter. Instead they gathered their own "general staff" and made their attacks in southwestern Oklahoma, starting on the night of August 3, 1917: a few bridges were burned, but the rebels proved incapable of making effective use of what dynamite they had. Sheriff's posses were quickly organized, and they arrested four or five hundred radicals before much damage could even be attempted. They were tried in federal court under the Espionage Act, with some of the informers whom Ameringer had warned them about testifying for the government. All were convicted. Most received suspended sentences upon their promises to return to their tenancies and behave, but eight of the leaders were given long prison sentences that they would still be serving well past the end of the war, until President Warren G. Harding took pity on them and their families and ordered their release.

The dragnet had not just gone after the Green Corn boys, but authorities had used the opportunity to also arrest thousands of Socialist Party members, chasing thousands more into hiding in the Winding Stair Mountains. The fact that the party had tried to discourage the rebellion didn't matter, and the organization was destroyed in Oklahoma. It would not fare much better in the rest of the nation. Economic and political conservatives recognized that its adamant antiwar stance made it vulnerable, and they would make the most of this opportunity to destroy it and other groups that were seen as long-standing threats. The American Protective League, guided by Chicago business interests and cooperating closely with the Bureau of Investigation, played a major role in targeting such groups. It was an alliance that would also bear fruit against a different enemy in the great Red Scare of 1919.

Green Corn rebels were not the only ones who believed that Big Bill Haywood's Industrial Workers of the World were planning to join in rebellion against the established order; the American government believed it, as did the German. There were sound military intelligence reports that German agents in Mexico were attempting to make contact with the IWW to coordinate sabotage, spying, and strikes, and many similar stories, true or false, were published in the newspapers accompanied by virulent editorials demanding the crushing of the union.[33] The IWW, like the Socialists, was outspokenly in opposition to the war, warning that any member who joined the army would be expelled from the union. Conditions in the lumber and mining camps had grown worse, not better, when the United States entered the conflict, and Wobblies exploited these circumstances to expand their influence among rough and ready workers in tough industries; for them the class war was still the only one worth fighting. The resulting strikes brought federal attention, but also local action by both elected officials and "volunteers." In Bisbee, Arizona, vigilantes led by the local sheriff and assisted by Phelps Dodge mining manager Jack Greenway—one of Roosevelt's favorite Rough Riders who would later serve as a general in the American Expeditionary Force—broke an IWW strike with the help of the American Protective League by forcing more than a thousand of the union men at gunpoint aboard cattle and freight cars, then shipping them into the desert without adequate food or water in the furnacelike temperatures of July. They had to be rescued by the U.S. Army. Roosevelt wrote to Greenway that the IWW was "criminal" but that it should have been the government instead of a private force that "proceeded with utmost rigor against the I.W.W.'s."[34] The *Los Angeles Times* editorialized on July 15, 1917, "The citizens of Cochise County, Arizona, have written a lesson that the whole of America would do well to copy." And on the same day, the *Sacramento Bee* attacked Woodrow Wilson for criticizing the mob action and appointing a committee headed by Felix Frankfurter to investigate what had happened, writing that one doesn't "confer with a mad dog. He shoots the dog."[35]

Actually, though these men suffered from heat, thirst, and hunger, they were treated more humanely than some. In other parts of the West many IWW members were beaten or shot, and in Butte, Montana, organizer Frank Little was pulled from his boardinghouse, dragged behind an automobile until his kneecaps were torn off, then hanged from a railroad trestle. Haywood remembered Little as "an energetic worker, part Cherokee Indian, black-eyed, hot-blooded, and reliable."[36] He had come to Butte to agitate for justice in the wake of a mine fire that had burned to death 160 miners, many dying because the Anaconda Copper Mining Company had not provided escape holes in the concrete bulkheads. No one was ever brought to account for the deaths of the miners or the lynching of Frank Little. Some newspapers, especially in the West, condoned the vigilante action, while others, mainly in the East, deplored it. The *New York Times*, however, though finding the lynching "detestable," felt it had to point out, on August 4, 1917, that "the I.W.W. agitators are in effect, and perhaps in fact, agents of Germany." And, like Theodore Roosevelt, the *Times* argued that "the Federal Authorities should make short work of these treasonable conspirators against the United States." It would not take long before they did.

Militant crusades do not easily tolerate dissent. Repression fit with the progressive fervor for commitment by the public to higher causes, and with the belief in the expansion of federal power in aid of "The Good." Just as the government should suppress those who unconscionably exploited child labor, lured women into "white slavery," ignored or fought laws for pure food or worker safety, now it needed to direct its disciplinary attention to those who deliberately tried to sabotage the war effort.

In September, the Bureau of Investigation, forerunner to the FBI, began a nationwide roundup of the union's leaders and members. Hundreds would be convicted under the Espionage Act, including Haywood, who was sentenced to twenty years in prison and fined $30,000 by Judge Kenesaw Mountain Landis, who told the labor leader and the nation: "When the country is at peace, it is a legal right of free speech to oppose going to war and to oppose even preparation for war. But when once war is declared this right ceases."[37] Haywood wrote to Jack Reed: "The big game is over we never won a hand. The other fellow had the cut, shuffle and deal all the time, personally we didn't lose much just a part of our lives. . . . All in the world they had against us was morsels of fragmentary evidence, not enough to convict a ward heeling politician, but we were off our field, we will do better when we get organized and can tie into them on the Industrial ground."[38] But Big Bill decided that the odds weren't too good on that ground, either; he later obtained bail, then fled to revolutionary Russia, dying there in 1928 of alcoholism, diabetes, and disappointment.

Of course these men *were* unquestionably radicals, bragging often and loudly of their willingness to use violence to overthrow the economic system and as to how they did not care if they harmed the war effort. They, like the Green Corn rebels, should have known that provocative actions provoke. Others, however, who tried to use provocative words, free speech, and rational argument to dissent from the war fared little better. Attorney General Thomas W. Gregory was widely quoted as warning those who refused to support the crusade: "May God have mercy on them, for they need expect none from an outraged people and an avenging government."[39] Here again, Kaiser Bill's money was suspected to be at work suborning the war effort, just as before 1917 it had been used to buy political influence, blow up American factories, and sink American ships with time bombs. Socialist Party publications, along with those of many other individuals and groups, were denied use of the U.S. mail at the direction of Albert Sidney Burleson, the postmaster general. Though it took a very loose interpretation of the Espionage Act to find such authority, this was an interpretation that a unanimous Supreme Court would support in several cases decided in 1919.

Socialist leaders such as Eugene Debs, Kate Richards O'Hare, Oscar Ameringer, and former congressman Victor Berger would all fall victim to federal prosecution under the Espionage Act. Berger was reelected to Congress in 1918, in a heavily German American district of Milwaukee, running on the argument that the country should immediately withdraw from the war, but by a vote of 309 to 1, the House refused to seat him. The next year, he would be convicted of aiding the enemy and sentenced to twenty years in prison, the judge in the case, again Landis, publicly lamenting that he could not instead "have Berger lined up against a wall and shot."[40] Eugene Debs, who had won 6 percent of the national vote as his party's presidential candidate in 1912, was made a particular target for his speeches against the war; convicted, he was sentenced to ten years of confinement. He, too, would wait in prison until Harding felt confident enough to pardon him.

Entangled in this repression were the bohemian radicals of *The Masses.* Jack Reed, seeing the causes of war in narrow economic terms, was puzzled and frustrated by how easily the workers ignored what he and his fellow socialists were explaining to them: that this was a war solely for the profit of the big capitalists. Even his own family was immune to his arguments. Brother Harry Reed immediately volunteered for the army, writing Jack: "I have done this because I consider it my duty, not because I want to be a soldier or fight. I wish you could see a little more clearly just what the situation is in this country and how useless it is to try to buck what can't be changed."[41] And his mother lamented, "It gives me a shock to have your father's son say that he cares nothing for his country and his flag. I do not want you to fight . . . for us, but I do not want you to fight against us, by word and pen, and I can't help saying that if you do . . . I shall feel deeply ashamed. I think you will find that most of your friends and sympathizers are of foreign birth; very few are real Americans, comparatively."[42] Later she would threaten suicide over his politics.

Reed's political opinions also made earning a living more difficult after war was declared. Few of the richly paying mass-market publications now found his views acceptable, and he was willing to take a reduction in salary to join the staff of the *New York Mail* in May 1917, a newspaper that seemed less unthinkingly patriotic than the others. He did not realize, nor evidently did its German American editor Edward Rumely, that one reason for its neutral point of view was that it had been secretly bought in 1915 with German government funds as part of its propaganda campaign. Reed was given a relatively free hand, writing a column and covering news such as an execution at Sing Sing, gang murders over control of the kosher meat industry, and local color pieces on New York, though he occasionally complained to Louise about some assignments: "I've got to interview a damned actress about her damned marriage to a damned prizefighter."[43] *The Mail* editorialized for the excess profits tax, and sent Reed to Washington to study the legislation. He found the city energized and exciting, and that his name still gained him access to representatives, senators, and even the president for interviews. "No group or class of Americans should be permitted to have a vested interest in war," he wrote in his first piece in the series, "nor should they be permitted at the expense of the people to amass enormous sums of money out of the slaughter of mankind." And he went on to argue that the motto of the Senate was: "Make the poor and the future pay for the war."[44] While in the capital, he was offered a job by the Hearst editor Arthur Brisbane at the *Washington Times* and was also asked by his old friend George Creel to join the Committee on Public Information, but he turned them both down.

Reed was feeling restless, wondering if instead of continuing in journalism he shouldn't really act on his feelings against the war, to "raise hell and go to jail."[45] Most of his hell-raising was in *The Masses,* where he wrote of the Bisbee deportations, attacks by soldiers and sailors on Socialist parades and meetings, a vicious race riot in East St. Louis, the tainted trial and conviction of Tom Mooney for the Preparedness Day bombing, and the general suppression of free speech that was taking place. "In America," he wrote in the September 1917 issue, "the month just passed has been the blackest month for freedom our generation has known. With a sort of hideous apathy the country has acquiesced in a regime of judicial tyranny, bureaucratic suppression, and industrial barbarism, which followed inevitably the first fine careless rapture of militarism." When Emma Goldman and Alexander Berkman were arrested for obstructing the draft, Reed, Max Eastman, and *The Masses* came to their defense. Reed testified to their good character at the trial, which did not stop their being convicted and sentenced to two years in prison and a $10,000 fine each. And by then Reed and his friends needed their own defense.

Reed had been uninspired by the March revolution in Russia, seeing it at first as a "bourgeois" move for power, but he changed his mind as he read reports of radical governing bodies, or soviets, being established by workers and soldiers. These then immediately agitated for a Russian withdrawal from the war. This was going to be, he passionately wrote in the May 1917 issue of *The Masses,* "the establishment of a new human society upon the earth," and he decided he had to go there as a witness to what promised to be a world-changing revolution. His desire was further encouraged by his old mentor Lincoln Steffens, who returned from Russia in June. After reporting to President Wilson about what was going on there, he also talked enthusiastically with Reed about the most militant of the parties,

*Emma Goldman and Alexander Berkman waiting to be sent
to the penitentiary in 1917*

the Bolsheviks. Louise Bryant had been covering the war in Europe for the
Bell Syndicate news service, partly to escape the troubles she and her husband had brought on themselves through sexual dalliances with others;
now she returned home, as eager to see the revolution as Jack was. The
couple made up their differences, and began to plan for Russia.

One hurdle was Jack's draft status, but that was cleared when the government conceded that having only one kidney was grounds for deferment.
That same day they applied for passports. An even greater problem was
money and accreditation. Max Eastman, eager to have Reed reporting on
Russia for *The Masses,* and Eugene Boissevain, widower of the Amazonian
feminist Inez Milholland, used their charms to convince a wealthy socialite
to contribute $2,000.[46] Louise was able to continue with the Bell Syndi-
cate, while Reed, now notorious for his antiwar arguments, could claim
only his favorite left-wing magazines. They sailed at the end of August, and
such were the wartime conditions that it took four weeks of hard traveling
before they finally pulled into the Finland station in Petrograd, the old St.
Petersburg, where Lenin, helped by the Germans, had arrived in April. Just

before they reached the city, a suspected coup by the reactionary General Lavr Georgiyevich Kornilov had been repulsed with help by the Bolsheviks. Inspiring, and so too was the hand-printed sign on their breakfast table: "Just because a man must make his living by being a waiter, do not insult him by offering him a tip."[47]

Heady days, and they became even more exciting as Bolshevik revolutionary forces gathered themselves to seize power from the weakening Kerensky government. Jack and Louise's language skills and political understanding were enhanced through the émigré radicals who had returned to take part in the revolution, some of them members of the IWW who organized meetings and protests to educate Russians about the prison sentences of Tom Mooney, Emma Goldman, and Alexander Berkman. A particular help was Albert Rhys Williams, a well-educated, native-born American socialist who had for a while been minister of a Boston church and was now a correspondent for the *New York Post*. In Russia since June, Williams was a knowledgeable guide to the ins and outs of the constantly changing political scene. Reed and Bryant moved between the various parties, factions, and classes, observing and taking notes, but also trying to contribute to the revolution. When this partisanship became known to the American embassy, the ambassador not only had Reed followed, but evidently also ordered that his pocket be picked to better discover what he was up to.[48] And the pace of what he was up to increased, as did the pace of Bolshevik plotting. At a factory meeting of a soviet, Reed and Williams gave enthusiastic greetings from America as one of the committeemen addressed a thousand workers, warning: "Now is the time for deeds not words. The economic situation is bad, but we must get used to it. . . . [Reactionaries] are trying to provoke us. But let them know . . . [that] if they dare to lay their hands upon the organizations of the proletariat we will sweep them away like scum from the face of the earth!"[49]

In October the sweeping began in earnest. Lenin had been forced into hiding in Finland, but through smuggled messages he guided his followers' preparations for insurrection, while other Bolshevik factions seemed to have trouble making up their minds; all came together early in the morning on October 24 (by the Julian calendar; November 6 by ours, the Gregorian).[50] Bryant and Reed ran into one of their IWW friends, Bill Shatov, who called to them, "We're off!" as he went with other militants to shut down "the bourgeois newspapers!"[51] The couple spent the next few months, sometimes together but often apart, trying to cover as much of the story as they could. They filled their notebooks and their memories with what they knew were historic events, using their American passports and various passes to go where they wanted amid the chaos. Reed was particularly aggressive, taking such chances that at one point he was put up against a wall by illiterate Red Guards who were going to shoot him before a comrade who could read his papers stopped them. He joined Karl Radek's Bureau of International Revolutionary Propaganda, gave speeches pledging to promote the Bolshevik cause when he returned to America, and at one point carried a rifle in case of a countercoup. Young Red Guards, armed workers, soldiers who disobeyed their officers to join the revolutionaries—it seemed that the revolutionary dream had finally come true. As he watched a funeral procession for slain Bolsheviks, he had his sudden realization that the Russian people were building a heaven on earth. Jack, just months before in despair because he could discern no real purpose or achievement in his life, had found what he had been longing for.

———◇———

CHAPTER EIGHTEEN

Force

*Force, Force to the utmost, Force without stint or limit, the right-
eous and triumphant Force which shall make Right the law of the
World, and cast every selfish domination down in the dust.*

Woodrow Wilson, April 6, 1918[1]

Les premiers Américains ont été tués.

General Bordeaux calling out to Major Marshall[2]

I will show you fear in a handful of dust.

T. S. Eliot, *The Waste Land*

THE JAZZ MUSICIANS forced from Storyville were only a small part of
the migration of African Americans out of the South. The war had virtu-
ally ended immigration at the same time that orders for food and clothing
and arms and so much more had caused the economy to boom. In 1914,
more than a million foreign workers had entered the country, but only
around 300,000 landed the next year, and the number continued to drop for
the duration of the fighting. Whenever given an option, employers would
pick an immigrant over an American-born black; now they had little
choice. As word spread through the oppressed shantytown ghettos of Mississippi, Alabama, Georgia, and other states of the South that there were
good-paying jobs to be had up north, the long, difficult journeys began.[3]

It took awhile for the southern white establishment to understand that
the region was losing an essential part of its economic and social order. The
Macon Telegraph sounded the alarm: "Everybody seems to be asleep about
what is going on right under our noses—that is, ever[y]body but those
farmers who waked up mornings recently to find every negro over twenty-
one on their places gone—to Cleveland, to Pittsburgh, to Chicago, to Indi-

anapolis."[4] Thousands, then tens of thousands, ultimately five or six hundred thousand African Americans eagerly took to the road, full of hope that they were leaving behind the racism, the poverty, and the resulting lack of education and opportunity that had marred generations of their people's lives. In the North they did find that at least they could register and vote, but they also discovered that few northern whites welcomed their arrival, especially in the booming industrial areas already suffering a severe shortage of housing. There were riots in major cities such as Washington, Philadelphia, and New York, with a particularly bad one in the summer of 1918 in Chicago that left hundreds injured and twenty-three blacks and fifteen whites dead.

The East St. Louis race riot of July 1917 was probably the worst of all. A strike had been called in April by the union of white workers in an aluminum plant in the city, but plant owners had successfully blamed the job action on the IWW and German agents, hired strikebreakers, then convinced the state government to issue injunctions against the union that were backed by the Illinois National Guard. When the strike was crushed, union members turned on African Americans, some of whom had provided scab labor at the plant and almost all of whom were newcomers to the already crowded city. The trouble started first as random small-scale acts of violence, but on the night of July 1 a carload of whites drove through a black neighborhood firing into houses. Police were called, and when they arrived in an unmarked patrol car a crowd of angry blacks, thinking they were the returning attackers, fired into the automobile, killing two officers. Rumors quickly spread that not only had blacks murdered white policemen, but that they had been urged on by German agents. Furious mobs went on a rampage, dragging black men, women, and children off streetcars and out of their houses or any other sanctuary they sought, beating and sometimes killing them. It is impossible to know how many white and black citizens died in East St. Louis, but there were probably more than a hundred, and many more hundreds injured, the vast majority of the casualties African American.[5]

The army was the one service that accepted black draftees and some volunteers; the navy had about five thousand serving in menial positions, and the marines allowed none. Of course, the army followed its tradition of keeping separate units for whites and blacks, and resisted expanding its minuscule corps of black officers. Lieutenant Colonel Charles Young, who had served so well in the Punitive Expedition and elsewhere, was given a medical discharge when it was discovered that he had high blood pressure, but there is reason to believe that at least part of the reason that some use wasn't found for him on active duty was because the authorities did not want an African American of such high rank. Young, who had endured decades of military racism without flinching, did not give up easily, making a well-publicized journey first on horseback, then afoot, from his last posting in Ohio to Washington to prove his health; it did no good.[6]

The army also resisted training black junior officers, but under pressure from the National Association for the Advancement of Colored People, the War Department set up such a school at Fort Des Moines, Iowa, which, in combination with promoting Regular Army sergeants, eventually produced about 1,200 black company-grade officers. The army was having trouble convincing draftees of the need to salute even white officers and follow workaday orders with any degree of enthusiasm, so aside from innate institutional racism there must have been fear of far more severe discipline problems. There were sometimes fistfights or worse between white and black soldiers, but the more dangerous battles were when African American troops ran into southern civilian prejudice, as at Camp MacArthur, near Waco, Texas, where six rebellious black recruits fired their rifles at authorities in the downtown area in late July 1917. The tragedy of East St. Louis had taken place just a few weeks before and may have sparked some of the anger. There were no casualties thanks to a brave, quick-thinking army officer who stepped in and disarmed the men.[7] A deadlier rebellion happened the next month at Camp Logan in Houston, when African American soldiers, reacting to rumors that a black soldier had been murdered and that a threatening white mob was gathering, took their rifles and attacked the city, killing seventeen civilians. Only the rushing in of white troops and the swift execution of thirteen ringleaders prevented a white riot. Another sixteen were sentenced to be executed, but Woodrow Wilson commuted ten of those death sentences to life imprisonment.[8]

These incidents and others reinforced prejudice against African American soldiers, giving support to a plan to use them only as laborers and stevedores, and that is how the majority did serve. But, again because of protests by the NAACP, two black combat divisions were also formed: the Ninety-second and the Ninety-third. The Ninety-second, which was poorly trained, equipped, and led, turned out to be a disaster in combat. That this failure was also in part due to racism is shown by the far different story of the Ninety-third, regiments of which were attached to French units and fought with such spirit that they won numerous French medals for valor.[9]

Of course, antiblack prejudice was not the only prejudice at work in early twentieth-century America, and among all the tribal feelings, the hatred of things German reached epidemic proportions during the war. Billy Sunday, the colorful fundamentalist preacher, roared that this was a struggle between a good people and evil: "All this talk about not fighting the German people is a lot of bunk. . . . [It is] Germany against America, Hell against Heaven. . . . Either you are loyal or you are not, you are either a patriot or a blackhearted traitor."[10] One of the most popular posters issued by George Creel's Committee on Public Information was entitled *Spies and Lies,* which was also reproduced in literary magazines. It began: "German agents are everywhere," and went on to urge citizens to report anyone "who spreads pessimistic stories, divulges—or seeks—confidential military information, cries for peace, or belittles our effort to win the war."[11]

The exposure of German governmental acts of sabotage and the spurring on of Mexican attacks on the United States were bad enough, but the real key to understanding the intensity of the hatred, aside from a certain self-righteousness in the American cast of mind, is the cooperation of some German Americans with these acts. In a country of immigrants of diverse and often contending racial, ethnic, and religious origins, this treasonous alliance with foreigners was seen as the unforgivable betrayal, opening the possibility of schism, of civil war, of the breaking apart of the whole society founded on words and ideals instead of shared blood and religion. And once that fear took the actual form of German Americans acting as agents of a distant fatherland, it was not forgotten. The press often played on the theme, as when *Life,* supposedly a humor magazine, published on June 13, 1918, a cartoon showing a paunchy, mustachioed man with a document labeled "Plans of Forts" sticking out of his jacket pocket. Across his expansive gut ran the label "German-American," and he was declaiming the "German-American Version" of "My Country, 'Tis of Thee," which went:

> *My country over sea,*
> *Deutschland is sweet to me;*
> *To thee I cling.*
> *For thee my honor died,*
> *For thee I spied and lied,*
> *So that from every side*
> *Kultur might ring.*[12]

Some of the inflamed prejudice, however, had more mundane and local origins, as when a businessman of Anglo descent with several generations in America might spark a whispering campaign against a German

American competitor, or resentment over long-ago struggles now flared again as happened in Missouri when unreconstructed Confederate sympathizers took a chance for revenge against the German Americans, who had been a regional bulwark of the Union. Prohibitionists also recognized a chance to profit from the weakness of their old opponents, the brewers. "We have German enemies across the water," one pointed out. "We have German enemies in this country too. And the worst of all our German enemies, the most treacherous, the most menacing are Pabst, Schlitz, Blatz, and Miller."[13]

Suddenly all things German were objectionable: sauerkraut became liberty cabbage; German shepherds now were to be called police dogs or Alsatians; frankfurters were hot dogs; hamburgers liberty steak; and so on to the point of patriotic lunacy as German measles was renamed by a physician in Massachusetts liberty measles.[14] Towns changed their names: East Germantown, Indiana, became Pershing, while Berlin, Iowa, adopted the name Lincoln; individuals followed suit. Arguments, labeled "childish" by Woodrow Wilson, were made to drop German-language instruction from schools.[15] The American Defense Society, one of the numerous volunteer patriotic organizations, argued that German music was "one of the most dangerous forms of German propaganda, because it appeals to the emotions and has power to sway an audience as nothing else can."[16] Evidently agreeing, the California State Board of Education directed that all German folk songs were to be literally cut out of music textbooks; German orchestral and operatic works were dropped by such first-rate companies as the Philadelphia Orchestra and the Metropolitan Opera of New York.

The threat of violence hung over all such suppression, and there were occasions when bullies beat those suspected of lack of patriotism or made them kiss the flag, but there seems to have been only one lynching of a German American. A drunken mob in Collinsville, Illinois, on the evening of April 4, 1918, grabbed a young, rather slow-witted man named Robert Prager, a native of Dresden, Germany, with plans to tar and feather him because of the suspicious way he had been behaving. Collinsville was only a few miles from East St. Louis, where German agents were rumored to have instigated the race riots of the year before. Questions were shouted at Prager: "Are you a German spy?" "Did you steal powder from the Maryville mine?" "Who else is mixed up with you in this business?"[17] The mob became more unruly and drunken as the night went on. Just past midnight, after allowing him to write a letter to his parents in Germany and listening to his request to be buried in the American flag, men threw an automobile towing rope over a tree limb and hanged him. There was a national cry of outrage at the murder, the *New York Times* editorializing that the miscreants responsible had to be brought to justice "to vindicate the name of America" and "to stamp out lynching as a demonstration of patriotism."[18] Leaders of the mob were tried, but found not guilty by a jury that evidently did see lynching as a patriotic demonstration. Useful in the murderers' defense had been the earlier widely reported exchange between Ambassador James Gerard and Foreign Minister Zimmermann. When Zimmermann had warned that there were half a million trained German reservists in the United States who would with the help of the Irish start a revolution, Gerard had coolly replied: "In that case there are half a million lamp-posts to hang them on." Attorneys used this as support for the argument that the defendants had been acting under an "unwritten law" to protect themselves from the domestic German threat.

The fact that many who sought to avoid war service because of religious beliefs, such as the Mennonites, were of German origin was also used against the German American community. And it did not help that the most notorious of all draft dodgers was Grover Cleveland Bergdoll, scion of a wealthy German American brewing family. He not only refused to report for induction, but while in hiding sent the authorities postcards mocking their vain pursuit of him. The national press joined the hunt by printing rumor after rumor of the whereabouts of this "Super-Slacker," which just added to the flood of false information pouring in from concerned citizens. Not until January 1920 would he be tracked down and arrested, and even then, using family money and influence, he managed to escape custody and flee to Germany.

But, of course, the vast majority of German Americans were not only patriotic but also eager to serve in the armed forces. There were countless such, including Medal of Honor–winner Eddie Rickenbacker, who anglicized his name by dropping an *h;* a gifted major named Dwight Eisenhower, who in spite of repeated attempts to get to France was felt to be too valuable as a Stateside training officer; and the commander in chief himself, whose family name had originally been Pfoershing until an ancestor changed it. Sometimes this contribution would be publicly, if confusingly, celebrated, as when patriots forced Germantown, Texas, to change its name, but accepted "Schroeder" after a local German American soldier killed in France.[19]

VALOR, as well as training and equipment, was much on the mind of Pershing and his officers as they and the Stateside camps tried to prepare their troops for the industrial efficiency of the modern killing field. Pershing—no doubt partly inspired by Wilson's urging to do "the thing that is audacious to the utmost point of risk and daring. . . . You will win by the audacity of method when you cannot win by circumspection and prudence"—had decided that the American rifleman could break the German lines. There was much evidence to the contrary, of course. Both sides had tried to break through every year of the war, and the result was slaughter on an inhuman scale, but he felt that his soldiers, properly inspired and using supporting artillery and airplanes, could do it.

Pershing had always been a martinet in his demand for discipline, but there was a need for it in this new army. Early on, it became apparent that American youth, with their democratic social ease, had little understanding or respect for the punctilio of uniforms, saluting, and military hierarchy; strict training would modify some of that individualistic behavior. On everyone's mind, Americans, Allies, and Germans, was the question, How well would they fight? A preliminary answer came on November 2, 1917, when a German raiding party struck at Company F of the Sixteenth Infantry near Verdun, where they had been sent to train in a quiet section of the trenches. French officers, who had overall command of the area, would not allow the neophytes to patrol in front of their lines, which made them vulnerable to surprises such as the one that took place. The attack opened with a heavy and accurate artillery "box" barrage, which kept reinforcements out, then two hundred raiders poured into the trenches.

One, wearing an American uniform and evidently speaking with an American accent, shouted at a young soldier emerging from a dugout: "Who are you?"[20]

"An American, don't shoot!"

"You are the one I am looking for," said the German, and then shot him dead.

Fighting was at close quarters with rifle butts, bayonets, fists, and grenades. Two Germans were killed and seven wounded, but they left behind three dead Americans and took eleven prisoners to interrogate, which was the purpose of the raid.

George C. Marshall, along with General Bordeaux, who had called out to Marshall that the first Americans had been killed, went together to inspect the scene, the general asking so many questions that Marshall guessed that he was worried that the Americans had not resisted enough. "I told General Bordeaux that he need entertain no fears with regard to the fighting of our men; that we might worry over their lack of technical skill, but that there could be no question regarding their individual bravery."[21]

Both officers would have felt better had they been able to read the after-action debriefing of the raid leader, a Lieutenant Wolf, who reported: "The enemy was very good in hand to hand fighting."[22]

It was at around this time that propagandist George Creel asserted, "I would rather be an American, killed in the unpreparedness that proved devotion is to declared principles, than a German living as the result of years of lying, sneaking, treacherous preparation, for a wolf's spring at the throat of an unsuspecting world."[23]

AS THE ACTION became more intense in France, the stumbling of the war effort in the United States became more obvious. Industrial production was uncoordinated, railroads were so entangled that they would not have been able to bring further production to the jammed ports or to deliver enough coal to power steam engines, smelt steel, or warm houses. Harry Garfield, son of a martyred U.S. president and himself president of Williams College, had been appointed fuel administrator by his mentor Woodrow Wilson, who evidently felt scholars could also make good managers. Lacking any particular expertise in business or knowledge of coal or petroleum, he imitated many of the voluntary conservation techniques used by Herbert Hoover at the Food Administration, asking for "Heatless Mondays," as well as "Gasless Sundays" to limit automobile driving—Wilson began going to church in a horse-drawn carriage. But these efforts weren't enough, especially since the price of coal had been fixed too low, which kept marginal mines closed. On January 16, 1918, Garfield illustrated his incompetence as well as the severity of the crisis, partly brought on by an unusually harsh winter, when he announced without explanation that all factories east of the Mississippi River were to be closed for a week. They would then reopen, but only for five-day workweeks. The White House did not learn of this until a reporter telephoned Joe Tumulty at midnight to ask the half-asleep presidential secretary "about the drastic order."

A storm of criticism washed over the administration, even after the belated explanation was given that this was designed to quickly provide coal for the hundred loaded freighters and troop carriers being held in harbors unable to sail for lack of it. Tumulty expressed his worries about "the consequences upon the morale of the people" to the president, who responded, "We must just bow our heads and let the storm beat."[24] But the storm was beating harder and harder, and it was over the next few months that the administration reorganized its war effort by bringing in Peyton March as chief of staff of the army, and putting Bernard Baruch in charge of the War Industries Board. Treasury Secretary William Gibbs McAdoo, in addition to all his other tasks, was given power over national transportation when the president nationalized the railroads, and appointed him their "czar." McAdoo harbored his own ambitions for the presidential race of 1920, and, as Wilson's son-in-law, began to be called "the Crown Prince." Dr. Garfield, on the other hand, became popularly known as "the Professor," never a complimentary term in the United States.

Politically there was now a war on for control of the war. Republicans, and some Democrats, pushed for a congressional joint committee to guide the effort, which the president, remembering how Lincoln had been plagued by congressional interference, used great skill in thwarting. "I honestly think," he wrote an influential senator, "that it would be impossible for me to conduct the war with success if I am to be placed under daily espionage."[25] Wilson, accused of being dilatory and indecisive, blamed much of the industrial disorganization on lack of executive power and managed to have the Overman Act passed on May 20, 1918, giving him almost dictatorial authority over the war effort for the duration and six months after. The emphasis was still on voluntary cooperation with business executives, but now there was also some muscle to use in enforcement.

Bernard Mannes Baruch had been born in Camden, South Carolina, in 1870, son of an immigrant German Jewish doctor who had served as a combat surgeon in the Confederate army and a mother whose ancestors, also Jewish, had served with George Washington. The family moved to New York ten years later, where Baruch took up boxing to defend himself from the tough, anti-Semitic neighborhood boys; it was an interest he kept all his life, shadowboxing every morning until he was eighty years old. The young man, brilliant but a rather lazy student, graduated from tuition-free City College, then joined a Wall Street investment firm as a clerk. One of the most remarkable in an age of remarkable men, it did not take long before he made his own fortune by speculating in, among other things, raw materials. Tall, athletic, charming, and startlingly handsome, he was a womanizer unrestrained by his marriage or children. But he also had an interest in public service, especially through the Democratic Party, telling a newspaper reporter in 1912: "Of course, I was born a Democrat, a Southerner, and a Confederate."[26] Baruch had admired Wilson's stand against the exclusive clubs at Princeton, and initiated a warm friendship based on their shared southern background and dislike of the arrogant rich. He had contributed time and money to the campaign of 1912, then outdid himself in 1916, when he gave the enormous sum of $50,000 for Wilson's reelection. "I wish we had a lot more like him," said one Democratic politician when he learned this.[27] Great diplomatic skill at forming a team of talented people and letting them alone to get things done was one key to his success at the War Industries Board, but so was his experience as a "speculator," his extensive network of friends, his high intelligence, and his astonishing memory—everyone who admired him seems to have commented on his command of figures and "facts."[28] He also had an unusual ability to read character; "wiser than a treeful of owls," was how George Creel summed him up.[29]

The WIB, as Baruch later wrote, "mobilized more than three hundred and fifty industries, from asbestos through caskets to lumber and zinc. No steel, copper, cement, rubber, or other basic materials could be used without our approval."[30] And he gives a good sense of a few of the complex difficulties involved: "Should locomotives go to Pershing to carry his army to the front or should they go to Chile to haul nitrates needed to make ammunition for Pershing's troops? Should precedence be given to destroyers needed to fight the U-boats or to merchant ships whose numbers were being decimated by the German subs? Should nitrates be allocated to munitions or to fertilizer? Should the Railroad Administration or the Fuel Administration get the tank cars both were claiming?"

Most industrialists cooperated, but the two most defiant groups were steel and automobile executives. "Not even the fact of war was sufficient to win them from their laissez-faire convictions that government intervention was somehow un-American." Baruch finally forced steel prices lower by threatening the bosses with a government takeover of their plants. One of the most powerful, Elbert Gary, asserted, "You haven't got anybody to run the Steel Company."

"Oh," Baruch threatened, "we'll get a second lieutenant or somebody to run it."

The head of the WIB also called a meeting with the leading automobile manufacturers, including Horace Dodge, William C. Durant, and representatives of Ford, to ask that they reduce pleasure-car production by 75 percent to save steel. They rejected his patriotic arguments, implying that government interference with industrial decisions was socialistic, and bragging that they had stockpiled enough steel and coal to proceed without the administration's cooperation.

Frustrated, Baruch finally picked up the telephone and called his close friend McAdoo. "Mac," he told the railroad czar in front of the defiant automobile makers, "I want you to take down the names of the following factories, and I want you to stop every wheel going in and out." Then he gave the names of the plants of everyone in the room. Calls to Baker and

Garfield arranged for commandeering the hoarded steel and coal. "That did it. Billy Durant, head of General Motors, said, 'I quit.'" The others, after failing in an effort to use political influence to flank Baruch, finally capitulated—Ford, the most defiant, last of all.

Baruch, like so many of the progressives, hoped that government action such as taxation of corporations and the WIB would tame freewheeling businessmen into having a sense of social responsibility, making the society and economy fairer, not just during the war but far into the future. He felt that the War Industries Board had "demonstrated the effectiveness of industrial cooperation and the advantage of government planning and direction. We had helped inter the extreme dogmas of laissez-faire, which had for so long molded American economic and political thought. Our experience taught that government direction of the economy need not be inefficient or undemocratic, and suggested that in time of danger it was imperative." There were some victories, to be sure, but most of the gains would be quickly reversed after the war, and Baruch himself would become a favorite target of Henry Ford's well-funded anti-Semitic campaign in the early 1920s. It would not be until the administration of Franklin Delano Roosevelt during the Great Depression that such a strong government role in the economy would be again attempted.

McAdoo, unable to hide his ambitions to succeed his father-in-law, seemed to be everywhere doing everything, or at least his name seemed to be everywhere on documents directing the wartime lives of Americans, "with" as he himself remarked, "an authority as nearly absolute as any power can be in America."[31] Railroad and other industrial tycoons had reason to fear this authority, but Arthur Guiterman, a leading composer of humorous doggerel, wrote a widely quoted piece that mocked both the power and the ambition:

> The Who, preeminently Who
> Is William Gibbs, the McAdoo.
> (Whom I should like to hail but daren't,
> As Royal Prince and Heir Apparent.)
> A man of high intrinsic Worth,
> The Greatest Son-in-Law on Earth—
> With all the burdens thence accruing,
> He's always up and McAdooing.
> From Sun to Star and Star to Sun,
> His work is never McAdone.
> He regulates our Circumstances,

Our Buildings, Industries, Finances,
And Railways, while the wires buzz
To tell us what he McAdoes. . . .
I don't believe he ever hid
A single thing he McAdid!
His name appears on Scrip and Tissue,
On bonds of each succeeding issue,
On coupons bright and posters rare,
And every Pullman Bill of Fare.[32]

The various elements of the effort began falling into place. Everyone expected the decisive year of the war to be 1919, and by that time all was to be flowing so smoothly that neither Allied nor American soldiers would be lacking for anything necessary for victory. The Germans, who also recognized this, pushed aggressively against the Russians, anticipating that Lenin, whom they had helped return to Russia, would quickly appeal for peace. Negotiations began in December 1917 at Brest Litovsk, but the Bolsheviks delayed settlement at first, fantasizing about a great worker rebellion that would bring down not just enemy belligerents but world capitalism from the inside. Finally, the Germans began to use diplomatic tactics that divided Poland, the Baltic states, and the Ukraine from the Russians while also resuming military offensives. Lenin then capitulated. The resulting Treaty of Brest Litovsk was an immense land grab by the Germans and Austrians, stripping Russia of about one-third of its territory, including some of its most valuable resources, requiring that its army and navy be demobilized, and forcing favorable trade arrangements for the Central Powers. As soon as the treaty was signed in March 1918, the Germans began shifting hundreds of thousands of men and their equipment to the west.

JACK REED returned to the United States at the end of April 1918; it had been a long, frustrating journey thanks to the American ambassador and the State Department, which had put pressure on the Norwegian government to hold him in Christiana (Oslo) for more than two months. When he finally arrived in New York, Reed was met by government agents who searched his baggage, then seized all the boxes of records, publications, and papers he had collected for a book on the Bolshevik Revolution.

The Masses had been one of the first magazines banned from the mails by Postmaster General Burleson, who was offended by antiwar comments in the August 1917 issue. Though the publishers obtained a restraining order from federal judge Learned Hand, Burleson still refused to allow *The Masses* to use its second-class mailing privileges, now twisting logic to argue that since the August issue had been suppressed, or "skipped," it was no longer a periodical. Without this ability to mail issues to subscribers, the magazine soon went broke, but there was more trouble to come. The federal government then charged the editors and business manager of the magazine with conspiracy to violate the Espionage Act, to discourage recruiting and create disloyalty in the armed forces. Reed, held in Norway, had missed the first trial; that had ended in a hung jury, ten to two for conviction, the day before he landed in New York. He was quickly arraigned, then released on $2,000 bail to await the second trial; while waiting he gave talks on the revolution to whatever audiences he could find. No regular lecture bureau or hall would have him, but his message was enthusiastically received by immigrant workers in grimy industrial towns who eagerly asked questions about the new regime. His old mentor Lincoln Steffens tried to make him see that the times were not ripe, that "the public mind is sick" because of the war and the accompanying fear: "Jack you do wrong to buck this thing. . . . We must wait. . . . Write but don't publish."[33]

But he would talk and write and publish, and the authorities be damned: "All movements have had somebody to start them, and, if necessary, go under for them."[34] When denied permission to speak at a hall, he would speak in the street, which resulted in arrest in Philadelphia for "inciting to riot." Once the Allies and American forces intervened in northern Russia and Siberia, he became even more bitterly impassioned, condemning what he saw as an attempt to crush the Bolsheviks; as a result, he was arrested in New York for using "disloyal, scurrilous and abusive language about the Military and Naval Forces of the United States." Revolution would soon sweep the United States, he was sure, and there was no need to worry about spending an extended time in prison. He refused to compromise even with his friends. Max Eastman had started a new magazine, *Liberator,* still radical but edited with discretion so as to keep mailing privileges. Jack served as a contributing editor, but after several months resigned, writing Eastman: "I cannot in these times bring myself to share editorial responsibility for a magazine which exists upon the sufferance of [Postmaster] Burleson."[35] Eastman understood, but also feared that Jack had lost the joie de vivre that had made him so appealing to his Greenwich Village friends: "The trouble with you is you're getting too damned adult," he told Reed, when lectured at once too often.[36] The self-righteousness must have been particularly galling to these men and women who felt it was their role to correct dullards of the middle class while guiding workers to the correct path of action. Now here was this "poet-revolutionary" arrogantly correcting and trying to herd them to the true course. Even his beloved and respected Steffens, who advised presidents, was not spared. Meeting by accident one night under a New York street lamp, Steffens gave his favored boy a joyous greeting, which brought forth only "a stiff and sorrowful approach," followed by an angry "Why don't you join us? We are trying to do what you used to talk and write about."[37]

The major struggle at hand was the second *Masses* trial, which began in late September 1918. He sat with the lawyers helping to pick a jury by passing notes: "An exploiter," described one businessman; "Son of a bitch," another.[38] On trial with Reed were Eastman, the writer Floyd Dell, the cartoonist Art Young, and the business manager Merrill Rogers. Reed's crime was putting a headline over an article reprinted from the *New York Tribune* about soldiers suffering from shell shock: "Knit a Strait-Jacket for Your Soldier Boy." All but Rogers took the stand, waxing eloquently to the judge, jury, and friendly attendees, which included Louise, and Floyd Dell's beautiful new girlfriend, the poet and heartbreaker extraordinaire Edna St. Vincent Millay. The judge, Martin Manton, was sympathetic but no pushover, asking hard questions and not allowing Reed to wriggle away in a cloud of generalities. Finally, Judge Manton, after establishing that Reed opposed the war, asked directly: "Were you opposed to our obtaining the military forces [to fight it]?"

Reed had been warned by the lawyers what would come from answering honestly; feeling the need to keep his freedom to continue his fight for the revolution, he lied: "No."

"Didn't you think this article, in which you throw fear into the mothers and families of boys that might go to the front, was something in opposition to gathering military forces?"

"No."

The jury divided seven to five for conviction, and after this second failure the government dropped its case. The defendants had been helped by being tried in New York City, and by a fair-minded judge, especially since the fighting in Europe had intensified and the newspapers were now full of lists of American dead and wounded, whose ordeal had been made worse by the Bolsheviks' accommodation with the Germans.

In September, just before the trial began, Eastman had written to the president, arguing that repression in the country had gone beyond any reasonable need to protect the war effort; Wilson responded that the line between legitimate dissent and treason had to be drawn somewhere, "and

I cannot say that I have any confidence that I know how to draw it. I can only say that . . . we are trying, it may be clumsily but genuinely, to draw it without fear or favor or prejudice."[39] But Eastman recognized that the intellectually freewheeling country of his youth was gone: "Like all my radical friends, I had mistaken for final reality the brief paradise of America at the turn of the century. . . . It was . . . a protected little historic moment of peace and progress that we grew up in. We were children reared in a kindergarten, and now the real thing was coming."[40]

EXPERIENCE of the Real Thing had come to American troops in Europe. The German divisions that had been moved from the eastern front smashed into Allied lines in France in the spring of 1918, using new assault tactics of surprise and infiltration to deal with defensive machine guns and artillery. This technique had worked well against the Russians at Riga and the Italians at Caporetto in 1917, and initially they had such great success against the French and British that Pershing temporarily reversed his stand against amalgamation and offered his troops without restriction to the Allies. The British, sent reeling, also ended their long resistance to having a unified command, and placed their forces under French field marshal Ferdinand Foch.

Some American units were rushed to serve with British and French forces, but the First Division also launched its own offensive to capture the town of Cantigny in late May, the first real battle of the American Expeditionary Forces (AEF). It was a victory, but a bloody one. Others, even bloodier, swiftly followed. Pershing was determined to return aggressive movement to the battlefield and break the stalemate of the trenches. When the Germans seemed close to punching through in the Chemin des Dames region, threatening Paris, the Second Division was ordered forward. The fighting around Belleau Wood would become famous for the raw courage and discipline of the marine brigade of that division. The Third Division did similar service at Château Thierry, less than fifty miles from the French capital, and so did other divisions at other contested crossroads. By fall the Germans had spent their reserves, and the Allies struck back, with the increasingly experienced Americans, now two million strong, providing a limitless supply of manpower. As a German general wrote after the war, "The American soldier showed himself full of courage, even if he lacked experience. Fresh, well-fed, and with strong nerves that had known no strain, he advanced against the German Army, which was exhausted by the unprecedented efforts of four years of war. This and in the great numerical reinforcements which the Americans brought . . . at the decisive moment lies the importance of America's intervention."[41]

These words about courage, fighting, and movement read so easily on paper, but of course the reality faced by the men on the ground and in the air was anything but easy. Army life no longer was the "moving flower garden" described by Pershing on the previous Fourth of July in Paris. Blood, guts, severed arms and legs, shattered bodies of comrades littered the fields across which soldiers advanced or fled or lay shaking in rage and fear, the screams of those comrades often piercing the roar of exploding shells, the whining of bullets and shrapnel. Two examples will do to bring home some of this pain and chaos.

Dan Edwards had been a wide-ranging adventurer from Texas, working as a cowboy, a whaler, and a sea cook before serving with the army in Veracruz. An unusual man in his fighting spirit and breadth of combat experience, his account gives a sense of the variety of deaths available.[42] At Cantigny he handled a machine gun, and things went relatively smoothly until the Germans counterattacked and killed his two flank guards. "The first I knew anything was wrong, a big German . . . loomed above me . . . and began forking at me with a haggle-tooth bayonet. . . . I yelled '*Kamerad!*' to beat hell. You have no idea what it feels like, cold steel stabbing into you." Edwards managed to pull his pistol and shoot. "He kneeled down slowly on the edge of the pit, and a mighty change came over his face. All the pleasure left it. He looked surprised, and then disappointed, and then, just as he keeled over, he looked completely hopeless." The German had bayoneted him four times, with one wound so deep that it "had reached the lining of my belly." Wet with blood, Edwards lacked bandages but gouged some clay from the side of his fighting hole, slapped it over his wounds, and made it stick with one of his uniform leggings.

Evening came, but "steady streams of flares kept going up, and big searchlights kept weaving back and forth continually, all over the ground and up across the sky. Signal rockets of every color were soaring in the air, and airplanes zooming this way and that overhead, running into the searchlights and turning silver colored. Now and then a couple of planes would put on a dogfight. And let me tell you an airplane scrap at night is something to write home about."

Heavy shelling continued all through the hours of darkness, keeping American reinforcements away, then intensified the next morning just before another counterattack. "I caught a bullet in my thigh. . . . Then . . . I got a machine-gun bullet through my right foot. It came from an enemy airplane which was spraying our trenches." Short on ammunition, Edwards sent his buddy Vick to get more. But then the ammo dump blew: "It seemed as if the end of the world had come. The concussion almost jarred me to pieces. . . . I looked back over my shoulder, and there was a great big gob of smoke. Chunks of boxes, equipment, dirt, rocks, along with arms and legs and so on raining down out of the sky all around. Suddenly I saw a tall black thing come plunging out of the smoke. It was Vick. He was singed all over, his tin hat was gone, and his head streaming blood. . . . His face was a smear of black and blood." A few minutes later "a machine-gun bullet slapped me in the face and smashed my cheek bone all to hell. . . . [Then] a bullet caught me in the right knee, and that hurt to beat hell." As he finally crawled to the rear he found a close friend buried by a shell blast with just the top of his helmet sticking out. Edwards scrabbled frantically at the dirt to dig him out, but found that "he wasn't buried alive because a piece of shell had just about cut his head off."

As soon as he was physically able, Edwards went absent without leave from the hospital to rejoin his comrades on the line. At the battle of Soissons he was wounded several more times and lost his right forearm, but still managed to bring in four German prisoners. For these incredible acts of heroism he was awarded a slew of medals, including the Distinguished Service Cross and the Medal of Honor. "Yes, and I recovered from my wounds as well as I ever can," he reported some ten years after the war,

Night attack with phosphorus bombs during
maneuvers in France, 1918

"and I received scads of military glory, and all that remains to bother me now is the financial side of life. . . . But it's all right. I'm used to tough sledding." Heavy drinking was also a problem for him, but it always had been.[43]

Franklin Delano Roosevelt spent three months of 1918 touring the front; his letter to Eleanor describing his visit to Belleau Wood soon after the marines had won their fight has the bleak power of a Hemingway short story.

> In order to enter the wood itself we had to thread our way past water-filled shell holes and . . . up the steep slope over outcropping rocks, overturned boulders, down trees, hastily improvised shelter pits, rusty bayonets, broken guns, emergency ration tins, hand grenades, discarded overcoats, rain-soaked love letters, crawling lines of ants and many little mounds, some wholly unmarked, some with a rifle stuck bayonet-down in the earth, some with a helmet, and some, too, with a whittled cross with a tag of wood or wrapping paper hung over it and in a pencil scrawl an American name.[44]

And so we gain a slight sense of the cost exacted to break the German line. The spirit required for such an effort is epitomized by Gunnery Sergeant Dan Daly's battle cry at Belleau Wood as he rallied his marines to advance against enemy machine-gun fire: "Come on, you sons of bitches. Do you want to live forever?"[45]

CHAPTER NINETEEN

---◄◊►---

Victory and Defeat

The joy of the Armistice, which caught everyone up in its tidal sweep, was perhaps his last experience with unalloyed happiness.

George Creel on Woodrow Wilson[1]

Better a thousand times to go down fighting than to dip your colors to dishonorable compromise.

Woodrow Wilson[2]

Russia. Russia. That's where the weather is coming from.

Winston Churchill to Bernard Baruch in Paris, 1919[3]

IN EARLY MARCH 1918, a wave of "flu" struck the young soldiers at Camp Funston, Kansas, bringing fever and severe pain that made them miserable for a few days before they improved enough to be sent back to duty. Other military camps and some prisons and factories also reported the illness, places where large numbers of people were kept closely confined. But the disease was not widespread or marked by a great upsurge in deaths, and in a few weeks it all but vanished in the United States, like innumerable other waves of colds and respiratory infections in the past.[4]

But the flu then reappeared in the American Expeditionary Forces in France a month later, evidently brought over on troopships, and swept with phenomenal speed across Europe, mutating into such a virulent killer along the way that efforts were made to censor news of the epidemic. Spain, a noncombatant with no censorship, published stories about the suffering of millions of its people, and thus the disease came to be known as Spanish Influenza. It struck the exhausted, poorly nourished armies with incredible force, not only stripping them of able-bodied men, but burdening them with soldiers who needed constant treatment. "The dead were dead, and that was that . . . ," writes Alfred Crosby. "But flu took good men and made them into delirious staggering debits whose care required the diversion of healthy men from important tasks. Few things could be more troublesome to a front-line squad than a trench mate with a temperature of 104."[5] Some units temporarily lost 40 to 50 percent of their strength. Hospitals of all the belligerents, already overwhelmed by the wounded, tried but could do little for this new flood of the disabled who died by the tens of thousands. Only a few months were necessary for Spanish Influenza to make its way around the globe, becoming a pandemic with a death toll worse than the bubonic plague of medieval times. Soldiers on the battlefield, sailors at sea, civilians in the great cities of Europe, Asia, and Africa fell in hecatombs; estimates of total deaths range from twenty million to more than fifty million, many of them in parts of the world that did not keep statistics.

In late summer of 1918, the deadly new form arrived in the United States and found fertile ground for its harvest. Cities teeming with war workers, Liberty Bond rallies, Win the War for Freedom parades, induction and training centers, factories that never rested, movie theaters, baseball stadiums, even churches provided perfect sites for infection to take place.[6] No one knew how to treat the disease, though rumors of suddenly discovered cures would be published in newspapers over the next few weeks, and entrepreneurs would advertise that they, and they alone, could sell victims pills or lotions that would protect them against the plague. People hoped that masks, incense, tobacco, or whiskey would help, but to no avail. Most diseases attack the weak, those very young or very old or already ill, but this one killed the strong and healthy; in just eight weeks it would destroy 500,000 American men, women, and children, then in the next few months another 250,000 would be added to the total. The most likely to die were in their twenties and thirties, the age of parenthood, so families lost a father or mother, and often both, leaving thousands of orphans behind. Morgues and cemeteries, in spite of resorting to mass graves, could not keep up with the flow of bodies; cities were forced to rent warehouses and cold-storage facilities to try to keep them off the streets, though even then bodies could go uncollected for days. This was particularly true in Philadelphia, which was the worst-hit city in the country because of wartime overcrowding and a corrupt and inept Republican municipal government. There the morgue, built for 36 bodies, held more than 200 stacked three or four deep; doors were left open to disperse the stench, presenting a shocking sight to passersby.[7]

One condition shared nationwide was the lack of physicians and nurses because so many had been called to the colors, and as in endeavors of this war, great reliance had to be placed on volunteers: automobile clubs coordinated cars and drivers for ambulance service and for doctors and nurses to make house calls; middle-aged men, when off work, came forward to serve as stretcher bearers; department stores set up emergency telephone lines for people who needed help; health-care students, as at the Philadelphia College of Pharmacy and the University of California, left their classes to labor in the overwhelmed hospitals. Journalists lauded the voluntary effort, one arguing that "for the progress made in meeting the situation, credit must be given [to] the private associations."[8]

Even the most remote communities were hit: "Like a grass fire the disease swept the Indian country," wrote Hilda Faunce from her trading post on the huge Navajo reservation. "Every day some one told of deaths. The exhausted medicine men seemed to rest only when they stopped at the store to be warmed and fed, while they told of treatments and deaths. . . . The survivors . . . were thin and weak and pathetic."[9] Navajos, with their fear of ghosts and dead bodies, suffered greatly, as they had to abandon any dwelling in which someone had died, even if it meant living outdoors. "It was truly terrible. Where one day I saw ponies in the corral, children in the dooryard, and warm smoke curling from the roof of a hogan, the next day there would be no vestige of daily living; but instead the cold rain falling on an absolutely deserted home or an overturned pan or basket placed before the door of a hogan, empty save for an unburied body."

And then, as suddenly and mysteriously as the plague had arrived, it left. Though returning in sporadic outbreaks through 1920, the worst was over by early 1919. After decades of scientific detective work, it is now believed that the disease somehow leaped from pigs to humans and mutated into the deadliest killer ever known. There were charges at the time that the Germans were somehow behind its appearance, but though German agents had tried to spread glanders and anthrax in the area of St. Louis to destroy horses and mules at the source instead of just aboard transports, it seems that the cold winters had prevented the diseases from establishing themselves. There had also evidently been German attempts to inflict earlier forms of influenza on American war-plant workers, but the details are unknown.[10]

Oddly, just as the plague disappeared, so did any real discussion of its disastrous visit. Spanish Influenza became a matter of personal memory, of stories passed down in families of uncles and aunts and parents who died leaving children to be looked after by survivors, but not of public remembrance.[11] It faded so fast and so completely from the collective consciousness that most history books give at most only a passing reference to it. Part of this comes from the sheer horror of the experience, an unwillingness to look too closely at death from such an inglorious cause; part from the speed with which it came, killed, and went; and part because, since its victims were the young, few famous or powerful people died. "It killed the daughter of General Edwards of the 26th Division of the AEF," points out Alfred Crosby, "but not the General. It killed a daughter and son of Senator Albert B. Fall, but not the Senator. It killed the daughter of Samuel Gompers, President of the American Federation of Labor, but left America's most powerful labor leader alive."[12]

The strongest reason for the lack of resonance was that it was killing civilians in the streets and homes of America while newspaper headlines told of the most important battles of the war raging in France. The AEF pushed the Germans back from the St. Mihiel salient in early September 1918, and while that fight was still under way, were ordered by Field Marshal Ferdinand Foch to prepare for the "grand offensive" in the Meuse-Argonne region, sixty miles to the north. With George C. Marshall in charge of planning, roads were soon jammed with trucks and horse-drawn wagons, men marched at night without rest to the new front, and recently formed inexperienced divisions were wheeled on line. The great attack along a twenty-four-mile front began at 5:30 a.m. on September 26 against deep defenses the Germans had spent three years perfecting, making brilliant use of the rugged, heavily forested terrain with mutually supporting machine-gun positions and all key points registered for mortars and artillery. The fighting was savage, in spite of heavy rain and many soldiers sick with influenza, and immediately newspapers were full of dramatic tales of heroism backed up by long casualty lists. Eventually 1.2 million Americans would be engaged in the battle, with more than 120,000 falling dead or becoming wounded, ill, or missing. The agony was so prolonged as the fighting stretched through October that even a man as hard as Pershing was strained close to the breaking point, covering his face in his hands as he was being driven back from the front and calling his dead wife's name: "Frankie . . . Frankie . . . my God, sometimes I don't know how I can go on."[13] Bridgeheads were finally established over the Meuse River on November 7, and the German railroad line bringing supplies to the front was cut. Even before this, however, British and French politicians and generals had begun minimizing the American contribution to victory in the war.

In January 1918, Woodrow Wilson had proposed a peace based on Fourteen Points. There should be open diplomacy that rejected secret treaties, freedom of the seas, limitation of weapons, free trade, the resolution of colonial claims with the welfare of the colonized recognized, and, most important, a League of Nations established to ensure continued peace. Then there were eight specific recommendations regarding terri- tory, such as the evacuation of Belgium and the return of Alsace-Lorraine to France. These, and some later elaborations, amounted to a detailed restatement of Wilson's earlier desire for a "peace without victory" and was, at the very least, a brilliant piece of psychological warfare against the Ger- mans.[14] Wilson also understood that a totally defeated Germany would make his desire for a just peace impossible, that to prevent a "peace of the victors," that country had to retain at least some defensive capabilities. Theodore Roosevelt immediately responded to the Fourteen Points with a demand for a march on Berlin leading to Germany's unconditional surren- der: "Let us dictate peace by the hammering guns and not chat about peace to the clicking of typewriters."[15] Now, as the numbers of dead and dying Americans mounted in France, some of even Wilson's generosity and trust dissipated. The Germans grew desperate as their defenses weakened, their civilians starved because of the British blockade, and their allies Bul- garia, Turkey, and Austria-Hungary began asking for terms. When German representatives approached Wilson on October 6 requesting an armistice based on his Fourteen Points, he was rightly suspicious that they merely wanted time to rebuild their strength. "They have said that they agree to my terms," Wilson wrote a British official, "and if they were respectable people I should be obliged to meet them in a conference. Of course, we do not trust the present German Government; we can never trust them, and we do not want to discuss peace with them."[16]

One way they lost their respectability was through the Carthaginian peace they had forced on Russia at Brest Litovsk, which stripped that coun- try of so much of its territory, people, and wealth while freeing German troops for the western front. Wilson felt that the real German response to the Fourteen Points had been the spring offensive that had been launched two months after that speech, which proved that the military autocracy rul- ing the country desired peace only through conquest. It was then that he had urged "force. Force to the utmost," as an answer. What he did not know was that Generals Hindenburg and Ludendorff, panicking as they recog- nized that victory was now impossible and defeat likely, had maneuvered to have themselves removed from their posts so that the shame of asking for an armistice would fall on a new civilian government.

In his response to the German note, Wilson had to be careful. Earlier German sabotage, the efforts of the Committee on Public Information, and a growing list of dead and maimed had resulted in an angry desire for revenge in the American people, and congressional elections were only a few weeks away. There were also complications from the possibility of a Bolshevik-type revolution if the kaiser's government collapsed, and the suspicions of British and French leaders that Wilson would be too generous with Germany, denying them both revenge for and profit from the sacrifices of their peoples. Wilson began an exchange of notes testing the sincerity of the German request, and sent his adviser Edward House to confer with Allied leaders.

Meanwhile the killing continued, but so did the Allied advance. Pershing opposed the granting of an armistice, feeling that unless undeniable victory was won on the battlefield the German military would evade responsibility for the defeat. This is exactly what did happen, with the right wing, led by Adolf Hitler, later gaining popular support by claiming the army had been "stabbed in the back" by Jews, profiteers, malingerers, and liberal politicians. But Wilson—after the kaiser abdicated in late October and a German republic was declared—was willing, as were the leaders of the Allies; the guns fell silent on November 11, though they roared with murderous effect right up to the last minute. Slowly, cautiously, men emerged from their trenches, bunkers, and shell holes and moved toward one another. "The rolling plain was alive with cheering men, friends and enemy alike," wrote one American journalist. "Germans and Americans were coming along the narrow stretch of ground so fiercely fought over, some shyly and awkwardly, like embarrassed schoolboys."[17]

Marshal Ferdinand Foch, overall commander of the Allied armies, had established the immediate concessions required from the Germans, and they were harsh: northern France and Belgium to be evacuated quickly, leaving behind military equipment; Alsace-Lorraine, taken from France in the Franco-Prussian War, also to be evacuated; German submarines and surface fleet to be surrendered or otherwise neutralized; a large percentage of their artillery and machine guns also to be surrendered; Allied and American occupation of the left bank of the Rhine with three strong Allied bridgeheads across that river; and the treaty of Brest Litovsk revoked. The most severe, and inhumane, requirement was that the food blockade, already starving millions of Germans, would continue. The final peace treaty was to be negotiated later at a conference in Paris.

Wilson had hoped that the importance of the American combat role, most of which came from the numbers and freshness of its soldiers, which promised great victories in 1919, as well as its already huge contributions of money and matériel, would allow him to guide the treaty process to a peace that would endure. But there were a number of things working against him. The British, French, Italians, Japanese, and other Allies were determined to gain territory from the defeated Central Powers, and the French were adamant that, after having 1.4 million of their men killed and another 4.5 million wounded, Germany must be left too weak to threaten them ever again. They would resist any attempts by the president to hinder those goals, and as part of their negotiating strategy, they had already begun, aided by the British, to downplay the significance of American aid in the victory.

But Wilson also had problems at home. In May 1918, while asking Congress to act on a progressive tax program, the president had announced that "politics is adjourned. The elections will go to those who think least of it."[18] That was a foolish hope, but might have developed into something if he had really acted on it. Wilson, however, was very much a party man, and could not make the leap, especially since feelings between him and Republican leaders, particularly Lodge and Roosevelt, were so bitter. Aside from a couple of relatively unimportant appointments, he did not reach out to the Republicans to help run the war in a bipartisan way, nor would he ask for their help in making the peace. That meant he needed to strengthen the party's tenuous hold on the House and Senate. In an incredible series of misfortunes, eight Democratic senators had died during the Sixty-fifth Congress, including Paul O. Husting, killed in a hunting accident, whose seat would normally not have been up for election until 1920.[19] Wilson and the Democrats scrambled to find candidates to run, including one of the oddest of all: Henry Ford.

The automaker had continued to fund his peace crusade until Germany's submarine policy made it likely that the United States would enter the war. Then, in just a few days, he had reversed his pacifist position, spoke of the need to support his country, and offered to put his industrial empire to work making the very instruments of death that he had been railing against for years, even telling the *New York Times* of an idea he had for a little one-man submarine that could sneak up on a battleship and blow it out of the water.[20] Though, as we have seen, he tried to insist on continuing to make cars for the civilian market, he also built ammunition boxes, steel helmets, gas masks, tractors, the Liberty airplane engine, and "Eagle" boats, a brainchild of Franklin Roosevelt's for hunting submarines. The Model T, with its jaunty ability to pull through muddy wastes, also went to war, serving as staff car and ambulance, while enduring attempts to turn it into an armored attack vehicle. Though Ford had publicly pledged he would not make "one cent of profit" on the work, much of this varied production was taking place at his huge new Rouge River plant, designed by Albert Kahn and partially built with government money.

There had been some midwestern murmurings about drafting Henry Ford to run for president in 1916, but he had refused, instead spending $50,000 to help Wilson win reelection. Now, with Democrats faced with the likelihood of losing control of Congress, he was drafted on direct appeal from Wilson himself to run for senator in Michigan. It was a strange campaign in a number of ways, but especially striking was Ford's refusal either to make a personal effort to be elected by giving speeches and attending rallies or to spend money on the race. His one public statement was on his support for women's suffrage, a cause that had grown increasingly popular during the war.[21] Michigan allowed cross-filing in the primary, so Ford was listed for both the Republican and Democratic nominations, but lost the GOP position to Truman H. Newberry, a Detroit businessman. Republicans poured far more money into the race than was legal, while Ford attempted to stay above the fray, even when things turned very ugly in October and early November. He had always been loose-lipped, impulsively blurting out the unconsidered thought of the moment; now these came back to haunt him as every crackpot remark was resurrected, sometimes distorted, and spread wide and far through expensive advertising. One would think there would be little need for additional ammunition, but his son, Edsel, was viciously attacked for having received a draft deferment, and when it was found that a top company engineer had been born in Germany, the Republican State Central Committee pulled out all the stops, running newspaper ads across Michigan just days before the election: "Carl Emde, a German alien and sympathizer [Emde was not an alien but a citizen, and emphatically protested his loyalty], is boss of the drafting work on the Liberty motor. . . . If Carl Emde wishes to make plans and photographs of the Ford plant or the Liberty motor for use by the enemies of the United States, Henry Ford is willing to give him the chance to do it."[22] Ford lost the election, but only by a few thousand votes, so had he really made an effort he would probably have won. As it was, he later went after Newberry ferociously in the courts, charging him with breaking expenditure limits; in 1922 Newberry resigned from the Senate because of the case. Ford was convinced that he had been defeated by the machinations of his old enemy Big Capital as represented by Wall Street, but he also identified a new element in the forces against him, claiming that Newberry had been the front man for an "influential gang of Jews."[23]

The Democrats went down to a broader defeat in 1918, losing six seats in the Senate, and thirty in the House of Representatives, though many of these races, like Ford's, were decided by just thousands of votes. Republicans gained control of both chambers, an ominous portent for the presidential election in 1920. It is normal for the party out of power to gain in midterm elections, but the Republicans had added to the usual victory by outspending the Democrats by a wide margin, and taking advantage of the resentment of midwestern and western farmers who felt that southerners had too much influence in the administration's high-price supports for cotton while the government underpaid for wheat. The GOP also made much of "Kitchinism," saying that party provincialism weakened the war effort, while also claiming that Wilson and his party were not after real victory, but for a "soft" peace.

To make matters worse, in response to Republican attacks, the president had abandoned what little bipartisanship had remained between the parties just before the election, pleading for the public to support him by choosing a Democratic majority so that he could remain their "unembarrassed spokesman in affairs at home and abroad." The Republicans had dangerously different ideas on the course to follow, he argued, and if they gained control that would "certainly be interpreted on the other side of the water as a repudiation of my leadership."[24] That is exactly the way the defeat was interpreted by leaders abroad, an interpretation abetted by Roosevelt's virulent attacks. "Our allies and our enemies and Mr. Wilson himself should all understand that Mr. Wilson has no authority whatever to speak for the American people at this time. His leadership has been emphatically repudiated by them. . . . Mr. Wilson and his Fourteen Points and his four supplementary points and his five complementary points, and all of his utterances every which way, have ceased to have any shadow of right to be accepted as expressive of the will of the American people."[25] This astonishingly irresponsible statement from an ex-president was then followed by a passage downplaying the country's military contribution to victory. Prime Minister David Lloyd George certainly sensed Wilson's weakened position, writing in his memoirs that the president's threats against the Allies at the conference "conveyed no real menace. There was no real assurance that his country would support him in a break with the Allies on any issue."[26]

Some of Wilson's closest advisers argued that he should not personally attend the Paris conference, feeling that, as one pointed out, he would lose "all the power that comes from distance and detachment. Instead of remaining the great arbiter of human freedom he becomes merely a negotiator dealing with other negotiators."[27] And these negotiators, Clemenceau and Lloyd George especially, were seasoned, dogged, and wonderfully adept at deception, manipulation, and the wearing down of opponents. If he had stayed home, the argument went, he could use the bully pulpit of the White House to preach the moral course, while also taking credit for achievements or disavowing mistakes by his representatives.[28] But such hack political manipulation had never been Wilson's way. Though he was not in good health and disliked personal confrontations, there was no representative he trusted to realize his vision of a treaty that would establish a just peace and extend democracy by creating a League of Nations while blunting the revenge that would breed resentment.[29]

At first his decision to travel to Europe seemed a brilliant stroke as he was greeted that December 1918 by frenzied crowds—two million cheering people lined his route in Paris, including some American soldiers on leave. One of them, a young captain of artillery named Harry Truman, would remember it through a life filled with such demonstrations as the greatest he had ever seen.[30] Millions more would excitedly applaud him when he later toured the Continent, seeing in the tall, lean figure both the symbol of American aid that had made victory possible and the man, or perhaps "messiah," able to bring about fulfillment of their desires, wildly contradictory though these desires were. Bernard Baruch, who accompanied him to Paris, recounts how everyone wanted to meet the president, even an Indian maharaja who asked for an audience so "he could tell his people that the 'light of Wilson's countenance had shone upon him.' "[31]

But, of course, that glow could not last. As the negotiations finally began in January 1919 at the Palace of Versailles, the differences between the hopes of Wilson and the fear and vengeful selfishness of his associates in the war became clear. "The genes of a thousand years of inbred hate and fear . . . were in their blood," wrote Herbert Hoover, who was also in Paris. "Revenge for past wrongs rose every hour of the day. It was not alone the delegates that were thus inspired. These emotions of hate, revenge, desire for reparations, and a righteous sense of wrong were at fever heat in their peoples at home."[32] The French planned to break off other parts of Germany besides Alsace-Lorraine to diminish its military power while the British targeted the navy. Both wanted enormous reparations and to strip Germany of its colonies in Africa and Asia, while Japan—which had joined the war only as an excuse to seize Shantung, Germany's possession in China—was demanding that its grip there and over some of the Pacific-island colonies now be made permanent. Italy insisted on receiving the Austrian regions it had been promised for joining the Allies; Romania had its own ambitions.

The Big Four at the Paris Peace Conference, May 1919.
From left, David Lloyd George of Great Britain, Vittorio Orlando
of Italy, Georges Clemenceau of France, and Woodrow Wilson.

Germany had fallen into revolutionary chaos before establishing a
weak democracy, its army had disintegrated, thereby providing no counter-
weight to the victors, and rendering Wilson's implied threats of striking a
separate peace ineffectual. Wilson resisted these demands as best he
could, compromising on some because he thought that his vision of a
League of Nations would be thereby insured, and that the League could
resolve any injustices that would result from these compromises. For
example, Georges Clemenceau, whose country had been invaded twice by
German troops since 1870, was insistent on his plan to break Germany
apart. He had a tigerish fierceness toward the Germans, as Herbert Hoover
explained: "His soul contained to his dying day all the bitterness of the sufferings of the French people. The widows, orphans, and ruined homes in
France were the lenses he looked through. To him the turn of Germany to
democracy was a fraud; the only way to deal with Germans was to make
them impotent forever."[33]

But when the president threatened to leave the conference and ordered steam to be raised in his ship's boilers, Clemenceau, fearing the complications and delays this might bring, backed down. He dropped his demand that Germany be broken into various republics and that a permanent French occupation of the Rhineland be established. In return, France won approval for a fifteen-year occupation there, along with British and American guarantees that in the immediate future they would help protect France from attack by Germany. The British insisted that Japan receive Shantung and that Italy be rewarded with the strategically important Brenner Pass on the Austrian frontier. Wilson was forced to acquiesce, while extracting an agreement that Japan would soon return Shantung to Chinese sovereignty. He blocked Italy from obtaining Fiume, which was instead to be the port of the newly created Yugoslavia, and also insisted that former German colonies be administered through a new mandate system under the League of Nations that would eventually lead to their independence. Behind much of Wilson's action was the need to quickly rebuild stability in Europe so it could better resist the appeals of the Bolshevik Revolution. He was warned by William C. Bullitt, the young former journalist now in the diplomatic service who had just returned from Eastern Europe, that people were losing faith in the treaty process, and in him: "They turn, therefore, to Lenin."[34]

And so it went from issue to issue, Wilson standing firm where he could on points of major importance to him, but willing to compromise; always, though, fighting to establish the League of Nations, insisting that the covenant establishing the League form the first part of the treaty so that it could not be separated from the general peace terms. He was sure that once the passions of the war had time to diminish, the League would eventually ensure a just peace that would bring Europe and the world back to an even keel. Wilson came home briefly in late February as Congress was about to adjourn to sign bills, bringing with him the League Covenant and hoping to have it accepted by the Senate. Henry Cabot Lodge responded, however, with a letter signed by thirty-seven senators, enough to block the treaty, demanding changes. The president, though furious, returned to Paris and successfully had adjustments made that met most of the concerns: a nation could refuse to accept a colonial mandate; the League could not regulate immigration or other domestic issues; League policies would not affect the Monroe Doctrine; and any member could withdraw after giving two years' notice.

That Wilson accomplished all this while suffering from various illnesses makes it all the more impressive. He had never been particularly robust, and under pressure often fell ill. It should be remembered that when Wilson had taken office in 1913, the great expert in nervous diseases Silas Weir Mitchell had predicted that Wilson would not live through his first term. His physician, Admiral Cary T. Grayson, had kept him alive and usually healthy by guiding his diet and insisting he relax and take regular exercise. This program fell apart at Versailles as the stress of overwork took its toll; the president took an active part in meetings all day and often into the night. Grayson pleaded with the sixty-two-year-old man to slow his pace, but Wilson felt too much urgency. "Give me time. We are running a race with Bolshevism and the world is on fire. Let us wind up this work here and then we will go home and find time for a little rest and play and take up our health routine again."[35] He suddenly collapsed on April 3, either from influenza or a mild stroke or a combination of the two, and spent the next four days in bed. Though he returned to the negotiations, he seemed greatly changed. Herbert Hoover, among a number of others, made note of the effects: "Prior to that time . . . he was incisive, quick to grasp essentials, unhesitating in conclusions, and most willing to take advice. After, . . . [others as well as I] found we had to push against an unwilling mind."[36] It was during this period that he made his greatest deviation from the Fourteen Points, when he allowed the British and French to carry the argument for heavy German reparations that would pay not only for civilian damages they had caused but also for military pensions for Allied widows and for maimed soldiers. After the Germans were forced to sign the document in late June, Wilson, still suffering from the effects of his illness, returned to Washington to lay the accomplished treaty before the Senate, confident that everyone would recognize that in spite of many imperfections it was the best that could have been achieved and that it would be easily approved. Then he would finally be able to rest.

JACK REED had not rested. As soon as *The Masses* trial was over and his confiscated papers returned, he had secluded himself in an attic room in Greenwich Village and begun to write of all he had witnessed during the Bolshevik Revolution. The words poured out as he relived the excitement of those days in Petrograd and Moscow: the intellectual and spiritual stimulation of listening to Lenin and Trotsky expound on the inevitable path of history, the physical dangers of his trips to contested areas, the inspiring sacrifices he had witnessed made by workers and common people of all sorts. But, making full use of the documents he had brought back, Reed did not make it a personal adventure story like *Insurgent Mexico*. Instead it was the "adventure" of the Bolsheviki, "one of the most marvelous mankind ever embarked upon, sweeping into history at the head of the toiling masses and staking everything on their vast and simple desires."[37] By constant injections of caffeine and tobacco, Reed was able to finish the book in just over two months. Max Eastman, crossing Sheridan Square, came across his friend taking a rare break from the writing, appearing "gaunt, unshaven, greasy-skinned, a stark sleepless half crazy look on his slightly potatolike face," but there was also "unqualified, concentrated joy in his mad eyes," the look of a man "doing what he was made to do."[38] Published on March 19, 1919, the book vividly evokes the drama of those revolutionary days. While not hiding his biases, Reed claimed it was the work of "a conscientious reporter, interested in setting down the truth."[39] Biased it certainly was, and full of numerous errors, but it was also a magnificent piece of propaganda that prompted positive reviews from liberal and even some conservative newspapers and magazines. Former socialist activist Charles Edward Russell found great fault in it for the *New York Times,* but most reviews saw the work as both prophecy of what the rest of the twentieth century would bring and, also, *The New Republic* claimed, "a handbook of reference" for revolutionaries.[40] Enthusiastic huzzahs poured in from the radical Left: IWW members wrote him from Leavenworth; Emma Goldman, serving her sentence in the Missouri state penitentiary, found the book so "engrossingly thrilling" that she was transported to Russia "caught by her fierce storm. . . . Reed's narrative was unlike anything else I had read about the October Revolution . . . a social earthquake whose tremors were shaking the entire world."[41] Vladimir Lenin was so impressed that he contributed an introduction to later editions that read in part: "Unreservedly do I recommend it to the workers of the world. Here is a book which I should like to see published in millions of copies and translated into all languages. It gives a truthful and most vivid exposition of the events so significant to the comprehension of what really is the Proletarian Revolution." Some of this excitement can also be sensed from Reed's later biographers. Granville Hicks, writing in the 1930s when he himself was a member of the Communist Party, quoted Reed's reply to the Russell review in the *Times:* "You are correct when you call information about Russia Bolshevik propaganda, for the great majority of persons who learn the truth about Russia become convinced Bolsheviki." Hicks admitted that the claim might be a bit exaggerated, but pointed out that "it would not be easy to compute the number of persons whose interest in Communism dates from a reading of *Ten Days That Shook the World.*"[42] Robert A. Rosenstone, writing during the early 1970s, recognized that the book is "inaccurate in details, biased in point of view," but believes it "conveys the kind of truth that is beyond fact, that creates fact. More than history, it is poetry, the poetry of revolution."[43]

Reed and Bryant had been struggling financially, but *Ten Days* sold five thousand copies within the first three months, and Louise had published her own book on the revolution, *Six Red Months in Russia,* which had also been well received.[44] Reed was able to redeem his father's gold watch from a pawnbroker, send money to his mother, and devote himself anew to the revolution, writing long pieces with titles such as "Why Political Democracy Must Go" that ran in the *New York Communist,* which he had founded. He also wrote a satirical play, "The Peace That Passeth Understanding," published in Max Eastman's *Liberator,* that mocked Wilson's efforts at Versailles. The Provincetown Players mounted a weeklong production that he regarded as a success.

WOODROW WILSON came home to a country in turmoil. Some contentious issues had seemingly been resolved: the Eighteenth Amendment to the Constitution, which would ban all consumption of alcohol, including wine and beer, was working its way through ratification by the states. It had been adopted nationally as a wartime conservation measure in 1917, but now would be made permanent. Congress passed the Volstead Act in the summer of 1919, legislation to establish how the amendment would be enforced; Wilson used his veto power, but was overridden by a large margin. The Women's Suffrage Amendment, finally advocated by both the president and Theodore Roosevelt, had gathered even wider support because of the contributions of women to the war effort and was also making its way through the ratification process. Both these amendments would become law in 1920.

Many citizens were gratified by this continuing social progress, though others were irritated. The country at large was particularly impatient for the wartime controls, which had brought the government into so many areas of their lives, to be ended. Bernard Baruch, among other emergency administrators, recognized that feeling: "Let's turn industry absolutely free," he said when the fighting stopped. "Everything that made us possible is gone, the war spirit of cooperation and sacrifice, the vast purchasing power of the government, the scant legal authority we have had, and the support of public opinion."[45] Industry, which had made enormous profits during the war, was turned free quickly as the war agencies closed down, but so were prices, which Baruch had kept under some limited control.

"Had WIB been empowered to carry on its direction of the economy," he later argued, "much of the waste and disorder accompanying reconversion might have been avoided."[46] Particularly suffering from the waste and disorder were millions of increasingly resentful soldiers being demobilized as fast as possible with no plan for having them reintegrated into society and with scant opportunities for employment. Constantly appearing in newspaper headlines during this time were the initials HCL, which every reader knew from bitter experience stood for "high cost of living." Using 1913 as a base, the cost of living had risen 97 percent by 1919; the next year it leaped to 102 percent. Food costs, especially burdensome for those with families, had increased 84 percent, with milk jumping from nine cents a quart to fifteen cents, steak from twenty-seven cents a pound to forty-two cents, while rents had gone up even more.[47] Salaries of workers, blue collar or white collar, did not keep even close to the rise in costs, with the result that in 1919 the United States was being riven by the worst strikes in its history.

The range of workers who took to the picket lines showed the depth of discontent. From actors in the Broadway theaters to police in Boston to the hard-labor industries of logging, mining, and steelmaking, over four million workers walked off their jobs that year for a total of 2,600 strikes. The first important action was in Seattle, when local unions made the prodigious mistake of calling a general strike, almost unprecedented in American history. *All* workers in *all* jobs were to stop work at 10 a.m. on Thursday, February 6, 1919. "We are undertaking the most tremendous move ever made by Labor in this country," bragged a union newspaper. "We are starting on a road that leads, NO ONE KNOWS WHERE!"[48]

It led to disastrous failure, as the public, fearing that food or medicine would not be available for their children, their old folks, or themselves, rushed shops to empty the shelves of everything, including guns. Also immediately disappearing was any sympathy for the legitimate grievances of the workers, who just wanted enough money to keep up with inflation and a diminishment of the long hours spent on the job. The strike worked in the sense that the city, except for essential services, did shut down. There was no violence, the union men guaranteed that food and milk would be available and that the garbage would be picked up. But the mayor, Ole Hanson, claiming that the IWW was directing the strike, called for federal troops to prevent a Bolshevik revolution; he got 7,500 of them. "The time has come," announced the mayor, "for the people in Seattle to show their Americanism. . . . The anarchist in this community shall not rule its affairs."[49] Moderate unions, guided by the American Federation of Labor, pulled back, the strike collapsed, and Hanson became a national hero as a fearful middle class became convinced that the same wave of revolution washing across parts of Europe had reached these shores. The Red Scare was on.

An even more traumatic event occurred in Boston when the police went on strike on September 9, for better pay and working conditions, and to have a recognized union affiliation with the AF of L. This time, events did get out of control: stores were looted, thugs rioted, men were assaulted and killed, women were raped. The State Guard clumsily restored order, all the strikers were fired, and when the governor, Calvin Coolidge, declared, "There is no right to strike against the public safety by anybody, anywhere, any time," he became even more of a national hero than Hanson, and would soon sit in the White House.[50]

The steel industry was as great a devourer of men as mining. In 1919, the average steelworker spent seventy hours a week in the hot, clanging, dangerous plants, while about half of them were there for twelve hours a day, seven days a week. For this they received about $1,450 a year when the minimum required for a family of five was estimated at $1,575.[51] Elbert Gary, head of United States Steel, the boss of bosses of the industry and the same industrial titan that Bernard Baruch had humbled, refused to discuss any improvements with the steelworker unions, or even to officially acknowledge their existence, though the company had earned a net income of $224 million in 1917. Instead, determined not to be humbled again, he and his associates in the steel trust literally prepared for war by surrounding the plants with barbed wire, hiring heavily armed guards, and using his political influence to swear in thousands of deputy sheriffs.

The workers, demanding the right of union representation, an eight-hour day, six days a week, and a living wage, walked out on September 22; within a week, more than 365,000 were taking part in the strike. Violence began almost immediately as union meetings were disrupted and pickets attacked while company spies and agents spread pernicious rumors about union sellouts. They also tried to promote racism and ethnic strife in the ranks; it was deliberate steel-trust policy to use African American strikebreakers whenever possible to create worker dissension.[52] There were labor riots in several cities, the worst occurring in Gary, Indiana, the town named for Elbert Gary, that resulted in an unknown number of dead and wounded. Again federal troops were called in, this time under the command of General Leonard Wood. By late November the strike was broken, and the men returned to the same dreadful working conditions still unprotected by union representation. A similar defeat was inflicted on the United Mine Workers when they tried to strike in the bituminous coalfields that fall.

Business leaders and politicians had learned how to meet the drive for unionism and better wages for shorter hours: by adapting the techniques used during the war to the new struggle. Unions, it was asserted in newspaper advertisements and political speeches, all of them from the conservative AF of L to the IWW, were in thrall to a foreign ideology. This was no longer Kaiserism, but Bolshevik Communism, which, business organizations charged, was trying to overthrow the government with the help of foreign and domestic radicals and establish a soviet dictatorship. A public already angry at German sabotage and mourning its war dead was vulnerable to the argument; the campaign of defamation was well financed, intelligently directed, and overwhelmingly effective.

A great part of its effectiveness came with help from the radicals themselves. Inspired and reinvigorated by the example of the Bolsheviks, the extreme Left suddenly bounced back after the repression of the war years; many of them were as convinced as the conservatives that Red revolution would soon sweep the old order out of power. Deadly letter bombs were sent to leading political, legal, and business figures in late April 1919, followed by more in June, fitting into the dynamite rhetoric of anarchists such as Emma Goldman and Alexander Berkman.[53] On May Day, fights broke out between parading leftists and veterans who had just returned from Europe. The worst of these riots took place in Boston, when a radical workers' group waving red flags defied the requirement for a permit and marched regardless. Authorities and private citizens tried to stop them. The marchers pulled knives; three policemen and a civilian were wounded, and a policeman was stabbed to death.[54] When word spread, mobs destroyed Socialist Party headquarters and attacked any radicals they could identify. Similar fighting took place in Cleveland, New York, and other cities. These riots were seen by some newspaper editorial writers as "dress rehearsals" for the coming Red revolution.

In Portland, Oregon, a group called the Council of Workers, Soldiers, and Sailors was organized to help with the government's overthrow, a move hailed by the *Soviet World,* a publication based in Philadelphia that predicted the "next two years would see the birth of the Socialist Soviet Republic of the United States."[55] There were in late 1919, the Justice Department claimed, 471 such radical publications advocating violent revolution.[56] Optimists on the extreme Left not only looked to the increasing number of American strikes, but the uprisings going on in Europe. They took confidence from the fact that there had been only ten thousand or so Bolsheviki in Russia in May 1917, yet within six months they had forced their way to power. John Reed was so certain that the workers, under proper direction, would soon rise that he advised Roger Baldwin, just sentenced for being a conscientious objector, not to worry, that they would free him before he had spent much time in jail.[57]

Reed did all he could to bring that revolution about, including trying to found an organization to serve as vanguard. At first he joined with allies in an attempt to capture the Socialist Party for its left wing, but at the national convention in Chicago on August 30, 1919, he and his friends were involved in an altercation with the credentials committee that quickly became a fistfight. That struggle was resolved, ironically enough, by the Chicago police, who expelled the challengers. Now the need was clear for a new organization, and the ejected activists immediately formed the Communist Labor Party. But here, too, there were problems, as the radicals fought among themselves, the major split being between the foreign-language faction and the native-born socialists. There ended up being two groups: the Communist Labor Party with only ten thousand members, being led by native radicals such as Reed, and the Communist Party, with over 90 percent of its sixty thousand members being foreign-born, very few of whom were even able to speak English. Both applied to the Communist International, or Comintern, for recognition, and Reed, who knew all the important Bolsheviks, was sent to argue for the CLP. Disguised and using the name Jim Gormley, he worked his way to Norway as a stoker on a freighter, then was smuggled by the Communist underground across Scandinavia into a Russia being torn by civil war.

The fear of revolutionary fighting in the United States spurred the federal government to action. A. Mitchell Palmer, the pacifist Quaker whom Woodrow Wilson had wanted to make secretary of war in 1913, did consent to be attorney general in March 1919. He was among the public figures who were sent bombs in April, along with Oliver Wendell Holmes, Jr.; Judge Kenesaw Mountain Landis, famous for sending radicals, including Big Bill Haywood, to prison; Postmaster General Albert S. Burleson, who had barred radical publications from the mails; and two enormously wealthy capitalist juniors: John D. Rockefeller and J. P. Morgan. Those packages had been intercepted, so on the evening of June 2, personal delivery was attempted. An enormous explosion blew the front off Palmer's house in the District of Columbia just after he and his family had gone to bed. Franklin and Eleanor Roosevelt, who lived across the street, were parking their car when the bomb detonated, evidently prematurely since it splattered its carrier across their front steps; it was FDR who called the police. Explosions, obviously well-planned and coordinated, went off simultaneously in eight cities, destroying homes, but luckily killing only two people. Federal and local judges were targeted, as were businessmen, police, and the Rectory of Our Lady of Victory. Palmer, unharmed, did not hesitate; over the next seven months the General Intelligence Division of the Bureau of Investigation, guided by an eager young bureaucrat named J. Edgar Hoover, began rounding up radicals without much concern about whether they were guilty of anything more than unpleasant rhetoric. The attorney general, whom friends in the press began calling "the Fighting Quaker," became yet another hero spawned by the dangers and fears of the time; dreams of the presidency soon followed.

This was the violent, chaotic, almost hysterical background to Woodrow Wilson's fight for the Versailles Treaty and the League of Nations. He addressed the Senate on July 10, pleading for swift passage because it was "the hope of the world. . . . Shall we or any other free people hesitate to accept this great duty? Dare we reject it and break the heart of the world?"[58] Henry Cabot Lodge cared little about the heart of the world, and a great deal about defeating a president he loathed while protecting the freedom of action of the United States. A particularly bothersome part of the treaty was Article X, or 10, which he interpreted to mean that the country could be unwillingly pulled into wars by other signatories, though Wilson showed him how the wording protected against that. The Republicans had sincere reservations, but they also saw the fight as a chance to prepare the ground for victory in the presidential campaign of 1920; at least two senators made public attacks on the League by likening it to Bolshevism.

But the aggravating and powerful voice of one sworn enemy of Woodrow Wilson had been stilled. Theodore Roosevelt had died in January at the relatively young age of sixty. He never stopped trying to get in the fighting, but had to be satisfied with sending his four sons to the AEF: Kermit was an artillery officer; TR, Jr., and Archibald, infantry officers, were both badly wounded; Quentin, a fighter pilot, was shot down and killed. The death hit TR with unexpected force. In ill health since an adventure to the Amazon after his electoral defeat in 1912, he now found little of interest in life, not even the likelihood of being the Republican candidate for president in 1920. Nevertheless, a fervent believer in "balance of power" international strategy, TR had before his death done all he could to smear both the president and what he was trying to accomplish at Versailles.

In spite of the early attacks on the treaty, the public at first seemed to support approval; Lodge, however, managed to delay consideration, and as time passed opposition forces grew. Many immigrants were angry over what their home countries either received or didn't receive from the pact, while citizens wanted a retreat to prewar isolationism, or as William Randolph Hearst had his newspapers put it, "one-hundred-percent-Americanism." Progressive men and women, on the other hand, were unhappy with Wilson's compromise "Covenant" because it had veered so far from the Fourteen Points, which had promised a genuine peace without victors. Liberal leaders had suffered harassment, prison, or worse during the war when their desire for peace was seen as traitorous, and their influence had been weakened. One of Wilson's advisers had written to Edward House earlier in 1919: "Most assuredly we cannot gain the Senate if, in addition to the opposition of the reactionaries we have the liberals dissatisfied."[59] Dissatisfied they were, feeling that the administration, which had refused to pardon Eugene Debs or other prisoners of conscience, had become reactionary. Now, partly in the interest of their pure idealism, they abandoned him and his soiled treaty.

Wilson handled none of the renitency well. He did meet privately with senators, but though he felt he was being patient in his teaching of the details of the treaty, a number were offended by his high-handed manner and unwillingness to compromise. Here again it is difficult to separate his innate stubbornness from the effects of his ill health; he seems to have been struck with another minor stroke in the middle of July.[60] Confident in the rightness of his cause, and encouraged by his faith in the moral and intellectual quality of the public, he decided to use the same tactic he had when faced with recalcitrant trustees at Princeton and in his earlier battles with the Senate: take to the road. Both Dr. Grayson and Wilson's wife recommended against the tour, warning of his exhaustion and bad health, but Wilson was adamant: "I cannot put my personal safety . . . in the balance against my duty," he replied. "I must go."[61] On September 3, the president departed, giving, over the next three weeks, almost forty speeches throughout the West to enthusiastic crowds of twenty to thirty thousand. He would also spend hours in rallies and parades, shaking hands with well-wishers, being particularly moved by mothers of sons lost in the war, who would weep when meeting him and, supporting his effort to ensure that such sacrifice would not be required again, say, "God bless you, Mr. President."[62]

Terrible headaches, a weakness in the limbs, tremors that shook his body—Wilson relied on his stern self-discipline to get him through most of the planned trip. However, on September 25, after giving major speeches in Colorado at Denver and Pueblo, he collapsed, suffering a minor stroke that caused him to admit to Joseph Tumulty that he was falling to pieces. In spite of his physical distress, he pleaded that the trip not be cut short:

"Don't you see that if you cancel this trip, Senator Lodge and his friends will say that I am a quitter and that the Western trip was a failure, and the Treaty will be lost."[63] But this time all those closest to him refused to be swayed. They returned to Washington, where a massive stroke on October 2 almost killed him. He survived, but was paralyzed on the left side of his body, and could barely speak or see. For six weeks he was bed-bound, the business of government handled by his wife, his aides, and the Cabinet officers; Dr. Grayson urged him to resign, but after wavering briefly, he refused, still holding to a now impossible hope that he might win the fight for his Covenant.

Epilogue

They . . . are weary of hearing highfalutin and meaningless words;
they sicken of an idealism that is oblique, confusing, dishonest and
ferocious. . . . Today no sane American believes in any official state-
ment of national policy, whether foreign or domestic. He has been
fooled too often, and too callously and impudently. Every idea that
has aroused him to sentimental enthusiasm and filled his breast
with the holiest of passions has been dragged down into the mud by
its propounders and made to seem evil and disgusting. He wants a
change. . . . Tired to death of intellectual charlatanry, he turns
despairingly to honest imbecility.

H. L. Mencken, 1920[1]

As soon as the armistice had been arranged, soldiers, vocally supported by their families, neighbors, friends, and congressmen, began clamoring to go home. "We've paid our debt to Lafayette," went the bitter refrain. "Who the hell do we owe now?" Like the rest of the country, they increasingly felt that they owed only themselves.

With victory, higher-ranking members of the government were also free to leave for the more rewarding fields of private enterprise. They, like soldiers and workers, fervently believed that the time of sacrifice should be over. In February 1919, Secretary of the Interior Franklin Lane resigned from the Cabinet to take a job with Edward L. Doheny's Pan-American Petroleum Company for the enormous salary of $50,000 a year.[2] Lane happily boasted, at a luncheon with other Cabinet members, that he would never again feel the "dishonor" of being poor. He was spared by an early death from knowing the dishonor of scandal that would attach to Doheny's name a few years later when it was discovered that the oilman had bribed government officials, including then president Warren G. Harding's secretary of the interior, Albert B. Fall, to secure access to the naval oil reserves at Teapot Dome, Wyoming.

Wilson's secretary of the treasury and son-in-law William McAdoo also felt the financial pinch of government service. "I was spending more than I earned, several times more, and my financial means were dwindling. The cost of living in Washington had gone up to fabulous heights; the monthly deficit made a tremendous hole in my assets."[3] McAdoo returned to private enterprise, still harboring well-founded ambitions for the presidency. He moved to California, where one of his first jobs, early in 1919, was to help the movie stars Douglas Fairbanks, Mary Pickford, and Charlie Chaplin join with director D. W. Griffith to form United Artists so they could produce and market their own films. Though these pioneer celebrities drew salaries of $10,000 or so a week, that was as nothing compared to the millions that the studios earned from their talents. Perhaps in McAdoo's eyes it was another case of the "little guy" taking on the greedy capitalists, but he would also work for Edward Doheny, and that would mar his later political career.

Attorney General A. Mitchell Palmer had his own ambitions, of course, and worked hard to fulfill them. In early 1920, he proudly informed the nation that the "blaze of revolution" that had been "sweeping over every American institution of law and order a year ago" had now more or less been quenched.[4] Aided by his loyal assistant J. Edgar Hoover, Palmer had "discovered upwards of 60,000 . . . organized agitators of the Trotzky doctrine" and was continuing to sweep "the nation clean of such filth." That sweeping had gathered up thousands of anarchists and Communists, most of them aliens, without bothering about proof of criminal activity. Almost nine hundred of these foreign agitators would be forced to leave the country, many on the SS *Buford* in December 1919. The "Soviet Ark," as it was nicknamed by the press, carried 249 radicals to exile in the Soviet Union, including Alexander Berkman and Emma Goldman. She was defiant: "I do not consider it punishment to be sent back to Soviet Russia. I consider it an honor to be chosen as the first political agitator to be deported from the United States."[5]

Palmer devoted himself to the task of cleansing America of these "Russian and German" agents. "There is almost no other nationality represented among them." It was not a completely single-minded effort, for he still had presidential ambitions. But then the wind shifted, fear of Reds subsided, and the "Fighting Quaker" began to be mocked as the "Quaking Fighter." The ridicule was not enough to take him completely out of the race, but it was a distraction.

So President Wilson lost some of the men he most respected and listened to at a time when their advice could have been crucial in the fight for the League, for the October stroke had, along with its physical effects, deprived him of his sense of political balance. To take a pure stance on an issue had been a familiar tactic with Wilson, who would then, after principle had been established, be willing to compromise on details. Now: no compromises. Stories were printed claiming that Edith Wilson along with Dr. Grayson was governing the country, and there was some truth to them; comments in her handwriting are to be found in the margins of state papers, though she may have been taking notes for a president who could no longer write. Even worse rumors circulated that he had died or gone insane and that this was being hidden from the public. Wilson did finally allow two Republican senators to meet with him under special, limited conditions, and they were fooled into reporting that he was fine and taking care of business. Lodge and his allies tried to bargain, but Wilson refused to seriously deal with them, ordering loyal Democrats to vote against any attempt to change the treaty. As McAdoo noted admiringly about his father-in-law: "Like Andrew Jackson, he was a good hater, and when he saw that a man was capable of duplicity, and was playing the part of a hypocrite or a demagogue, he crossed him off . . . and the crossing-off was final."[6] And the crossing-off meant an end to trust or cooperation. The result was that the Versailles Treaty did not pass and the United States never joined the League of Nations.

It is difficult to know just how much difference U.S. membership in the League would have made. Perhaps what could have been a postwar period of peace became instead merely a prewar pause, but that might have happened anyway. After a war that killed upward of fifteen million people, maimed the lives of tens of millions more, shattered empires, and released titanic forces of discord and hatred, there was probably no man or group of men that could have put things back together again. The League quite possibly would have ended as an example of the same misplaced faith in signed scraps of paper that William Jennings Bryan had indulged in with his arbitration treaties.

Disillusionment with the Great Crusade was widespread, partly because in their innocence people—urged on by government propaganda—had allowed expectations to grow out of all proportion to reality. But there was also a broader rejection of uplifting campaigns and attempts to find humane solutions to inhumane conditions. Members of the middle class, who had scorned politics as vulgar and debased throughout the latter part of the nineteenth century, had re-entered the arena during the progressive movement, providing its core strength. Now they exited again. The myriad social evils that had seemed susceptible to rational reform through education and political action now stood revealed as requiring far more complex responses. Truth alone did not make men free. After two decades of reform, slums still existed, corrupt bosses still ruled the cities, giant corporations had grown even larger and more powerful. Confidence was lost as well in the mass public, which had earlier seemed so open to progressive ideas. The achievements of the Committee on Public Information in promoting a blind, unquestioning patriotism had exposed the ignorance, irrationality, and eager conformity that a determined, well-funded government or private advertiser could direct for its own purposes.

Then there were progressive successes such as women's suffrage and Prohibition. The first was a good reform, most people came to realize, but the second was obviously a victory for small-town, self-righteous bluenoses, and it was viewed by city sophisticates as provincialism run wild. Now there were many more such city folk. The Census of 1920 would show for the first time that the urban population of the United States was larger than the rural, and this trend would continue apace over the coming decades. As a popular song from 1918 asked:

> *How 'ya gonna keep 'em down on the farm, after they've seen Paree?*
> *How 'ya gonna keep 'em away from Broadway,*
> *Jazzin' a-roun', and paintin' the town?*

Not everyone gave up the fight to improve the world. Jack Reed had returned to Soviet Russia to argue that his Communist Labor Party should be recognized as the agent to bring Bolshevism to America. He lost the argument, but not his faith. Reed advised Lenin on American radicalism, and traveled through the chaotic Russian countryside to study the party's solutions to worsening conditions of famine, disease, and combat, becoming hardened to the savageness of the civil war. "I have learned one mighty expressive Russian word," he crowed to Emma Goldman after she arrived on the *Buford*. "*Razstrellyat!*"—execute by shooting.

"Stop, Jack! Stop!" she cried. "This word is terrible enough in the mouth of a Russian. In your hard American accent it freezes my blood. Since when do revolutionists see in wholesale execution the only solution to their difficulties?"[7] He assured her that she was confused by all the theory she had studied, that this was "revolution in action."

Reed attended the Second Congress of the Communist International during the summer of 1920, where he was elected a member of its Executive Committee. He died a few weeks later of typhus, just three days short of his thirty-third birthday. Many of his comrades in American socialist groups had also transferred their allegiance to the exciting but disciplined new movement being organized by the Bolsheviks. Lincoln Steffens encouraged these enlistments, telling anyone who would listen that he had been to Russia and he knew what he had seen: "I have been over into the future, and it works."[8]

Most youth, though, would not be interested in such causes for the next decade; there were more rewarding personal things to do, and they, like most of the society at large, had lost their innocent enthusiasm and withdrawn from the social struggle. When Woodrow Wilson had ventured out from Paris on Christmas Day 1918 to speak to soldiers in the field, the customary winter rain of northern France had poured down. Together they had braved the elements, one of the greatest orators of his generation assuring his warriors that their sacrifices would result in a firm yet just peace. But the well-trained professorial voice rolling out abstractions made these men and their comrades aware that they were of a very different generation from the president. As Ernest Hemingway would write in *A Farewell to Arms,* his novel of the war: "I was always embarrassed by the words sacred, glorious and sacrifice, and the expression in vain. We had heard them, sometimes standing in the rain almost out of earshot, so that only the shouted words came through. . . . The things that were glorious had no glory and the sacrifices were like the stockyards at Chicago if nothing was done with the meat except to bury it."

Alienation would grow even stronger for many when they returned home to find the parades over, the good jobs taken, and appreciation of their efforts forgotten. Defiance was a common reaction. John F. Carter wrote a piece entitled "These Wild Young People: By One of Them," for the September 1920 *Atlantic Monthly,* in which he charged that the older generation "had certainly pretty well ruined this world before passing it on to us. They give us this Thing, knocked to pieces, leaky, red-hot, threatening to blow up." Then, "these sentimental old world-wreckers" complained about the lack of "Chivalry and Modesty" with which the burden was received. "Now my generation is disillusionized," he explained, "and . . . brutalized, by the cataclysm which *their* complacent folly engendered. . . . We have seen man at his lowest, woman at her lightest, in the terrible moral chaos of Europe. . . . We have seen the rottenness and shortcomings of all governments, even the best and most stable. We have seen entire social systems overthrown, and our own called in question. In short, we have seen the inherent beastliness of the human race revealed in an infernal apocalypse."

As a result of being forced to grow up fast, Carter wrote, "Our music is distinctly barbaric, our girls are distinctly *not* a mixture of arbutus and barbed-wire. We drink when we can and what we can, we gamble, we are extravagant—but we work. . . . We're men and women, long before our time, in the flower of our full-blooded youth. We have brought back into civil life some of the recklessness and ability that we were taught by war. . . . Terrible mistakes will be made, but we shall . . . make them intelligently and insist . . . on doing pretty much as we choose now."

This youthful rebellion was intensely individual, and though its adherents might be cynical about corporations, they harbored no moral outrage over their sins. In fact, the Red Scare had been a strong signal that the two decades of struggle to control big business was now at an end. The United States had come out of the war no longer a debtor but instead a great creditor nation, and as the country regained its economic confidence, the contributions of volunteer dollar-a-year men were celebrated, perhaps more than the mental and physical sufferings of the combat troops were recognized. Certainly it now seemed that businessmen could do no wrong. Early in 1921 an article in *The Independent* began: "Among the nations of the earth today America stands for one idea: *Business*. . . . In this fact lies, potentially, the salvation of the world."[9] That faith would be briefly shaken by the terrifyingly sudden and severe recession that struck the country later that year, but then would rebound quickly with the economy and last until the real accounting began in 1929.

The election of 1920 reflected all the changes sweeping the United States, from rejection of the League to rejection of an energetic reform movement and a turning to purely personal ambitions. With Theodore Roosevelt dead, the Republicans lacked an obvious candidate, though his good friend General Leonard Wood tried hard for the nomination. The decision was made under the direction of the party professionals, and it was for Warren Gamaliel Harding, senator from Ohio and perhaps the most unqualified candidate, up to that time, to have ever run for the presidency. The party hacks were denied the vice-presidential selection they wanted when a mild revolt on the convention floor insisted that Calvin Coolidge, famous thanks to the Boston police strike, be on the ticket. Harding, a handsome, genial womanizer whom H. L. Mencken sympathetically called the "Marion stonehead" after the candidate's hometown, was strongly advised to run a "front porch" campaign reminiscent of William McKinley's in 1896 and 1900. "Keep Warren at home," insisted one old pro. "Don't let him make any speeches. If he goes out on a tour, somebody's sure to ask him questions, and Warren's just the sort of damn fool that'll try to answer them."[10] This is the strategy he pretty much followed, staying in Marion, holding a solemn flag-raising ceremony every morning, and having his supporters come to him.

Woodrow Wilson, unable to recognize the obvious signs of disenchant-ment with all that he stood for, entertained the fantasy of being drafted to run for a third term, and so withheld his endorsement from William McAdoo. The Democratic convention in San Francisco saw McAdoo, Attorney General Palmer, and Ohio governor James M. Cox battle through ballot after ballot until Palmer finally withdrew and Cox took the nomina-tion on the forty-fourth vote. The young Franklin Delano Roosevelt won the vice-presidential spot. Both were energetic, valiant campaigners, trav-eling thousands of miles and personally addressing millions of voters. But this was not enough to overcome the appeal that Republicans made for a rejection of "Wilsonianism," while obfuscating the League question, and promising a return to "normalcy." "Mr. Wilson and his dynasty," demanded Henry Cabot Lodge, "his heirs and assigns, or anybody that is his, anybody who with bent knee has served his purpose, must be driven from all control of the government and all influence in it."[11]

The Democrats were driven from control as the voters handed them an overwhelming defeat: 404 electoral votes for Harding and only 127 for Cox, with Harding winning 61 percent of the popular vote, and Cox 34 percent, the worst defeat for a Democrat since Stephen A. Douglas had lost to Abra-ham Lincoln. In addition, Republican domination of both houses of Con-gress became even stronger. The Socialist Party had also taken part in the election, running Eugene Debs from his federal cell in Atlanta. Amazingly, he won 920,000 votes. There had been great hopes that women would keep alive the flame of the progressive crusade, but even they showed little interest in social and political questions; only 49 percent of eligible voters had gone to the polls. It was the first presidential election in U.S. history where less than a majority had lived up to their civic duty.

To elect a man such as Warren Harding after presidents of the stature of Theodore Roosevelt and Woodrow Wilson was to emphatically reject the social achievements of the previous twenty years, then add gratuitous insult to that injury. Mencken's comment about "honest imbecility" turned out to be only half right, since several members of Harding's Cabinet would resign in criminal disgrace, though Mencken's point about the administration's lack of intelligent guidance would hold true. But so great was the nation's desire for "normalcy" that not much was made of these scandals. Harding would die in 1923, perhaps never knowing the full scale of the betrayal by his friends. Woodrow Wilson followed the next year, without having recovered his health or his reputation.

On the evening of the great defeat, Jonathan Daniels, son of Wilson's secretary of the navy, watched the dismal election returns come in for hours, then wandered off into the night, feeling that "an age had ended. . . . My father, like reform, seemed suddenly very old and out of date, defenseless and innocent."[12]

American crusading, for now, was at an end.

Acknowledgments

During the six years it has taken to write this introduction to the American Century, there has been ample opportunity to incur obligations. The University of the Sciences in Philadelphia has been unfailingly supportive of my writing, providing leave time as well as money for research trips. Philip Gerbino, Barbara Byrne, Charles Gibley, and Reynold Verrett are to be thanked, as is Robert Boughner, head of the Humanities Department. Allen Misher, Garnett McCoy, and William T. Walker also deserve recognition for their support of the humanities. Patricia Hass, Ashbel Green, and Luba Ostashevsky at Alfred A. Knopf were essential in seeing the book into its final form.

As every scholar knows, librarians and archivists are invaluable allies. At both the Joseph W. England Library of the University of the Sciences and the University of Pennsylvania libraries they provided important bibliographic services. The staffs at Harvard's Houghton Library, at the Military History Institute in Carlisle, Pennsylvania, and the Morgan Library in New York were unfailingly polite and efficient as they guided me through their manuscript collections. Over the years, the National Endowment for the Humanities, the Smithsonian Institution, the Fulbright Commission, and the Camargo Foundation in Cassis, France, provided me with experiences that deepened my understanding of both American and European history.

It would be impossible to write without the help of friends who both challenge and support. Ideas in the book were discussed with, among others, Anthony and Susan Scirica, Anne Taylor and Caruso Kimballi, Robert and Diana Harding, David and J. B. Greenway, Robert and Susan Peck, Sam Gugino and Mary Lee Keane, and Anne Scott Ranck. John and Carolyn Friedman also loaned family documents. Discussions with Thomas Santorelli of Santorelli Historical Media helped me to better understand the pioneer moviemaker J. Stuart Blackton and his Vitagraph film company. The late Peter Braestrup spent hours trying to educate me about many things, but especially the fighting spirit and skill of the U.S. Marines. Those efforts bore more fruit in my book on the year of the Spanish-American War, but also have relevance here. Edward McIlvain, Samuel McIlvain, and Joshua McIlvain provided books, insights, and music. Rosemary Ranck discovered sources, read and reread the chapters, and gave counsel that improved the text. She made the book possible.

But for all this help from strangers, friends, and family, the flaws, eccentricities, and opinions in this work are mine alone.

Notes

ABBREVIATIONS

GD   *Official German Documents Relating to the World War. The Reports of the First and Second Subcommittees of the Committee Appointed by the National Constituent Assembly to Inquire into the Responsibility for the War.* 2 vols. New York: Oxford University Press, Carnegie Endowment for International Peace, 1923.

FRUS   Department of State. *Papers Relating to the Foreign Relations of the United States, 1913, 1914, and Supplements, World War, 1914–18.*

IPH   Seymour, Charles, ed. *The Intimate Papers of Colonel House.* 4 vols. Boston: Houghton Mifflin, 1926–28.

JRP   The John Reed Papers at the Houghton Library, Harvard University

MHI   Military History Institute, Carlisle Barracks, Carlisle, Pa.

NYT   *New York Times*

PWW   Link, Arthur S., ed. *Papers of Woodrow Wilson.* 68 vols. Princeton, N.J.: Princeton University Press.

TRW   *The Works of Theodore Roosevelt.* 24 vols., memorial ed. New York: Charles Scribner's Sons, 1919–26.

CHAPTER ONE: AMERICAN RENASCENCE

1. Baker, *American Chronicle,* 83.
2. Quoted in Nevins and Hill, 1:531–32.
3. Quoted in Cooper, *Pivotal,* 18.
4. Quoted in Traxel, *1898,* 315.
5. Quoted in Robinson, 50. There are a number of good biographies of Roosevelt, the most recent of which is Kathleen Dalton's fine study.
6. Roosevelt, *Autobiography,* 63.
7. Quoted in Chessman, 42.
8. Quoted in Morris, 555. This and the companion volume form a splendid biography of TR.

9. For a variety of details, see the NYT for February 3, 7, 9, 10, and 11, 1897.
10. Rockefeller, 152–54.
11. Quoted in Crunden, 45–6. Other versions of the speech I have read are not as direct in expressing such views.
12. See Hackett, *Fifty Years of Best Sellers.*
13. Addams, 90.
14. Taylor, 8.
15. Baker, *American Chronicle,* 213.
16. White, *Autobiography,* 390.
17. Theodore Roosevelt, *Autobiography,* 302. For more on political machines, see Traxel, *1898,* 267–75.
18. A particularly good biography that brings out the strengths and weaknesses of these reformers is Crundon's study of Whitlock.
19. Quoted in Pringle, *Taft,* 223.
20. See Bishop, 1:184–85.
21. Reprinted in the *Literary Digest,* August 30, 1902, 258.
22. Quoted in Harbaugh, 169.
23. For a brief, clear account of the part Roosevelt played in this strike, see Chessman, 88–92. See also TR's own account in his autobiography, 504–11.
24. Quoted in Baker, *American Chronicle,* 253.
25. Quoted in Harbaugh, 155.
26. See Traxel, *1898,* 53. Pinchot's struggle with Muir for the soul of the conservation movement is laid out in this book.
27. Quoted in Beale, 311.
28. Wister, 124.
29. Wharton, *Backward Glance.* See her admiring portrait of him, 311–17.
30. Quoted in Cooper, *Warrior,* 138.
31. Pringle, *Taft,* 1:400–1.
32. Quoted in Chessman, 160.

CHAPTER TWO: THE BATTLE

1. TRW, 17:18.
2. Quoted in Davidson, 491.
3. Quoted in Chessman, 161.
4. Taft quoted in Hays, 169.
5. Quoted in Harbaugh, 384. Letter to William Kent.
6. Quoted in Harbaugh, 384.
7. For a detailed study of the Ballinger-Pinchot controversy, see Hays, 147–74. For Pinchot for president, see Harbaugh, 386.
8. TRW, 7:69–74.
9. Quoted in Wharton, 317.
10. Quoted in Sullivan, 4:428.
11. Quoted in Harbaugh, 388.
12. For Osawatomie speech, see TRW, 17:18.
13. Villard, 227.
14. *Philadelphia North American,* February 4, 1912. See this issue for a description of

the senator's collapse, and the next few days for reactions. Also see Villard, 227, who believed La Follette was "confused" by drink.

15. Quoted in Harbaugh, 424, on March 20 in St. Louis.
16. Victor Rosewater, an active Taft supporter, thought so. See his book, 54–55.
17. Quoted in *Philadelphia North American*, April 26, 1912.
18. Quoted in Harbaugh, 430.
19. Ibid.
20. The whole poem is quoted in Rosewater, 93, who was one of the leaders of the Taft forces.
21. The barbed wire was discovered when the Progressives were later holding their own convention at the Coliseum. See White, *Autobiography*, 483.
22. Harriman, 99.
23. Quoted in Rosewater, 139.
24. See James E. Amos, *Theodore Roosevelt: Hero to His Valet* (New York: John Day, 1927), 140.
25. Quoted in Chessman, 182.
26. Quoted in Harbaugh, 435.
27. William McAdoo, 143. His book gives a good sense of the convention from the Wilsonian point of view.
28. Quoted in Lord, 305.
29. Harriman, 109.
30. White, 477.
31. Ibid., 478.
32. Quoted in Lord, 309.
33. Letter to Adrian F. Joline, April 29, 1907, PWW, 17:124. This letter was published during the primary season in order to drive Bryan and Wilson apart, but obviously did not succeed.
34. Quoted in Baruch, 7.
35. Quoted in Harbaugh, 443.
36. White, 483.
37. For a description of some of the battles over the platform, see White, 484–88.
38. NYT, August 7, 1912.
39. PWW, 25:255.
40. See Baker, *American Chronicle*, 272.
41. Creel, 148.
42. See Radosh, 58.
43. See Thompson, 291.
44. See Walworth for both the background of the rumor and the TR quote, 1:247.
45. See the NYT, October 15, 1912.
46. TRW, 17:320–23.
47. Quoted in Walworth, 250.
48. Quoted in McAdoo, *The Woodrow Wilsons*, 172.

CHAPTER THREE: THE NEW SPIRIT

1. Quoted in Sullivan, 4:249.
2. Ibid., 4:244.

3. Quoted in Furia, 91.
4. Quoted in Sullivan, 4:255.
5. Langner, 68.
6. Quoted in Angle, 57.
7. Ibid., 58.
8. Roosevelt's review is in TRW, vol. 12.
9. See his essay in Heller and Rudnick, 172.
10. Sanger, 70–71.
11. Ibid., 79–80.
12. The poem was privately published in book form in 1913, and reprinted in Mabel Dodge Luhan, *Movers and Shakers,* 171–85.
13. Luhan, 83–84.
14. Eastman, *Enjoyment of Living,* 523.
15. Luhan, 36.
16. Steffens, *Autobiography,* 654–55.
17. Quoted in Parry, 278.
18. For descriptions of the peyote evening, see Luhan, 265, and Eastman, *Enjoyment of Living,* 525–26.
19. Luhan, 39.
20. Sanger, 73.
21. Quoted in Heller and Rudnick, 32–33. Robert A. Rosenstone's biography is a well-written, scholarly study of John Reed's life and a good guide to the Reed papers at Harvard and elsewhere. The Granville Hicks study is also still useful.
22. Reed, "Almost Thirty." Reed goes on to say, "Since then I have gone to him with my difficulties and troubles, and he has always listened while I solved them myself in the warmth of his understanding."
23. Steffens, *Speaking,* 313.
24. See Reed, "Almost Thirty."
25. See Reed, "War in Paterson," *The Masses,* June 1913. All the following Reed quotes about Paterson are from this piece.
26. Weeks also had a great influence on the artist and political radical Rockwell Kent. See Traxel, *An American Saga.*
27. *The Masses,* December 1912. Also Parry, 286.
28. *The Masses,* January 1913. Reed helped write this editorial. Also Parry, 287.
29. Eastman, *Enjoyment of Living,* 399.
30. Quoted in Parry, 281.
31. The quotes are from Mabel Dodge's memoir, but her claims to have come up with the idea have been questioned. See the note in Rosenstone, 126.
32. Hapgood, 351.
33. Elizabeth Flynn, *I Speak My Own Piece,* 156.
34. See Sanger, 84. Actually, a number of others, conservative and radical, thought Haywood had lost some of his revolutionary zeal through associating with the crowd at Mabel Dodge's salon. See Luhan, 87.
35. Langner, 68.
36. Floyd Dell, writing in the April 1917 issue of *The Masses.*
37. Quoted in Luhan, 224.

38. Hapgood, 351.
39. JRP, see the letter from Reed to Fred Bursch in June 1913.
40. Luhan, 212–13. All immediately following quotes are from this part of her book.

CHAPTER FOUR: A SOUTHERN GENTLEMAN

1. PWW, 25:348. The various works of Arthur S. Link comprise the most complete study of Woodrow Wilson, but Heckscher provides a good long single volume biography, while Clements also deals expertly with the life in a much shorter format. A brilliant comparison of Wilson and Roosevelt is made in Cooper's *The Warrior and The Priest.*
2. Quoted in Walworth, 1:86.
3. PWW, 27:148–52. For details of all the inaugural events, see the NYT, March 4 and 5, 1913.
4. Quoted in Walworth, 1:73.
5. PWW, 4:472.
6. WW to Ellen Axson, PWW, 3:349.
7. PWW, 3:303.
8. Ibid., 17:330.
9. Quoted in Walworth, 1:18.
10. Walworth, 1:20.
11. The article is reprinted in PWW, 1:493–510.
12. PWW, 2:500–501.
13. Quoted in Walworth, 1:24.
14. PWW, 2:343.
15. On Roosevelt and Putnam's, see Cooper, *Warrior,* 45–46, and George Haven Putnam, "Roosevelt, Historian and Statesman," in TRW, 9:xvi.
16. PWW, 2:322.
17. Quoted in Walworth, 1:35.
18. PWW, 3:504.
19. Ibid., 7:752.
20. Ibid., 2:552.
21. See *Congressional Government,* in PWW, 4:167 and on.
22. See Walworth, 1:46.
23. Ibid., 55.
24. See Vesey for a brilliant study of higher education during this period.
25. PWW, 3:418.
26. Quoted in Walworth, 1:65.
27. PWW, 10:323.
28. Quoted in Walworth, 1:65.
29. Ibid., 67.
30. Ibid., 86.
31. Quoted in McAdoo, *The Woodrow Wilsons,* 59–60.
32. Hibben quoted in Walworth, 109. For an excellent account of the struggle, see Heckscher, 163–73.
33. Quoted in Walworth, 1:113.

34. Quoted in Heckscher, 185.
35. Heckscher, 186.
36. This was a speech given in New York, November 30, 1904. Reprinted in PWW, 15:547.
37. This was in a speech at Pittsfield, Massachusetts, on October 8, 1908. PWW, 18:441.
38. On the details of this maneuvering, see Cooper's chapter "Spokesman and Critic," in his *Warrior,* a book that is essential in understanding Wilson and Roosevelt.
39. *Constitutional Government* is reprinted in PWW, vol. 17.
40. See Cooper, *Warrior,* 135.
41. Quoted in PWW, 27:253.
42. William McAdoo, 183.
43. Quoted in Walworth, 1:273, note 9.
44. William McAdoo, 191.
45. Ibid., 197.
46. PWW, 27:270–71.
47. Quoted in Walworth, 1:296.
48. PWW, 27:473.
49. Quoted in Walworth, 1:298–99.
50. PWW, 27:572.
51. Quoted in Walworth, 1:326.
52. Quoted in Link, *Wilson: The Road to the White House,* 501.
53. Quoted in Williamson, 381.
54. PWW, 31:300.

CHAPTER FIVE: TESTING

1. Said to his friend E. G. Conklin, quoted in Baker and Dodds, *Woodrow Wilson,* 4:55.
2. Reed, "Almost Thirty." The emphasis is in the original.
3. For a clear, if somewhat dry, examination of arbitration treaties proposed by various American statesmen, see the relevant chapters in Boyle. Bryan explained his own treaty in a speech in New York City on May 9, 1913, the details of which were reported in the *New York Times.*
4. Quoted in Boyle, 125.
5. Quoted in Paxson, 1:33.
6. Quoted in Johnson, 38.
7. Quoted in Link, *Woodrow Wilson and the Progressive Era,* 109. For a good, readable overall study, see Eisenhower, *Intervention!: The United States and the Mexican Revolution, 1913–1917.*
8. Hendrick, 1:204.
9. Baker and Dodds, 4:305, 273.
10. All quotes are from Mabel Dodge Luhan, 246.
11. JRP, Reed to Eddy Hunt, December 16, 1913.
12. Reed, *Insurgent Mexico,* 29. Unless otherwise noted, all Reed quotes in this chapter are from this book.

13. It is not clear who the friend was. The letters were later printed in *Metropolitan* magazine in February 1914, quoted in Rosenstone, 153.
14. See Reed, "Almost Thirty."
15. Ibid.
16. Steffens, *Autobiography*, 2:715.
17. JRP, Mexican Notebooks.
18. Quoted in Rosenstone, 163. The letters are in Moscow.
19. The pass is in the JRP.
20. JRP, Lippmann to Reed, March 25, 1914.
21. These reviews are quoted in Rosenstone, 167.
22. JRP, Dave Carb to Reed, March 21, 1914.
23. Mayo to Zaragoza, April 9, 1914, FRUS, 448.
24. Bryan to Wilson, April 10, 1914, FRUS, 449.
25. MHI, Delano Papers, letter dated April 20, 1914.
26. FRUS, 1914, 474–76.
27. MHI, Delano Papers, letter dated May 2, 1914.
28. Sweetman, 126. The Mexican figures seem low both to Sweetman and myself.
29. Quoted in Eisenhower, 119.
30. Quoted in Walworth, 1:373.
31. White, 142.
32. MHI, Delano Papers, letter dated April 29, 1914.
33. Prostitutes quoted in Sweetman, 153.
34. Eisenhower, 137.
35. Quoted in Eisenhower, 134–35.
36. Ibid., 131.
37. Mowrer, 219.
38. Quoted in the NYT, April 15, 1914.
39. The exchange is given in Reed, *Insurgent Mexico*, 34.
40. See the unsigned "confidential memorandum" to the ambassadors reprinted in PWW, 29:507.
41. See Link, *Woodrow Wilson and the Progressive Era*, footnote on 127.

CHAPTER SIX: MASSACRE

1. Rockefeller, 152–54.
2. Quoted in Gorn, 216. This biography is both well researched and very readable.
3. For details of the strike, see Traxel, *1898*, 257–63.
4. See Gorn, 90.
5. Brophy, 74.
6. Quoted in Gorn, 194.
7. NYT, June 1, 1913.
8. Quoted in Chernow, *Titan*, 572.
9. Quoted in McGovern and Guttridge, 54. This book provides a clear, well-researched account of the strike, but is marred by a lack of specific source notes, and an astonishingly incomplete index.
10. Quoted in Chernow, *Titan*, 575.

11. Quoted in Gorn, 207.
12. Ibid., 210.
13. Quoted in Chernow, *Titan,* 576.
14. Quoted in McGovern and Guttridge, 166–67.
15. Reed in *Metropolitan,* July 1914.
16. See McGovern and Guttridge, 172.
17. *The Masses,* June 1914.
18. *Metropolitan,* July 1914.
19. Goldman, 2:536.
20. Ibid., 2:538.
21. McGovern and Guttridge, 267.
22. JRP has the unpublished interview. See also PWW, 30:232–33.

CHAPTER SEVEN: THE SMASH UP

1. Quoted in Williams, 49.
2. Davis, 97.
3. Quoted in Mowrer, 159.
4. Mowrer, 133. See also Whitlock.
5. Mowrer, 213–14.
6. Quoted in Williams, 25.
7. Quoted in Watt, 53, but see his note.
8. Quoted in Lord, 335. Even Mildred Aldrich, a sophisticated journalist living in France, thought along somewhat similar lines, writing to a friend: "Well, I imagine that Austria will not grieve much—though she may be mad—over the loss of a none too popular crown prince, whose morganatic wife could never be crowned, whose children cannot inherit, and who could only have kept the throne warm for a while. . . . If a man will be a crown prince in these times he must take the consequences." Aldrich, *A Hilltop on the Marne* (Boston: Houghton Mifflin, 1917), 37–38.
9. Williams, 39.
10. Mowrer, 222.
11. Ibid., 223–34. Tuchman in *Guns of August* provides a very readable account of the opening events of this catastrophe. For a good history of the diplomacy, see Fromkin, and also Remak.
12. Williams, 48, 40.
13. Gibson, 3. All Gibson and Whitlock quotations are from their respective published journals.
14. The German note is translated and reproduced in Gibson, 16–19, as is the Belgian reply.
15. Fortescue, 31–35. All Fortescue quotes are from his book. I have to admit to having originally doubted his account, as did some of his contemporaries, but it does match with what happened. For example, see the Belgian officer's description of the German attack quoted in Tuchman, *Guns of August,* 174, "They made no attempt at deploying but came on line after line, almost shoulder to shoulder, until as we shot them down, the fallen were heaped on top of each other in an

awful barricade of dead and wounded that threatened to mask our guns and cause us trouble. . . . They got no farther than halfway because our machine guns and rifles swept them back." It is unlikely Fortescue would have had a chance to interview any participants before newspaper publication. Also see Gibson's journal for August 6, where he notes what Fortescue described upon his return to Brussels.

16. This observation of Caesar's was much on people's minds. King Albert quoted it when he issued an inspiring proclamation to his troops on the fifth: *"Horum omnium fortissime sunt Belgae,"* which Whitlock translated as "The bravest of all these are the Belgae."

17. Tuchman, *Guns of August,* 176.

18. Walworth, 1:399.

19. Sullivan, 5:40.

20. Quoted in Walworth, 1:399–400.

21. This was the Cedar Rapids, Iowa, *Gazette,* quoted in Lord, 339.

22. This was in the issue of August 13, 1914, but many *Life* pieces about the war from the beginning to American entry were collected in Martin, *Diary of a Nation.*

23. PWW, 30:332.

24. Williams, 51.

25. For this paragraph, see Gerard, 101–7.

26. Huard, 253.

27. Russell, 265.

28. This was "Lodi, the confessed German spy, who was shot in the Tower of London." Gerard, 114.

29. Quoted in Gibson, 52.

30. Aldrich, *A Hilltop on the Marne,* 53. Wells's novel was published in 1908.

31. Wood, 149, 53. Granville Fortescue later interviewed the German aviator who dropped the bombs on Paris, a Lieutenant Werner, whom he regarded as a "pirate" for these attacks on noncombatants. "Does this man know the cowardice of his deed?" he asked himself, but the lieutenant was called away before the question could be properly put to him, 128. Fortescue, too, was reminded of H. G. Wells's *War in the Air.*

32. Cobb, *Paths of Glory,* 87.

33. Williams, 52.

34. Davis, 11.

35. Gibson, 86.

36. It has been reprinted many times. A version is in Davis, beginning on page 22.

37. Whitlock, 42.

38. See Davis, 13, and Cobb, *Paths of Glory,* 70.

39. For example, see Cobb, *Paths of Glory,* 61, 66, and Read, 87–88. See also Horne and Kramer on German atrocities.

40. Fortescue, 185, 196.

41. Cobb, *Paths of Glory,* 77. Fortescue, 87, noted that the French "trousers stood out as striking as claret stains on a clean tablecloth."

42. NYT, August 14, 1914.

43. Quoted in Irwin, 230.

44. Cobb, *Speaking of Prussians,* 28.
45. Ibid., 61–64.
46. *Buffalo Courier,* quoted in Sullivan, 5:30.

CHAPTER EIGHT: PEACE AND PROSPERITY

1. Told in Sullivan, 5:1.
2. Quoted in Link, *Woodrow Wilson and the Progressive Era,* 145.
3. Quoted in NYT, September 27, 1914.
4. Quoted in Paxson, 1:127.
5. Quoted in Tuchman, *Guns of August,* 129.
6. Hoover, 141–42.
7. Hoover, 136–37. I have changed the order somewhat.
8. See Traxel, *1898,* 216–18.
9. For a charming depiction of, among other things, the strength of turn-of-the-century American love of German musical culture, see Nathalie Dana's *Young in New York: A Memoir of a Victorian Girlhood* (Garden City, N.Y.: Doubleday & Co., 1963).
10. White, 506.
11. Quoted in IPH, 1:288.
12. Davis, ix–x, but some of the same words opened his dispatch of September 2, 1914, in the *New York Tribune.*
13. For his account of the crisis, see William McAdoo, 290–92.
14. PWW, 30:372–73.
15. Quoted in *The Literary Digest,* August 8, 1914.
16. This quote is from an article he published in *Outlook,* September 23, 1914.
17. PWW, 30:372–73.
18. FRUS, 1914, 580, and Devlin, 176.
19. PWW, 32:41.
20. Irwin, 251. All following Hoover quotes are from Irwin unless otherwise noted.
21. Ibid., 251.
22. See R. M. Crundon's biography of Whitlock for a good brief history of the CRB.
23. Quoted in Crundon, 270.
24. See C. E. Persons, "Women's Work and Wages in the United States," *Quarterly Journal of Economics,* May 1915.
25. William McAdoo, 299.
26. Davis, 204.
27. William McAdoo, 304.
28. Baker and Dodds, 5:126.
29. This from a NYT interview on October 14, 1935, quoted in Chernow, *House of Morgan,* 186.
30. FRUS, 1914, 580.
31. Davison quoted in Colby, 187.
32. Quoted in Graham, 64.
33. Finnegan, 8.
34. Ibid., 198, note 5.

35. NYT, December 8, 1914. The piece was headlined, "This Is Not Militarism."
36. Quoted in NYT, November 10, 1915.
37. Quoted in Rosenstone, 182.
38. Mabel Dodge Luhan reports his "excitement and enthusiasm," 292. Unless otherwise noted, all her following quotes are from this section of her book.
39. Hicks, 162.
40. This and other quotes are from two Reed articles in *Metropolitan*: "German France" in March 1915, and "In the German Trenches," April 1915.

CHAPTER NINE: PRIDE AND SELF-RESPECT

1. Quoted in NYT, May 8, 1915.
2. PWW, May 10, 1915, 33:149.
3. Heckscher, 373.
4. Quoted in Martin, *Cissy*, 137.
5. Quoted in William J. Flynn, head of the Secret Service during these years, in *Liberty* magazine. He gives a detailed account of the procedures and results of the tapping.
6. Quoted in Martin, *Cissy*, 148.
7. Martin, *Cissy*, 137.
8. PWW, 31:467–68.
9. See Link, *Wilson: The Struggle for Neutrality*, 558–60.
10. Read, 190–92.
11. Quoted in Paxson, 1:172.
12. See Devlin, 414, for an account of the atrocity, which took place in August 1915, and the quote.
13. Quoted in Seymour, *American Neutrality*, 33.
14. The novel is set in the 1920s, but the point holds.
15. Quoted in Brinnin, 397.
16. The notices are reproduced in Link, *Woodrow Wilson and the Progressive Era*, 165.
17. Quoted in Brinnin, 417.
18. Sullivan, 5:118–19.
19. Ibid., 5:118.
20. NYT, May 8, 1915.
21. Quoted in Millis, 172.
22. PWW, 30:133.
23. Ibid., 33:151.
24. Papen, 42.
25. Bernstorff, 151.
26. Quoted in Millis, 174.
27. Quoted in Harbaugh, 477.
28. Quoted in Nevins and Hill, 2:23.
29. PWW, 33:147–50. Actually, his mother had used such language in a letter to him when he was a student at Princeton. See PWW, 1:228.
30. Quoted in D'Este, 152.
31. Quoted in Harbaugh, 477.

32. PWW, 33:154.
33. Ibid., 33:160.
34. Quoted in Millis, 180.
35. PWW, 33:182.
36. Quoted in Doerries, 293, note 14.
37. For the best account of the *Lusitania* controversies, see Bailey and Ryan.
38. See Paxson, 1:250.
39. Quoted in Seymour, *American Neutrality,* 12.
40. Quoted in IPH, 1:454–55.
41. GD, 1:253–54.
42. Quoted in Link, *Progressive Era,* 165, note 46.
43. Quoted in Doerries, 66.
44. Adler, 2:201. Also Doerries, 277, note 166.
45. Churchill, 2:306.
46. Quoted in NYT, September 2, 1915.
47. As John Milton Cooper points out: "Bryce's reliance on Wilson's assessment of the diffusion of power and his comparison with the British system bordered on plagiarism." *Warrior and Priest,* 59.
48. Whitlock, 139, 141.

CHAPTER TEN: THE WAR COMES HOME

1. See Brownlow, 566.
2. Quoted in Brownlow, 38.
3. See Chernow, *House of Morgan,* 189.
4. See the relevant papers at the Morgan Library, New York City.
5. Chernow, *House of Morgan,* 194.
6. Quoted in Chernow, *House of Morgan,* 194.
7. William McAdoo, 327–28.
8. Ibid., 328.
9. Papen, 38.
10. Quoted in William McAdoo, 330.
11. This dialogue is recorded in Papen, 46.
12. The complete letter is reprinted in Doerries, 341, note 270.
13. See the book Voska wrote with journalist Will Irwin, *Spy and Counterspy.*
14. This was widely quoted in the press, but see Paxson, 1:271.
15. This sweet scene is described in a talk that John Rathom, one of Voska's British directors, later gave. See *The Empire Club of Canada: Speeches, 1916–1917,* 570–87. Voska names a different German official as the would-be seducer, but his account was written more than twenty years later.
16. At one time or another, for example, there were 325 ambulance drivers in the various volunteer organizations who had attended Harvard, 187 from Yale, 181 from Princeton, and 68 from the University of California. See Charles Fenton.
17. Sweetser, 167–79.
18. Thomson, 23. Thomson, whose book is one of the best studies of Hollywood, is particularly perceptive on Mayer.
19. See Clements, 100, and PWW, 32:267, note 1.

20. Brownlow, 32. I also gained a great deal of insight into J. Stuart Blackton from discussions with Tom Santorelli, who is producing and directing a documentary about the Vitagraph film company.
21. The scene is from Brownlow, 32, who got it from Blackton's unpublished autobiography.
22. Brownlow, 36, says they are marines, but that would have been outside of Wood's jurisdiction and under the Department of the Navy.
23. NYT, August 7, 1915.
24. *Variety,* August 13, 1915.
25. Quoted in Brownlow, 37.
26. Finnegan, 96.
27. See the ad in NYT, April 23, 1916.
28. Quoted in Brownlow, 37.

CHAPTER ELEVEN: HENRY FORD AND THE PEACE SHIP

1. Quoted in Wik, 233.
2. Quoted in Hershey, x.
3. *Literary Digest,* October 14, 1899.
4. Wharton, 153.
5. White, 302.
6. McGerr, 229.
7. Faunce, 25.
8. Burns and Dun, 116.
9. Post, 3. All Post quotes are from this book.
10. Quoted in Traxel, *1898,* 57.
11. Ford, 33.
12. Quoted in Ford, 51. Oldfield became so famous that a particularly noteworthy wagon driver in Mexico during the Punitive Expedition was given the nickname Barney Oldfield. See Tompkins, 204–5.
13. Quoted in Nevins and Hill, 1:579.
14. Post, 24.
15. See Appendix II, "Total Sale of Ford Cars," in Nevins and Hill, 1:644.
16. *Detroit Free Press,* July 28, 1903, quoted in Nevins and Hill, 1:299. They give an excellent account of the patent fight.
17. Quoted in Nevins and Hill, 1:428.
18. Ford, 83.
19. See the tables in Nevins and Hill, 1:644, 646.
20. Ford, 83.
21. Quoted in Nevins and Hill, 1:536.
22. Quoted in Nevins and Hill, 1:534.
23. *Wall Street Journal,* January 7, 1914.
24. Quoted in Marquis, 152–53.
25. Quoted in Nevins and Hill, 1:545.
26. Quoted in Lacey, 126.
27. Quoted in Marquis, 153.
28. Ford, 147.

29. Quoted in Hounshell, 259.
30. See chapter 7.
31. NYT, April 11, 1915.
32. See Kraft, 29, for an excellent overall study of the adventure. She donated her research material for the book to the Swarthmore College Peace Collection.
33. For details about the remarkable Ms. Wales and her plan, see Kraft.
34. See Kraft, 60.
35. For the interview, see Lochner, and Kraft, 65–67.
36. NYT, November 27, 1915.
37. Quoted in Lacey, 139.
38. Lochner, 66.
39. Quoted in Kraft, 90.
40. The departure is described in the next day's newspapers, Kraft, Nevins and Hill, and Hershey, among many other sources.
41. For Pease, see Hershey, 24–25.
42. Quoted in Nevins and Hill, 2:39.
43. Kraft, 146.
44. PWW, 35:297–306.
45. Quoted in Nevins and Hill, 2:42.
46. Bullitt in the *Philadelphia Public Ledger,* January 3, 1916.
47. Quoted in Nevins and Hill, 2:46.

CHAPTER TWELVE: UNPREPARED

1. Hart, 104.
2. Quoted in Finnegan, 121.
3. Quoted in the *New York Evening Post,* December 4, 1915.
4. Quoted in Daniels, 181.
5. Starling and Sugrue, 62.
6. PWW, 35:399.
7. See her letter in the Patton Papers at the MHI.
8. Quoted in Devlin, 361, but see *PWW,* 4:31.
9. Quoted in PS, 473.
10. Hart, 103.
11. Ibid., 104.
12. PWW, 36:32.
13. Quoted in Palmer, 1:10.
14. This was on May 8, 1916. PWW, 36:634–48.
15. PWW, 36:79.
16. Quoted in Link, *Woodrow Wilson and the Progressive Era,* 133, note 54.
17. See Harris and Sadler, 76.
18. Ibid., 79.
19. Quoted in Heckscher, 387.
20. See Harris and Sadler, 81.
21. Quoted in Doerries, 169–70.
22. Quoted in Tuchman, *Zimmermann Telegram,* 86 (emphasis on original).
23. Quoted in Tompkins, 52. Tompkins, who was involved in every phase of the Villa

campaign, is an invaluable source. Lucas became an important general in the Second World War.

24. See Doerries, 170–71, and Katz, 332–38.
25. Quoted in Palmer, 1:11.
26. FRUS, 1916, 490, also quoted in Tompkins, 70.
27. PWW, 36:285–86.
28. Bullard, *Personalities,* 42.
29. Quoted in Traxel, *1898,* 209.
30. Quoted in Doerries, 124.
31. See Doerries, 306, note 157.
32. See PWW, 35:81.
33. See Devlin's excellent brief discussion of the blacklist, 513–17.
34. Devlin, 517.
35. PWW, 37:466–67.
36. Quoted in IPH, 2:317.
37. Quoted in Devlin, 490.

CHAPTER THIRTEEN: WAR ABROAD AND WAR AT HOME

1. Quoted in Eisenhower, 262.
2. JR to Fred Bursch, June 14, 1915, JRP.
3. See Tompkins for order of battle details and much else. See also the relevant sections of Clendenen and Eisenhower.
4. Tompkins, 75.
5. Quoted in Glines, 68; also in Eisenhower, 256. See as well Foulois's own report on his unit's operations, which is in Tompkins, Appendix B.
6. Tompkins, 109.
7. See the Patton file at MHI. Letter from Anne Patton to "Tante," dated April 11, 1916.
8. Entry dated only May 8, Richard H. McMaster diary at MHI.
9. See the "Recollections" of B. G. Chynoweth, 7, at the MHI.
10. See the Richard H. McMaster Papers at the MHI, letter dated "May 21, 16."
11. See Tompkins, 128–44, for a vivid account of the action and the casualties. The suspected German is mentioned on page 138.
12. Quoted in Eisenhower, 275.
13. This is from the *New York Journal,* June 19, 1916, quoted in Swanberg, 354.
14. For this raid's link to the Plan of San Diego, see Katz, 340.
15. Langhorne had an odd connection to the German secret service. While serving as military attaché in Berlin, he had sent some of his coded reports through German channels, which Rintelen claims to have decoded and then inserted pro-German passages in them. The British regularly intercepted German communications, and evidently complained about the officer's "prejudice." Langhorne was recalled in spring of 1915. See Doerries, 177.
16. See Finnegan on this, 165–71.
17. Pershing quoted in Clendenen, 303.
18. Both quotes in Eisenhower, 295–97.
19. "Recollections" of B. G. Chynoweth, 7, at the MHI.

20. See the NYT for June 26, 1916, and also Knock, 82–83.

21. PWW, 37:333.

22. Cheynoweth, 13, MHI. He was writing of a particular officer who "got too much to drink, saddled up, and made a personal mounted charge" on a nearby Mexican position. They "gathered him in, and returned him to us."

23. See Tompkins, 211.

24. Quoted in Chynoweth, 10, MHI. For Parker's actions at San Juan, see Traxel, *1898*, 191.

25. Quoted in Doerries, 171.

26. Quoted in Hicks, 183.

27. Reed, *The War in Eastern Europe*, 49. All quotes, unless otherwise noted, are from this book.

28. See Hicks, 188, as well as *The War in Eastern Europe*.

29. Quoted in Hicks, 197–98. Both Hicks and Rosenstone defend Reed's trying for this "artistic" truth, but the fact that this was a running argument shows that Robinson, who was there, was really not convinced.

30. See "The Rights of Small Nations," in *The New Republic*, November 27, 1915.

31. JR to Sally Robinson, December 5, 1915, JRP.

32. Ibid., December 18, 1915, JRP.

33. The words are Robert Rosenstone's, 241, based on a letter he found in the Hicks Papers.

34. This is as Virginia Gardner put it, 47, based on an interview with Dell.

35. For this affair, see Gardner, 18–19.

36. From an unpublished article in the JRP.

37. See "The Legendary Villa," *The Masses*, May 1917, and Hicks, 219, and Rosenstone, 243.

38. *The Masses*, July 1916.

39. See the Shulman edition of Goldman's writings, 301, 305.

40. Goldman, 2:578.

41. For remarks on cities and New York and the House quote, see Finnegan, 148–49.

42. PWW, 37:223.

43. The area called Black Tom has been renamed Liberty Park, and now is where tourists board ferries to the Statue of Liberty.

44. Landau, 78.

45. NYT, July 30, 1916, and Witcover.

46. See Landau and Witcover, and the Mixed Claims Commission publications on German sabotage. Few serious historians used them.

47. Quoted in Witcover, 311.

CHAPTER FOURTEEN: PROGRESS AND PEACE

1. Quoted in Cooper, *Warrior*, 306.

2. See Jonathan Daniels, who as son of the secretary of the navy spent his youth in Washington.

3. Wilson also appointed the first Jew, Samuel Kalisch, to New Jersey's Supreme Court.

4. PWW, 36:609–10.
5. Quoted in Knock, 88.
6. NYT, August 30, 1916.
7. NYT, August 15, 1916.
8. Quoted in Dalton, 464.
9. Ibid., 463.
10. White, 513.
11. Quoted in Heckscher, 398.
12. See Cooper, *Warrior*, 306.
13. NYT, June 16, 1916. Also in Heckscher, 400.
14. Quoted in Link, *WW and the Progressive Era*, 234.
15. Quoted in Tumulty, 225–26.
16. Lippmann, "The Case for Wilson," in *The New Republic*, October 14, 1916.
17. Quoted in Knock, 94, who has a very good brief section on radical support for Wilson.
18. Quoted in Knock, 95.
19. NYT, October 14, 1916, then reprinted in the December 1916 issue of *The Masses*.
20. See Nevins and Hill, 2:117.
21. PWW, 38:347, but see the whole section for words on this theme.
22. JR to Louise Bryant, no date, JRP.
23. Quoted in Rosenstone, 253.
24. Quoted in Gardner, 315, note 19.
25. Quoted in Rosenstone, 254.
26. Quoted in Hicks, 223.
27. Quoted in Hicks, 223–24.
28. Walworth, 2:61.
29. PWW, 38:286.
30. Brownlow, 77.
31. This was William Cochrane, the committee's press agent. See Ramsaye, 728.
32. NYT, November 9, 1916.
33. See William Allen White, *Autobiography*, 532, who understood Kansas better than anyone before Thomas Frank.
34. See Knock's excellent discussion of the vote, 101.
35. PWW, 38:90.
36. Ibid., 40:70. This was part of the draft of a peace note in November 1916 that was never used.
37. Quoted in Baker and Dodds, 6:391.
38. The Germans planned on demanding large sections of Belgium and Poland, and the whole Belgian Congo, among other areas. See GD, 2:1059–62.
39. See Cooper, *Warrior*, 292, where he says that Lansing was "the worst appointment Wilson ever made," and Link, *Woodrow Wilson: Revolution, War, and Peace*, 57, who called the sabotage "one of the most egregious acts of treachery in American history."
40. Quoted in IPH, 2:412.
41. PWW, 40:533–39.
42. Ibid., 41:55.

43. See Knock, 115, and NYT, January 27, 1917.
44. Quoted in NYT, January 29, 1917.
45. See the telegram from Frederick Funston to the secretary of war in Tompkins, 216.
46. Tompkins, 214.
47. Quoted in Blumenson, 1:362.
48. See the Chynoweth recollections at MHI. The claim is probably true, for Pershing respected those who stood up to him, as can be seen in his relationship with George Marshall.
49. See Finnegan, 168.
50. Quoted in Finnegan, 166.
51. Chester E. Baker, 2.
52. Quoted in Finnegan, 169.
53. Palmer, 71.

CHAPTER FIFTEEN: THE WEB OF WAR

1. Quoted in GD, 1:525. Also see Doerries, 195.
2. Quoted in Clements, 166.
3. Quoted in Rosenstone, 263–64.
4. Doerries, 192. For mistaken American assessments, see Tuchman, *Zimmermann Telegram*, 108–10.
5. GD, 2:1320. All quotes regarding the meeting at Pless are from this document unless otherwise noted.
6. Quoted in Doerries, 193.
7. Ibid., 214.
8. PWW, 41:3. Italics in original.
9. Quoted in Doerries, 207.
10. Tumulty, 254–56.
11. William McAdoo, 367.
12. PWW, 41:108.
13. See the excerpt from the House diary printed in PWW, 41:86–89.
14. PWW, 41:111–12.
15. This is the term Wilson used in his address to Congress, reprinted in PWW, 41:283–87.
16. See PWW, 41:89–92.
17. NYT, February 25, 1917.
18. Quoted in Doerries, 225. Italics in original.
19. PWW, 41:3–4.
20. The telegram is reproduced, among many other sources, in GD, 2:1337. For a full account of the telegram, see Tuchman, *Zimmermann Telegram*, relevant pages in Doerries, and Katz, 350–78.
21. Tuchman is particularly good on this complex deception.
22. PWW, 41:282.
23. Ibid., 41:320.
24. For a description of the swearing-in and the signing, see Thomas W. Brahany's diary excerpt in PWW, 41:327–31.

25. PWW, 41:329–30.
26. Both quotes from Daniels, 210.
27. See Murphy, 55, who sees these acts as attacks on American civil liberties, but makes no mention of German sabotage or spying.
28. See Tuchman, *Zimmermann Telegram*, 176.
29. See NYT, March 4, 1917.
30. PWW, 41:321–27.
31. Tuchman, *Zimmermann Telegram*, 180.
32. Baker and Dodds, 5:39, and the remark to Daniels quoted in Cooper, *Warrior*, 320.
33. Quoted in Baker and Dodds, 6:507. There has been some controversy about the truth of this quotation, which Link disposes of quite effectively in "That Cobb Interview," *The Journal of American History* 72 (June 1985): 7–17.
34. See Lansing's Memorandum on the Cabinet meeting, reprinted in PWW, 41:436–44.
35. Reed, "Almost Thirty."
36. See his undated letter to her from Baltimore, JRP.
37. Gardner, 56–58, has a particularly intelligent discussion of the infection.
38. Quoted in Hicks, 228.
39. Quoted in Hicks, 229. Rosenstone quotes only the part on lack of friendship.
40. See Millis, 433–34, and NYT, April 3, 1917.
41. William McAdoo, 371.
42. Tumulty, 265. Gilding the lily, Tumulty goes on to claim that Wilson then broke down in tears. This seems unlikely.
43. Quoted in Hicks, 233.
44. Quoted in the *Congressional Record* for April 4, 1917, 212, 214.
45. Quoted in Cedric Cummins, *Indiana Public Opinion and the World War 1914–1917* (Indianapolis: Indiana Historic Bureau, 1945), 251.

CHAPTER SIXTEEN: CRUSADE

1. Fosdick, 132.
2. Quoted in PWW, 41:558.
3. There are a number of books that deal with the United States in the war, but those by David Kennedy, the Harries, and Robert Ferrell stand out. They provide good overviews, and excellent guides to sources. The first two are still in print, and the third one certainly should be. Also valuable is Anne Venzon's encyclopedia on U.S. involvement.
4. Quoted in Palmer, 1:120.
5. William McAdoo, 376–77.
6. Ibid., 368.
7. His son, Rene Comte de Chambrun, would visit the United States in 1940 in the vain hope of gaining support for a France again under attack by Germany.
8. William McAdoo, 397.
9. Ibid., 376.
10. Joffre, 2:568.
11. PWW, 41:556.

12. Quoted in Cooper, *Warrior,* 324.

13. Tumulty, 285–88.

14. White, 534.

15. The news of Funston's death was carried to the president, who was dining at Newton Baker's, by Major Douglas MacArthur. They asked his opinion of who should be the replacement, and he said "unquestionably . . . General Pershing." MacArthur, 46–47. Many years later, Baker remembered MacArthur recommending both Pershing and Peyton March.

16. This was James Reed of Missouri, quoted in Sullivan, 5:296.

17. Quoted in Chambers, 165, who has an excellent account of the Great War version of the draft.

18. See Pershing, 1:13–14.

19. See Hicks, 234–35, and U.S. House of Representatives, Committee on Military Affairs, *Hearings on . . . Conscription System,* 65th Congress, April 7–17, 1917, 31–3.

20. Quoted in Jensen, 36.

21. Quoted in Chambers, 158.

22. PWW, 40:70–71.

23. Ibid., 42:325.

24. See Chambers, 212.

25. March, 237–38.

26. Quoted in Dorothy and Carl Schneider, 272. The Schneiders' book is an excellent place to start in studying women's roles in the war.

27. Kitchin quoted in William McAdoo, 375.

28. William McAdoo, 372.

29. Ibid., 374.

30. See Richard Schickel's highly stimulating discussion of modern fame, *His Picture in the Papers.*

31. Quoted in Kennedy, 108, who has a good, brief depiction of the tax battle. See Gilbert for a more detailed study.

32. Quoted in Kennedy, 109.

33. Creel, 160.

34. Quoted in Vaughn, *Holding Fast the Inner Lines,* 144. This is by far the best work on the committee, marked by intelligence and solid research.

35. PWW, 41:526, 528.

36. Quoted in Kennedy, 25.

37. Quoted in Murphy, 76.

38. PWW, 41:620.

39. Baker to Woodrow Wilson, April 2, 1917, PWW, 41:527.

40. See Fosdick, 136–57.

41. For an excellent study of British-American naval relations during the war, see Trask.

42. PWW, 43:427–31. See also Heckscher, 448–50.

43. All figures in this paragraph are from Trask, 81. Sims, however, thought that Daniels and the Navy Department were far too slow in understanding the danger

and adapting to submarine warfare, an unsettling fear that he passed on to Pershing. See Pershing, 1:48–49.

44. Quoted in Baruch, 141.

CHAPTER SEVENTEEN: PREPARING

1. Marshall, 19–20.
2. Reed, *Ten Days*, 259.
3. Pershing, 1:73.
4. Marshall, 11.
5. Pershing, 1:92.
6. Quoted in Coffman, 4.
7. Marshall, 13.
8. Ibid., 12. "I am very beautiful today."
9. Ibid., 44.
10. Quoted in Coffman, 134.
11. Keene, 108. This is a valuable study that should be widely read.
12. Wynn, 122, and Furia, 81.
13. Marshall, 20.
14. Quoted in Coffman, 133.
15. For example, see Pershing, 1:62, 64.
16. Marshall, 37.
17. Pershing, 1:16.
18. See Palmer, 1:128–29.
19. Requin, 23.
20. Pershing, 1:185.
21. Hoover, 241.
22. Ibid., 242.
23. Ibid., 244.
24. For a complete study of his programs, see Mullendore. Kennedy has a good short treatment.
25. Hoover, 246. Ruth Hunter, a woman living in Spencer, Massachusetts, wrote her brother about one of the many speakers sent around to raise civilian morale: "He used to be a minister and so his talk was sort of a sermon. He talked quite a lot about the war, the faith we should have in our President, our government, Mr. Hoover and God. He told us we should be willing to go without sugar in order to keep our soldiers supplied with it. Did you know how necessary it is for a soldier to have plenty of sugar? Why, [he] said the German soldiers were each given a pound of sugar a day. Mr. Davis don't believe that story." Family papers of Carolyn Friedman.
26. Quoted in Shannon, 97.
27. Ibid., 95.
28. Quoted in Chambers, 208.
29. Spargo quoted in NYT, June 2, 1917.
30. Shannon, 106.
31. Ameringer, 349.

32. Ibid., 347–56.
33. For a well-documented account of some of these German activities, see Harris and Sadler, 114–29.
34. Quoted in Dalton, 485.
35. Quoted in Peterson and Fite, 55.
36. Haywood, 301.
37. Quoted in Murphy, 173.
38. Haywood to JR, September 1, 1918, JRP.
39. Quoted in NYT, November 21, 1917.
40. See Shannon, 113, and 290, note 21.
41. Harry Reed to JR, April 1917, JRP.
42. Margaret Reed to JR, April 5, 1917, JRP.
43. Quoted in Hicks, 235.
44. Both quotes in Hicks, 240.
45. Quoted in Hicks, 242.
46. See Rosenstone, 282.
47. Gardner, 83.
48. See Rosenstone, 289–90.
49. Quoted in Hicks, 264.
50. After seizing power, the Bolsheviks changed to the Gregorian system.
51. Shatov quoted in Gardner, 110.

CHAPTER EIGHTEEN: FORCE

1. PWW, 47:270.
2. "The first Americans have been killed," quoted in Marshall, 45.
3. See Henri, *Black Migration*.
4. Quoted in Sullivan, 5:486.
5. For a scholarly account of the riot, see Rudwick.
6. Young's kidneys had been damaged by the high blood pressure, and he died in 1922. However, he could have served, as some unhealthy white officers did, in a Stateside training post during the war.
7. See the article by Garna L. Christian.
8. See Haynes for full details.
9. The Harrieses have a good discussion of the divisions.
10. NYT, February 19, 1918.
11. Quoted in Vaughn, 155.
12. The cartoon and doggerel are reproduced in Luebke, 276.
13. Quoted in Timberlake, 179.
14. Flexner has a very good section on this and other word contributions resulting from the war.
15. Quoted in Vaughn, 51.
16. Quoted in Luebke, 249.
17. Ibid., 9, who gives details of the wretched event, 3–24.
18. NYT, April 6, 1918.
19. See Flexner, 170.
20. Quoted in Harries and Harries, 4. They have a good brief section on the raid.

21. Marshall, 47. See his account of the visit, 45–50.
22. Quoted in Coffman, 140. Ironically, Wolf was then captured on the first day of the St. Mihiel offensive, the first major American action. See Marshall, 50.
23. See the entry for Creel in Venzon.
24. See Tumulty, 361–64.
25. PWW, 43:246.
26. Quoted in Coit, 140.
27. Ibid., 144.
28. For a detailed account of Baruch's career in public service, see Schwarz's study.
29. Creel, 154.
30. Baruch, 72. All subsequent relevant quotes are from this book.
31. William McAdoo, 447. He lays out in great detail the problems faced and solutions attempted.
32. Reprinted in Sullivan, 5:464, and in McAdoo's own *Crowded Years,* 501–2.
33. Steffens to JR, June 17, 1918, JRP.
34. JR to Steffens, June 29, 1918, JRP.
35. This was printed in the September 1917 issue, and reprinted in Hicks, 312.
36. Quoted in Rosenstone, 328.
37. Steffens wrote this in a letter that amounted to a review of Granville Hicks's biography of Reed. It was first published in *The New Republic,* May 20, 1936, and reprinted in *Lincoln Steffens Speaking,* 307–10.
38. The notes are in the JRP. Both Rosenstone and Hicks have good accounts of the trial partly based on the official transcript.
39. PWW, 44:210.
40. Eastman, *Enjoyment of Living,* 586.
41. General Kuhl, quoted in DeWeerd, 392–93.
42. Years after the war, his story was written by Lowell Thomas. The following is from Thomas, 210–18.
43. Ibid., 315.
44. Elliott Roosevelt, ed., 407–8.
45. Quoted in Gibbons, 304. Daly had already twice won the Medal of Honor. The journalist Floyd Gibbons himself was wounded three times in the battle, and lost an eye to a ricocheting machine-gun bullet.

CHAPTER NINETEEN: VICTORY AND DEFEAT

1. Creel, 254.
2. Quoted in Bailey, 184.
3. Quoted in Baruch, 122.
4. I am following Crosby on the early stages of the disease.
5. Crosby, 160. There were of course many things—such as shrapnel, poison gas, machine guns—that were more "troublesome," but the point is still a good one.
6. The following account, unless otherwise noted, is based on issues of NYT, the *Philadelphia Inquirer,* and the *Philadelphia Public Ledger* between September and November 1918.
7. See *The Survey,* October 19, 1918, 75.
8. Ibid., 76.

9. Faunce, 397–98.

10. See Witcover, 126–27, Landau, 169–70, and Doerries, 189, and 344, note 296.

11. This was made clear to me when I wrote a piece on the 1918 influenza outbreak in Philadelphia for the *Philadelphia Inquirer* and received letters, telephone calls, and e-mails from people wanting to relay stories of family tragedies resulting from the epidemic.

12. Crosby, 322.

13. Quoted in Ferrell, 85. Wounded from the fighting so overwhelmed medical facilities that instant decisions had to be made about treatment. One alert medic, Baghdasar Goolkasian, noticed that a soldier who had been tagged for the amputation of a leg, was not that severely injured. Goolkasian was able to delay the operation until a surgeon had a closer look and decided that the limb could be saved. Years after the war, the soldier looked up Goolkasian to thank him. Interview with his grandson Ara DerMarderosian.

14. See PWW, 45:534–39.

15. Quoted in Baker and Dodds, 3:510.

16. PWW, 51:347.

17. Quoted in Crozier, 269.

18. Quoted in Kennedy, 111.

19. See Kennedy, 237, who has a particularly good few pages on the election of 1918. The most thorough study is Livermore's book.

20. See NYT, February 10, 1917.

21. See Nevins and Hill, 119.

22. Advertisement quoted in Nevins and Hill, 79.

23. Quoted in Lacey, 161.

24. PWW, 51:381–82.

25. Quoted in Creel, 255.

26. Quoted in Crosby, 175.

27. Frank Cobb quoted in PWW, 51:590.

28. Some historians have supported these arguments. For a good example, see Ferrell, 135–38.

29. For a very good brief explanation of Wilson's reasoning, see Clements, 197–98.

30. See Crosby, 173.

31. Baruch, 126.

32. Hoover, 437.

33. Ibid., 449.

34. Quoted in Crosby, 189.

35. Ibid., 188. See Crosby's discussion of Wilson's health in Paris, 171–200.

36. Hoover, 468.

37. From Reed's preface to *Ten Days*.

38. Quoted in Rosenstone, 335.

39. See Reed, *Ten Days*, preface.

40. See Rosenstone for quotes from reviews, 349.

41. Goldman, 2:684.

42. Hicks, 341.

43. Rosenstone, 337.

44. See Rosenstone on the sales, 349.
45. Quoted in Schwarz, 106.
46. Baruch, 91–92. An example of wartime profits is clearly seen in the case of Bethlehem Shipbuilding, which earned an average annual profit of $6 million from 1910 through 1913; from 1914 to 1918 it averaged $49 million. See Ferrell, 195.
47. See the *Bulletin of the U.S. Bureau of Labor Statistics,* May 1924. Also the comparison of prices in newspaper and magazine advertisements between 1913 and 1920 makes startlingly obvious the soaring inflation.
48. Quoted in Murray, 60, which is the standard work on the Red Scare. See also Coben.
49. Quoted in Murray, 63.
50. See Coolidge, 134.
51. See Soule, 192.
52. See Murray, 146.
53. Sixteen of the original bombs were not delivered due to insufficient postage. They were discovered thanks to an alert postal clerk named Charles Kaplan. See NYT, May 1, 1919, for his story. Two were delivered, maiming two people; eighteen others were intercepted.
54. Murray, 74.
55. Hicks, 343.
56. See Murray, 53–54.
57. Hicks, 324.
58. PWW, 61:426–36.
59. Quoted in Knock, who has an excellent account of the ratification battles, 233.
60. See Heckscher, 587.
61. Quoted in Clements, 214.
62. He incorporated these weeping mothers into his speeches. See Tumulty, 449–50.
63. Quoted in Tumulty, 447.

EPILOGUE

1. Mencken, 31.
2. See Daniels, 312.
3. William McAdoo, 498.
4. Palmer, "The Case Against the Reds." All Palmer quotes are from this article.
5. Quoted in Murray, 208.
6. William McAdoo, 515.
7. This scene and dialogue are from Goldman, 2:741.
8. To Bernard Baruch the wording was a little different: "I have seen the future and it works." Baruch, 195.
9. Edward Earl Purinton in *The Independent,* April 16, 1921.
10. This was former senator and party boss Boies Penrose of Pennsylvania. Quoted in Ferrell, 226.
11. Quoted in Ferrell, 228.
12. Daniels, 321.

Select Bibliography

Addams, Jane. *Twenty Years at Hull House*. New York: Macmillan, 1910. Reprint, New York: New American Library, 1960.

Adler, Cyrus. *Jacob H. Schiff: His Life and Letters*. 2 vols. Garden City, N.Y.: Doubleday, Doran, 1929.

Ameringer, Oscar. *If You Don't Weaken: An Autobiography*. New York: Henry Holt, 1940.

Angle, Paul M. *Crossroads: 1913*. New York: Rand McNally, 1963.

Anonymous. *A Red Triangle Girl in France*. New York: George H. Doran, 1918.

Asinoff, Eliot. *1919: America's Loss of Innocence*. New York: Donald I. Fine, 1990.

Baker, Chester E. *Doughboy's Diary*. Shippensburg, Pa.: Burd Street Press, 1998.

Baker, Ray Stannard. *American Chronicle: The Autobiography of Ray Stannard Baker*. New York: Charles Scribner's Sons, 1945.

Baker, Ray Stannard, and William E. Dodds, eds. *Woodrow Wilson: Life and Letters*. 8 vols. Garden City, N.Y.: Doubleday, Page, 1927–39.

Bailey, Thomas A., and Paul B. Ryan. *The Lusitania Disaster: An Episode in Modern Warfare and Diplomacy*. New York: Free Press, 1975.

Baruch, Bernard M. *Baruch: The Public Years*. New York: Holt, Rinehart and Winston, 1960.

Basinger, Jeanine. *Silent Stars*. New York: Alfred A. Knopf, 1999.

Beale, Howard K. *Theodore Roosevelt and the Rise of America to World Power*. Baltimore: Johns Hopkins Press, 1956. Reprint, Collier paperback, 1973.

Beck, James M. *The Years That Were*. New York: Pageant Press, 1965.

Bernstorff, Johann Heinrich, Count von. *My Three Years in America*. New York: Charles Scribner's Sons, 1920.

Bishop, Joseph B. *Theodore Roosevelt and His Times Shown in His Own Letters*. 2 vols. New York: Charles Scribner's Sons, 1920.

Blumenson, Martin, ed. *The Patton Papers*. 2 vols. Boston: Houghton Mifflin, 1972.

Boyle, Francis Anthony. *Foundations of World Order: The Legalist Approach to International Relations, 1898–1922*. Durham, N.C.: Duke University Press, 1999.

Brinnin, John Malcolm. *Beau Voyage: Life Aboard the Last Great Ships*. New York: St. Martin's Press, 1981.

Brophy, John. *A Miner's Life*. Madison: University of Wisconsin Press, 1964.

Brownlow, Kevin. *The War, the West and the Wilderness*. New York: Alfred A. Knopf, 1979.

Bullard, Robert Lee. *Personalities and Reminiscences of the War.* Garden City, N.Y.: Doubleday, Page, 1925.

Bullard, Robert Lee, in collaboration with Earl Reeves. *American Soldiers Also Fought.* New York: Longmans, Green, 1939.

Burk, Kathleen. *Britain, America, and the Sinews of War, 1914–1918.* Boston: G. Allen and Unwin, 1984.

Burns, James MacGregor, and Dunn, Susan. *The Three Roosevelts: Patrician Leaders Who Transformed America.* New York: Atlantic Monthly Press, 2001.

Chambers, John Whiteclay. *To Raise an Army: The Draft Comes to Modern America.* New York: Free Press, 1987.

Chernow, Ron. *House of Morgan.* New York: Simon & Schuster, 1991.

———. *Titan: The Life of John D. Rockefeller, Sr.* New York: Random House, 1998.

Chessman, G. Wallace. *Theodore Roosevelt and the Politics of Power.* Prospect Heights, Ill.: Waveland Press, 1969. Reprint, 1994.

Christian, Garna L. "The Ordeal and the Prize: The 24th Infantry and Camp MacArthur." *Military Affairs* 50, 2 (April 1986): 65–70.

Churchill, Winston Spencer. *The World Crisis, 1911–1918.* 4 vols. New York: Charles Scribner's Sons, 1923–27.

Clements, Kendrick A. *Woodrow Wilson, World Statesman.* Chicago: Ivan Dee, 1999.

Clendenen, Clarence C. *Blood on the Border.* New York: Macmillan, 1969.

Cobb, Irvin S. *Paths of Glory: Impressions of War Written at and Near the Front.* New York: George H. Doran, 1915.

———. *Speaking of Prussians.* New York: George H. Doran, 1917.

Coben, Stanley. "A Study in Nativism: The American Red Scare of 1919–1920," *Political Science Quarterly,* vol. 79, no. 1 (March 1964): 52–75.

Coffman, Edward M. *The War to End All Wars: The American Military Experience in World War I.* Madison: University of Wisconsin Press, 1968.

Coit, Margaret L. *Mr. Baruch.* Westport, Conn.: Greenwood Publishing, 1975.

Colby, Gerard. *DuPont Dynasty.* Secaucus, N.J.: Lyle Stewart, 1984.

Coolidge, Calvin. *Autobiography.* New York: Cosmopolitan Book Corporation, 1929.

Cooper, John Milton, Jr. *Pivotal Decades.* New York: W. W. Norton, 1990.

———. *The Warrior and the Priest: Woodrow Wilson and Theodore Roosevelt.* Cambridge, Mass.: Harvard University Press, Belknap Press, 1983.

Creel, George. *Rebel at Large: Recollections of Fifty Crowded Years.* New York: G. P. Putnam's Sons, 1947.

Crosby, Alfred W. *America's Forgotten Pandemic: The Influenza of 1918.* Cambridge, U.K.: Cambridge University Press, 1989.

Crozier, Emmet. *American Reporters on the Western Front, 1914–1918.* New York: Oxford University Press, 1959.

Crunden, Robert M. *A Hero in Spite of Himself: Brand Whitlock in Art, Politics, and War.* New York: Alfred A. Knopf, 1969.

Cuff, Robert D. *The War Industries Board: Business-Government Relations During World War I.* Baltimore, Md.: Johns Hopkins University Press, 1973.

Dalton, Kathleen. *Theodore Roosevelt: A Strenuous Life.* New York: Alfred A. Knopf, 2002.

Daniels, Jonathan. *The End of Innocence.* Philadelphia: Lippincott, 1954.

Davidson, John Wells, ed. *A Crossroads of Freedom: The 1912 Campaign Speeches of Woodrow Wilson*. New Haven, Conn.: Yale University Press, 1956.

Davis, Richard Harding. *With the Allies*. New York: Charles Scribner's Sons, 1914.

Department of State. *Papers Relating to the Foreign Relations of the United States, 1913, 1914, and Supplements, World War, 1914–18*. (Referred to in Notes as FRUS.)

D'Este, Carlo. *A Genius for War: A Life of George Patton*. New York: Harper Trade, 1995.

Devlin, Patrick. *Too Proud to Fight: Woodrow Wilson's Neutrality*. London and New York: Oxford University Press, 1974.

DeWeerd, Harvey A. *President Wilson Fights His War: World War I and the American Intervention*. New York: Macmillan, 1968.

Doerries, Reinhard R. *Imperial Challenge: Ambassador Count Bernstorff and German-American Relations, 1908–1917*. Chapel Hill: University of North Carolina Press, 1989.

Dreiser, Theodore. *A Traveller at Forty*. New York: Century Co., 1913.

Eastman, Max. *Enjoyment of Living*. New York: Harper, 1948.

———. *Love and Revolution: My Journey Through an Epoch*. New York: Random House, 1964.

Eisenhower, John S. D. *Intervention!: The United States and the Mexican Revolution, 1913–1917*. New York: W. W. Norton, 1993.

The Empire Club of Canada Speeches, 1916–1917. Toronto, Canada: Empire Club of Canada, 1917.

Faunce, Hilda. *Desert Wife*. Lincoln: University of Nebraska Press, 1981 (reprint).

Fenton, Charles. "Ambulance Drivers in France and Italy: 1914–18." *American Quarterly* 12 (1960): 326–43.

Ferrell, Robert H. *Woodrow Wilson and World War I, 1917–1921*. New York: Harper & Row, 1985.

Finnegan, John Patrick. *Against the Specter of a Dragon: The Campaign for American Military Preparedness, 1914–1917*. Westport, Conn., Greenwood Press, 1974.

Flexner, Stuart Berg. *I Hear America Talking*. New York: Simon & Schuster, 1979.

Flynn, Elizabeth Gurley. *I Speak My Own Piece*. New York: Masses and Mainstream, 1955.

Flynn, William J. "Trapped Wires." *Liberty*, June 2, 1928.

Ford, Henry, with Samuel Crowther. *My Life and Work*. Garden City, N.Y.: Doubleday, Page, 1923.

Fortescue, Granville. *At the Front with Three Armies*. London: Andrew Melrose, 1914.

Fosdick, Raymond B. *Chronicle of a Generation*. New York: Harper, 1958.

Fromkin, David. *Europe's Last Summer: Who Started the Great War in 1914*. New York: Alfred A. Knopf, 2004.

Furia, Philip. *Irving Berlin: A Life in Song*. New York: Schirmer Books, 1998.

Gardner, Virginia. *"Friend and Lover": The Life of Louise Bryant*. New York: Horizon Press, 1982.

Garrison, Dee. *Mary Heaton Vorse: The Life of an American Insurgent*. Philadelphia, Pa.: Temple University Press, 1989.

Gerard, James W. *My Four Years in Germany*. New York: Grosset and Dunlap, 1917 (special edition, with different page numbering than the original).

Gibbons, Floyd. *And They Thought We Wouldn't Fight.* New York: George H. Doran, 1918.

Gibson, Hugh. *A Journal from Our Legation in Belgium.* Garden City, N.Y.: Doubleday, Page, 1917.

Gilbert, Charles. *American Financing of World War I.* Westport, Conn.: Greenwood, 1970.

Gitelman, H. M. *Legacy of the Ludlow Massacre: A Chapter in American Industrial Relations.* Philadelphia: University of Pennsylvania Press, 1988.

Glines, Carrol Y. *The Compact History of the United States Air Force.* New York: Hawthorn Books, 1963.

Goldman, Emma. *Living My Life.* 2 vols. New York: Alfred A. Knopf, 1931.

Gorn, Elliott J. *Mother Jones.* New York: Hill and Wang, 2001.

Graham, Otis L., Jr. *The Great Campaigns.* Englewood Cliffs, N.J.: Prentice-Hall, 1971.

Hackett, Alice Payne. *Fifty Years of Best Sellers.* New York: R. R. Bowker, 1945.

Hapgood, Hutchins. *A Victorian in the Modern World.* New York: Harcourt, Brace, 1939.

Harbaugh, William Henry. *Power and Responsibility: The Life and Times of Theodore Roosevelt.* New York: Farrar, Straus and Giroux, 1961.

Harries, Meirion, and Susie Harries. *The Last Days of Innocence: America at War, 1917–1918.* New York: Random House, 1997.

Harriman, Florence. *From Pinafores to Politics.* New York: Henry Holt, 1923.

Harris, Charles H., and Louis R. Sadler. *The Border and the Revolution: Clandestine Activities of the Mexican Revolution: 1910–1920.* Silver City, N.M.: High-Lonesome Books, 1988.

Hart, Albert Bushnell, ed. *Selected Addresses and Public Papers of Woodrow Wilson.* New York: Boni and Liveright, 1918.

Haynes, Robert V. *A Night of Violence: The Houston Riot of 1917.* Baton Rouge: Louisiana State University Press, 1977.

Hays, Samuel P. *Conservation and Efficiency: The Progressive Conservation Movement, 1890–1920.* Cambridge, Mass.: Harvard University Press, 1959.

Haywood, Big Bill. *Bill Haywood's Book: The Autobiography of William D. Haywood.* New York: International Publishers, 1929.

Heckscher, August. *Woodrow Wilson: A Biography.* New York: Charles Scribner's Sons, 1991.

Heller, Adele, and Lois Rudnick, eds. *1915: The Cultural Moment.* New Brunswick, N.J.: Rutgers University Press, 1991.

Hendrick, Burton J., ed. *The Life and Letters of Walter H. Page.* 3 vols. Garden City, N.Y.: Garden City Publishing, 1924–26.

Henri, Florette. *Black Migration: Movement North, 1900–1920.* Garden City, N.Y.: Anchor Press, 1975.

Hershey, Burnet. *The Odyssey of Henry Ford and the Great Peace Ship.* New York: Taplinger Publishing, 1967.

Hicks, Granville. *John Reed: The Making of a Revolutionary.* New York: Macmillan, 1937.

Hofstadter, Richard. *The Age of Reform.* New York: Alfred A. Knopf, 1955.

Hoover, Herbert. *The Memoirs of Herbert Hoover: Years of Adventure, 1874–1920.* New York: Macmillan, 1951.

Horne, John, and Alan Kramer. *German Atrocities, 1914: A History of Denial.* New Haven, Conn., Yale University Press, 2001.

Hounshell, David A. *From the American System to Mass Production, 1800–1931*. Baltimore, Md.: Johns Hopkins University Press, 1984.

Houston, David F. *Eight Years with Wilson's Cabinet, 1913–1920*. 2 vols. New York: Doubleday, Page, 1926.

Huard, Frances Wilson. *My Home in the Field of Mercy*. New York: George H. Doran, 1917.

Irwin, Will. *The Making of a Reporter*. New York: G. P. Putnam's Sons, 1942.

Jacobs, Lewis. *The Rise of the American Film*. New York: Teachers College Press, 1968.

Jensen, Joan M. *The Price of Vigilance*. Chicago: Rand McNally, 1968.

Joffre, Marshal Joseph Jacques. *The Memoirs of Marshal Joffre*. 2 vols. London: Geoffrey Bles, 1932.

Johnson, William Weber. *Heroic Mexico: The Narrative History of the Twentieth Century Revolution*. Rev. ed. San Diego: Harcourt, Brace, Jovanovich, 1968.

Johnston, Johanna. *Mrs. Satan*. New York: G. P. Putnam's Sons, 1967.

Katz, Friedrich. *The Secret War in Mexico: Europe, the United States, and the Mexican Revolution*. Chicago: University of Chicago Press, 1981.

Keegan, John. *The First World War*. New York: Alfred A. Knopf, 1999.

Keene, Jennifer D. *Doughboys, the Great War, and the Remaking of America*. Baltimore, Md.: Johns Hopkins University Press, 2001.

Kennedy, David M. *Over Here: The First World War and American Society*. New York and Oxford: Oxford University Press, 1980.

Knock, Thomas J. *To End All Wars: Woodrow Wilson and the Quest for a New World Order*. Princeton, N.J.: Princeton University Press, 1992.

Kraft, Barbara S. *The Peace Ship: Henry Ford's Pacifist Adventure in the First World War*. New York: Macmillan, 1978.

Lacey, Robert. *Ford: The Men and the Machine*. New York: Ballantine, 1986.

Langner, Lawrence. *The Magic Curtain*. New York: E. P. Dutton, 1951.

Landau, Captain Henry. *The Enemy Within: The Inside Story of German Sabotage in America*. New York: G. P. Putnam's Sons, 1937.

Lewis, Sinclair. *Dodsworth*. New York: Harcourt, Brace, 1929.

Link, Arthur S., ed. *Papers of Woodrow Wilson*. 68 vols. Princeton, N.J.: Princeton University Press. (Referred to in Notes as PWW.)

Link, Arthur S. *Wilson: The Road to the White House*. Princeton, N.J.: Princeton University Press, 1947.

———. *Wilson: The Struggle for Neutrality*. Princeton, N.J.: Princeton University Press, 1960.

———. *Woodrow Wilson: Revolution, War, and Peace*. Wheeling, Ill.: Harlan Davidson, 1979.

———. *Woodrow Wilson and the Progressive Era, 1910–1917*. New York: Harper & Brothers, 1954.

Lippmann, Walter. *Early Writings*. New York: Liveright, 1970.

———. *Public Opinion*. New York: Macmillan, 1922.

Livermore, Seward W. *Politics Is Adjourned: Woodrow Wilson and the War Congress, 1916–1918*. Middletown, Conn.: Wesleyan University Press.

Lochner, Louis P. *Henry Ford: America's Don Quixote*. New York: International Publishers, 1925.

Lord, Walter. *The Good Years: From 1900 to the First World War.* New York: Harper and Brothers, 1960.

Luebke, Frederick C. *Bonds of Loyalty: German-Americans and World War I.* De Kalb: Northern Illinois University Press, 1974.

Luhan, Mabel Dodge. *Movers and Shakers.* New York: Harcourt, Brace, 1936.

MacArthur, Douglas. *Reminiscences.* New York: McGraw-Hill, 1964.

March, Peyton C. *The Nation at War.* Garden City N.Y.: Doubleday, Doran, 1932.

Marquis, Samuel S. *Henry Ford: An Interpretation.* Boston: Little, Brown, 1923.

Marshall, George C. *Memoirs of My Service in the World War, 1917–1918.* Boston: Houghton Mifflin, 1976.

Martin, Edward S. *The Diary of a Nation: The War and How We Got into It.* Garden City, N.Y.: Doubleday, Page, 1918.

Martin, Ralph G. *Cissy: The Extraordinary Life of Eleanor Medill Patterson.* New York: Simon & Schuster, 1979.

McAdoo, Eleanor Wilson, ed. *The Priceless Gift.* New York:McGraw-Hill, 1962.

McAdoo, Eleanor Wilson. *The Woodrow Wilsons.* New York: Macmillan 1937.

McAdoo, William Gibbs. *Crowded Years: The Reminiscences of William G. McAdoo.* Boston: Houghton Mifflin, 1931.

McGerr, Michael. *A Fierce Discontent.* New York: Free Press, 2003.

McGovern, George S., and Leonard F. Guttridge. *The Great Coalfield War.* Boston: Houghton Mifflin, 1972.

Mencken, H. L. *A Carnival of Buncombe: Writings on Politics.* Chicago: University of Chicago Press, 1984.

Millis, Walter. *Road to War: America, 1914–1917.* Boston: Houghton Mifflin, 1935.

Morison, Elting E., and John Blum, eds. *The Letters of Theodore Roosevelt.* 8 vols. Cambridge, Mass.: Harvard University Press, 1951–54.

Morris, Edmund. *The Rise of Theodore Roosevelt.* New York: Ballantine Books, 1980.

Mowrer, Paul Scott. *The House of Europe.* Boston: Houghton Mifflin, 1945.

Mullendore, William Clinton. *History of the United States Food Administration, 1917–1919.* Stanford, Calif.: Stanford University Press, 1941.

Murphy, Paul L. *World War I and the Origin of Civil Liberties in the United States.* New York: W. W. Norton, 1979.

Murray, Robert K. *Red Scare: A Study in National Hysteria, 1919–1920.* New York: McGraw-Hill Paperback, 1964.

Nasaw, David. *The Chief: The Life of William Randolph Hearst.* Boston: Houghton Mifflin, 2000.

Nevins, Allan, and Frank Hill. *Ford: The Times, the Man, and the Company.* Vol. 1. New York: Charles Scribner's Sons, 1954.

———. *Ford: Expansion and Challenge, 1915–1933.* Vol. 2. New York: Charles Scribner's Sons, 1957.

Official German Documents Relating to the World War. The Reports of the First and Second Subcommittees of the Committee Appointed by the National Constituent Assembly to Inquire into the Responsibility for the War. 2 vols. New York: Oxford University Press: Carnegie Endowment for International Peace, 1923. (Referred to in Notes as GD.)

O'Neill, William L. *Echoes of Revolt: The Masses, 1911–1917.* Chicago: Quadrangle Books, 1966.

Palmer, Frederick. *Newton D. Baker: America at War.* 2 vols. New York: Dodd, Mead, 1931.

Papen, Franz von. *Memoirs.* Trans. Brian Connell. New York: E. P. Dutton, 1953.

Parry, Albert. *Garrets and Pretenders: A History of Bohemianism in America.* Rev. ed. New York: Dover, 1960.

Paxson, Frederic L. *American Democracy and the World War.* 3 vols. Boston: Houghton Mifflin, 1936–48. Reprint, New York: Cooper Square Publishers, 1966.

Pershing, John J. *My Experiences in the World War.* 2 vols. New York: Frederick A. Stokes, 1931.

Peterson, H. C., and Gilbert C. Fite. *Opponents of War, 1917–1919.* Seattle: University of Washington Press, 1957.

Pinchot, Gifford. *Breaking New Ground.* New York, 1947.

Post, Emily. *By Motor to the Golden Gate.* New York: D. Appleton, 1916.

Pringle, Henry F. *The Life and Times of William Howard Taft.* 2 vols. New York: Farrar and Rinehart, 1939.

———. *Theodore Roosevelt: A Biography.* New York: Harcourt, Brace, 1931.

Radosh, Ronald, ed. *Debs.* Englewood Cliffs, N.J.: Prentice Hall, 1971.

Ramsaye, Terry. *A Million and One Nights.* New York: Simon and Schuster, 1926. Reprint, 1964.

Read, James Morgan. *Atrocity Propaganda, 1914–1919.* New Haven, Conn.: Yale University Press, 1941.

Reed, John. "Almost Thirty." *The New Republic,* April 15, 1936. (There is a slightly different unpublished version in the Reed Papers.)

———. *The Day in Bohemia.* Privately published, 1913.

———. *Insurgent Mexico.* New York and London: D. Appleton, 1914. Reprint, New York: International Publishers, 1969.

———. *Ten Days That Shook the World.* New York: Boni and Liveright, 1919.

———. *The War in Eastern Europe.* New York: Charles Scribner's Sons, 1916. Reprint, 1948.

Remak, Joachim. *The Origins of World War I, 1871–1914.* Fort Worth, Texas: Harcourt Brace College Publishers, 1995.

Requin, Colonel E. *America's Race to Victory.* New York: Frederick A. Stokes, 1919.

Robinson, Corinne Roosevelt. *My Brother Theodore Roosevelt.* New York: Charles Scribner's Sons, 1929.

Rockefeller, John D. *Random Reminiscences of Men and Events.* Garden City, N.Y.: Doubleday, Doran, 1933.

Roosevelt, Elliott, ed., assisted by James N. Rosenau. *FDR: His Personal Letters, 1905–1928.* New York: Duell, Sloan and Pearce, 1948.

Roosevelt, Theodore. *An Autobiography.* New York: Macmillan, 1919.

———. *The Works of Theodore Roosevelt.* 24 vols., memorial ed. New York: Charles Scribner's Sons, 1919–26.

Rosenstone, Robert A. *Romantic Revolutionary: A Biography of John Reed.* New York: Alfred A. Knopf, 1975.

Rosewater, Victor. *Backstage in 1912: The Inside Story of the Split Republican Convention.* Philadelphia: Dorrance, 1931.

Rudwick, Elliot M. *Race Riot at East St. Louis, 2 July 1917.* New York: Atheneum, 1972.

Russell, Charles Edward. *Bare Hands and Stone Walls: Some Recollections of a Sideline Reformer.* New York: Charles Scribner's Sons, 1933.

Sanger, Margaret. *An Autobiography.* New York: W. W. Norton, 1938.

Schickel, Richard. *His Picture in the Papers: A Speculation on Celebrity in America, Based on the Life of Douglas Fairbanks, Sr.* New York: Charterhouse, 1973.

Schlereth, Thomas J. *Victorian America: Transformations in Everyday Life.* New York: HarperCollins, 1991.

Schneider, Dorothy, and Carl J. Schneider. *Into the Breach: American Women Overseas in World War I.* New York: Viking, 1991.

Schwarz, Jordan A. *The Speculator: Bernard M. Baruch in Washington, 1917–1965.* Chapel Hill: University of North Carolina Press, 1981.

Senate Documents. Judiciary Committee. *Hearings on Brewing and Liquor Interests and German and Bolshevik Propaganda.* 2 vols. 66th Congress, 1st Session, Senate Document 62, Washington, D.C., 1919.

Seymour, Charles. *American Neutrality, 1914–1917.* New Haven, Conn.: Yale University Press, 1935.

Seymour, Charles, ed. *The Intimate Papers of Colonel House.* 4 vols. Boston: Houghton Mifflin, 1926–28. (Referred to in Notes as IPH.)

Shackleton, Robert. *Russell Conwell: His Life and Achievements.* New York, 1915.

Shannon, David A. *The Socialist Party in America.* New York: Macmillan, 1955.

Shulman, Alix Kates, ed. *Red Emma Speaks: Selected Writings and Speeches by Emma Goldman.* New York: Vintage Books, 1972.

Soule, George. *Prosperity Decade.* New York: Rinehart, 1947.

Starling, Colonel Edmund, with Thomas Sugrue. *Starling of the White House.* New York: Simon & Schuster, 1946.

Steffens, Lincoln. *Autobiography.* New York: Harcourt, Brace, 1931.

———. *Lincoln Steffens Speaking.* New York: Harcourt, Brace, 1938.

Stout, Ralph, ed. *The Works of Theodore Roosevelt.* New York: Charles Scribner's Sons, 1919–26. (Referred to in Notes as TRW.)

Sullivan, Mark. *Our Times: The United States, 1900–1925.* 6 vols. New York: Charles Scribner's Sons, 1926–1935.

Swanberg, W. A. *Citizen Hearst: A Biography of William Randolph Hearst.* New York: Charles Scribner's Sons, 1961.

Sweetman, Jack. *The Landing at Veracruz, 1914.* Annapolis, Md.: U.S. Naval Institute, 1968.

Sweetser, Arthur. *Roadside Glimpses of the Great War.* New York: Macmillan, 1916.

Taylor, Frederick W. *The Principles of Scientific Management.* New York: Harper and Brothers, 1911.

Thomas, Lowell. *This Side of Hell: Dan Edwards, Adventurer.* New York: Doubleday, Doran, 1932.

Thompson, Charles Willis. *Presidents I've Known.* Indianapolis: Bobbs-Merrill, 1929.

Thomson, David. *The Whole Equation: A History of Hollywood.* New York: Alfred A. Knopf, 2005.

Timberlake, James H. *Prohibition and the Progressive Movement, 1900–1920.* Cambridge, Mass.: Harvard University Press, 1963.

Tompkins, Col. Frank. *Chasing Villa: The Story Behind the Story of Pershing's Expedition into Mexico.* Harrisburg, Pa.: Military Service Publishing Company, 1934. Reprint, 1996.

Trask, David F. *Captains and Cabinets: Anglo-American Naval Relations, 1917–1918.* Columbia: University of Missouri Press, 1972.

Traxel, David. *An American Saga: The Life and Times of Rockwell Kent.* New York: Harper & Row, 1980.

———. *1898: The Birth of the American Century.* New York: Alfred A. Knopf, 1998.

Tuchman, Barbara. *The Guns of August.* New York: Macmillan, 1962.

———. *The Zimmermann Telegram.* New York: Viking Press, 1958.

Tumulty, Joseph P. *Woodrow Wilson As I Know Him.* Garden City, N.Y.: Doubleday, Page, 1921.

Vaughn, Stephen. *Holding Fast the Inner Lines: Democracy, Nationalism, and the Committee on Public Information.* Chapel Hill: University of North Carolina Press, 1980.

Venzon, Anne Cipriano, ed. *The United States in the First World War: An Encyclopedia.* New York: Garland Publishing, 1995.

Vesey, Laurence. *The Emergence of the American University.* Chicago: University of Chicago Press, 1965.

Villard, Oswald Garrison. *Fighting Years.* New York: Harcourt, Brace, 1939.

Vorse, Mary Heaton. *A Footnote to Folly: Reminiscences of Mary Heaton Vorse.* New York: Farrar and Rinehart, 1935.

Voska, Emanuel Victor, and Will Irwin. *Spy and Counterspy.* New York: Doubleday, Doran, 1940.

Walworth, Arthur. *Woodrow Wilson.* 2 vols. New York: W. W. Norton, 1978.

Watt, Richard M. *Dare Call It Treason.* New York: Simon & Shuster, 1963.

Wharton, Edith. *A Backward Glance.* New York: D. Appleton, 1934.

White, William Allen. *The Autobiography of William Allen White.* New York: Macmillan, 1946.

Whitlock, Brand. *The Journal of Brand Whitlock.* New York: Appleton-Century, 1936.

Wik, Reynold M. *Henry Ford and Grassroots America.* Ann Arbor: University of Michigan Press, 1972.

Williams, Wythe. *Dusk of Empire: The Decline of Europe and the Rise of the United States, as Observed by a Foreign Correspondent in a Quarter Century of Service.* New York: Charles Scribner's Sons, 1937.

Williamson, Joel. *The Crucible of Race: Black-White Relations in the American South Since Emancipation.* New York: Oxford University Press, 1984.

Wister, Owen. *Roosevelt: The Story of a Friendship.* New York: Macmillan, 1930.

Witcover, Jules. *Sabotage at Black Tom: Imperial Germany's Secret War in America, 1914–1917.* Chapel Hill, N.C.: Algonquin Books, 1989.

Wood, Eric Fisher. *The Notebook of an Attaché: Seven Months in the War Zone.* New York: A. L. Burt Company, 1915.

Wynn, Neil A. *From Progressivism to Prosperity: World War I and American Society.* New York and London: Holmes and Meier, 1986.

Zurier, Rebecca. *Art for The Masses: A Radical Magazine and Its Graphics, 1911–1917.* Philadelphia, Pa.: Temple University Press, 1988.

Index

Page numbers in *italics* refer to illustrations.

PHOTOGRAPHIC CREDITS

Grateful acknowledgment is made to the following for permission to reproduce photographs appearing on the pages indicated:

Houghton Library, Harvard University: 246 (By permission of the Houghton Library, Harvard University: bMs Am 1091[239].)
Library of Congress: 294
The National Archives: 17, 32, 46, 102, 163, 195, 225, 261, 279, 285, 300, 309, 328, 340
The Philadelphia Museum of Art: 44 (© 2004 Artists Rights Society [ARS], New York/ADAGP, Paris/Succession Marcel Duchamp.)
Tamiment Institute Library, New York University: 55, 108

A NOTE ON THE TYPE

This book was set in Fairfield, a typeface designed by the distinguished American artist and engraver Rudolph Ruzicka (1883–1978). In its structure Fairfield displays the sober and sane qualities of the master craftsman whose talents were dedicated to clarity. Ruzicka was born in Bohemia and came to America in 1894. He designed and illustrated many books, and was the creator of a considerable list of individual prints in a variety of techniques.

Composed by North Market Street Graphics, Lancaster, Pennsylvania

Printed and bound by Berryville Graphics, Berryville, Virginia

Designed by Robert C. Olsson